THE
TOSEFTA

THE

TOSEFTA

TRANSLATED FROM THE HEBREW

SIXTH DIVISION

TOHOROT

(The Order of Purities)

BY

JACOB NEUSNER

University Professor
Professor of Religious Studies
The Ungerleider Distinguished Scholar of Judaic Studies
Brown University

KTAV PUBLISHING HOUSE INC.
NEW YORK
1977

Library of Congress Cataloging in Publication Data

Tosefta. English
  The Tosefta.

    Includes bibliographical references and index.
    CONTENTS:
—division 6. Tohorot.
    I. Neusner, Jacob 1932—
BM508.13.E5   1977   296.1'262   77-4277
ISBN 0-87068-430-2 (v. 6)

MANUFACTURED IN THE UNITED STATES OF AMERICA

For
Maurice Glicksman

CONTENTS

THE TOSEFTA
SIXTH DIVISION
TOHOROT

PREFACE

I. *Purpose and Redactional Character of Tosefta*

Tosefta, meaning "supplement," is a corpus of materials correlative to Mishnah. Standing apart from Mishnah, the greater part of Tosefta's materials is incomprehensible gibberish, bearing no autonomous meaning to be discovered wholly within the limits of a discrete passage. Tosefta's units relate to corresponding ones in Mishnah in one of three ways: 1. Tosefta cites Mishnah verbatim and then supplies glosses or further discussions of Mishnah's rules; 2. Tosefta complements Mishnah without directly citing the corresponding passage; 3. Tosefta supplements Mishnah with information relevant to, but in theme and meaning autonomous of, the principal document.

The first sort of relationship characterizes about half of the pericopae of our Order, the second about another third, and the last, about a sixth. Tosefta's aggregations of materials normally are grouped in accord with their respective relationships to Mishnah. A sequence serving a given chapter of Mishnah, for example, may begin with pericopae in which Mishnah is cited, then proceed to another set in which Mishnah is complemented, and finally, present materials in which Mishnah is given supplementary but essentially separate materials. The formulary traits of Tosefta run parallel to those of Mishnah in the first, and, to a lesser extent, the second sort of materials. But in the main Tosefta in language is a far less formalized document than Mishnah. Mishnah's redaction tends to produce aggregates of materials characterized by a common formulary pattern and a common theme. So far as Tosefta may be divided into sizable groups of materials, by contrast, it is redacted primarily in accord with a single relationship to Mishnah exhibited by a sequence of otherwise formally and thematically discrete units.[1] In size, Tosefta is approximately four times larger than Mishnah.[2]

Tosefta is important within Rabbinical literature for two reasons. First, pericopae of Tosefta (or versions of pericopae, attributed to authorities of the first and second century, strongly resembling those now found in Tosefta) commonly form the foundation of the treatment, by both Palestinian

---

1. See my *History of the Mishnaic Law of Purities. XXI. The Formulation and Redaction of the Order of Purities in Mishnah and Tosefta* (Leiden, 1977: E. J. Brill). M. D. Herr, "Tosefta," *Encyclopaedia Judaica* 15, pp. 1283–85, finds five relationships between Tosefta and Mishnah, but these do not differ materially from the three given here.

2. Herr, *op. cit.*, p. 1283.

and Babylonian Talmuds, of the corresponding pericopae in Mishnah. Indeed, the Toseftan supplement to a Mishnah often stands at the outset, and generates the two Talmuds' analyses of that same Mishnah. Second, the entire exegetical tradition of Mishnah in later times depends upon Tosefta's original exegesis of that document at all points at which Tosefta is available and cited. If, therefore, one wants to understand how Mishnah has been interpreted for nearly eighteen centuries, the place to begin is in Tosefta. It hardly needs saying that Tosefta, separate from its importance within the other principal documents of Rabbinic Judaism, contains innumerable sayings which bear considerable value of their own. For the period after the redaction of Mishnah and before the conclusion of the Talmuds, from *ca.* 200 to *ca.* 600, Tosefta, and, especially, formulations of sayings which ultimately found their way into Tosefta, constitutes a document of paramount importance. It is second only to Mishnah as a definitive corpus of the thought of the formative minds of Judaism.

II. *Origin and Development*

We do not know who compiled and redacted Tosefta or when the work reached its present form. On this matter we presently rely upon the judgment of M. D. Herr:

> Very often a *baraita* quoted in the Talmud in a corrupt form is found in the Tosefta in its original coherent form. Furthermore, very often there is a discussion in the Talmud about the exact meaning of the words of a certain *tanna* (either in the Mishnah or in the *baraita*), while the parallel statement as found in the Tosefta is manifestly clear. It would therefore seem obvious that the Tosefta in its present form was not edited before the end of the fourth century C.E. and cannot therefore be identified with any of the . . . earlier collections of *beraitot*. It is certain that the Tosefta was composed in Ereẓ Israel, since the *beraitot* which it contains resemble more those of the Jerusalem Talmud than those of the Babylonian Talmud.[3]

The many textual problems of Tosefta itself, however, leave room for other interpretations of the data to which Herr makes reference, not to mention quite different theories of the character of the sayings themselves and the interrelationships of their diverse versions. For the present purpose it suffices to note that Tosefta reaches its present shape some time between the redaction of Mishnah, about A.D. 200, and that of the Palestinian Talmud, two and a half centuries later, about A.D. 450. These are no more than guesses.

3. *op. cit.,* p. 1284.

III. *Text*

We know little about the transmission of Tosefta thereafter. Most of the pericopae of the Order of Purities are cited by Samson of Sens (*ca.* 1150—1230), in his commentary to the Mishnah of the present Order, and many are quoted by Maimonides in his *Mishneh Torah* (1180), principally in the *Book of Cleanness.*[4] The first modern text was that of M. S. Zuckermandel (1881), following the Erfurt Manuscript. For our Order in particular, the preferred text is the version of the Vienna Manuscript, edited by Karl Heinrich Rengstorf.[5]

The present translation is based upon Rengstorf's text, but also includes pericopae in the version of Samson of Sens. The extant text is further revised, in my translation, in the light of the unparalleled exegetical text of Saul Lieberman, *Tosefeth Rishonim. A Commentary Based on Manuscripts of the Tosefta and Works of the Rishonim and Midrashim in Manuscripts and Rare Editions.* III. *Kelim-Niddah* (Jerusalem, 1939: Bamberger and Wahrmann) and IV. *Mikwaoth-Uktzin* (Jerusalem, 1939: Mossad Rabbi Kook Press). Where I diverge from the text supplied by Rengstorf, that fact is noted under the *sigla: Sens,* or *TR* (+ volume and page reference).

Since in the main it is Rengstorf's edition which is carefully followed, the names of those responsible for the several tractates should be given: *Kelim Baba Qamma, Baba Meṣia, and Baba Batra:* Walter Windfuhr; *Ahilot:* Walter Windfuhr; *Negaim:* Walter Windfuhr and Karl Heinrich Rengstorf; *Parah:* Gerhard Lisowsky; *Niddah:* Emanuel Schereschewsky and Günter Mayer; *Miqvaot:* Gerhard Lisowsky; *Tohorot:* Emanuel Schereschewsky and Günter Mayer; *Makhshirin:* Gerhard Lisowsky; *Zabim:* Günter Mayer; *Yadayim:* Gerhard Lisowsky and Karl Heinrich Rengstorf; *Tebul Yom:* Gerhard Lisowsky; *Uqsin:* Gerhard Lisowsky. Rengstorf's edition includes a complete and thoroughly annotated translation into German and extensive notes, as well as an index.

Among commentaries systematically consulted are Isaac Pardo (1718—1790), *Ḥasdé David.* IV.*Tohorot* (Jerusalem, 1970), and Elijah ben Solomon Zalman ("Elijah Gaon," "Vilna Gaon," or "GRA"), (1720—1797), printed in the Mishnah, ed. Romm (Vilna, 1887) and in the text of Tosefta of the Order of Purities in Volume XX of the Vilna edition of the Babylonian Talmud.

An exegesis of each pericope, together with explanation of both the text as translated and its meaning, is found for each tractate in the relevant

---

4. *The Code of Maimonides. Book Ten. The Book of Cleanness,* translated from the Hebrew by Herbert Danby (New Haven, 1954: Yale University Press).

5. *Die Tosefta. Text. Seder VI: Ṭoharot. In Zusammenarbeit mit* Frowald Hüttenmeister, Gerhard Lisowsky, Günter Mayer, Emanuel Schereschewsky, *und* Walter Windfuhr, *herausgegeben von* Karl Heinrich Rengstorf (Stuttgart, 1967:W. Kohlhammer Verlag).

volumes of my *History of the Mishnaic Law of Purities.*[6] There is no need to extensively annotate each pericope because the requisite information on the relationship of each pericope to Mishnah's counterpart, textual problems and emendations, and the meaning of the given passage, is supplied there. The unavoidable length of such annotation would greatly increase the size of the translation but add nothing new. Accordingly, the footnotes simply refer the reader to the correlative pericope of Mishnah for each unit of Tosefta for which there is a relevant passage in the principal document.

Bibliography for the study of Tosefta is given by M. I. Abramski in *Qiryat Sefer* 29, 1953−4, pp. 149−161. In addition, the works of Ḥ. Albeck, *Meḥqarim biveraita vetosefta* (Tel Aviv, 1944) and *Mavo lattalmudim* (Tel Aviv, 1969) and of Y. N. Epstein, *Mevo'ot lesifrut hattannaim* (Jerusalem and Tel Aviv, 1957), pp. 241−263, are to be consulted.[7]

IV. *Arrangement*

While the interpretation of Tosefta depends upon Mishnah, the sixth division of Tosefta does not follow the order of tractates of the corresponding division of Mishnah, nor are Tosefta's tractates divided into chapters equivalent either in number or at point of demarcation to Mishnah's. The order of tractates and number of chapters in each document are as follows (an asterisk marks a tractate of Tosefta out of Mishnah's order):

Mishnah		*Tosefta*		
Kelim	30	Kelim Baba Qamma	7	
		Kelim Baba Meṣia	11	25
		Kelim Baba Batra	7	
Ohalot	18	Ahilot	18	
Negaim	14	Negaim	9	
Parah	12	Parah	12	
Tohorot	10	*Niddah	9	
Miqvaot	10	Miqvaot	7	
Niddah	10	*Tohorot	11	
Makhshirin	6	Makhshirin	3	
Zabim	5	Zabim	5	
Tebul Tom	4	*Yadayim	2	

6. I−III. *Kelim* (1974); IV−V. *Ohalot* (1975); VI−VIII. *Negaim* (1975); IX−X. *Parah* (1976); XI−XII. *Tohorot* (1976); XIII−XIV. *Miqvaot* (1976); XV−XVI. *Niddah* (1976, 1977); XVII. *Makhshirin* (1977); XVIII. *Zabim* (1977); XIX. *Tebul Yom and Yadayim* (1977); XX. *Uqsin* (1977).

7. Herr, *op. cit.*, p. 1285.

| Yadayim | 4 | *Tebul Yom | 2 |
| Uqsin | 3 | Uqsin | 3 |

Clearly Mishnah's tractates are arranged in order of length. Tosefta's are indifferent both to length and to Mishnah's corresponding sequence.

The tractates of Mishnah-Tosefta are organized around legal topics, and the chapters among which Mishnah is divided generally follow suit. The division of Mishnah, therefore of Tosefta, into tractates and chapters is fundamental and integral to its structure. The sixth division encompasses nearly the whole of Mishnah's and Tosefta's material on purity. It furthermore rarely introduces any theme found elsewhere in Mishnah. Other divisions of Mishnah and Tosefta treat purity as background for quite different inquiries, and scarcely a single important conception of cleanness finds its primary locus outside the sixth division. The twelve tractates before us (treating *Kelim* in Tosefta as one) are carefully demarcated by thematic boundaries. They are further defined by a distinctive problematic, an area of concern quite internal to, and imposed upon, the topic or theme of the tractate. A single topic is common to only two tractates of the sixth division, Tohorot and Uqsin, both of which attend, but in different aspects, to uncleanness of food.

To be sure, brief tractates at the end of the division develop ideas laid down in longer ones at the beginning. The laws of Zabim are secondary to those of Niddah. The generative conceptions of Yadayim depend upon those of Parah. The problem of the Tebul Yom is a consequence of the datum of Miqvaot, that immersion pools do purify. Uqsin, as noted, carries forward concerns of Tohorot. Parah and Miqvaot, for their part, contain exactly complementary ideas. In general the shorter, secondary and younger tractates, like the longer, primary and older ones, are self-contained. They work out the logic of their theme in a manner autonomous of the ways in which the primary and older tractates do theirs. Accordingly, the definitive redactional principle by which the tractates of the sixth division, both Mishnah and therefore Tosefta, are organized is theme, given concreteness and distinctiveness by an inner problematic. The theme therefore will explain why some materials are included and others excluded.

V. *Topics*

The principal themes of the twelve tractates of the sixth division are as follows:

Kelim	the capacity to receive uncleanness of various sorts of domestic, non-cultic utensils (Lev. 11:29−35, 15:4−6, 9−12, 19−27; Num. 19:14−15, 31:19−24)

Ohalot	the uncleanness imparted to persons and objects by reason of their location within the tent of, which is to say, under the same roof as, a corpse (Num. 19:14−19).
Negaim	the uncleanness of the *meṣora'* ("leper") (Lev. 13:1−14:59) and of the *nega'* ("plague"), the latter of which is deemed to be distinct from, but wholly analogous to, the former.
Parah	preparation of the purification-water and ashes of the red cow (Num. 19:1−13, 20−22).
Niddah	the uncleanness of the menstruating woman and others of similar status (Lev. 12:1−8, 15:19−24, 25−31).
Miqvaot	immersion-pools, in which uncleanness is removed (Lev. 11:31−2, 36, 15:13, 16; Num. 31:23).
Tohorot	uncleanness affecting foods, with particular reference first, to matters of doubt about contamination of food, second, to the *ḥaber* ("associate") and *'am ha'areṣ* (ordinary person) and, third, to the uncleanness of olives and grapes.
Makhshirin	liquids which render dry produce capable of receiving, or susceptible to, uncleanness (Lev. 11:34, 38), and the conditions under which the application of liquid imparts susceptibility to uncleanness.
Zabim	the uncleanness of a man who has a discharge, the Zab (herein treated as a substantive not to be translated or italicized) (Lev. 15:1−15).
Yadayim	the way in which hands are made clean.
Tebul Yom	the uncleanness of a person or object which has been immersed in an immersion-pool, between the time of said immersion and sunset of that very same day, at which time the process of purification is deemed to be complete (Lev. 11:24, 25, 28, 32, 22:6−7).
Uqsin	cleanness of foods, with regard, in particular, to the status of subsidiary parts of pieces of fruit or vegetable, connected to, but separate from, the principal parts of said pieces of fruit or vegetable.

VI. *Purpose of the Translation*

The translation aims at extreme literalness and closely follows the word-order and simple meaning of the Hebrew text. There is very little, if any, effort at paraphrase, or at restating material in smooth English. It should be easy for the student to follow the Hebrew text along with the English translation, with the proviso, already noted, that the text which is translated at some points is not that of Rengstorf and his co-workers. Consultation with the version in Samson of Sens' or Maimonides' parallels, and, especially, with Lieberman's exegetical and textual commentary, will account for the difference between the translation and Rengstorf's text. These passages do not comprise a major part of the whole.

I have diverged from the policy of paraphrase followed by Danby,[8] specifically so that the actual formulary traits of the Hebrew may be grasped by the reader, whose study of the way in which Tosefta expresses its ideas in syntactical and grammatical patterns of its own may thereby be facilitated. This 'philosophy' of translation does not produce a smooth version in English of the Hebrew original. It has therefore to be explained, since, in most other translations of classical Rabbinical literature, a contrary policy is followed.

The fact is that Mishnah-Tosefta expresses its conceptions as much through the *way* things are said as through *what* is said. The style is highly formalized and particular to the document. "Mishnaic" Hebrew, that is, Middle Hebrew, is a supple and rich everyday language. The Hebrew of Mishnah-Tosefta, by contrast, is reduced to recurrent formularies, and depends upon a very small repertoire of syntactic patterns, which are inseparable from the ideas expressed in those patterns. One simply cannot understand the full meaning of Mishnah-Tosefta merely by knowing in paraphrase the gist of what is said, for the grammatical and syntactic modes of expression are integral and essential to the concrete meanings of the document. If the Hebrew is not smooth, then the English should not be smooth. If the Hebrew relies upon disconnected clauses (apocopation) and repetitious ones, then so should the English translation.

In my judgment the contrary policy, which is to paraphrase the Hebrew and render it into "something like" the original but also into very good English, obscures one of the paramount points of interest of the document itself, which is, its very peculiar and particular mode of formalized speech. Moreover, by following the Hebrew as literally as possible, I avoid making exegetical commitments to the meaning of difficult or obscure passages. Paraphrase, by contrast, involves supplying the Hebrew with a definite meaning or interpretation, which, as I said, the Hebrew itself may sustain but does not explicitly invite. Danby's translation of Mishnah seems deliberately to obscure all of the most interesting traits of Mishnaic discourse, e.g., the dispute form, the persistent use of the present tense in attributive formulae, the mixture of tenses, and many other formal and rhetorical policies. The net result is a handsome document in English, related to the Hebrew in matters of substance; but obscuring for the English reader the distinctive and engaging linguistic character of what is translated.

---

8. Herbert Danby, *The Mishnah. Translated from the Hebrew with Introduction and Brief Explanatory Notes* (London, 1933:Oxford University Press).

Moreover, Danby in Mishnah takes a position on numerous exegetical problems, nearly always in line with *Tif'eret Yisra'el*'s commentary, without clearly indicating alternative approaches to interpretation—and therefore to translation—and also without making obvious the fact that his translation is more of a commentary than it needs to be. It may be quite fairly argued that Danby's translation of Mishnah produces a more intelligible version than this translation of Tosefta. In reply I may point out that Danby makes Mishnah more intelligible than its other commentaries find it to be. My version of Tosefta on every page preserves the obscurity of Tosefta when read out of correlation with Mishnah. In my view, we should let Tosefta be *tosefta*—a supplement to Mishnah, as I have explained, dependent for meaning and full clarity upon Mishnah. If it is to be translated at all, then, in my view, this is how the work should be done. Paraphrase is not translation, and translation is always what its name says it is, rather than the occasion to transform and transcend an obscure and difficult text and to produce a smooth and facile one.

What is conceived, moreover, as facility and smoothness need not be defined solely by the contemporary reader and translator. This is the way the people who made up Tosefta formulated their thoughts, so far as I am able to render their language and thoughts into corresponding English words. It may not be deemed to be an elegant translation, but it *is* the way they wanted to say things. As deeper study of Tosefta (all the more so, of Mishnah) will persuade the reader, there is a certain reason and logic behind their, to us, somewhat gnarled and difficult linguistic and syntactical preferences. Tosefta is not a document of piety or literature but of highly sophisticated, subtle, and often brilliant exegesis of Mishnah,and a translation which through paraphrase renders it into what it is not does not, in my judgment, serve any important purpose.

Although I have taken a very different route toward the translation of Tosefta, I have generally made use of Danby's choices of English equivalents to Hebrew technical terms, names of objects, and the like. Substantives not translated, such as *ḥaber* and *'am ha'areṣ* and Zab, seem to me to bear a technical meaning for which English lacks any accurate counterpart. But here too, consulting Danby's Mishnah-translation will provide an acceptable English alternative. It follows that a far more felicitous English version of Mishnah is available than that herein provided for Tosefta. In my judgment what is lost is more than compensated by what is gained, which is accuracy and precision in respect to what is translated.

Division of pericopae into their constituent phrases and cognitive components, and designating each by a letter, are intended to facilitate the literary- and form-analysis of the text. That division normally is into the smallest meaningful phrases and clauses. It is entirely my own. Readers who consult my *History of the Mishnaic Law of Purities* also will observe that I have revised the division of pericopae, as a fresh look showed me other possibilities than those originally proposed. I have also improved the translation given there in a great many small points and have made numerous minor, and some major, corrections. Nonetheless, the net result, entirely in phase with Mishnah and without regard to Tosefta's own sequence and order, is essentially the same as that given in my *Purities*.

To repeat the words, inserting *Tosefta* where called for, with which Danby begins his preface to Mishnah: "The object of this translation is to render the contents of Tosefta easily accessible in their entirety." While, however, Mishnah had been translated in large part before his time, to my knowledge no complete division of Tosefta is in English, and the present division of Tosefta exists, outside of Hebrew, only in the excellent German translation under Rengstorf's editorship. So, returning to Danby: "Such fragmentary presentation of the contents of Tosefta fails to give a true idea of its nature and may easily give a wrong idea. Tosefta as we now have it was planned and systematically compiled as a single whole, and it is only by studying it as a single whole [alongside Mishnah] and understanding somewhat of the system governing its compilation that we can hope to estimate aright the value of the traditions which it has preserved. The annotations to the present translation aim only at explaining allusions [to Mishna in particular] ... they do not pretend to be an adequate commentary. Thus no account is taken of the wealth of illustrative material contained in the literature, history, religion, jurisprudence, handicrafts, beliefs, superstitions, and folklore contemporary with the Mishnah [and Tosefta]; and in no case do the notes trace the logical processes which underlie many of the recorded opinions. ... Even with their very limited purpose the present annotations have been kept as few and brief as possible."

Danby's translation of Mishnah is a model for all who propose to render into English important documents of earlier Rabbinic Judaism, just as his translation of the tenth book of Maimonides' *Mishneh Torah* is worthy of the elegance and stylistic lucidity of the Hebrew original. For reasons amply spelled out, I do not claim to have attained equivalent success and hope only that this work will prove half as useful to English-speaking students of Rabbinic literature as has Danby's.

It remains to thank my colleague, Professor Richard S. Sarason, for reading and criticizing the draft of this translation, both in the context of work on *A History of the Mishnaic Law of Purities* and in that of sizable revisions for the present volume. His help has been indispensable. Brown University paid the cost of typing the manuscript, for which I am most grateful.

The work is dedicated to a friend and colleague, who, in the familiar tradition and spirit of the Brown University administration, has done everything he could to foster and facilitate my work as teacher and scholar.

As Dean of the Graduate School and, now, Dean of the Faculty, Maurice Glicksman has given counsel, sound advice, and concrete and vital support to the work of the Department of Religious Studies in general, and to mine in particular. Time and again, decisions are made and implemented which make possible fruitful and cordial conditions of labor for us all, faculty, students, scholars. This small token of respect and esteem is offered in appreciation.

J. N.

24 September 1976
29 Elul 5736

List of Abbreviations and Glossary

[ ]	= Words supplied by translator.
( )	= To be deleted from the Hebrew text.
[?]	= Translation uncertain.
Ah.	= Ahilot (Tosefta's title for Ohalot).
Albeck	= Ḥanokh Albeck, *Seder ṭohorot* (Jerusalem and Tel Aviv, 1958. *Shishah sidré mishnah,* VI).
'Am ha'areṣ	= Ordinary person, *paganus.* Specifically: One who does not observe the laws of tithing and who does not eat ordinary food, that is, food which is not consecrated as one of the priestly gifts, in a state of cleanness such as is required for the eating of consecrated food.
b.	= ben, son of.
b.	= Babylonian Talmud.
B.B.	= Baba' batra'. Last "gate," that is, unit.
B.M.	= Baba' meṣi'a'. Middle "gate."
B.Q.	= Baba' Qamma'. First "gate."
Chron.	= Chronicles.
Dan.	= Daniel.
Deut.	= Deuteronomy.
'Erub	= Mixture, combination. If sufficient food for two meals is deposited in an accessible place on the eve of the Sabbath, that place becomes a person's temporary abode, permitting a range of 2,000 cubits from that place.
Etrog	= A kind of citron.
Ex.	= Exodus.
Ezek.	= Ezekiel.
Fingerbreadth	= About 2 1/3 centimetres.
Gen.	= Genesis.
Ḥaber	= Associate, fellow. One who observes the laws of tithing meticulously and also who eats his unconsecrated food in a state of cleanness, as if it were heave-offering. Compare *'Am Ha'areṣ.*
Ḥaliṣah	= The removal of a shoe. The ceremony prescribed in Deut. 25:7−9 in the case of a man who refuses to marry the widow of his brother who has died without children. The sister-in-law who has survived removes the surviving brother's shoe, etc.

Ḥaluṣah	= A woman who has carried out the rite of *ḥaliṣah*.
Ḥallah	= Dough-offering.
Handbreadth	= Four fingerbreadths, about 9 1/3 centimetres.
Heave-offering	= *Terumah*, the portion of the yield of the harvest which must be given to priests (Num. 18:8ff., Deut. 18:4). It is the first tax on the crop. It is to be eaten in a status of cleanness by priests and their relations.
If water be put	= Lev. 11:38: "If water be put on the seed, and any part of their carcass falls on it, it is unclean to you." Food which is dry is insusceptible to uncleanness. Food which is wet down is subject to uncleanness and made unclean when in contact with a source of uncleanness. Makhshirin uses "If water be put" as the apodosis for various cases.
Is.	= Isaiah.
Jer.	= Jeremiah.
Kel.	= Kelim.
Kokh	= Burial-niche.
Kor	= A *kor*'s space is 75,000 square cubits.
Land	= The Land, the Land of Israel.
Lev.	= Leviticus.
Litres/*litras*	= half a *log*.
Log	= the contents, in liquid measure, of six eggs.
M.	= Mishnah.
M'ŚH (+B/Š)	= *Ma'aśeh* is a meaningless form which signifies that that which follows is a precedent or story. It is left untranslated, but could be given as "A story is told+B: "concerning so-and-so" or Š: "*that* so-and-so *did* such-and-such."
Maddaf	= Uncleanness conveyed by the Zab, etc. (Lev. 15:2, 25) to what lies above him, even though he does not directly touch the object, specifically pertaining to food, drink, and an object not used for lying and sitting.
Mak.	= Makhshirin.
Meṣora', meṣora'at	= A skin-disease, (mis)translated "leprosy."
Midras	= Pressure-uncleanness, imparted by the Zab, the menstruating woman and others of a similar status (Lev. 12:2, 15:2, 25), to any object which can be used for lying or sitting, when said Zab etc. will lie or sit on such an object. *Midras* also is used to mean "susceptible to *midras*-uncleanness," that is,

an object generally used for lying or sitting.

Miq.	= Miqvaot.
Nazir	= One who has taken the vow specified at Num. 6:1–21.
Neg.	= Negaim.
Nid.	= Niddah.
Notar	= Portions of sacrifices left over beyond the legal time and supposed to be burned.
Oh.	= Ohalot.
Par.	= Parah.
Peruṭot	= Small coins.
Piggul	= A sacrifice rendered loathsome and unfit because a priest has formed the intention to make unfit use or inappropriately to dispose of said sacrifice.
Ps.	= Psalms.
Qab	= Four *logs* = the volume of 24 eggs.
Qartob	= 1/64th of a *log*, about a tenth of an egg in liquid volume.
R.	= Rabbi.
ŠWB	= *Once more*, part of the formulary of M'ŚH ("*Another* story concerning").
Ṣara'at	= "Leprosy."
Se'ah	= Six *qabs*, 36 eggs in liquid volume.
Sela'	= Two *sheqels*, a somewhat large coin.
Sens	= Samson of Sens. See Preface.
Sit	= Two handbreadths (4 2/3rds centimetres).
T.	= Tosefta.
TR	= Saul Lieberman, *Tosefet Rishonim*. See Preface.
T.Y.	= Tebul Yom.
Tammé	= Cultic materials which are made unclean.
Tebul Yom	= One who has immersed in a fit immersion-pool and awaits sunset to complete the process of purification.
Ṭerefah	= Flesh of a beast which was wounded so that it could not survive for twelve months after the wound, or which suffered an abnormality or defect; flesh of an animal slaughtered sloppily yet acceptably, as distinct from *nebelah,* carrion, a clean beast which suffered violent death or was improperly slaughtered.
Uqs.	= Uqsin.
Y.	= Yerushalmi, Palestinian Talmud.
Yad.	= Yadayim.

Zab (F: Zabah;
  Pl.:Zabin, Zabot) = A man or woman who has suffered a flux as specified at Lev. 15:1−15, 25−30.

Zuckermandel = M. S. Zuckermandel, *Tosephta. Based on the Erfurt and Vienna Codices* (Repr.: Jerusalem, 1963).

KELIM BABA QAMMA

1:1 A. [There is a] more stringent [trait] in [regard to] the creeping thing than in regard to semen, and in regard to semen than in regard to the creeping thing.

B. The more stringent trait in regard to the creeping thing [is] that the creeping thing's uncleanness is undivided, but the semen's uncleanness is divided.

C. The more stringent trait in regard to semen [is] that semen renders unclean in any quantity, but the creeping thing renders unclean only in the quantity of a lentil.

1:2 A. There is a more stringent trait in regard to the carrion than in regard to purification-water, and in regard to purification-water than in regard to carrion.

B. For a small quantity of purification-water is unclean, and a small quantity of carrion is clean.

C. The more stringent trait in regard to the carrion [is] that purification-water which has dried up — lo, it is clean. [As to] carrion which has dried up, if it can be soaked and stand in its former condition, lo, this is unclean.

1:3 A. There is a more stringent trait in regard to one unclean by a corpse than in regard to one who has intercourse with a menstruating woman, and in regard to one who has intercourse with a menstruating woman than in regard to one made unclean by a corpse.

B. For one made unclean by a corpse requires sprinking on the third and seventh days, which does not apply to the one who has intercourse with a menstruating woman.

C. The more stringent trait in regard to one who has intercourse with a menstruating woman [is] that one who has intercourse with a menstruating woman renders unclean the lowest spread as the uppermost one, which is not so of one made unclean by a corpse.

D. R. Yosé says, "The flux of a Zab, his spit, his semen, and his urine are like the saddle.

E. "The more stringent trait in regard to them which does not apply to the saddle, and to the saddle which does not apply to them [is]

F. "that touching and carrying them is the same so far as rendering man and clothing unclean, which [capacity for contamination] does not apply to the saddle.

G. "There is more stringent trait in regard to the saddle, for the saddle renders unclean [even what lies] under a heavy stone, which does not apply to them."

1:4 A. The more stringent trait in regard to an olive's bulk [of a corpse]

1

than to [an entire] corpse is that, for an olive's bulk, an opening [in a room] of one handbreadth square [affords protection], but for the corpse, [a much larger] opening, [namely] four handbreadths [is required to protect other openings from uncleanness].[1]

B. R. Nathan said, "He [who] went and became unclean on account of a corpse [is unclean so as] to render unclean at two removes and to render unfit at one [a third]."[2]

1:5 A. In three ways is Syria [subject to the same legal status] as the Land of Israel, and in three [ways is Syria subject to the same legal status] as foreign territory.

B. Its dirt imparts uncleanness as [does dirt of] foreign territory.

C. And he who brings a writ of divorce from Syria is like one who brings [a writ of divorce] from foreign territory.

D. And he who sells his slave to [purchaser in] Syria is like him who sells [a slave] to [a purchaser] in foreign territory.

E. [In] three [ways is Syria subject] to [the same legal status as] the Land of Israel,

F. for he who purchases a field in Syria is like one who purchases [a field] in the suburbs of Jerusalem.

G. And it [produce grown in Syria] is liable for tithes and for [the observance of] the Seventh Year.

H. And if one can bring [something] into it in a state of cleanness, it remains in a state of cleanness.

1:6 A. "Those whose hands and feet are not washed enter [the area] between the porch and the altar," the words of R. Meir.

B. And sages say, "They do not enter."[3]

C. Said R. Simeon the Modest before R. Eliezer, "I entered [the area] between the porch and the altar without having washed [my]hands and feet."

D. He said to him, "Who is more beloved, you or the high priest?"

E. He was silent.

F. He said to him, "You are ashamed to say that [even] the dog of the high priest is more beloved than you!"

G. He said to him, "Rabbi, you have said it."

H. He said to him, "By the [sacred] service! Even the high priest [who without washing hands and feet enters the area between the porch and the altar] — they break his head with clubs. What will you do that the guardsman not find you!"

I. R. Yosé says, "Just as everyone keeps separate [from the area] between the porch and the altar during the time of burning incense, so they keep separate in the time of the laying on of blood."[4]

---

1. M. Kel. 1:1—3.   2. M. Kel. 1:5.   3. M. Kel. 1:9.
4. M. Kel. 1:9.

J. ([That is to say, the laying on of blood of] the cow of the anointed priest and the cow which is offered in behalf of the community [because of an error of the congregation], and the goats offered on account of the sin of idolatry, and the blood of the Day of Atonement).

K. What particular distinction applies to [the area] between the porch and the altar and the Temple? But [into the area] between the porch and the altar do people enter both for the sacrificial service and not for the sacrificial service. But [into the area of] the Temple people enter only for the purpose of the sacrificial service alone.

1:7 A. Abba Saul says, "The upper chamber of the house of the Holy of Holies is subject to a more stringent rule than the house of the Holy of Holies [itself].[5]

B. "For [as to] the house of the Holy of Holies, a high priest enters therein once a year for the sacrificial service of the Day of Atonement four times in the day. And if he entered five [times], he is liable to the death penalty.

C. "But into the upper chamber of the house of the Holy of Holies people enter only [once in seven] years to know what it requires."

D. They said to him, "This is no particular distinction."

1:8 A. [If] lepers enter [the area] beyond the wall, they incur forty stripes.

B. [If] *Zabin* and *Zabot*, menstruating women, and women unclean by reason of childbirth enter the Temple mount, they incur eighty stripes.[6]

C. One who is unclean by reason of corpse-uncleanness enters the Temple mount, and not one unclean by corpse-uncleanness alone have they said, but even the corpse itself,

D. as it is said, "And Moses took the bones of Joseph with him"[7] —

E. with him into the camp of the Levites.

F. R. Simeon says, "The rampart and the women's court are [subject to] a special distinction in the eternal house. But unclean people who entered [that] area are free [of punishment]."

1:9 A. The entire court is suitable for eating Most Holy Things and for slaughtering Lesser Holy Things.

B. He who slaughters unconsecrated [animals] therein — they [the animals] are prohibited for [his] use.

C. It was the courtyard of the tent within the veils which were in the wilderness.

1:10 A. All unclean people who entered [the area] from Nicanor's Gate and inward, even if they have not yet completed atonement, lo, they are liable, [if they did so] deliberately, for extirpation, and, [if they did so] inadvertently, for a sin-offering.

B. And one does not have to say [that the same rule applies to] those who have immersed and await sunset [the Ţebul Yom].

---

5. M. Kel. 1:9.   6. M. Kel. 1:8.   7. Ex. 13:19.

C. And as to all other unclean people who entered beyond their limits, lo, they are subject to warning.

D. [If] they entered into the holy place, lo, they are liable to the death penalty.

E. R. Judah says, "[For entering into] the area before the holy place, [they are subject to] the death penalty. And [for entering] the whole rest of the house, [they are subject to] warning."

1:11 A. All enter to build and to repair [the Temple building] and to remove uncleanness.

B. [If] it is the duty for priests [to carry out the dead, and if] there are no priests there, Levites enter. [If] there are no Levites, Israelites enter. [If] it is the duty for clean people [to carry out and if] there are not clean people there, unclean people enter. [If] it is the duty of unblemished [people] [and if] there are no unblemished people, blemished people enter in.

C. And so it says, "And the priests entered the house to purify it and they brought out all the uncleanness."[8]

D. R. Judah says, "[The area] of the cellars which are under the Temple is unconsecrated area, but the roof of the Temple is sacred.

E. "They do not eat there Most Holy Things, and they do not slaughter there Lesser Holy Things, and unclean people who entered there — lo, they are free [of punishment]."

1:12 A. And just as in the wilderness were three camps, the camp of the Indwelling Presence of God, the camp of the Levites, and the camp of the Israelites, so there were in Jerusalem [three camps]:

B. From the gate of Jerusalem to the gate of the Temple Mount is the camp of Israel.

C. From the gate of the Temple Mount up to Nicanor's gate is the camp of the Levites.

D. From the Nicanor's gate and inward is the camp of the Indwelling Presence of God.

E. And that [corresponded to the place within] the curtains in the wilderness.

F. In the time of journeying, no aspect of sanctity applied to them, and people were not liable concerning them on account of uncleanness.

1:13 A. And how much [flesh] is sufficient to bring about healing?[9]

B. They compare it to a young shoot of a fig tree which was torn off but is still attached to the tree by a small rind.

C. If it can live from it [the connection formed by the rind], it is unclean, and if not, it is clean.

1:14 A. R. Menaḥem b. R. Yosé says, "Cities surrounded by a wall are more holy than the Land of Israel.

---

8. II. Chron. 29:16.   9. M. Kel. 1:5.

B. "For they send forth lepers from their midst.

C. "And the house is sold permanently in their midst [only] after twelve months.

D. "And they carry the corpse around in their midst so long as they like.

E. "[If] it has gone forth, they do not bring it back."[10]

F. And so [Scripture] says, "And Uzziah rested with his fathers, and they buried him in the burial field belonging to the kings, for they said that he was a leper, and Jotham his son reigned after him."[11]

G. R. Simeon says, "Just as *Zabin* and *Zabot,* menstruating women and those who have given birth do not enter the Temple mount, so too their seat and couch are according to their [status]."[12]

2:1   A. Vessels of alum-crystal —

B. The House of Shammai say, "They convey uncleanness from their inside and from their airspace like clay vessels, and from their outer parts like rinsable utensils."

C. And the House of Hillel say, "Vessels of alum-crystal — lo, they are like clay vessels in every respect."

D. R. Simeon b. Eleazar says [this tradition] in another formulation:

"The House of Shammai say, 'They are made unclean like a half-utensil and convey uncleanness like a whole utensil.'

"And the House of Hillel say, 'Vessels of alum-crystal — lo, they are like clay vessels in every respect.' "[13]

2:2   A. [Those fragments which] set without supports — their size [when broken, for the sherd to remain susceptible to uncleanness] is sufficient [oil] for anointing [a small finger of] a child. [And this measure applies to vessels which, when whole, hold] up to a *log.*

B. [A vessel the size of a] *log* and less than it [follows the foregoing rule].

C. From [a vessel which holds] a *log* to [one which holds] a *se'ah* [the measure to be held by the sherd for the remnant to remain susceptible to uncleanness is] a quarter [*log*].

D. [A vessel which holds a] *se'ah* and less than it [follows the foregoing rule].

E. From [a vessel which holds] a *se'ah* to [one which holds] two *se'ahs* [the measure to be held by the sherd for the remnant to remain susceptible to uncleanness is] a half-*log.*

F. [A vessel which holds] two *se'ahs* and less than it [follows the foregoing rule].

G. From [a vessel which holds] two *se'ahs* up to [one which holds] five *se'ahs* [the measure to be held by the sherd for the remnant to remain

10. M. Kel. 1:7.   11. II Chron. 26:23.   12. M. Kel. 1:8.
13. M. Kel. 2:1.

susceptible to uncleanness is] a *log*.

H. [A vessel which holds] five [*se'ahs*] and less than that [follows the foregoing rule].

I. [1] R. 'Aqiva says, "From [vessels of the type of Beth]leḥem to large jars [the measure, etc.] is a *log*. Henceforward [likewise the measure, etc.] is a *log*."

J. The matters were forgotten and now are not stated.

K. R. Nehemiah and R. Eliezer b. Jacob say, "[As to] large jars — their measure is two *logs*."

L. Cruses and *gelulin* [?] and the storage-jars which are [used] in Judah have bottoms but do not have sides.[14]

2:3   A. Gutter spouts and roof-tiles in which water or pebbles have made a receptacle are unclean.[15]

B. A reading desk —

C. folded up, is clean;

D. spread out, lo, this is unclean.[16]

E. The chair and the stool and everything on which one may lie [which are] clay vessels are clean.

F. R. Yosé says, "Also the ship and the potter's mould."[17]

G. And R. Nehemiah says, "The matters are reversed."

2:4   A. A metal funnel, whether of householders or of peddlers, is unclean.

B. And one of wood, bone, and glass, belonging to house holders, is clean, and one belonging to peddlers is unclean.

C. "Because it is [used as] a measure," the words of R. Judah b. Betera.

D. And R. 'Aqiva says, "Because he puts it on its side, and the buyer smells from it."[18]

2:5   A. The cover of wine-jars and oil-jars and the cover of a small jar and a papyrus [cover] —

B. [if] used at random and tossed away, are clean, and if adapted for use, are unclean.

C. A breadbasket-cover and a cover for a stewpan, when they are perforated and have a pointed top, are clean; when they are not perforated and do not have a pointed top, are unclean,

D. because she drains the vegetables into it.

E. R. Eleazar b. R. Ṣadoq says, "Because she turns the stewpot on it."[19]

F. This is the general rule: Whatever serves as a cover for a clay utensil is clean.

2:6   A. A spoiled jar which split in the furnace — how [do we know its status]?

---

14. M. Kel. 2:2.   15. M. Kel. 2:3.   16. M. Kel. 16:7.
17. M. Kel. 2:4.   18. M. Kel. 2:4.   19. M. Kel. 2:5.

B. They make an estimate of it.

C. If its sherds were equal [to one another in size] and its inside is red, it is ascertained that after its manufacture was completed, it was split.

D. If its sherds are not equal [to one another in size] and its inside is red, it is ascertained that before its manufacture was completed, it was split.[20]

2:7 A. A wooden spice-box made in two compartments and not having a rim —

B. [if] one of them [the two compartments] is made unclean by liquid, it is unclean and its fellow clean. And [if it was made unclean] by a creeping thing, the entire [utensil] is unclean.

C. [If] liquids fell on its breadth —

D. R. Yosé says in the name of R. Yoḥanan b. Nuri, "They divide its thickness. That part which serves the unclean [compartment] is unclean, and that part which serves the clean [compartment] is clean."

E. [If] liquids fell on its outer rim, it is adjudged as [a segment of] the outer part.[21]

F. [If] it was [permanently] affixed with a nail, [the nail] serves as a connector for [rendering the object] unclean and for [rendering it clean through] sprinkling.

G. [If] it was fastened, that [nail] serves as a connector for [rendering the object] unclean, but not as a connector for sprinkling.

H. [If] one takes off and returns [the object to that to which it is suspended], [the nail is a connector] neither for uncleanness nor for sprinkling.

2:8 A. As to the comb of a water-cooler —

B. R. Eliezer says, "It does not contract uncleanness through its airspace."

C. And sages say, "It conveys [and contracts] uncleanness through its airspace."[22]

D. That which is made for both [liquid and foodstuff], for example the breadbasket-cover, and the cover of a stewpan, and the jar —

E. they judge it according to its more stringent [rule]:

F. to admit and give forth uncleanness [with respect] to other things [if there is a hole sufficient to] admit liquid.

G. But it itself is clean only [if the perforation is of sufficient size to] release olives alone.[23]

2:9 A. Leather sacks for wine — their measure [of a hole to render them clean] is with liquids.

B. And R. Simeon says, "With seeds."

C. A lamp — its measure is liquids.

20. M. Kel. 2:6.   21. M. Kel. 2:7.   22. M. Kel. 2:8.
23. M. Kel. 3:1.

And R. Simeon says, "With seeds."

D. A spoiled jar — its measure is liquid.

E. The cruses of Galilee, with which they bring oil to the bath, and watercoolers, and tumblers that cannot stand,

F. before they have been fired are clean,

G. and after they have been fired are unclean.

H. And [if] they have been fired, and they are beautiful, they are unclean.[24]

2:10 A. A sherd which broke off of a jug or a jar,

B. if it contains according to measure, is unclean, and if not, it is clean.

C. [If] it was perforated and repaired with a pitch, it is clean.

D. For a clay utensil which is clean for one instant never again is subject to uncleanness.[25]

3:1 A. [If one] brought sherds of a clay utensil and glued them together and made an oven of them and made for them a plaster surface, whether on the inside or on the outside, and then fired them, even though in no one [of the sherds] is [the specified] measurement, they all [together] are [capable of becoming] unclean through contact and airspace.[26]

3:2 A. The large baskets which one plastered with scutch-grass and with earth, lo, these are not a connector.

If he immersed them, lo, it interposes on it.[27]

B. A clay utensil which one plastered so as to boil with it, lo, this [plaster] is not a connector.

C. And the tar-kettles which one plastered to boil pitch in them, lo, these are a connector.[28]

D. Sages agree with R. Meir and R. Simeon concerning a kettle which was plastered up to the place which flame reaches, that it [the plaster] is a connector; and [if it was plastered] up to the place which the flame does not reach, it [the plaster] is not a connector. [In the former case] if one immersed it [the kettle], it [the plaster] does not interpose on it.[29]

3:3 A. In [respect to] the hoop of the gourd that is whole, lo, this is a connector.[30]

B. The plaster lining, lo, this is not a connector.

C. [If] one immersed it [the hoop and the gourd], it does not interpose on it.

D. Downy hair of a child, lo, this is not a connector. [If] one immersed it, it does not interpose on it.

E. Excrement which is on the toilet [is not a connector; if one immersed it], it [the excrement] does not interpose on it [the toilet].

---

24. M. Kel. 3:2.   25. M. Kel. 3:4.   26. M. Kel. 3:4.   27. M. Kel. 3:6.
28. M. Kel. 3:8.   29. M. Kel. 3:5.   30. M. Kel. 3:5.

F. The limb and the flesh which hang from a man, lo, these are not a connector. [If] one immersed, they do not interpose on him.

3:4 A. Pitch is a connector on something to which it is appropriate [something used for cold water], but [as to] something to which it is not appropriate [something used for hot water], lo, it is not a connector.

B. How so? A [metal] ladle which was perforated and repaired with pitch, lo, this [pitch] is not a connector, [for hot water is put in the ladle]. If he immersed it [the ladle], lo, this [pitch] interposes.[31]

C. But a [clay] jar which was perforated and repaired with tin, or with a lead and tin mixture, or with sulphur, or with pitch, or with plaster, or with gypsum — this [lining] is a connector.

D. But all other things are not connectors.

E. And R. 'Aqiva declares unclean in the case of wood, because it [pitch] is its [wood's] genre.[32]

3:5 A. A large trough of earthenware, even though it comes in the measure [sufficient to be insusceptible], is unclean.

B. [If] it is broken so that it releases olives, even though she may place it on its side and knead in it, it is clean,

C. for in the first place it was not made for that purpose.[33]

3:6 A. He who brings chests and ovens and bowls and clay utensils from foreign territory to the land [of Israel] —

B. [if he did so] before they were heated up, they are subject to uncleanness in respect to [the uncleanness of] foreign territory, but insusceptible to uncleanness as earthenware utensils.

C. [If he did so] after they were heated, they are susceptible to uncleanness as earthenware utensils but insusceptible in respect to [the uncleanness pertaining to] foreign territory.

D. You turn out to rule: When they are subject to uncleanness pertaining to foreign territory, they are insusceptible to uncleanness as earthenware utensils, and when they are susceptible to uncleanness as earthenware utensils, they are insusceptible in respect to [the uncleanness pertaining to] foreign territory.

E. [If] he brought dirt from a place of uncleanness and kneaded it in a place of cleanness, or from a place of cleanness and kneaded it in a place of uncleanness, it is unclean. [If] he kneaded it on rock, even in a place of cleanness it [nonetheless] is unclean.

3:7 A. He who makes bricks in a grave-area — [if he does so] in a place of uncleanness, it is unclean. [If he does so] in a place of cleanness, it is clean.

B. R. Simeon says, "Even a brick from a grave area, from a place of uncleanness, is clean.

C. "For they have stated only [that the dirt of the grave area is unclean] when the clod is as it was when it was created [but not after manufacture]."

3:8 A. The assumption concerning sherds which are found anywhere is that they are clean,

B. except for those found in the pottery-works,

C. because most of them [sherds found anywhere] are from the spoiled vessels.

3:9 A. [As to] a sherd which breaks off from the side of a jar or from the side of a jug —

B. R. Simeon b. Eleazar says in the name of R. Meir, and so would R. Judah say according to his [Meir's] words, "[If it functions in its normal] way of receiving [something], it is unclean, but if [it does not function] according to [its normal] way of receiving something, it is clean."

C. [If] the handle is removed or the pointed end is broken —

D. R. Judah declares unclean.

E. And sages declare clean,

F. for a clay vessel which was clean one instant never again is subject to uncleanness.[34]

3:10 A. [As to] a jar which was diminished [through the breaking of its bottom] but which holds [something while lying] on its side, or which was divided like two troughs —

B. R. Judah declares clean.

C. And the sages declare unclean,[35]

D. for from the first place it was made for this purpose, so that one may tip it on its side and pour out what is in it to the sides.[36]

E. And if it was a spoiled jar, lo, it is clean, for they did not say there may be remnants to remnants, but only remnants to [whole] vessels.

F. What is a 'spoiled jar'?

G. Any [jar] whose handles have been split, and even one of them.

H. [If] it [the jar] was split below its handles, even though its handles stand, lo, this is [still] like a spoiled vessel.

I. But if in the first place it was made without handles, it is regarded as a [whole] jar.

J. [If] it was lying on its side like a kind of throne, this is the rule:

K. Any part with which one may receive water when he pours liquids into it [the jar] is subject to uncleanness through contact and through airspace.

L. Any part with which one may not receive water when he pours liquids into it is subject to uncleanness by contact but is not subject to uncleanness through airspace.[37]

3:11 A. The bottoms of *Qurpadot* [?], and the bottoms of Sidonian bowls,

34. M. Kel. 4:1.   35. M. Kel. 4:1.   36. M. Kel. 4:2.
37. M. Kel. 4:3.

and any sherd whose bottoms are sharp —

B. and, according to the words of R. Nathan, the oil-vessel and the Babylonian wooden bowl —

C. which split above and receive [hold] according to measure below, even though they cannot set without supports, are unclean.

D. For it was for this purpose that they were made to begin with.[38]

3:12   A. The bottoms of wooden, bone, glass vessels, if one scraped them, polished them, and made them into vessels, [and if] they receive [hold] any [thing] whatever, are unclean.

B. [If] they were equal, [the space] from the inner lip and inward is unclean, and from it and outward is clean.[39]

3:13   A. Earthenware utensils — from what point [in their manufacture] do they receive uncleanness?

B. "From [the point at which] their manufacture is completed," the words of R. Meir.

C. R. Judah says, "When they have been fired in the furnace."[40]

D. [If] one fired them, even with olive-refuse, they are unclean. One does not take account of the possibility that liquids dripped into them.

E. And in respect to being in the domain of an 'am ha'areṣ one does not scruple, for the ḥaber may come even after three days and take [the utensils, and they are assumed to be clean].

3:14   A. [If] one removed the covering and found dust on the utensils [which proves no one had touched them], lo, this one takes [one] of them.

B. [If, however] one of them has been removed, all of them are deemed to be in the possession of the 'am ha'areṣ.

C. In a place in which they plaster the beautiful ones with white plaster and a ḥaber supervises the plastering, the column [of pots the plastering of which] he has supervised is not unclean — but only that column alone [is clean].[41]

D. A ḥaber stands above, and an 'am ha'areṣ stands below and draws out [a pot] and gives it to him [the ḥaber], and the 'am ha'areṣ is believed to state, "I did not make it unclean," because he is assumed to be appropriately supervised.[42]

4:1   A. [As to] an oven for little girls — its [susceptibility at the] beginning [of its manufacture] is any [height] whatsoever, and its remnants [to remain susceptible to uncleanness] are at [the measure] of the larger part [of the whole oven].

B. And R. Meir says, "Its beginning is four [handbreadths] and its remnants [remain susceptible to uncleanness if they are at the height of] four

38. M. Kel. 4:3.   39. M. Kel. 4:4.   40. M. Kel. 5:1.
41. T. Par. 5:2, M. Par. 5:1.   42. T. Par. 5:3.

[handbreadths]."[43]

4:2   A. [As] to an oven — from what point [in the process of manufacturing it] does it receive uncleanness?

B. From the time that it has been heated sufficiently so as to bake sponge cakes in it.

C. R. Yosé says, "They regard the wood with which it is heated after the removal of the loaf."[44]

D. Rabban Simeon b. Gamaliel says in the name of R. Yoḥanan HaSandlar, "When it will be completed."[45]

E. The plastering of the oven — to what extent is it deemed [integrally] connected to the oven? To the extent that it serves the need [of the oven].

F. And how much [plaster] is needed [by the oven]?

G. In the case of an oven, a handbreadth, and in the case of a stove, three fingerbreadths.

4:3   A. [As to] three stones which one joined to one another and made into an oven and covered with plaster, whether on the inside or the outside

B. "They are made unclean through contact and airspace," the words of R. Meir.[46]

C. R. Judah says, "[If the plaster is] on the inside, they are made unclean through contact and airspace, and [if it is] on the outside, they are made unclean through contact and are not made unclean through airspace."

D. [If] one fixed them to the oven but did not fix them to one another, they are unclean.

E. [If] one fixed them to one another and did not fix them to the oven, lo, they are like the fender.

F. [If] one dug into the ground and made them a fender, they are clean. And the fender of the stove is clean.[47]

4:4   A. An oven which one heated so as to roast in it is unclean; [if it was heated so as] to place within it raw bundles of flax, it is clean, for one does not [in heating flax] do work with the oven itself.

B. An oven which was heated before its manufacture was completed is unclean.

C. R. Judah says it is clean.

D. Said R. Judah "This was a case in regard to the ovens of Kefar Signa, and Rabban Gamaliel did declare [them] unclean, and the sages clean."[48]

4:5   A. Why is the chimney piece of the oven of bakers susceptible to uncleanness? Because on it one rests the roasting spit.[49]

B. R. Judah says, "Because one suspends a kettle on the spit and puts it [the spit] on it [the oven]."

43. M. Kel. 5:1.   44. M. Kel. 5:1.   45. So *TR* III, p. 14.   46. Compare M. Kel. 7:4.
47. M. Kel. 5:3.   48. M. Kel. 5:4.   49. M. Kel. 5:5.

C. Rabban Simeon b. Gamaliel says in the name of R. Yoḥanan HaSandlar, "The [lowest height of a] chimney piece of the oven [to be susceptible to uncleanness] is a handbreadth. The [lowest height of the] chimney piece of the kettle of olive-seethers is two handbreadths."[50]

D. And it becomes unclean through airspace only in relationship to the chimney piece.

E. And from what point does it become unclean? When one begins to seethe them.

4:6　A. [As to] an oven in which one put dirt up to its mid-point —

B. "From the dirt and downward [the space] becomes unclean through contact. From the dirt and upward [the space] becomes unclean through airspace," the words of R. Meir.

C. And sages say, "They do not divide clay utensils, but the entire [oven] becomes unclean through contact and airspace."[51]

D. (R. Yosé says R. Eliezer says, "'From the dirt and downward is unclean through contact, from the dirt and upward is unclean through airspace,' the words of R. Meir. And sages say, 'They do not divide clay utensils, but the entire oven becomes unclean through contact and airspace.'")

E. Said R. Judah, "Under what circumstances? When one put dirt in it and afterward heated it. But if one heated it and afterward put in dirt, the entire oven is unclean through contact and airspace."

F. And R. Judah agrees with the sages concerning an oven which one placed over the mouth of the well or over the mouth of the cellar, and under which one put a stone, and which one plastered with mud from the sides, that it is unclean.

G. And sages say "In either case it is unclean."[52]

4:7　A. [As to] an oven which one partitioned into two, one part of which was heated and made unclean —

B. That one is unclean, but its counterpart is clean.

C. [If] both were heated, and one of them was made unclean —

D. R. Yosé says in the name of R. Yoḥanan ben Nuri, "They divide its breadth. That [part of the partition] which serves the unclean part is unclean, and that which serves the clean is clean."

E. Under what circumstances?

F. When one divided it and afterward heated it. But [if] one heated it and afterward divided it, the whole became unclean through contact and airspace.

G. [If] one of them becomes unclean through contact with a liquid, lo, its counterpart is clean. [If it was made unclean] by a creeping thing, the whole is unclean, and the thickness which is between them is entirely unclean.

50. M. Kel. 5:5.　　51. M. Kel. 5:6.　　52. M. Kel. 5:6.

4:8   A. An oven which one divided into two is unclean, because it is not possible to do it exactly.[53]

    B. And if it is possible to do it exactly, it is clean.

4:9   A. A cracked oven, the crack of which one put facing the corner [of a room] and which one plastered with plaster on the sides [to the walls of the room] —

    B. R. Nathan declares unclean, because the corner joins [the whole thing] together.

    C. And sages declare clean.

    D. The ledge of an oven which one placed in the corner [of a room] so as to bake with it is clean.

    E. And if the larger part of an oven is on it, it is unclean.

4:10   A. A cracked oven, on each crack of which one spread plaster, and the place of the cracks [of which] remains apparent, is unclean.

    B. [If] one put [in] dirt or pebbles, it is clean.

    C. [If] one put plaster on the crack, it is unclean.

    D. [If] one put earthenware on the crack, it is clean.

    E. [If] one plastered it with plaster on the top [surface of the earthenware], or made a lining for it on the outside, it is unclean, because the lining makes the whole thing into one [oven].

4:11   A. [If] one put on it [a crack in an oven] clay, lime, dirt, plaster, and gypsum, in any amount at all, and even at the craftsman's house, it is unclean. [If one put on it] fine clay, sulphur, wax, wine-lees, dough, or clods, or anything with which one does not make ovens, it is clean.

    B. The general rule is this: Whatever substance is not used for making ovens does not serve to join the crack together.

4:12   A. An oven which came broken into pieces from the house of the craftsman, [and for which] one made hoops, which one placed on it, is clean.[54]

    B. [If] one plastered it [the oven and hoops] with plaster, it is unclean when he will have heated it sufficiently to bake sponge cakes in it.

    C. And R. Simeon declares it unclean forthwith.[55]

    D. [If it was] unclean [and if] one removed the hoops, it is clean.

    E. [If] one restored them to it, it is clean.

    F. [If] one plastered it with plaster, it receives uncleanness, and one does not need to heat it, for it has already been heated.

4:13   A. [As to] an oven of rings, each of which is less than four handbreadths [in height], and among which was one which was four handbreadths in height, that one becomes unclean through contact and through airspace, and the remainder become unclean through contact, but not through airspace.

---

53. M. Kel. 5:7.   54. M. Kel. 5:9.   55. M. Kel. 5:8.

4:14 A. An oven cut into rings, each of which is less than four handbreadths [in height], and there was among them one which was four handbreadths in height — that one renders unclean through contact and not through airspace, and the remainder are clean.[56]

4:15 A. Rabban Simeon ben Gamaliel says, "He who wishes to make for himself an oven in [a state of] cleanness brings a cracked oven and brings a new oven [which has not been heated] and dresses it from the outside and puts dirt or pebbles between them, and even though he has made a lining for the outer one, it is clean."[57]

4:16 A. A large jar which one smoothed and rounded off, and which one has used as an oven, and for which one has made a plaster lining on the outside, even though it is able to contain [something] on its sides in accord with the prescribed measure, is clean.

4:17 A. When does it[58] receive uncleanness?

B. When it will have been heated sufficiently to bake sponge cakes in it.

C. And R. Simeon declares [it] unclean forthwith.

D. Rabban Simeon ben Gamaliel says in the name of R. Shila, "When its manufacture will be completed."

E. [If] one plastered it in a state of insusceptibility to uncleanness and it became unclean, from what time is its purification?

F. R. Ḥalafta of Kefar Ḥanania said, "I asked Simeon b. Ḥananiah, who asked the son of R. Ḥananiah ben Teradion, and he said, 'When one will have moved it from its place.'

"And his daughter says, 'When he will have removed its garment.' "[59]

And when these things were reported before R. Judah b. Baba, he said, "Better did his daughter rule than did his son."

4:18 A. A metal oven for which one made a lining, and for which one made a chimney-piece, and which one divided into two, and one part of which was made unclean through airspace — it is unclean, and its counterpart is clean.[60]

B. [If] a creeping thing touched it [the metal oven] on the inside, it becomes unclean through contact and through airspace, and its counterpart becomes unclean through contact, but does not become unclean through airspace. And its [the second part's] lining is clean.

C. [If] a creeping thing touched it from its outer part, the whole thing [is unclean in the first remove and so] renders unclean through contact at one [further] remove and renders [heave-offering] unfit at one [still further] remove.

D. [If] an olive's bulk of a corpse touched it on the outer part, the whole thing renders unclean through contact at two [removes] and renders [heave-

56. See TR III, p. 16.   57. M. Kel. 5:8.   58. The jar of T. 4:16.
59. M. Kel. 5:7.   60. M. Kel. 5:11.

offering] unfit at a one [further] remove, because it has been made into a Father of uncleanness. And it renders his body unclean.

E. "And its airspace renders unclean foods and liquids and hands," the words of Rabbi.

F. R. Ishmael the son of R. Yosé says in the name of his father, "It does not render unclean foods and liquids and hands, for a clay utensil does not impart uncleanness from its outer side."

4:19 A. [If] it [a metal oven] was perforated, damaged, or cracked, and one repaired it with plaster of any amount, it is unclean.[61]

B. [If] a creeping thing fell into its airspace, the entire [oven] is unclean through contact and airspace.

C. [If] an olive's bulk of a corpse fell into it, not in a tent, the entire [oven] renders unclean foods and liquids and hands, whether from its inside or its outer side.

D. The general principle is this: So long as it is subject to uncleanness as a clay utensil, it is adjudged according to the rules applying to a clay utensil. [If it is unclean] as a metal utensil, it is adjudged according to the rules pertaining to a metal utensil.

E. [If] one plastered it with plaster, whether inside or outside, it is clean.

F. R. Judah says, "[As to] the inside: if one can plaster it so that it will stand on its own, it is unclean, and if not, it is clean.[62]

G. "But one way or the other it is unclean on grounds of being a metal utensil."

4:20 H. A stove of metal for which one made a stand or for which one made clay props is clean.

I. [If] one plastered it with plaster, whether inside or outside, it is clean.

J. R. Judah says, "[As to plaster] on the inside, if one can plaster it so it will stand by itself, it is unclean, and if not, it is clean.

K. "But one way or the other it is unclean on grounds of being a metal utensil."

5:1 A. Three [metal] nails, three [wooden] pegs, [or] three [clay] props, which one set in the ground and joined with clay so as to set the cooking pot on them —

B. it is unclean.

C. And R. Judah declares clean until he will join them to one another with clay.

D. And R. Judah agrees that if one set them on the stone and joined them to it, that it is unclean, because the stone joins them together.[63]

5:2 A. Three stones which one joined to one another but [which] one did not attach to the earth, [or] attached to the earth but did not attach to one

61. M. Kel. 5:11.   62. M. Kel. 5:10.   63. M. Kel. 6:1.

another, are unclean.

B. And R. Judah declares clean until one will join them to one another and join them to the earth.

C. And how much [plaster] is [required to] join them?

D. Any amount of plaster.[64]

5:3   A. As to two large stones [or] two barrels which one arranged so as to suspend on them a large cauldron or a large kettle —

B. only the [part] necessary [for that purpose] is unclean.

C. And how much is necessary?

D. The place for setting — a handbreadth.[65]

E. [As to] two jars, two stewpans, two pots which one made into a stove—

the space between them is subject to uncleanness through contact and airspace, but their inside is clean.

F. As to the thickness between them, they divide it:

G. that which serves the unclean [part] is unclean, and that which serves the clean part is clean.

H. R. Judah says, "On it [a wall] and on the projection — if the wall is removed and the projection stands by itself, it is clean, and if not, it is unclean."

5:4   A. A stove which one placed on top of the stand [for a portable stove] of stone is unclean only in regard to the required part.

B. And how much is required?

C. Rabban Simeon b. Gamaliel says in the name of R. Judah, "The required part is three fingerbreadths."

D. R. Nathan says, "If the stove was removed and the stand which is on it goes up with it, it is a connector. And if not, it is not a connector."[66]

5:5   A. The fire-basket of householders which was diminished [hollowed out], lo, this is clean.

B. And how much is its measure?

C. In the scattering of its coals.[67]

D. The court of the double-stove —

E. R. Simeon says, "[If] the stove is made unclean, the court is made unclean. [If] the court is made unclean, the stove is not made unclean.

F. "And if it was separated, it is clean."[68]

G. R. Judah says, "If it may be taken as one [piece], it is unclean, and if not, it is clean."

5:6   A. "The socket for oil, spices, and the light, which are built on the stove —

B. "Their inside is adjudged as [is] the outer part of the stove.

64. M. Kel. 6:1.   65. M. Kel. 6:3.   66. M. Kel. 6:4.
67. M. Kel. 7:1.   68. M. Kel. 7:3.

C. "The socket for the light which extends from the stove —

D. "Up to three fingerbreadth is unclean. More than that is clean," the words of R. Meir.[69]

E. And R. Simeon declares [the whole] clean.

5:7   A. A chair which one has made into an ash-box, even though one makes use of it [for sitting], is clean.

B. [If] it was unclean and one made it [into] a box, it remains unclean until one will affix it with a nail.

C. A metal box belonging to householders, even though the plaster goes down into its midst, is clean.

D. [If] one made for it props, it is unclean.

5:8   A. A metal hive [large round vessel] of householders which is used as a basket, even though the plaster goes down into it, is clean. [If] one made for it clay props, it is unclean.

B. A box of the bath-house attendants, even though one made props for it, is clean.

C. For it is made only to be used with [on] the ground.

5:9   A. "Four props of a stove, two of which were removed crosswise —

B. "the second two are susceptible to uncleanness through contact and airspace, because one sets the saucepan and the pot on them," the words of R. Meir.[70]

C. And R. Simeon declares clean.

D. For R. Simeon would say, "Any clay props of a stove which are not subject to uncleanness through contamination of airspace are not subject to uncleanness through contact."

6:1   A. A clay vessel is made unclean only by a Father of uncleanness or liquids.

B. Whatever is at one time a Father of uncleanness [through being connected to a Father of uncleanness], and on which one has come to lighten [the burden of uncleanness], even not through immersion [but through separating the object from the source of uncleanness to which it is attached], so that it renders unclean at one remove and unfit at one remove, does not render men and utensils unclean.

C. Whatever is at one time a Father of uncleanness [and] on which [one] has lightened the burden of uncleanness only through immersion, [before it is immersed] renders unclean at two removes and unfit at one,

D. lo, this renders men and clay utensils unclean.

6:2   A. Whatever makes a man unclean makes a clay vessel unclean, and whatever does not make a man unclean does not make a clay vessel unclean, except for liquids.

---

69. M. Kel. 5:3.   70. M. Kel. 7:5.

B. Whatever is made unclean in a clay utensil on its inside is made unclean on its outside.

C. And uncleanness applies to a clay vessel only from its airspace or through its being moved by a *Zab* or on top of a heavy stone.

D. And it makes unclean only food, liquids, and hands.

6:3 A. [As to] a hive [which was] broken down [and] patched with straw and hung down in the airspace of an oven, with a dead creeping thing inside it —

B. the oven is unclean.

C. [If] a dead creeping thing is in the oven,

D. foods which are in it are unclean.

E. And R. Eliezer declares [them] clean.

F. Said R. Eliezer, "[We may construct an argument] *a fortiori*: If it [the broken hive] affords protection from the power of the Tent of a corpse, which is stringent, will it not afford protection from the power of a clay utensil, which is lenient?' "

G. Said R. Yoḥanan b. Nuri, "I stated to R. Eliezer, 'If Tents [partitions] afford protection from the power of Tents in connection with the Tent of a corpse — for indeed they do partition Tents — will Tents afford protection from the power of Tents in the Tent of a dead creeping thing for they do not partition clay utensils?' "[71]

6:4 A. Said R. Yosé, "I stated to R. Yoḥanan b. Nuri, 'I should be surprised if R. Eliezer accepted this answer from you. But an answer for the matter(s) [is thus]: If Tents afford protection from the power of Tents in connection with the Tent of a corpse — for [if] one makes a [space of] a handbreadth by a handbreadth with the height of a handbreadth in a house, [it is] clean — will Tents afford protection from the power of Tents in the case of a dead creeping thing? For [if] one makes [a space] for a handbreadth by a handbreadth in a clay utensil, it is unclean.' "

B. Said Rabbi, "The answer of R. Yosé is the same as the answer of R. Yoḥanan b. Nuri."[72]

6:5 A. Everything affords protection from the power of a clay utensil, even a utensil made of dung or a utensil made of stones or a utensil made of dirt — except for man.

B. How so?

C. A clean person who had foods and liquids in his mouth and poked his head into the airspace of an unclean oven —

D. they [the liquids] are made unclean.

E. And they do not take account of the possibility that they are attached to the spring.[73]

6:6 A. [As to] the mattress and the wrap which were placed on the top of the oven [and] sunk down into it.

B. [if] a dead creeping thing is in them,

C. the oven is unclean.

D. [If] a dead creeping thing is in the oven,

E. foods which are in them are unclean.[74]

F. You have nothing which affords protection from the power of clay utensils except utensils which have an inside, for example, the basket and the hamper and the goatskin.

6:7 A. [As to] the basket and the hamper and the goatskin [all made of leather] which were placed in the oven, and their mouth was above [the mouth of] the oven,

B. [if] the dead creeping thing is in them,

C. the oven is clean.

D. [If] the dead creeping thing is in the oven,

E. foods which are in them are clean.

F. [If] they were perforated, and one repaired them with plaster,

G. [and if] a dead creeping thing is in them,

H. the oven is unclean, for the [rule of the] tightly-covered stopper does not apply to [the egress of] uncleanness.

I. [If] a dead creeping thing is in the oven,

J. foods which are in them are clean.

6:8 A. [As to] a jar which was sunk into an oven and its mouth was above [the mouth of] the oven,

B. [if] the dead creeping thing is in it,

C. the oven is clean.

D. [If] a dead creeping thing is in the oven,

E. foods which are in it are clean.[75]

F. [If] it was perforated and one repaired it with plaster,

G. [and] a dead creeping thing is in it,

H. the oven is unclean, for the [rule of the] tightly-covered stopper does not apply to [the egress of] uncleanness.

I. [If] a dead creeping thing is in the oven,

J. foods which are in it are clean.

K. And if one repaired it with pitch, the oven is clean, for the pitch is a connector to it.

But as to all other utensils which one repaired with pitch, the pitch is not a connector to them.

6:9 A. [As to] a jar which is placed on top of the oven, [with] its mouth to this side and its bottom to that side,

B. [if] the dead creeping thing is in it,

C. [the] oven is clean.

D. [If] a dead creeping thing is in the oven,

74. M. Kel. 8:2.   75. M. Kel. 8:3.

E. foods which are in it [the jar] are clean.

F. [If] its side was crushed into its [the oven's] midst,

G. [and if] a dead creeping thing is in it,

H. [the] oven is unclean.

I. [If] a dead creeping thing is in the oven,

J. foods which are in it are unclean.[76]

6:10   A. [As to] a pot which is full of foods and liquids, and tightly stopped up and placed into an oven,

B. [if] a dead creeping thing is in the oven,

C. foods and liquids which are in the pot are clean.

D. [If] they were unclean,

E. the oven is unclean, for the [rule of the] tightly-covered stopper does not apply to [the egress of] uncleanness.[77]

6:11   A. A rinsable utensil which is tightly sealed and placed into the midst of an oven —

B. a dead creeping thing is in the oven —

C. lo, this is unclean.

D. For whatever does not afford protection in the Tent of a corpse does not afford protection in the Tent of a dead creeping thing.[78]

6:12   A. Three things afford protection in the Tent of a corpse: that which is swallowed, and that which is tightly sealed, and Tents.

B. There is [a rule] concerning that which is swallowed up which does not apply to that which is tightly sealed or to Tents. There is [a rule] concerning that which is tightly sealed and Tents which does not apply to that which is swallowed up.

C. That which is swallowed affords protection for clean things so that they should not become unclean, and affords protection for unclean things so that they should not convey uncleanness.

D. That which is tightly sealed and Tents afford protection for clean things from becoming unclean, but do not afford protection for unclean things from conveying uncleanness.

E. Things which are swallowed do not become contaminated through the carriage of a Zab, and that which is tightly sealed and Tents do become unclean through the carriage of a Zab.

F. The leather bag and the basket which have been damaged so as to allow pomegranates to fall through, even though they have ceased to be subject to the law of utensils, [still] afford protection in the Tent of the dead creeping thing.

6:13   A. [As to] the goatskin which is placed in the oven, with its mouth above the oven, and a bone about the size of a barley-corn wrapped in bast or in parchment [is] placed in it [the skin] —

76. M. Kel. 8:3.   77. M. Kel. 8:6.   78. M. Kel. 8:5.

B. it [the goatskin] is clean, and the oven is clean.

C. [If] the clean person came and took it and raised it,

D. he is made unclean and renders the goatskin unclean, [and] the goatskin goes back and renders the oven unclean.

6:14 A. Two ovens, one on top of the other, and a jar is extended downward between them, and its mouth is in the upper [oven] and its bottom in the lower [oven] —

B. [if] a creeping thing is in the jar, the ovens are clean.

C. [If] a creeping thing is in the lower [oven], foods and liquids which are in the jar are clean.

D. [If] a creeping thing is in the upper [oven], foods and liquids which are in the jar opposite the airspace of the upper [oven] are unclean.

6:15 A. An oven whose rims extend downward into its midst, and liquids fell there —

B. in the name of R. Neḥemiah have they said, "One brings a metal cubit or staff and places it [the cubit] on it [the rim]. From it [the cubit] and inward is unclean, from it and outward is clean."

C. [If] its lips turned downward toward its outer sides, it is regarded like the outer parts.

D. R. Aḥa says in the name of R. 'Aqiva, "It is judged like its inside."

E. The eye of the oven which one repaired with dirt or pebbles brings uncleanness to the oven only if it is a handbreadth square.[79]

F. [If the dead creeping thing is found] from the blocked up space and inward, it is unclean through contact and airspace. [If it is found] from the blocked up space and outward, it is unclean through contact, but it is not unclean through airspace.

6:16 A. A furnace of smiths which stands on the ground and which one attached [to the ground] with plaster so as to place the cooking pot on it is unclean.

B. But what is unclean is only that which is necessary for use.[80]

6:17 A. A stove which one set on top of the upper aperture, even though one may set the pot on it, is clean.

B. [If] one made for it clay props, it is unclean.[81]

C. A large furnace, lo, this is clean.

D. For it is made only to be used on the ground.

E. R. Meir says in the name of R. Gamaliel, "If it has a rim, it is unclean."

F. R. Judah says in the name of R. Gamaliel, "If it has a roof."

G. R. Yosé says in the name of R. Gamaliel, "If it has lips."

H. And all are for the same reason.[82]

79. M. Kel. 8:7.   80. M. Kel. 8:9.   81. M. Kel. 8:9.
82. M. Kel. 8:9.

6:18 A. Olive-peat which was prepared in [conditions of] cleanness and fell into the airspace of the oven, even when it [the oven] is heated — [the oven is] clean.

B. And [olive-peat] which was made in [conditions of] cleanness and became unclean and fell into the airspace of the oven —

C. when it [the oven] is heated, [the oven is] unclean.

D. When it [the oven] is not heated, [the oven is] clean.[83]

E. And R. Simeon declares it clean.

F. R. Eleazar b. R. Simeon says, "The House of Shammai declare unclean, and the House of Hillel declare clean.

G. "Under what circumstances?

H. "In the case of new [peat].

I. "But in the case of old [peat] all agree that it is clean."

J. What is old [peat]? After twelve months.

K. Abba Yosé ben Dosetai and R. Yosé b. HaMeshulam say, "[If] it has dried, [it is clean] after thirty days. [If] it has not dried, even after three years [it is still unclean]."

6:19 A. A wick which is full of unclean liquids and dried up on the outside and fell into the airspace of the oven —

B. when it [the oven] is heated, [the oven is] unclean.

C. When not heated, [the oven is] clean.

D. But [in the case of] a sponge, in either case [the oven] is unclean, because it [the sponge] is made to absorb [liquid].

E. R. Meir declares unclean in the case of reed-grass because [therewith] the market-inspectors examine the wine.

F. R. Yosé declares unclean in the case of reed-grass because the physician places it on the wound to draw up the liquid.[84]

7:1 A. A needle or a ring which were found in the stopper of the jar at the side of the jar,

B. if they were unclean, they have not made the jar unclean.

C. And if they were clean, the jar does not afford them protection in the Tent of the corpse.[85]

D. [If] they were found above the lip of the jar opposite the inside of the jar, whether the plaster flows under them or does not flow under them,

E. if they were unclean, they have not made the jar unclean.

F. And if they were clean, the jar affords them protection in the Tent of the corpse.

G. [If] they were found below the lips opposite the inside of the jar, when the plaster flows under them, if they were unclean, they have not made the jar unclean, but if they were clean, the jar does afford them protection in

83. M. Kel. 9:6.   84. M. Kel. 9:4.   85. M. Kel. 9:1.

the Tent of the corpse.

H. [If] the plaster does not flow under them, if they were unclean, they have made the jar unclean, and if they were clean, the jar does not afford them protection in the Tent of a corpse.

7:2   A. A dead creeping thing was found in the ashes of the oven below the bottom of the oven — it [the oven] is clean, because there is something on which to blame it.

B. [As to] a needle or a ring which were found in the ashes of the oven below the bottom of the oven,

C. [the oven is] unclean, because there is nothing on which to blame it.[86]

D. R. Simeon says, "In the case of the eye-outlet, [there are] two measures: from the middle, capable of entering, and from the side, not capable of entering."[87]

7:3   A. How do they examine clay utensils to know whether it is not [so perforated as to] admit liquid?[88]

B. One would fill a trough with water and place the jar in it, and if it does not admit [liquid], it is known that it is not so perforated as to admit liquid.

C. R. Judah says, "In the first instance one would cover the pot in the midst of the trough and allow water to flow over it, and if it did not admit it, it is known that it is not so perforated as to receive liquid.

"[Or] one would place it on the fire, and [if] the fire stops [the leakage], it is known that it is not so perforated as to admit liquid. [If] the fire does not stop [the leakage], it is known that it is so perforated as to admit liquid."

D. R. Yosé says, "If one places it on the hot ashes, and [if] the ashes stop it up, it is known that it is not so perforated as to admit liquid.

E. "[If] the hot ashes do not stop it up, it is known that it is so perforated as to admit liquid."

F. If it drips drop by drop, it is known that it is so perforated as to admit liquid.

7:4   A. [Utensils made from] (1) bones of birds and (2) unfinished metal utensils [which are insusceptible] and (3) clean wooden utensils afford protection with a tightly sealed cover.

B. And R. Yosé adds, "Also a convex chest which is [tightly] covered."

C. The hollow which is in the chip and which is in the beam, and the stopper which is in the jar do not afford protection when tightly covered.

D. And if there is in them [an empty space of] a handbreadth square, they do afford protection [as a Tent] if they are covered.[89]

7:5   A. A jar which one inverted against the wall and whose lips one plastered [to the wall] affords protection for what is inside it and for what is

86. M. Kel. 9:3.   87. M. Kel. 9:8.   88. M. Kel. 9:8 [M. Kel. 3:1].
89. M. Kel. 10:1.

opposite it in the wall.

7:6   A. [If] one overturned it and plastered down its lips to the earth,

B. it affords protection for what is inside it and for what is opposite it in the earth.

C. R. Eliezer says, "That which is turned upside down does not afford protection."

D. And R. Eliezer agrees concerning two saucepans or two pots which one inverted against each other and plastered together with plaster on the sides, that they afford protection as a tightly sealed cover.[90]

E. But if it was a small utensil and does not contain a handbreadth square and it is inverted on its mouth, it does not afford protection.

7:7   A. They do not stop up with tin, because it is a covering but is not tightly stopped up. And if one used it for reenforcing [the cover], lo, this affords protection.

B. Pots of fishbrine which one stopped up to the lip, and the lips of which protrude, even though the plaster extends downward into their midst as much as a full span of fingers, do not afford protection.[91]

C. For whatever does not afford protection in the Tent of the corpse does not afford protection in the Tent of a dead creeping thing.

7:8   A. R. Judah says, "A tightly stopped-up cover [cannot be arranged] from the inside."

B. And sages say, "A tightly stopped-up cover [can be arranged] from the inside."

C. How so?

D. A jar which was perforated and which the winelees have stopped-up

E. R. Judah says, "It does not afford protection."

F. And sages say, "It affords protection."

G. [If its plaster] is rubbed off but its pitch stands —

H. R. Judah says, "It does not afford protection."

I. And sages say, "It affords protection."[92]

7:9   A. The eye of an oven for which one made hoops on the inside —

B. R. Judah says, "It does not afford protection."

C. And sages say, "It affords protection."

D. A basket in which one placed plaster up to its middle and in which one sank the utensils —

E. R. Judah says, "It does not afford protection."

F. And sages say, "It affords protection."

G. [If] one turned it on the mouth of the jar and plastered its sides [together] with the sides of the jar,

H. it affords protection for what is in the jar and for what is between it and the jar.

---

90. M. Kel. 10:1.   91. M. Kel. 10:5.   92. M. Kel. 10:5.

7:10 A. A patch [of cloth] which one placed over the mouth of a jar, and the lips of which one plastered on to the sides of the jar affords protection for what is in the jar and for what is between it and the jar.[93]

B. R. Yosé b. R. Judah says, "It does not afford protection for what is in the jar until it will have been plastered with the lip [of the jar]."

7:11 A. The wine-jug [made] of the skin of the fish or papyrus with which one covered the jar and which one tied below, lo, [such as] this affords protection.

B. The skin of the fish and papyrus with which one covered the jar but which one did not tie below, even though one plastered with plaster from the sides, do not afford protection.

C. For whatever does not afford protection in the Tent of the corpse does not afford protection in the Tent of the dead creeping thing.

7:12 A. A pot which one turned over onto the mouth of a jar and the lips of which are plastered to the sides of the jar affords protection for what is in the jar and for what is between it and the jar.

B. [If] one placed it in its ordinary position [right side up] and it was made unclean —

C. an unclean utensil does not interpose.[94]

7:13 A. Two saucepans and two pots which one turned upside down into one another, and the upper one exceeds [the lower one's rim], even though one plastered it with plaster on the sides —

they do not afford protection.

B. For whatever does not afford protection in the Tent of the corpse does not afford protection in the Tent of the dead creeping thing.[95]

7:14 A. "A funnel, even when clean, does not afford protection with a cover," the words of R. Meir.

B. And sages say, "It affords protection with a cover."

C. And there is no purifying a clay utensil except through breaking it, and even if one attached it to the ground, and even if one affixed it with a nail, filled it with plaster or gypsum.

D. Rabban Simeon b. Gamaliel declares clean.

7:15 A. The broken bottoms of ladling jars and the broken bottoms of jars and the bottoms of utensils and their sides —

B. they [priests] do not draw [water for the heifer-ashes] with them, and they do not sanctify [mix water and ashes] in them, and they do not sprinkle from them [for purifying corpse-uncleanness], and they do not afford protection from the power of a clay utensil.

C. [If] one trimmed them, smoothed them, and made them into utensils, they draw [water for the heifer-ashes] with them, and they do sanctify in them, and they do sprinkle from them, and they afford protection when

93. M. Kel. 10:4.   94. M. Kel. 10:1.   95. M. Kel. 10:1.

tightly sealed, and they afford protection from the power of a clay utensil.

D. "And they receive uncleanness from then on," the words of R. Meir.

E. And sages say, "Every clay utensil which was clean for one moment never again is subject to uncleanness."

7:16   A. The broken bottoms of wooden utensils and bone utensils and glass utensils —

B. They do not draw with them, and they do not sanctify in them, and they do not sprinkle from them, and they do not afford protection when tightly sealed, and they do not afford protection from the power of a clay utensil.

C. [If] one trimmed them and smoothed them off and made them into utensils, they draw [water] with them and sanctify in them and sprinkle from them, and they afford protection when tightly sealed, and they afford protection from the power of a clay utensil.

7:17   A. Sherds of clay utensils which hold anything at all —

B. they do draw with them, and they do sanctify in them, and they do sprinkle from them, and they afford protection when tightly sealed, and they afford protection from the power of a clay utensil.

C. The sherds of metal utensils have returned to their former uncleanness.[96]

D. Unformed metal utensils, lo, they are like utensils, but they are clean.

96. M. Kel. 11:1.

KELIM BABA MEŞIA

1:1 A. Rabban Simeon ben Gamaliel says, "Not to all uncleanness, [does it return], but to the uncleanness of the soul."[1]

B. R. Simeon says, "Even a metal utensil which was unclean for the self-same day (*Ṭebul Yom*) returns to the status of uncleanness for the selfsame day."

C. And he who makes utensils from the anchor which is used to weigh down the ship, from the large utensil which one made to escape the taxes —

D. R. Meir declares unclean.

E. And sages declare clean.

F. R. Yosé says, "He who makes utensils from the scraps — they are unclean."

G. R. Yoḥanan b. Nuri says, "He who makes utensils from filings — they are unclean.[2]

1:2 A. Said R. Eleazar b. R. Yosé, "The House of Shammai and the House of Hillel did not dispute concerning nails which are known to have been made from vessels, that they are unclean.

B. "Or concerning nails which are known not to have been made from utensils, that they are clean.

C. "Concerning what did they dispute?

D. "Concerning the ordinary [nails], for

E. "The House of Shammai declare unclean.

F. "And the House of Hillel declare clean."[3]

1:3 A. He who makes utensils from filings, whether from the Land [of Israel] or from foreign territory — they are unclean.

B. R. Judah says, "He who makes utensils from filings from foreign territory — they are clean."

C. Clean utensils which one glazed with unclean glaze are clean.

D. He who makes utensils from unclean glaze — [the utensils] are unclean.

E. A spade which one made from the unclean [utensil], [with] (and) its adze [made] from the clean [utensil], is clean. [If] he made it from clean [material] and its adze from unclean, it is unclean.

F. Everything follows after [the status of the part of the object which actually] does the work.

G. [If] one made it from clean [material], even though it is covered [with metal] from the unclean, it is clean.[4]

---

1. M. Kel. 11:1.   2. M. Kel. 11:3.   3. M. Kel. 11:3.
4. M. Kel. 11:4.

1:4 A. A ladle [for drawing wine] which one made from the unclean [utensil], and its bottom from the clean, is clean. [If] one made it from the clean and its bottom from the unclean, it is unclean. Everything follows after the [status of the] receptacle.

B. "A laver which one made from cement, and its bottom from dung, is clean. [If] he made it from dung and its bottom from cement, it is unclean. Everything follows after the bottom," the words of R. Nathan.

C. Rabbi says, "Only if its bottom is a receptacle."[5]

1:5 A. [As to] cement and dung which one put together and with which one made utensils —

if the greater part is from the unclean, it is unclean.

If the greater part is from the clean [dung], it is clean.

B. Half and half —

C. R. Eleazar says, "They burn heave-offering on their account, but they are not liable on their account for uncleanness of the Sanctuary and its holy things."

D. Said R. Yosé, "R. Yoḥanan b. Nuri came to R. Ḥalafta. He said to him, 'What do you say concerning the metal spinner's coil?'

"He said to him, 'Unclean.'

"He said to him, 'So I say thus, but 'Aqiva declares it clean.'"[6]

1:6 A. A door bolt —

B. R. Ṭarfon declares unclean.

C. And sages declare clean.

D. And Beruria says, "One removes it from this door and hangs it on another on the Sabbath."

E. When [these] things were reported before R. Judah, he said, "Beautifully did Beruria rule."[7]

1:7 A. A plated double flute is clean.

B. [If] one made on it a receptacle for wings, it is unclean. And unclean is only that part which serves of necessity.

C. A plated recorder is clean.

D. [If] one made on it a receptacle for cups, it is unclean. And unclean is only that part which serves of necessity.

E. Its cups are unclean and are not a connector to it.

F. [If] its mouthpiece was of metal, the utensil is connected to the mouthpiece.[8]

1:8 A. A trumpet made of parts, lo, this [whole thing, when joined together] is unclean.

B. [If] it is taken apart, the upper part is unclean, and the lower part is clean.[9]

---

5. M. Kel. 11:4.   6. M. Kel. 11:4.   7. M. Kel. 11:4.
8. M. Kel. 11:6.   9. M. Kel. 11:7.

C. The nail with which one removes the wick and the tongs with which one crushes the wick are unclean. The nail with which one raises up and pushes down the branch for the base is unclean.

D. And Rabban Simeon b. Gamaliel declares clean.

E. [If] one made it with tin or with lead, it is a connector for uncleanness and for sprinkling. [If] one takes it and puts it back, it is a connector neither for uncleanness nor for sprinkling.

1:9   A. The scarabee which was breached, and the sting of which was removed, is clean.

B. [If] hooks remained on it from either side, it is unclean.

C. A necklace, the beads of which are of red coral and suspended on hooks of metal, lo, these are clean, for they are made only for reenforcement.

D. [If] it is broken, each one of them is clean by itself.

E. R. Eliezer says, "A hooklet of the nose is clean by itself."[10]

1:10   A. All sculptured images are unclean, and the thin image is clean.

B. [If] its lock is of metal, lo, this is susceptible to corpse-uncleanness.

1:11   A. All seals are clean.

B. Unclean is only the metal seal with which they actually seal alone.

C. A metal amulet, lo, this is susceptible to corpse-uncleanness. [If] the lower part broke, it is unclean. If the upper [broke], it is clean.

1:12   A. The leather with which one binds the amulet is unclean. [If] one spread it out, it is clean. It may be made unclean and then made clean even ten times a day.

B. Bowls[11] on which one writes the amulet are clean.

C. [If] one took a chip from it and made a ball for an ornament, it is unclean.

D. A sash which contains metal, lo, this is susceptible to corpse-uncleanness.

1:13   A. All ornaments of a beast, such as the chains and the nose-rings and the hooklets and the rings, are clean. Unclean is only the clapper which makes a sound for the man to hear.

B. One who makes bells for the mortar and for a cradle and for mantels for scrolls or for children's mantels — [lo,] they are clean.

[If] one made for them a clapper, they are unclean. [If] their clapper is removed, they are clean.

C. The bell of the door is clean, and of the beast is unclean.

D. The bell of a door which one made for a beast is unclean, and of a beast which one made for a door, even if one affixed it to the ground and even if one nailed it with a nail, is unclean.[12]

1:14   A. The presumption concerning bells which are found anywhere [is

10. M. Kel. 11:9.   11. *TR* III, p. 36.   12. M. Kel. 11:8.

that] they are unclean, except for those found in cities, because most of them [in cities] are for doors.

B. [If] one said to a craftsman, "Make for me two bells, one for the door and one for the cow," "Make for me two reed-mats, one for lying and one for tents," "Make for me two sheets, one for a tapestry [for pictures] and one for tents," — lo, these [both] are unclean until the time that he will distinguish between them.

And R. Simeon declares them clean until one will [actually] distinguish between them.

C. But the craftsman who makes and displays bells for a cow and bells for doors, and mats for lying and mats for tents, and sheets for tapestries and sheets for tents, if most of them are of the unclean variety, they are unclean until one will set them aside for a clean [purpose], and if most of them are of the clean [variety], they are clean until one will set them aside for the unclean [purpose].

2:1   A. A ring with which one fastens his breeches or affixes [the cloak] between his shoulders is clean.[13]

B. Unclean only is the ring of the finger alone.

C. A ring, whether incised or not incised, is unclean, but one which is plated is clean.

D. Said one disciple of the disciples of the Upper Galilee before R. Eliezer, "I have heard that they make distinctions between one sort of ring and another."

He [Eliezer] said to him, "Perhaps you heard only in regard to the Sabbath, that one who goes out [from one domain to another] with an incised one is liable, and [one who does so] with an unincised one is free of liability."

2:2   A. A needle whether perforated or not perforated is unclean, but one which is plated is clean.

B. Further did a disciple of the disciples of the Upper Galilee say before R. Eliezer, "I heard that they make distinctions between one needle and another."

C. He [Eliezer] said to him, "Perhaps you have heard only in respect to the Sabbath, that one who goes out with a perforated one is liable, and with an unperforated one, is free of liability."

2:3   A. A chain of saddlebags, lo, this is clean; and one of surveyors, lo, this is unclean, because with it one spreads out tents.[14]

B. And [as to the chains] of padlocks and of all other vessels, that which serves the unclean [vessel] is unclean, and that which serves the clean [vessel] is clean.

13. M. Kel. 12:1.   14. M. Kel. 14:3.

C. On what account is the chain of the wholesale graindealer unclean? Because it is used for tying up.

D. And as to that of householders, if one set it up for protection, it is unclean.[15]

E. R. Yosé says, "It is all the same with a rope, a chain, and a surveyor's rope."

2:4　A. A balance of retailers —

B. [if] it has weights and does not have hooks, [or if it] has hooks but does not have weights, it is unclean.

C. [If] its weights are removed, it is clean.

D. And when one attaches them, they are a connector for uncleanness and for sprinkling.

2:5　A. A balance which has a receptacle for coins is unclean. And unclean is only that [part] which serves of necessity.

B. Its cups of metal, whether or not they are able to serve as a receptacle, are unclean, and those of wood and of bone and of glass are unclean [if] they are able to serve as a receptacle, but are clean if not.

C. [If] one joined them to a beam and a beam to a balance, the entire [contraption] is one connector.[15]

2:6　A. A lantern which has a receptacle for oil is unclean; [one which has] a receptacle for a candlestick is clean. And unclean is only that part which serves of necessity.

B. Its pillars of metal, whether or not they are capable of serving as a receptacle, are unclean, and those of wood, bone, and glass which serve as a receptacle are unclean, and those which do not serve as a receptacle are clean.

2:7　A. A candlestick which has a receptacle for oil is unclean, and [one which has] a receptacle for a light is clean. And unclean is only that part which serves of necessity.

B. The nail on which one hangs the funnels is clean. But the funnels are unclean, and it is not connected to it.

2:8　A. Decorations which are on cupboards and frames, and their galleries and colonnades on turrets, lo, these are clean, since they are made only as an ornament.

B. The hook of a chest is unclean, but if it [the chest] was of sufficient size, it [too] is clean.[17]

2:9　A. Said R. Judah, "On what account is that [the hook] of the peddlers which is in front of him unclean? Because he hangs things from it. And the one behind him clean? Because it is made for guarding."[18]

B. A basket-cover of metal and of householders — Rabban Gamaliel

15. M. Kel. 12:1.　　16. M. Kel. 12:2.　　17. M. Kel. 12:2.
18. M. Kel. 12:2.

declares unclean.

And sages declare clean.[19]

C. And [a basket-cover] of wood is clean.

D. [If] it was sunk in up to its half or third, it is unclean, because it is like the lid of a cauldron.

E. Less than that is clean, because it is like the cover of a box.

F. And why is the cabinet door of physicians unclean? Because he places compresses on it or hangs the scissors on it.

G. R. Yosé b. R. Judah says, "Because he manipulates the child on it."

H. They said to him, "If so, let it be unclean [with] midras-uncleanness."[20]

2:10 A. And what are unfinished metal utensils which are clean? Any object which one is destined to smooth, to scrape, to hollow out, to adorn with designs, and to plane with a plane.

B. [If] they are lacking a cup, a border, and an ear, and a hand, they are clean.

C. [If] they [merely] lack covers, they are unclean.

D. What are tongs? Those with which the storekeeper stirs the pot.

E. What are firebars? Those which are affixed on the walls.[21]

2:11 A. A bowl of a storekeeper which is entirely made of nails, even if the whole thing is of wood and one is of metal, is unclean. And one of a householder, even if the entire thing is of metal and one of wood, is clean.

B. Rabban Simeon b. Gamaliel says, "[A bowl] of a storekeeper, even if the whole is of metal and one is of wood, is clean, for it is made only for use in connection with the ground."

C. R. Simeon b. Judah says in the name of R. Simeon, "A blood letter's nail is clean, for it is made only for use in connection with the ground."[22]

2:12 A. Said R. Nathan, "Rabban Gamaliel and sages did not differ concerning the hook of the scrapers of the bathhouses, that it is clean, for it is made only for use in connection with the ground.

B. "Concerning what did they differ?

C. "Concerning the scraper of metal of householders which is made like a ball, for:

D. "Rabban Gamaliel declares it unclean, because slaves scrape with it.

E. "And sages declare it clean."[23]

2:13 A. Said R. Judah, "Rabban Gamaliel and sages did not differ concerning a plate which was divided into two, and one of them was twice as large as the other, that the large one is unclean and the small one clean.

B. "Concerning what did they differ?

C. "Concerning the case in which one of them is not larger than the

19. M. Kel. 12:3.   20. M. Kel. 12:3.   21. M. Kel. 12:3.
22. M. Kel. 12:4.   23. M. Kel. 12:6.

other, or in which the two are equal, for:

D. "Rabban Gamaliel declares unclean.

E. "And sages declare clean."[24]

2:14 A. A nail which one twisted so as to open and close [a door] is unclean.

B. [If] one adapted it for protection, it is clean.[25]

C. [If] one made it for a lock or for a strigil, it is clean.

D. [If] one put it on a door-bolt so that the bolt should not move, it is unclean.

And Rabban Simeon b. Gamaliel declares clean.

E. [If] one placed it on the hand-mill or on the donkey-mill, it is unclean.

2:15 A. The hooks which hold the millstones above, lo, these are clean, for they are used only for strengthening.

B. The metal ball and anvil are unclean.

2:16 A. Weights which are broken, even though one restores them and weighs them, are clean.

[If] one set apart from them half-litres, third-litres, fourth-litres, they are unclean.

2:17 A. And what are the unfinished wooden objects which are unclean?

B. Whatever one is destined to smooth, to scrape, to hollow out, or to plane.

C. [If] they lacked a cup, a border, an ear, or a hand, they are unclean.

D. [If] they lacked hollowing, they are clean.[26]

2:18 A. A *se'ah*-measure which one is going to plane below is unclean; above, is clean.

B. Rabban Simeon b. Gamaliel says, "Wooden utensils do not receive uncleanness until their manufacture has been completed.

C. "And a *se'ah*-measure — once one will tie the tongs to it."

2:19 A. All unfinished wooden utensils are unclean, except those made of box-wood, because they lack heating.

B. R. Judah says, "He who makes utensils from branches of olive — they are clean because they lack heating, and they embitter what is in them."[27]

3:1 A. The javelin and the spear-head and the javelin-case and the helmet and the greaves, which were divided, lo, they are clean.[28]

B. A breast-plate which was divided lengthwise is clean; [when divided] breadthwise, if it serves its original function, it is unclean, and if not, it is clean.

---

24. M. Kel. 12:6.   25. M. Kel. 12:5.   26. M. Kel. 12:8.
27. M. Kel. 12:8.   28. M. Kel. 13:1.

C. When is its purification? When it will be worn out and no longer serve its original function.

D. [If] it wore out and there remains on it the greater part above, it is unclean; the greater part below, it is clean.

E. [If] one took a chip from it and made a bead for an ornament, it [the bead] is unclean.

3:2   A. Shears which may be taken apart, lo, this is unclean.

B. [If] it was separated, this-[one] is unclean by itself, and the other one is unclean by itself.

C. And when one joins it, it is a connector for uncleanness but it is not a connector for sprinkling.

3:3   A. Shears divided into two —

B. R. Judah declares unclean,

C. because in the first place one chops the branches with it and now one chops the branches with it.

D. And sages declare clean.[29]

3:4   A. A stylus whose stylus is removed is unclean because of the eraser.

B. [If] its eraser is removed, it is unclean because of the stylus.

C. [If] it was divided into two and there remained on the point [a sufficient part to] reach to the knuckles of his fingers, or on the eraser, one's entire palm, it is unclean. Less than that is clean.[30]

3:5   A. A kohl-stick whose point is removed, even though its receptacle is full of rust, is unclean.

B. [If] the receptacle is removed, if its point is full of rust, it is clean, because it will infect the eye.[31]

3:6   A. A soup-ladle whose spoon is removed is unclean because of [the] fork. [If the] fork is removed, it is unclean because of the spoon.

B. [If] it is divided into two, if it serves its original function, it is unclean, and if not, it is clean.[32]

3:7   A. A baker's shovel whose flat portion is removed is unclean because of the hook. [If] the hook is removed, it is unclean because of the flat portion. [If] it is divided into two, [and] if it serves its original function, it is unclean, and if not, it is clean.

B. A goad which is divided into two, and there remained on the coulter up to seven handbreadths, and on the leader up to four handbreadths, is unclean. Less than that is clean. And if in the first place one made it for this purpose, even less than that is unclean.

C. And the spade, even though its cutting edge is removed, is unclean.

3:8   A. A plane whose blade was removed, but on which there remained a full *sit* across its entire face, is unclean.

---

29. M. Kel. 13:1.   30. M. Kel. 13:2—4.   31. *ibid.*
32. *ibid.*

B. "[If] it is removed in its entirety," said R. Nathan b. R. Joseph, "in this case:

"The House of Shammai declare unclean.

"And the House of Hillel declare clean."

3:9 A. The scalpel of the plane is unclean by itself. When one attaches it, it is a connector for uncleanness, but it is not a connector for sprinkling.

B. The needle of the tax-collectors whose tip is removed is unclean because of its cavity.

C. [If] its cavity is removed, it is unclean because of its tip. [If] it is divided into two, if it serves its original function, it is unclean, and if not, it is clean.[33]

3:10 A. The sword and the knife which have rusted are clean. [If] one has polished them and sharpened them, they have returned to their original uncleanness.[34]

B. A tube of gold-smelters, and of glassblowers, and of smiths, and of those who make glass, which was divided lengthwise, is clean; [if] widthwise, if it serves its original function, it is unclean, and if not, it is clean.

3:11 A. [The] tongs of barbers, and of physicians, and of those who make glass, which are divided into two parts, are clean.

B. And [those] of smiths which are divided into two parts are unclean, because to begin with he stirs the coals with it, and now he [still] stirs the coals with it.

C. Rabban Simeon b. Gamaliel says, "Because to begin with he perforates the coals with it, and now he perforates the coals with it."

3:12 A. A nail-clipper is unclean. [If] it is divided into two, it is clean.

B. A siphon is unclean. [If] it is divided into two, it is clean. The nails and the attachments which are on it are connected for uncleanness and for sprinkling.

C. The funnel which was broken or the pipe of which one removed is clean. [If] it was divided into two and there remained on it a handbreadth, it is unclean.

D. The wards of a lock are clean. [If] one placed them in a lock, they are unclean.

E. [But if it is of a] revolving door and even if it is fixed on the door, they are clean.

3:13 A. A ring of metal and its seal of coral —

B. R. Neḥemiah declares clean.

For R. Neḥemiah held, "With a ring one follows after the [status of the] seal.[35]

"With the yoke they follow after its curved end.

"With the rack, after its nails; with the ladder, after its steps; with the

---

33. M. Kel. 13:4.   34. M. Kel. 13:5.   35. M. Kel. 13:6.

crib after its chains."

C. R. Simeon b. Eleazar says in the name of R. Yosé, "With a ladder, after the posts; with a rack, after the steps; and with a funnel, after the dish."

3:14   A. The furcated spear and the pronged pole and the mattock and the pinchers of launderers, one of whose teeth is removed and repaired with metal, lo, these are unclean.

B. Concerning all of them said R. Joshua, "A new thing did the scribes innovate, and I have no answer."[36]

3:15   A. A comb for flax, every other one of whose teeth was removed, is clean. [If] one tooth is removed from it, it is clean.

B. R. Simeon declares [the single tooth] unclean because one may write with it.

C. And if one adapted it so as to write with it, all agree that it is unclean.[37]

3:16   A. The shoemaker's last and the wrapping and the foil which are on teeth are clean. And that [wrapping] of wool which was divided, whether lengthwise or breadthwise, is unclean.

B. A gold tooth is susceptible to uncleanness, and they sprinkle on it in its place and go forth with it on the Sabbath.[38]

4:1   A. Metal utensils, such as the chest, the ark, and the cupboard, which come in measure [to be insusceptible, nonetheless], are unclean.

Their [= metal objects'] flat [forms], such as the table and the tray and the three-legged table of metal, are unclean. And their measure [to be so damaged as to be insusceptible to uncleanness is less than] a handbreadth.

B. "A metal utensil which lacks polishing is unclean," the words of R. 'Aqiva.

C. And sages say, "It is clean."[39]

D. A general principle did they state: Metal utensils which are damaged, if they serve their original function, are unclean, and if not, they are clean.

E. How so?

A bucket — sufficient to draw up [water] to drink.

A kettle — sufficient to warm up [water] with it to drink.

The jug — sufficient to serve guests with it.

The bowl — sufficient to rinse one of his feet in it.

F. [If] they were perforated:

A pot — sufficient to hold hot [water].

A kettle — sufficient to hold *selas*.

The stewpot — sufficient to hold jugs.

Jugs — sufficient to hold *peruṭot*.[40]

---

36. M. Kel. 13:7.   37. M. Kel. 13:8.   38. M. Kel. 13:6.
39. M. Kel. 14:1.   40. *ibid.*

4:2   A. Measures for wine and oil — their measure is with liquids.

B. R. Eliezer says, "With *peruṭot*."

C. A lamp — its measure is with liquids.

D. And R. Eliezer says, "With *peruṭot*."[41]

4:3   A. A club on the head of which one affixed a nail so as to be able to hold on to it in the place of the threshing is clean.[42]

B. And if [he did so] in order that the ground not wear it [the wood] away, it is unclean.

C. [If] one affixed a nail on its head so as to hit someone with it, it is unclean. [If] for ornamentation, it is clean.

4:4   A. R. Eleazar b. R. Ṣadoq says, "One row is unclean, and two rows are clean.

B. "A whip on the head of which one set a nail so as to smite [someone] with it is unclean; for ornament, it is clean.

C. "A band with which the saddle is fastened around the ass's belly which has on it a goad, lo, this is susceptible to corpse-uncleanness."

4:5   A. A claw of a carpenter with which one removes nails is unclean.

B. A siphon which one placed under the door, even though [the siphon is] used with it [the door], is clean.

C. [If] it was unclean and one affixed it under the door, it remains unclean, until the time that it will be purified.

D. And when is its purification?

E. "The House of Shammai say, 'When it will have been damaged.'

"And the House of Hillel say, 'When it will have been affixed,'" the words of R. Meir.

F. R. Judah says, "The House of Shammai say, 'When it will have been damaged and affixed.'

"And the House of Hillel say, 'When it will have been damaged, or when it will have been affixed.'"

G. R. Yosé b. R. Judah says, "A crowbar of a builder is clean, for it has been made only for use in connection with the ground."[43]

4:6   A. All utensils of the stone-cutter are susceptible to uncleanness, and the iron-tipped goads with them.

B. R. Judah says, "Except for the iron-tipped goads."

C. The cubit-measure and the eraser of metal are unclean, and those which are plated are clean.

4:7   A. A halter [which is plated] is clean. [If] one made a chain on it, it is unclean.

B. A chain which one made into a halter is unclean because it is like a bridle.

C. Three things are unclean in connection with the horse: the reins, the bit, and the bridle.

41. *ibid.*   42. M. Kel. 14:2.   43. *ibid.*

D. The bridle of the horse is unclean by itself. The cords and the thongs, when sewn, are a connector, and, when knotted, are not a connector.

4:8 A. A teethed strigil and a chain of figures and whatever does not circulate as a coin, lo, these are unclean.

B. A statue of a man which one made in the house, if [he made it] for an ornament, is clean. And if [he made it] to place the cup and the plate on it, it is unclean, because it is like a three-legged table.

4:9 A. A chain of a lamp is a connector on the comb. [If] there is no comb, it is a connector on the ring.

B. A chain of a large bucket [is unclean as part of the bucket for] four handbreadths, and [a chain] of a small bucket and of [a bucket of the kind used by] the immigrants from Babylonia is [unclean for] ten handbreadths.[44]

C. [If] one attached to it [the chain] a rope or a cord, whether above or below, even a hundred 'amah, the entire thing is a connector.

4:10 A. A saw, the teeth of which one placed in the hole of the door, even though one makes use of it [the saw], is clean.

B. [If] it was unclean and one affixed it to the hole of the door, it is unclean until one will affix it with a nail.

C. [If] one reversed it, whether upward or downward or sideways, it is clean.

4:11 A. The cover of a box and of a kettle, the cover of a basket and of an ink-well are unclean. And all other covers are clean.[45]

B. The rings which hold the ropes, lo, these are clean, for they are made only for ornamentation.

C. Those made to weight the straps and the straps which are suspended on them are unclean.

D. The iron which is under the neck of the beast and which is on the neck of the beast is unclean.

4:12 A. A nail with which one attaches the wheel so that it [the wheel] will not fall out is unclean.[46]

B. And Rabban Simeon b. Gamaliel in this case declares clean.

C. R. Judah agrees with sages in respect to the metal cover of a basket which one made into a mirror, that it is unclean.[47]

D. [If] it is broken and ceases to be useful for its purpose —

R. Judah says, "It is clean."

E. And sages say, "One way or the other, it is unclean."

4:13 A. A mirror which was broken, if it serves its original function, is unclean, and if not, is clean.

B. [If it] became dirty, if it shows most of the face, it is unclean, and if not, it is clean.[48]

---

44. M. Kel. 14:3.   45. *ibid.*   46. M. Kel. 14:4.

47. M. Kel. 14:6.   48. *ibid.*

4:14 A. R. Eliezer says, "[As to] metal utensil which was made unclean, and then broke, and which one forged [into a new utensil] — one sprinkles on it on the same day and repeats [the sprinkling] on it on the fourth.

"And that which was made unclean and on which one sprinkled and which then broke, and which one forged [into a new utensil] — one repeats [the sprinkling] on it that very day."[49]

B. R. Joshua says, "Sprinkling may take place only on the third and seventh days."

C. R. Nathan says, "R. Eliezer says, 'A metal utensil which was made unclean and which broke and then was reforged [into a new object], and on which one sprinkled, and which broke, and which one reforged — let [the owner] sprinkle on it on that very day.'

D. "R. Joshua says, 'Sprinkling is only on the third and seventh days.'"

4:15 A. A jointed lock which was broken in the midst of its joint —

B. R. Meir declares unclean.

C. And R. Judah declares clean.

D. And Rabban Simeon b. Gamaliel says, "Matters are reversed."[50]

4:16 A. A mustard strainer which was divided lengthwise is clean, and breadthwise, if it serves its original function, is unclean, and if not, it is clean.

B. Said R. Eleazar b. R. Ṣadoq, "The House of Shammai and the House of Hillel did not differ concerning a mustard strainer in which the three holes in the bottom merged into one another, that it is clean.

C. "Concerning what did they differ?

"Concerning two [holes which merged into one another], for —

"The House of Shammai declare unclean.

"And the House of Hillel declare clean."

4:17 A. A ladle for drawing wine, the mouth of which one is planning to close and to make like a duct, is clean until one will [actually] close the mouth.[51]

5:1 A. Utensils of dung and utensils of stone and utensils of dirt which come in [prescribed] measure —

R. Meir says, "Lo, they are like utensils."

And sages say, "Lo, they are like Tents."

B. R. Neḥemiah says, "Large boxes and large provision chests which have [flat] bottoms and hold forty *[se'ahs]* in liquid measure which are two *kors* in dry measure, lo, they are like utensils, for even though they are not carried when they are full, they are carried with what remains in them."[52]

C. And how much are they?

49. M. Kel. 14:7.   50. M. Kel. 14:8.   51. M. Kel. 14:5.
52. M. Kel. 15:1.

D. A cubit by a cubit by three cubits — they are six hundred and forty-eight handbreadths.

E. Evidence for the matter comes from the measurements of the [altar] table.

5:2 A. R. Yosé says, "In [reference to] the sea which Solomon made, it says, 'It holds three thousand baths' [II Chron. 4:5]. And in another place it says, 'It held two thousand *baths*' [I Kings 7:26].

B. "It is not possible to say 'two thousand,' for already 'three thousand' has been said, and it is not possible to say 'three thousand,' for 'two thousand' already has been said.

C. "On this basis state, 'Two thousand in liquid measure are three thousand in dry measure.'"

5:3 A. The boards used at weddings as tables which are in dining rooms — householders eat on them, for even though they are divided like the talon of a bird, they are unclean, because they are like a tray.

B. WM'ŚH B: A householder had boards in his house, and they would borrow them for a mourner's house or for a banquet-house. And the matter came before sages. They declared it clean. He saw that they needed them, and he gave them to them as a gift. And the matter came before the sages, and they declared them unclean.[53]

5:4 A. Why are baking boards of bakers unclean? Because they are designated as utensils. And [those] of householders are clean until one will designate them as a utensil.

B. R. Simeon says, "Why is the frame of bakers which is divided unclean? Because on it he cuts [dough] and brings the rolls to the oven.

"And one of householders — if he adapted it for cutting [dough] and bringing rolls on it to the oven, it is unclean."[54]

5:5 A. The frame with a rim of plated ropes, if it has handles, is unclean. [If] it does not have handles, it is clean.

B. R. Simeon b. Eleazar says, "Even though it does not have handles, it is unclean."[55]

C. Why is the sieve of millers unclean? Because one designated it as a utensil.

And [that] of householders is clean until one will designate it as a utensil.

D. R. Simeon b. Judah says in the name of R. Simeon, "Even that of millers is clean until he will designate it as a utensil."

E. R. Judah says, "That of hair-dressers is unclean with the uncleanness imparted by sitting, because it is still a utensil.

"Girls sit in it and fix their hair."[56]

5:6 A. All hangers which are perforated are connectors.

53. M. Kel. 15:2.   54. *ibid.*   55. *ibid.*
56. M. Kel. 15:3.

B. R. Yoḥanan b. Nuri said, "Also the wedged ones."[57]

C. Added to them [are] a belt-hanger and a small sword's [hanger], because they assist in the time of work.

D. The hanger of a flagon tray and a cup tray which is sewn is unclean. [If it is] tied and fastened by means of a loop, it is clean.

E. R. Simeon b. Eleazar says in the name of R. Meir, "All hangers are unclean. They did not declare clean the hanger of the sifter and the riddle of the householders, except in the time that he slides two heads to one side."

5:7 A. Every garter is clean. The garter of the plough is unclean.

B. All pieces [of fish] are unclean, but a piece of Iltith-fish is clean.

C. All the harps are clean, and the harps of song are unclean.

D. All liquids are unclean, and the liquids of the slaughter house [of the Temple] are clean.

E. And what are the liquids of the slaughter house which are clean? This is the blood and the water. [If] they were made unclean within, even though they went forth outside [the Temple court], they are clean. [If] they were made unclean outside and went into the Temple court, they are unclean.

5:8 A. The Scroll of Ezra which went forth outside [the court] renders the hands unclean.

B. And not only of the Scroll of Ezra alone did they speak, but even the Prophets and the Pentateuch.

C. And another scroll which entered there renders the hands clean.[58]

5:9 A. Cloths of the sons of Levi [used to cover harps] are clean. Similarly, a householder who made cloths to cover the walls and pillars — they are clean.[59]

B. Bed-frames of the sons of Levi are clean. Similarly, a householder who made a bed-frame to spread it from bed to bed and from crib to crib — it is clean.[60]

C. If he designated it for one particular bed —

D. R. Meir and R. Judah declare unclean.

E. R. Yosé and R. Simeon declare clean,

F. for one does not do any work with the object itself.

5:10 A. R. Judah says, "The *markof* [?] of song is clean, for it was made only to serve with the ground.

B. "[If] one made a nail on its head to hold on to it, it is unclean.

C. "At the place of the threshing, it is clean."[61]

D. R. Yosé b. R. Judah says, "The mouse-trap which has a receptacle is unclean."

E. The Babylonian tray and the plate and the wooden vessel for rubbish and the subdivided tray which were divided, even though they receive [food]

---

57. M. Kel. 15:4.   58. M. Kel. 15:6.   59. M. Kel. 24:14.
60. M. Kel. 18:3.   61. M. Kel. 15:6.

on their sides like stew-pots, are clean.[62]

5:11 A. The bed and the chair and the stool and the chair with a back and the cot which were untied are clean.

B. A bed which was untied piece by piece is unclean, each [piece] by itself.[63]

C. Sages agree with R. Meir and R. Simeon that ropes are not a connector to the bed until one will have knotted three knots in each direction.[64]

5:12 A. A cot — from what time does it receive uncleanness? From the time that its manufacture is completed.

B. And if one is destined to make a wagon for it, it is clean until one will make a wagon for it.[65]

5:13 A. A case for flagons and basket for cups [made] of palms which one has bound and smoothed on the outside, even though one has not smoothed on the inside, is clean, for thus they keep it.[66]

B. The small baskets and the handbaskets [are susceptible to uncleanness] once one has tied and smoothed [them].

C. The large baskets and the large *se'ah*-measures [for] which one has made two circling bands along their circumference, in addition to this one which is on the woven part, [are susceptible].

D. The willow basket, once one will have made two twists along its circumference, in addition to this one which is on the woven part, [is susceptible].

E. The rush basket, once one will have made on it one twist, in addition to this one which is on the woven part, [is susceptible].[67]

5:14 A. The baskets of camels [which] one has untied are clean. [If] one has tied them, they are unclean. They may be made unclean and purified even ten times in the day.

B. Utensils of twigs which one has not smoothed and which one uses at random are unclean. [If] one was destined to tie them up and to smooth them, even though one may [nonetheless] make use of them at random and throw them away, they are clean.[68]

C. And [this rule applies] solely [on condition that] one not practice deception. And if one has practiced deception, lo, these are unclean.

5:15 A. More strict [is the rule] concerning utensils made of papyrus than that concerning utensils made of twigs.

B. Utensils made of twigs receive uncleanness only after their manufacture has been completed.

C. But utensils made of papyrus, once one has made a single circling band along their circumference, are unclean.

---

62. M. Kel. 16:1.   63. M. Kel. 18:9.   64. M. Kel. 19:1.
65. M. Kel. 16:1.   66. M. Kel. 16:2.   67. M. Kel. 16:3.
68. M. Kel. 16:5.

6:1   A. Leather utensils — from what time do they receive uncleanness?[69]

B. The sandal — when one will have fastened the straps.

C. And the foot-covering — when one will have shaped [it] on the last.

D. And if one is destined to arch [them] — when one will have arched [them]. And [if] one is destined to cut patterns on it — when one will have cut patterns on it.

E. A leather apron — when one will have rinsed [it].

F. And the leather bed — when one will have cut patterns on it.

6:2   A. The leather of the cot for which one is destined to make an umbilicus is clean until one will make for it an umbilicus.

B. R. Judah says, "In respect to the pillow, there are no less than five [handbreadths], and in a mattress, there are no less than three [handbreadths]."[70]

6:3   A. Utensils of bone — when do they receive uncleanness? When their manufacture has been completed.

B. [If] they lack covers, they are unclean.

C. A shofar is clean. [If] one cut it off for a horn, it is unclean.

D. The horn which one uses and throws away is clean. [If] one gave thought to [continue to use] it, it receives uncleanness from that time onward.

6:4   A. A wicker wrapping of palms out of which one is destined to eat dates and [which one will] throw out is clean.[71]

B. [If] one gave thought to put [something] in and take out of it at home and in the field, it is unclean.

6:5   A. All utensils which are woven with a needle, like the purse and the socks, do not receive uncleanness until their manufacture is completed.

B. R. Judah says, "The basket — until it is woven sufficiently to receive a *peruṭah*. And the socks — until woven sufficiently to receive the coil."

C. All utensils which are woven on a needle, for example wickerwork (in the wine or oil press) and a trap, once one has made on them a receptacle [which serves] their use, are unclean.

6:6   A. The basket and the crates of camels and wide-meshed baskets which one made in the first place for holding [objects as large as] pomegranates are unclean.[72]

B. R. Simeon says, "Wide-meshed baskets which cannot be taken up by the sides to go out of the door are clean."

C. A new goat-skin, even though it holds pomegranates, is clean. [If] one sewed it, and it was torn, its measure [then] is with pomegranates.

D. R. Eliezer says, "[Its measure is] with warp-clews from four for a *mana*, which is forty for a *sela'*."

69. M. Kel. 16:4.   70. *ibid.*   71. M. Kel. 16:5.
72. M. Kel. 24:9.

6:7   A. A wringer on the door, lo, this is unclean, because one places [something] on it [on the top part] before the first [bottom part] is finished. [If] the bottom is taken off, it is unclean. [If] the top is taken off, it is clean. And its measure is a handbreadth.

B. R. Judah states concerning them three principles in the name of R. 'Aqiva: "That which is made to serve man, for instance, the ladder, and that which is made to serve utensils, for example, the rack, are clean. That which is made to serve both man and the things which serve man, for example, the table, the tray, and the three-legged table, is unclean."[73]

6:8   A. A tray for flagons and a tray for cups made of wood: [if] one [section] of them was damaged, it is clean, and it is not connected to it.

[If] the second is damaged, [that which is damaged] is clean, and it is not connected to it [the remainder]. If the three of them are damaged, the entire object is clean.

B. Four baskets which are in the haversack: [if] one of them was damaged, [the damaged one] is clean, and it is not connected to it. [If] the second was damaged, it is clean, and it is not connected to it.

C. [If] two were broken from one side, the whole broad part which is between them is clean.

D. [If] two of them were broken, one facing the other, they divide the broad part which is between them. That which serves the unclean [part] is unclean, and that which serves the clean [part] is clean. [If] two were broken diagonally, the whole broad diagonal which is between them is unclean.

6:9   A. A dung-basket, the middle part of which is high, and whose corners hang down, and which was broken on one side, is unclean, because it holds [something] on the second side. [If] it was broken on the second side, it is clean.[74]

B. And all other utensils which cannot hold olives, for example the tube and the small baskets —

C. "their measure [to be insusceptible to uncleanness] is [the breakage of] their greater part," the words of R. Meir.

D. R. Eleazar b. R. Simeon says, "With spices."

E. [If] they were broken through, their measure is with spices.

F. [If] they were worn away, their measure is in accord with what they are.

6:10   Said R. Judah, "The pomegranates of Ba'dan and the leek of Geba' [acquired] from among Kutim were mentioned only because they are tithed as certainly [untithed produce] in every place."[75]

6:11   A. R. Judah says, "One brings the largest of the large ones and the smallest of the small ones. One brings a cupful of water and brings foods which do not absorb [water]. And one puts them [the eggs] into it [the cup]

---

73. M. Kel. 6:7.   74. M. Kel. 19:10.   75. M. Kel. 17:5.

until the water will return to its former volume and goes and divides it [the water]."[76]

B. Said to him R. Yosé, "You have even set a measure to your measures. And who will inform me which is the largest or which is the smallest? But all is according to the opinion of the one who sees."

6:12 A. "With a spindle-staff" — with a middle-sized spindle-staff.

B. "With a spit" — with a middle-sized spit.

C. "With an ox-goad" — with a middle-sized ox-goad.

D. "With the thickness of the ox-goad" — with the thickness of two fingers. And its circumference is a handbreadth.

E. "A finger-breadth" — from four fingerbreadths in a handbreadth.

F. "A handbreadth" — from six handbreadths in a cubit.

G. A span which is mentioned in the Torah is a half-cubit of six handbreadths. And what is this? It is a middle-sized cubit. This is the cubit of five handbreadths.[77]

6:13 A. R. Meir says, "All the measurements of which the sages have spoken with reference to the vineyard, for example the waste-state of the vineyard, and untilled ground of the vineyard, an espalier which was destroyed in the middle, and the surplus lathes [of the espalier] — they all are [measured with] a cubit of five handbreadths;

B. "except for the golden altar and the horn, and the circuit and the base [of the altar], which are [measured] with a cubit of six handbreadths.

C. "As it is said, 'And these are the measurements of the altar, the cubit' [Ezek. 43:13] — that there should be two measurements for the altar. Might one say they should all be with a cubit of five handbreadths? Scripture says, 'With cubits, a cubit, a cubit and a handbreadth' — with a cubit which is longer than its fellow by a handbreadth."[78]

7:1 A. "A ladleful of corpse matter of which they spoke includes [the area] from the joint of one's fingers and upward," the words of R. Meir.[79]

B. And sages say, "One's handful."

C. A clod of dirt from clean earth and a clod from a grave-area and a clod from foreign territory — their measure is in accord with a large spindle of sack-weavers. They encompass the area equivalent to the upper side of the stopper of a Bethlehem-jar.

D. R. Ţarfon says, "[The measure of] dirt of a grave-area is [that volume] sufficient to cover therewith a bone the size of a barley-corn."

7:2 A. The fist of which they have spoken —

B. R. Ţarfon spreads out the tips of his fingers and shows [the size].

C. R. 'Aqiva closes the tips of his fingers and shows [the size].

76. M. Kel. 17:6.   77. M. Kel. 17:8.   78. M. Kel. 17:10.
79. M. Kel. 17:12.

D. R. Judah places his fingers on his big thumb and brings it down.

E. R. Yosé says, "It is as large as a large ram's head in Sepphoris."

F. Others say in his name, "A handbreadth and a third of a handbreadth."

G. And so did they measure before Ben Battiah came.[80]

7:3 A. The bags of wine and oil — their measure is with their large stopper.

B. And what is their large stopper? It is that which goes in them through their mouth.

C. Under what circumstances? [If the hole is] below. But [if the hole is] on the side, lo, these are unclean, because they [can] hold [liquid] from the hole and downward.

D. In their original form, they are not susceptible to uncleanness until one will blow it up and cut it off. [If] they have been cut off, their measure is in accord with what they are.

E. R. Simeon says, "[As to] skins, their measure is [determined by whether they can hold] liquids."[81]

7:4 A. He who makes utensils from that which grows in the sea — [they are] clean.

B. [If] one attached to them something which grows on the land in accord with the way they are [normally] attached, they are fitting for [receiving] uncleanness.

C. — but not utensils of dung, utensils of stone, and utensils of dirt

D. — something utensils made from which receive uncleanness is unclean; something utensils made from which do not receive uncleanness is clean.

E. R. Judah says, "Utensils [made from something which grows in the] sea are fitting for uncleanness, but they declared them clean, until you will find an excuse for them to be unclean."[82]

7:5 A. He who makes utensils from bones of the birds — they are clean.

B. [If] one attached to them [something] which grows on the earth, even a string, and even a thread, something which is susceptible to uncleanness — [it is] unclean.

C. Said R. Yohanan b. Nuri, "Why is the wing of the vulture different from all other wings, that it is subjected to a stringent [ruling]? But all wings which hold [something] are susceptible to uncleanness, and [all] those which do not hold [something] are not susceptible to uncleanness."[83]

7:6 A. The plated egg of the chicken is clean, because it is only [plated] so as to preserve it.

B. R. Simeon b. Eleazar says in the name of R. Meir, "Also the plated

80. *ibid.*   81. *ibid.*   82. M. Kel. 17:13.
83. M. Kel. 17:14.

egg of the chicken [which] holds anything at all is susceptible to unclean ness."

C. And the wing of the vulture and the egg of the ostrich are mentioned only with [reference to] existing [conditions].[84]

7:7 A. He who makes utensils from something which will last — it is unclean. [If he makes] from something which will not last — it is clean.

B. The turnip and the citron and the dried gourd which the children hollowed out so as to measure the dirt with them, or which they arranged as a spoon for the scales, are clean.

C. The pomegranate and the oak-nut and the nuts which children hollowed out so as to measure the dirt with them or which they made into a spoon for the scales are unclean.[85]

7:8 A. The cavity of the smith which has a receptacle for a limb [of the anvil] is clean. [If it is affixed] in its [normal] way, [that is] above, it is unclean [as a receptacle].

B. A tube which one cut and in which one placed the *mezuzah* and which one afterward set on the wall, even in the normal way of a receptacle, is clean.

C. [If] one affixed it onto the wall and afterward placed the *mezuzah* in it, even not in the normal way of a receptacle, it is unclean.

D. [If] not in the normal way of a receptacle, it is clean.

E. [If] he [permanently] affixed it even in the normal way of a receptacle, it is clean.[86]

7:9 A. The beam of the balance and the levelling-rod which have a receptacle for metal, and the carrying yoke which has a receptacle for coins, and the cane of the poor man which has a receptacle for water, and the staff which has a receptacle for a *mezuzah* or for a pearl —

B. the whole object is unclean only so far as it [the flat wood] serves the need [of the receptacle].

C. And concerning all of them said Rabban Yoḥanan b. Zakkai, "Woe is me, if I speak. If I speak, now I instruct the deceivers how to deceive. And if I do not speak, now I hold back learning and declare clean things unclean."

D. "Another matter: That the deceivers should not say that sages are not expert in their manner of actions."[87]

7:10 A. On what account is the base of gold-refiners unclean? Because one puts rubbish in it.

B. And of smiths, lo, this is clean.

C. But if one adapted it so as to put rubbish into it, all agree that it is unclean.

84. *ibid.* 85. M. Kel. 17:15. 86. *ibid.*
87. M. Kel. 17:16.

D. A whetstone which has a receptacle for oil, and a tablet which has a receptacle for wax — the whole [utensil] is unclean only in so far as it serves the need [of the receptacle].[88]

7:11 A. Matting — from what point does it become susceptible to uncleanness? Once one will have bound [it] round and smoothed [it] off.

B. R. Judah says, "When one will have tied up the tops of its knots."

C. If lumps were going forth from it, any one which is in the manner of knots is unclean, and any one which is not in the manner of knots is clean.[89]

7:12 A. A tube — from what point does it become susceptible to uncleanness?

B. When one will have bound it round and smoothed it off.

C. R. Judah says, "When one will bring forth pith from it."

D. The horn — from what point does it become susceptible to uncleanness? When its manufacture will have been completed.

E. R. Simeon b. Gamaliel says, "When one will have brought out the pith from it."

F. The gourd — from what point does it become susceptible to uncleanness? When its manufacture will have been completed.

G. Rabban Simeon b. Gamaliel says, "When one will have taken out the intestines from its midst."

H. And all of them which one found cut and smoothed are unclean. [If] one found them unformed, they are clean, for it is known that they are nothing.

8:1 A. A chest, the drawers of which are on the inside — they are measured with it. And [those] on the outside are not measured with it.

B. But one measures the empty space [of the drawers].

C. And R. Judah says, "One measures its place [that of the empty space] on the inside [of the chest]."

D. Its trundle — one slips it off and measures it [as part of the chest].

E. Said R. Simeon Shezuri, "The House of Shammai and the House of Hillel did not dispute concerning the thickness of the legs and the thickness of the rims, that they are not measured with it [the chest].

F. "Concerning what did they differ?

G. "Concerning [the spaces] in-between, for:

H. "The House of Shammai say, 'They are not measured.'

I. "And the House of Hillel say, 'They are measured.'"[90]

8:2 A railing which is in the cupboard and the cupolas which are in it — when they are affixed, they are measured with it, and when they are not fixed, they are not measured with it.[91]

88. M. Kel. 17:17.   89. ibid.   90. M. Kel. 18:1.
91. M. Kel. 18:2.

8:3   A. The boards of a couch, lo, these are clean.

B. The frames on which a couch is spread, even though they are separated and lying in four corners of the house, are unclean.

C. The four legs which are on its four corners are unclean, and the rest of its legs are clean.

D. The bed-base which is under the bed-frame and the bowls which are under the legs are clean.

E. The cups which are under the legs, even though they are hollowed out and receive [something], are clean, and they are not subject to the rule applying to a receptacle.[92]

8:4   A. The frame of the bed and of the cradle, the poles of the bed and boards of a straw-mattress, and the legs of a table, and the handle of the knife, when they are attached, are connected for uncleanness and for sprinkling.

B. [If they can] be removed and restored, they are not a connector either for uncleanness or for sprinkling.

C. The frame of a cradle which is equipped with knobs [and] which has legs is unclean.

D. [If] it is tied with ropes and does not have legs —

E. R. Meir and R. Judah declare unclean.

F. R. Yosé and R. Simeon declare clean, for one does not make use of the object itself.[93]

8:5   A. At first they used to say: A bed from which one cut off two tongues cross-wise, or two legs cross-wise, or from which one cut off a square handbreadth cross-wise, is clean.

B. Our rabbis said, "One cuts off from below until one diminishes it to less than a handbreadth [to render the bed insusceptible]."[94]

8:6   A. A bed, two tongues of which one made wide on a single side, is unclean. [If] one made the four of them wide, or [if] two of them were removed cross-wise, it is unclean.

B. [If] the short side and two legs were removed, it is unclean, because it is like the remnants of a bed, [so] one [may] prop [it] up and sleep on it.

C. And if in the first place one made it thus, it is clean, because it is like a pedestal.

D. [If one removed] the long board and two legs —

E. R. Neḥemiah declares unclean, because one leans it on the side of the bed or on the side of the stall and sleeps on it.

F. And sages declare clean.[95]

8:7   A. A bed from which one piece was separated and placed in the corner and replaced, and so with two, and so with three, and so with four,

92. M. Kel. 18:3.   93. M. Kel. 18:4.   94. M. Kel. 18:5.
95. ibid.

and so with five, and so with six, and so with seven, still is unclean with *midras*-uncleanness.

B. And if one replaced the eighth, it is clean of *midras*-uncleanness, but unclean with the uncleanness imparted by contact with *midras*-uncleanness.

C. [If] one goes back to the last and puts it into a corner and replaces it, and so with the second, and so with the third, and so with the fourth, and so with the fifth, and so with the sixth, and so with the seventh, it still is unclean with the uncleanness imparted by contact with *midras*-uncleanness.

D. And if one replaced the eighth, it is clean.

E. Under what circumstances?

F. When one began with the last.

G. But if one began with the first, even though one has not replaced the eighth, it is clean.[96]

8:8   A. "A bed is made unclean as a bundle, and purified as a bundle," the words of R. Eliezer.

B. And sages say, "It is made unclean in pieces and made clean in pieces."

C. How so?

D. "A leg which separated with the long piece and with the short piece

E. "R. Eliezer says, 'Lo, this is connected, and if one immersed it, it does not interpose.'

F. "And sages say, 'It is connected, and if one immersed it, lo, this interposes,'" — the words of R. Simeon.

G. Rabbi says, "R. Eliezer says, 'A bed is a bundle only when it is whole.'"

H. A bed which one divided into eight parts is unclean because one is going to restore it.

I. [If] one fastened it with a nail [in some other place], it is clean.[97]

9:1   A. A storage-bench of tailors is unclean with corpse-uncleanness. [If] one [side-] piece separated from it, it is [still] unclean. And [if] two pieces [separated from it], it is clean.

B. A crib of little girls, lo, this is susceptible to corpse-uncleanness. [If] it served for sitting and lying, lo, this is susceptible to *midras*-uncleanness.

C. A bed on which they sell utensils, lo, this is susceptible to corpse-uncleanness. [If] it served for sitting and lying, lo, this is susceptible to *midras*-uncleanness.

9:2   A. A bed, the inner parts of which were damaged, and to which the ropes are not tied, and on which there remained enough [space] for sitting and lying, lo, these [inner parts] are susceptible to *midras*-uncleanness.

B. [If] lumps were hanging from it, lo, these are unclean, because one

96. M. Kel. 18:8.   97. M. Kel. 18:9.

will restore them.

9:3   A. The rope which hangs over from [the webbing of] the bed —

B. up to five handbreadths is clean.

C. [Exactly] five are [regarded as] longer than it [the foregoing five].

D. From five to ten [are] unclean.

E. [Exactly] ten are [regarded as] shorter than it.

F. [If] one sprinkled on the rope within ten handbreadths, it [the bed] is clean.

G. And when one immerses the bed, he must immerse the rope for ten handbreadths.

H. A leg which is unclean with *midras*-uncleanness and which one attached to the bed —

I. [if] one sprinkled on the bed, the leg is clean.

J. And so with the bedgirth, and so with the tooth of the mattock.[98]

9:4   A. The rope with which one knots the bed, even a hundred handbreadths [long], is entirely a single connector.

B. [If] one fastened another rope to it, from the knot and inward is a connector. From the knot and outward is not a connector.

C. And [if] one inserted it into three rows of webbing, the entire [rope] is a single connector.

D. The rope which is tied to a fish-net, even a hundred handbreadths long, is entirely a single connector.

E. [If] one tied another rope to it, from the knot and inward is a connector. From the knot and outward is no connector.

F. Said R. Eliezer b. Jacob, "Under what circumstances? For bringing it up [out of the water] but for lowering it [into the water], even one [rope] tied to [still] another, attached [rope] is entirely a single connector."[99]

9:5   A. The thread which one threaded into the needle, even though it is fastened from two sides, lo, this is not a connector. [If] one inserted it [the needle] into the garment, the thread is a connector to the garment, and the needle is not a connector to the thread.

B. The thongs and the straps which are on the mantles of scrolls and in the diapers of babies, when sewn on, are a connector, and when tied on are not a connector.

C. Those which are in the handles of clay utensils, even though sewn, are not a connector, for there are no connectors to clay utensils.

D. The remnants of the legs of the bed, when tight, are a connector, but when loose, are not a connector.

E. And those in the hands of the Zab, even tight, are not a connector. This matter is more strict for *midras*-uncleanness than in connection with the Zab.[100]

98. M. Kel. 19:2.   99. M. Kel. 19:1.   100. *ibid.*

9:6 A. A bedgirth which one wraps around the bed and which one brought into the house in which a corpse is located, even though under the tent is any [small]   part of it [the girth] at all, even a hundred cubits [removed from the bed itself], the bed is unclean like utensils which have actual contact with the corpse.

B. [If] the Zab tread on it [the girth] beyond ten handbreadths [of the bed], it [the girth] is unclean, and the bed is clean.

C. A bedgirth which one wraps around the bed, and a corpse touched them — they are unclean with a seven-day uncleanness.

D. [If] it [the girth] was taken off, it [the girth] is unclean with a seven-day uncleanness.

E. [If] a creeping thing touched them, they are unclean with the uncleanness which passes at sunset. [If] it [the girth] was taken off, it is unclean with the uncleanness which passes at sunset.[101]

F. [If] unclean water touched them, they render [heave-offering] unfit. [If] they separated, they render [heave-offering] unfit.

G. This is the general rule: Every uncleanness to which a bed and girth are equally susceptible, for example, the corpse and the dead creeping thing and liquids — all are one connector, even to a hundred cubits.

And every uncleanness to which the bed and girth are not equally susceptible, for example the uncleanness of the Zab and Zabah — up to ten handbreadths are a connector for uncleanness. That which is made unclean by a Zab beyond this point is not a connector.[102]

H. R. Eleazar b. R. Şadoq says in the name of R. Gamaliel, "Up to seven handbreadths."

10:1 A. A box which is full of utensils and to which one attached a cover is unclean.

B. [If] it was empty and one attached a cover to it, it is clean.

C. To what is this likened? To an empty ball filled with air, which is clean.

10:2 A. A box which is unclean with corpse-uncleanness, and which one attached to [something susceptible to] *midras*-uncleanness is clean from every sort of uncleanness, but receives uncleanness from now on.

B. A box which is half open and half locked [closed off] is susceptible to *midras*-uncleanness and corpse-uncleanness.

C. [If] it is opened from above, it is unclean because it holds something from below.

D. If it was damaged from below —

E. R. Meir declares unclean.

F. And sages declare clean,

101. M. Kel. 19:6.   102. M. Kel. 19:4. Reading: *TR* III, p. 65.

G. because [if] the primary function is annulled, the secondary function is annulled.[103]

10:3   A. "A goatskin which was damaged, lo, this is unclean, because in the first place it serves for sitting and lying, and now it [still] serves for sitting and lying," the words of R. Meir.

B. And sages say, "Because [if] the primary function is annulled, the secondary function is annulled, [it is clean]."

C. Sages agree with R. Meir concerning the mattress and pillow of leather which were torn, that, even though they do not hold that which is within them, they are unclean [midras], and one need not add, pillows of woven cloth and sacking; not that they are unclean because of forming a receptacle, but because of woven matter.[104]

D. R. Yosé says, "The box of the bath-house attendants which is ten handbreadths high and which has a rim is unclean, for in the first place that is how it was made, so that one may climb up and sit on its top."

10:4   A. A box on which they sell oil in the bath is susceptible to corpse-uncleanness.

B. [If] one brought a board and affixed it to it [the box] from rim to rim so as to sit on it, [the box] becomes susceptible to midras-uncleanness.

C. And unclean is only that part which serves a need.

D. Four planks which are in its four corners, if they were a handbreadth wide, are unclean.

E. The upper plank on which they lay out the coins, even though it has a rim, is clean.

F. [If] one brought another plank and affixed it to it from rim to rim so as to be able to sit on it, it is unclean.

G. And unclean is only that part which serves a need.

10:5   A. A board of tailors [which] has sides is unclean, [and one which] does not have sides is clean.

B. [If] one brought a plank and affixed [it] from rim to rim to be able to sit on it, it is unclean.

C. And unclean is only that part which serves a need.

10:6   A. Tables which are in the cities, on which [people] eat, even though one affixed them [to the ground] with a nail, are unclean. [If] one brought a plank and affixed [it] on it [the table] from rim to rim so as to be able to sit on it, it is unclean.

And unclean is only that part which serves a need.

B. The seats which are on the [court-room] platform, lo, these are clean, for they are made only to serve with the ground.

C. The torture-block is clean, for it is only a painful place in which to sit.

103. M. Kel. 19:9−10.   104. M. Kel. 20:1.

11:1 A. A trough which is less than two *logs,* lo, it is like a dish, and its measure [for a perforation to render it insusceptible to uncleanness] is with olives.

B. And [as to] one of two *logs* to nine *qabs,* even Zabin and Zabot, menstruating women, and those who have given birth sit and lie in it, [and it is] clean.[105]

C. "If it is split and holds water only sufficient to rinse one foot in it, lo, it is susceptible to corpse-uncleanness and receives *midras*-uncleanness," the words of R. Yosé b. R. Judah.

D. Rabbi says, "After one will have given it thought [for such a purpose is it susceptible]."

11:2 A. R. Yosé says, "It [the trough] may be made unclean and purified even ten times a day. How so?

"[If] one left it in the rain and it swelled up, it is clean. [If one left it] in the east wind, it becomes unclean. So it becomes unclean and is purified even ten times a day."

B. [If] it was damaged so as to allow olives to drop through, it is insusceptible to any sort of uncleanness.

C. [If] one gave it thought —

D. Rabbi declares unclean.

E. And sages declare clean, until one will actually do something to it.

F. [As to] one larger than this which was split, even Zabin and Zabot, menstruating women, and those who have given birth sit and lie in its midst, [and it is] clean.

G. [If] it was damaged so as to let pomegranates drop through, it is clean from any sort of uncleanness.

H. [If] one gave it thought —

I. R. 'Aqiva declares unclean.

J. And sages declare clean, until one will smooth it off.

K. Said R. Yosé, M'ŚH Š: "They brought from Kefar 'Adim before Rabban Gamaliel more than sixty troughs, and he would measure them: a large one for a *se'ah,* a *se'ah,* and the small one, two *logs.* The measure of a *se'ah-se'ah* holds nearly nine *qabs.*"[106]

11:3 A. A trough for mixing mortar which is from two *logs* to nine *qabs*

B. The House of Shammai say, *"Midras."*

C. And the House of Hillel say, "Corpse-uncleanness."

D. And the goatskin —

E. The House of Shammai say, "[When] it is filled and stands [it is susceptible to *midras*-uncleanness]."

F. And the House of Hillel say, "[When] it is filled and bound."

G. R. Yosé b. R. Judah says, "Matters are reversed."[107]

---

105. M. Kel. 20:2.　　　106. *ibid.*　　　107. *ibid.*

11:4 A. The heft of an ax is a connector for uncleanness, whether in use or not in use. And if one did not affix it all that is necessary, lo, this is not a connector.

B. A staff which one put into an ax to cut with it for a time, when in use, is a connector, and when not in use, is not a connector.[108]

11:5 A. A nail which one placed in a yarn-winder so as to weave on it is a connector for uncleanness whether in use or not in use.

B. [If] one affixed it onto a post, when it is in use it is a connector, and when it is not in use, it is not a connector.

C. [If] one affixed a chair on it, unclean is only that part which is needed. And how much is needed? A place for sitting — a [square] handbreadth.[109]

11:6 A. A chair which one placed in a building and on which one built, [if he set it] in the way in which one sits on it, is unclean, and [if] not in the way in which one sits on it, is clean.

B. [If] one [permanently] affixed it, even in the way in which one sits on it, it is clean.

C. [If] one set it above [on the wall], even not in the way in which one sits on it, it is unclean. If one affixed it, [if] in the way in which one sits on it, it is unclean; [if] not in the way in which one sits on it, it is clean.[110]

11:7 A. The long side of a bed which one used for beams is unclean, and the bed [still] is unclean.

B. [If] one affixed it, it is clean, but the bed [still] is unclean.

C. Two long sides of a bed which one used for beams are unclean, and the bed is unclean.

D. [If] one affixed them, they are clean, and the bed is clean.

E. A mat which one used for beams, even though one makes use of it, is clean.[111]

F. [If] it was unclean and one used it for beams, it is unclean until one will have affixed it with a nail.

G. Under what circumstances? With a nail [knocked in] below.

H. But [if the nail is hammered in] above, [if] one [permanently] affixed it and did not place plaster on it, [or if] one placed plaster on it and did not [permanently] fix it, it is unclean.

I. [If] one fixed it and placed plaster on it, it is clean.

J. When is its purification?

K. "The House of Shammai say, 'When one will have damaged [it].'

L. "And the House of Hillel say, 'When one will have fastened [it],'" the words of R. Meir.

M. R. Judah says, "The House of Shammai say, 'When one will have

108. M. Kel. 20:3.   109. *ibid.*   110. M. Kel. 20:5.
111. *ibid.*

damaged and fastened [it].' And the House of Hillel say, 'When one will have damaged or fastened it.'"[112]

11:8 A. "A sheet which was unclean with corpse-uncleanness and which one made into a curtain, lo, this is [still] unclean with corpse-uncleanness but does not receive *midras*-uncleanness," the words of R. Yosé b. R. Judah.

B. R. Eleazar b. R. Simeon says, "It is clean of all uncleanness and receives uncleanness from now on."

C. And when is its purification?

D. When it is worn out and does not serve its [former] function.

E. [If] it wore out and there remains on it the greater part above, it is unclean; [if] the greater part below [remains], it is clean.

F. And if it was large and one cut it down and made it into a small door, it receives uncleanness from now on.[113]

11:9 A. "A sheet which was unclean with corpse-uncleanness and which one made into a sail for ship, — lo, it is unclean with corpse-uncleanness but does not receive *midras*-uncleanness," the words of R. Yosé b. R. Judah.

B. And R. Eleazar b. R. Simeon says, "It is clean of all uncleanness and receives uncleanness from now on."

C. And when is its purification?

D. When it is worn out and does not serve its [former] function.

E. [If] it wore out and there remains on it the greater part above, it is unclean; [if] the greater part below [remains], it is clean.

F. And if it was large, and one cut it down and made it into a sail for a small boat, it receives uncleanness from now on.[114]

11:10 A. Sheets and blankets which one placed on the ground so as to walk on them are unclean. [If] one affixed them with a nail, they are clean.

B. [If] one used them to cover projections and columns, walls and windows, they are susceptible to the uncleanness of Tents.

C. And if it was a reed mat, lo, this is clean.[115]

D. You have nothing which is made of wood that is susceptible to the uncleanness of Tents except for flax alone.

11:11 A. "A mat which one used for tents and which one then intended to use for lying is clean. [If] one made it for lying and then intended to use it for tents, until one has tied the heads of the end-knots, it is clean. After one has tied the heads of the end-knots, it is unclean," the words of R. Meir.

B. R. Judah says, "It may be made unclean and purified even ten times a day.

11:12 A. "How so? [If] one untied it, it is clean, and [if] one then tied it, it is unclean. So it may be made unclean and purified even ten times a day."

B. [If] one divided it lengthwise, it is clean; [if it was divided]

112. M. Kel. 20:6.   113. *ibid.*   114. *ibid.*
115. M. Kel. 20:7.

breadthwise and there remained on it three end-knots, which are six handbreadths, and a square handbreadth between one end-knot and the next, with a handbreadth on either side, it is unclean. And less than that is clean.[116]

C. And if to begin with one made it for that purpose, even less than that [will be] unclean.

D. R. Nathan says, "The remnants of a reed-mat are seven handbreadths, and the remnants of a mat are six handbreadths."

116. *ibid.*

KELIM BABA BATRA

1:1 That which touches the posts on the sides, from either side, and on the vise which is on the reeds, even though it is hollowed out and holds something, is clean. Unclean is only that which touches the iron alone.

1:2 A. A menstruating woman who drew the rope and stepped on the beam and leaned on the reed which goes up and down — the cloth is unclean with *midras*-uncleanness.

B. M'ŚH B: One woman was weaving a cloth in cleanness, and she came before R. Ishmael for inspection. She said to him, "Rabbi, I know that the cloth was not made unclean, but it was not in my heart to guard it [from impurity]." In the course of the questions which R. Ishmael asked her, she said to him, "Rabbi, I know that a menstruating woman came and pulled the rope with me." Said R. Ishmael, "How great are the words of sages, who would say, 'If one did not intend to guard it, it is unclean.' "

1:3 ŚWB M'ŚH B: One woman was weaving a covering in a state of purity, and she came before R. Ishmael, who inspected her [about it]. She said to him, "Rabbi, I know that the covering was not made unclean, but it was not in my heart to guard it." In the course of the questions which R. Ishmael asked her, she said to him, "Rabbi, I know that one thread was broken, and I tied it with my mouth." Said R. Ishmael, "How great are the words of sages who would say, 'If one did not intend to guard it, it is unclean.' "

1:4 A. A weasel which dragged the undyed wool thread which one would restore, and brought it into a house in which a corpse was found, even though it [the thread] is not under the tent more than any small amount — the garment [in which it is woven] is unclean with corpse-uncleanness.

B. [If] the Zab stepped on it within ten handbreadths, the garment [in which it is woven] is unclean with *midras*-uncleanness.

1:5 A. The warp, so long as one will weave [with it], is connected to what is woven. [When] one has completed weaving, unclean is only that part of it up to the place at which one will divide the ends of the web.

B. That which touches the separated threads of warp and of the woof, lo, this is not a connector.

C. R. Yosé says, "That which touches the separated threads of the warp up to three fingerbreadths is connected, because the expert fuller smoothes them into it."

1:6 A. That which touches the wool which is on the spool and the spun wool which is on the spindle is clean. [That which touches] the spindle-reed and the distaff is unclean.[1]

---

1. M. Kel. 21:1.

B. That which touches the black which is on the white or the white which is on the black is clean.

C. But if it was entirely black on one side, and one placed it over white, or if it was entirely white on one side, and one placed it over the black, it is unclean.

1:7   A. The tail piece which one separated from the pegs of the plough, lo, this is unclean, because one perforates the entrenchment around the well with it.

B. The eye which is on the ax and the eye which is on the plough, and the iron sheath of the ploughshare, when they are fixed, are connected for uncleanness and for sprinkling. When they are by themselves, they are clean.[2]

1:8   A. The thongs and the straps which are on the sharebeam, when sewn, are a connector, and, when tied, are not a connector.

B. The vise of the carpenter, when it is fixed, is a connector for uncleanness and for sprinkling.

C. [If] one takes it off and puts it on, it is not a connector either for uncleanness or for sprinkling.

D. R. Judah says, "Also: that which touches the frame of the large saw from one side or the other is clean. And unclean is only the place of the handgrip from either side toward the iron."[3]

1:9   A. The table and the tray and the end-table which were cut up and on which there remained two handbreadths [of usable space] are unclean.

B. A [double] table [in two parts, the upper part of which is used,] which one scraped — the lower part is clean, and the upper part is unclean. [If] it was separated, but it holds something, it is unclean from now on.

C. A tray which one scraped — the upper part is unclean, and the lower part is clean. [If] it was separated and holds something, it is unclean from now on.

D. A tray inlaid with wood which one nailed on is clean. [If] one overlaid it with [loosely attached] strips of wood, it is unclean.

1:10   A. A table which one covered with marble [intending] to eat on it, even though one made for it a wide [piece of] wood [with which] to attach the marble to it [the table], it [the table] is clean.

B. For he made it [the wood] only for strengthening, to be able to hold the marble on it.

1:11   A. The benches which are in the inns, even though they are perforated and people put the[ir] feet in them, are clean. [If] one affixed them [the legs of the benches] with a nail, they are unclean.

B. The benches of the teachers of children, even though they are perforated and one puts things on them, are clean. [If] one affixed them [the

2. M. Kel. 21:2.   3. *ibid.*

legs] with a nail, they are unclean.

1:12   A.   A bench which was separated [into its component parts] is clean. [If] one [repaired it and] tied it together with thongs or ropes, it is unclean.

B.   A side-board for which one made a wood like a fork so as to eat on it is clean. [If] he made on it a wide board for his own needs, it is unclean.

C.   A chair which one affixed onto a trough in such wise that one may sit in it is unclean. [If affixed] not in such wise that one may sit on it, it is clean.

D.   "That which is made in it [a chair carved into the trough itself] —

"The House of Shammai declare unclean.

"And the House of Hillel declare clean," the words of R. Meir.

E.   R. Judah says, "The House of Shammai and the House of Hillel did not differ concerning one which was made in it [in the trough itself], that it is clean. (And Shammai would declare unclean.)

"Concerning what did they differ?

"Concerning the case in which one brought [a chair] from another place and affixed it onto it [the trough], for

"The House of Shammai declare unclean.

"And the House of Hillel declare clean."

F.   Said R. Yosé, "I concur with the words of the House of Shammai, for I say that a frame even at the house of the craftsman is subject to uncleanness."[4]

1:13   A.   The seat of the wagon-driver, [if] one loosened it, is clean, and [if] one tied it, is unclean.

B.   And that which is on the back of the wagon, one way or the other, is clean, for it is only a painful place in which to sit.

C.   The sitting place of the stone cutter, if one loosened it [from the stone], is clean, and if one tied it [to the stone], is unclean. It may be made unclean and purified even ten times a day.[5]

1:14   A.   The leather of the toilet and its open space, lo, these are measured [together for] a handbreadth.

B.   The mule-hide and the panther-hide which are before the bed, lo, these are susceptible to *midras*-uncleanness.

C.   The plank on which they press the pressed olives, lo, this is susceptible to corpse-uncleanness.

D.   This is the general rule: Anything which may be removed without its legs being removed with it, whether of wood or of stone, is clean.

E.   And anything which is taken only [if] its legs are taken with it, [if made] of wood is unclean, and [if made] of stone is clean.

1:15   The vise of a shoemaker on which he stretches the leather and on which he leaves the stone, even though it is hollowed out and holds something, is clean and is not regarded as a receptacle.

---

4. M. Kel. 22:4.   5. M. Kel. 22:8.

2:1 A. A block — the part which is not a handbreadth high is clean.

B. And [the part] which is a handbreadth high —

C. R. Meir and R. Simeon declare unclean.

D. R. Yosé and R. Eleazar b. R. Ṣadoq declare clean.[6]

E. Said R. Meir, M'ŚH B: "One cut two blocks of date-palm to sit on them, and the matter came before sages, and they declared them unclean."

2:2 A. Said R. Simeon, M'ŚH B: "A person brought a stump of olive-wood which was planed like a cupboard before R. 'Aqiva, and he said to him, 'On this I was sitting.' And he declared it unclean for him. He saw his students astonished. He said to them, 'Why are you astonished? Something more inappropriate [for sitting] than this did R. Joshua declare unclean.'"

B. Said R. Yosé, M'ŚH B: "Four elders were sitting in the store of R. Eleazar b. 'Azariah in Sepphoris; R. Ḥuspit and R. Yeshebab, and R. Ḥalafta, and R. Yoḥanan b. Nuri. And they brought before them one head of a post which was removed with a chisel. He said to them, 'On this was I sitting.' And they declared it clean for him."

C. Said R. Eleazar b. R. Ṣadoq, "Heads of posts were on the Temple Mount on which craftsmen would sit and polish stones, and sages did not scruple concerning them in respect to any uncleanness."

2:3 A. And so did R. Eleazar b. R. Ṣadoq say, "Two blocks were in the house of father, one unclean, the other clean. I said to father, 'On what account is this unclean and the other clean?' He said to me, 'This one, which is hollowed out, is unclean, and the other, which is not hollowed out, is clean. And on it sat Haggai the prophet.'"

B. And all of them, if one did not hollow them out intentionally, are clean.

C. [If] one found them hollowed out and gave thought to them, they receive uncleanness from then on.

D. [If] a deaf-mute, an insane person, a minor, or a man to whom they do not belong gave thought to them [as seats], they are insusceptible to uncleanness.

2:4 A. The spoon with which the priests knead, and so the cover of a pot, if they are hollowed out and receive anything at all, are unclean, and if not, they are clean.

B. M'ŚH B: The butcher of Onqelos the Proselyte brought his cover [or block] before Rabban Gamaliel, and eighty-five elders were in session there. Rabban Gamaliel took it and looked at it, and gave it to his colleague, and his colleague to his. When he saw that no one said anything about it, Rabban Gamaliel took a thread from the cloak of a disciple who was sitting before him and stretched it [the thread] on it [the block], and found it hollowed out ever so little, and declared it unclean for him.

6. M. Kel. 22:9.

C. And in all instances, if one did not deliberately hollow them out, they are clean. [If] one found them hollowed out and gave thought to them, they receive uncleanness from then on.

[If] a deaf-mute, an insane person, a minor, or a man to whom they do not belong gave thought to them, they are insusceptible to uncleanness.

2:5   A. One who trims [something] for lying — there must be no less than three-by-three [handbreadths]; and for sitting, a handbreadth; and for a place to stand, any amount at all.

B. [If the object is] of wood — [it is clean] until one will hollow it out or until one will make legs.[7]

2:6   A. The ball and the shoe last and the amulet and phylacteries and the round pillow which were torn, if they [nonetheless] hold what is in them, are unclean.

B. R. Joshua b. Qorḥa says in the name of R. Eleazar b. 'Azariah, "One immerses them just as they are."[8]

2:7   A. The saddle is subject to uncleanness on account of sitting, and its handle is subject to uncleanness on account of that which is ridden on.

B. And all other saddles which are on the sides, if they are a handbreadth wide, are unclean.

C. R. Simeon says, "Three [things] are unclean because of that which is sat upon, and three things are unclean because of that which is ridden upon:

D. "The Askelon girth, and the Median mortar, and the saddle — these three [are susceptible to *midras*] as that which is ridden upon.

E. "The seat of the female camel and of the horse and the saddle — these three [are susceptible to *midras* because of that which is] sat upon."[9]

2:8   A. The bed, the pillow, and the mattress of the corpse —

B. R. Meir says, "They are not susceptible to [*midras*] uncleanness."

C. And sages say, "They are subject to *midras*-uncleanness because the women sit on them and bewail their dead."

D. And all agree that they are subject to corpse-uncleanness.[10]

2:9   A. There are three [kinds of] beds:

B. That which is used for lying is susceptible to *midras*-uncleanness.

C. That on which they sell utensils is susceptible to corpse-uncleanness.

D. And that of the frames of the sons of Levi is wholly clean.

E. There are three [kinds of] cribs:

F. That which is used for lying is susceptible to *midras*-uncleanness.

G. And that of little girls is susceptible to corpse-uncleanness.

H. And that of plasterers and of moulderers is wholly clean.[11]

2:10   A. There are three [kinds of] nets:

B. That of the old woman is susceptible to *midras*-uncleanness.

7. *ibid.*   8. M. Kel. 23:1.   9. *ibid.*
10. M. Kel. 23:4.   11. M. Kel. 24:9.

C. And that of the little girl is susceptible to corpse-uncleanness.

D. [And that which is] torn and does not hold most of the hair is wholly clean.[12]

2:11 A. There are three kinds of sandals:

B. That of man is suceptible to *midras*-uncleanness.

C. That of metal and of cattle is susceptible to corpse-uncleanness.

D. And that of cork and of goats-hair is wholly clean.

E. R. Yosé says, "All leather-gloves are clean."

F. And sages say, "There are three kinds of gloves:

G. "That of hunters of beasts is susceptible to *midras*-uncleanness.

H. "That of hunters of birds is susceptible to corpse-uncleanness.

I. "And that of fruit-gatherers is wholly clean."

2:12 A. R. Eleazar b. R. Simeon says, "A cup of scales unclean with corpse-uncleanness, and which one patched on to the bottom of a cauldron on the inside, whether perforated [the cauldron] or not perforated, is unclean.

B. "[If one patched it] on the outside, [if the cauldron is] perforated, it is unclean, [and if] it is not perforated, it is clean.

C. "[If] one patched it on its [the cauldron's] side, on the inside, [if the cauldron is] perforated, it [the cauldron] is unclean; and [if the cauldron is] not perforated, it [the cauldron] is clean.

D. "[If one patched it on the side] from the outside [of the cauldron], whether it [the cauldron] is perforated or is not perforated, it [the cauldron] is clean."[13]

3:1 A. A mattress which was turned inside out, so that its outer part became its inside and its inside [became] its outer part, and a basket which one turned inside out, so that its outer part became its inside and its inside, its outer part —

B. R. Meir says, "Any object which has seams has outer parts and an inside, [and any which] does not have seams has no outer parts or inside."

C. R. Judah says, "Any which has a face — its face is its inside."[14]

3:2 A. "The serving tray on part of which liquids fell is entirely unclean," the words of R. Meir.

B. R. Judah says, "[If] they fell on its inner part, it is entirely unclean. [If they fell] on its outer part, only its outer part is unclean.

C. "[If] they fell on its broad side, one dries it and it is clean."[15]

3:3 A. "A smooth side-board or a smooth tray on part of which liquids fell is entirely unclean," the words of R. Meir.

B. R. Judah says, "[If] they fell on its inside, it is entirely unclean. [If

---

12. M. Kel. 24:16.　　　13. M. Kel. 24:17.　　　14. M. Kel. 25:1.
15. *ibid.*

they fell] on its outer part, unclean only is the outer part alone.

C. "[If] they fell on its broad side, one dries it, and it is clean."[16]

3:4 A. A table on part of which liquids fell is entirely unclean. [If] they fell on its outer part, unclean is only the outer part. [If] they fell on its leg, one dries it, and it is clean.

B. Said R. Judah, "I state a law from the days of the priests: 'They did not refrain from placing the leg of a table on unclean liquids.' (They said,) 'Because as to a leg, one dries it, and it is clean.' "[17]

3:5 A. "The ox-goad on part of which liquids fell is entirely unclean.

"[If] they fell on its outer part, unclean is only its outer part," the words of R. Meir.

B. And sages say, "[If] they fell on the broad blade, unclean is only seven [handbreadths of the goad], and [if they fell] on the point, unclean is only four [handbreadths]."[18]

3:6 A. A soup-ladle on the inside of which liquids fell is entirely unclean. [If] they fell on its outer part, unclean is only its outer part. The inside and the fork and the handle are clean.

B. [If] they fell on the fork, they divide the handle. That which serves the unclean part [the fork] is unclean, and that which serves the clean part is clean.

C. [If] they fell on the handle, one dries it, and it is clean.[19]

3:7 A. A basket on the inside of which liquids fell is entirely unclean. [If] they fell on its outer parts, its outer parts are unclean. Its inside and ear are clean. [If] they fell on the ear, one dries it, and it is clean.

B. But the priests were accustomed not to keep bottoms unclean, because of the possibility of trouble.

3:8 A. The quarter[*log*] and half-quarter[-*log*] —

B. [if] one hollowed out the quarter and was planning to hollow out the half-quarter, it [the whole measure] is clean until one will [actually] hollow out the half-quarter.

C. [If] the outer sides of the quarter are made unclean with liquids, the outer sides of the half-quarter are unclean.

D. And when one immerses the quarter, he needs to immerse the half-quarter.

E. [If] there was on it something which interposes, and one immersed it, he has done nothing.

F. The quarter which one inlaid with wood and affixed —

G. Rabban Simeon b. Gamaliel and Rabbi declare unclean until one will have affixed it with a nail.[20]

3:9 A. Said R. 'Aqiva, "They made mention of the holding place only for cups,

"so that one should not drink, and [it result that] each drop render the next unclean.

B. "Unclean liquids which were put in the holding place of a cup, and which a clean loaf touched —

"the loaf is made unclean.

C. "Clean liquids which were put at the holding place of the cup, and which an unclean loaf touched —

"the liquids are made unclean.

D. "Unclean liquids which were put on the ground, and a cup, the outer sides or holding place of which were unclean, touched them —

"the liquids are made unclean."

E. R. Meir says, "For unclean hands:

F. "How so?

G. "It is not possible to say [that we are dealing] with dry [hands], for hands do not render unclean when they are dry. It is not possible to say [the hands render unclean] when full of liquids, for before one will touch them, the liquids [already] were made unclean.

H. "It therefore follows that [if] one's hands were unclean, and the outer parts of the cup were clean, and liquid was dripping on the outer parts of the cup, one holds it [the cup] on its holding place and does not take account lest the liquids which are on the outer parts of the cup be made unclean on account of his hands and go and make the cup unclean."[21]

3:10 A. R. Yosé says, "Concerning clean hands:

B. "How so? [If] one's hands were clean and on them was some moisture, and the outer parts of the cup were unclean — one takes it [the cup] with its holding place and does not worry lest the liquids which are on his hands be made unclean on account of the cup and go and make his hands unclean."[22]

3:11 A. R. Ṭarfon says, "A large trough of wood has a holding place.

B. "This is the general rule: [If one] takes it with one [hand], its holding place is with one [finger]. [If one] takes it with two, its holding place measures two [fingers]. The place at which one takes hold of it — there is its holding place."

C. R. Judah says, "A utensil which has a rim and an ear and a handle has no holding place."[23]

3:12 A. Utensils used for Holy Things have no [distinctions among] an outer part or an inner part and have no holding place, and they do not immerse utensils in the midst of [other] utensils for Holy Things.

B. Said R. Yosé, "This is redundant: Whatever has outer parts and an inner part has a holding place, and [whatever] does not have outer parts and

---

21. M. Kel. 25:7—8.   22. *ibid.*   23. *ibid.*

an inside does not have a holding place.

"In this respect, the Holy Things of the sanctuary and the Holy Things of the provinces are governed by the same rule."[24]

3:13 A. All utensils descend to their uncleanness with [mere] intention, but do not ascend from their uncleanness without an act which changes them.

B. R. Judah says, "An act which changes them for the worse."[25]

4:1 A. A phylactery — when does it receive uncleanness?

B. When its manufacture has been completed.

C. If one has cut it, even though he will later on put the strap on it, it is unclean.

D. And when is its purification?

E. That of the hand: when one will have untied [it] in three directions. And that of the head: when one will have untied [the knot] between one capsule and the next.

4:2 A. A bag inside of a bag, one [bag] of which is made unclean — that one is unclean, but its fellow is clean.

B. Under what circumstances?

C. When they are both the same size.

D. But if the outer one was larger than the inner one, [then if] the inner one is made unclean, the outer one is made unclean. [But if] the outer one is made unclean, the inner one is not made unclean.

E. Under what circumstances?

F. In the case of [unclean] liquid.

G. But [if] in the case of a creeping thing, they are both equal.[26]

4:3 A. Said R. Nathan, "R. Eliezer and sages did not differ concerning a bag for coins, that it is clean.

"Concerning what did they differ?"

"Concerning a bag for pearls, for

B. "R. Eliezer declares unclean.

C. "And sages declare clean."[27]

D. A bag for pearls, when it [a pearl] is in it [the bag], is unclean. In flat [form] it is clean.

E. It may be made unclean and purified even ten times a day.

4:4 A. A leather-hide which one prepared as a rug for placing on his heart during the harvest because of the heat,

B. if it is five-by-five [handbreadths], is unclean.

C. If not, it is clean.

D. [If one prepared it] for his heel and his toes, if it covers most of the

24. M. Kel. 25:9.   25. *ibid.*   26. M. Kel. 26:2.
27. *ibid.*

foot, it is unclean. And if not, it is clean.

4:5   A. A sandal made of straw —

B. R. 'Aqiva declares unclean. And the woman performs ḥaliṣah with it; and they go out in it on the Sabbath.

C. And they did not agree with him.

D. A sandal, whose [two] straps were broken and whose strappings were torn, or from which even one sole separated, is clean.

If one of its ears tore, or one of its strappings, or if the larger part of one sole [was] separated from it, it is unclean.

E. R. Judah says, "[If it is] the inner one, it is unclean. [If it is] the outer one, it is clean."[28]

4:6   A. A sandal which was damaged and still holds the larger part of the foot, [or] a shoe which tore open and which [nonetheless] covers the larger part of the foot, or the thongs of which were torn or the arch of which was removed, is unclean.

B. [If] it was damaged and does not hold the larger part of the foot, [or if] it was torn and does not cover the larger part of the foot, or [if] its ears were torn, it is clean.[29]

4:7   A. A shoe on the last —

B. R. Eliezer declares clean.

C. And sages declare unclean.

D. Said R. Simeon Shezuri, "R. Eliezer and sages did not differ concerning a shoe on the last, that it is clean.

"Concerning what did they dispute? Concerning [a case in which] one removed it from the last, for

"R. Eliezer declares unclean.

"And sages declare it clean, because the woman laces it up and returns it to the last."[30]

4:8   A. A leather [for an] ass, and a leather [apron] of an ass-driver, and the leather apron of the flax-worker, and the leather apron of the physician, and the leather apron of the heart of a child, and the leather on which the girls spin, if it is five-by-five [handbreadths], is unclean, and if not, is clean.

B. A leather rug and a leather [piece for] the crib, and the leather used as the lower covering of a bed, and the leather of the mattress and the leather of the pillow, even though not five-by-five [handbreadths] — it is unclean.

C. Rabban Simeon b. Gamaliel says, "If there are five-by-five [handbreadths], it is unclean, and if not, it is clean, for leather [to be susceptible to uncleanness] cannot be less than five-by-five."[31]

4:9   A. A piece of leather which one made for a cover, even if it is of any size at all, is susceptible to uncleanness.

---

28. M. Kel. 26:4.   29. ibid.   30. ibid.
31. M. Kel. 26:5.

B. Said R. Eleazar b. R. Yosé, "The House of Shammai and the House of Hillel did not differ concerning a leather bag of purple and the wrapper for purple, that they are unclean.

C. "Concerning what did they differ?

D. "Concerning the leather bag for clothing and a wrapper for clothing for

"the House of Shammai declare unclean [*midras*].

"And the House of Hillel declare clean [of *midras*]."[32]

4:10 A. (1) A wrapper for purple, when [it is] inside, is unclean. [When it is] spread out, it is clean. It may be made unclean and may be made clean even ten times a day.

B. A leather bag of wool and a knapsack which come from abroad, even though they come in [requisite] measure, are unclean.

C. The chest, box, and cupboard of bone and of leather —

D. Rabbi declares unclean.

E. And R. Yosé b. R. Judah declares clean.[33]

F. R. Simeon b. Menasia says, "A fur-skin which one is going to cut and from which one is going to remove the tail is clean.

G. "And all of them which lack stretching onto a frame and drying are clean.

H. "[If] they lack anointing, they are unclean."

4:11 A. A mat [in] the house, whether of the thief or of the robber — the intention [of the thief or robber] renders it susceptible to uncleanness, because the owners give up hope [of recovering it].

B. The [leather] cover of a tray for flagons and of a tray for cups, even though it is five-by-five [handbreadths square] is clean, for it is only a cover.

C. And [if it serves to] keep the utensils together, it is unclean.[34]

4:12 A. A hide which is before an ass, even though it measures five-by-five [handbreadths], is clean, for it is only a cover.

B. Its pillow is clean.

C. [If] it was sewn to the saddle, it is unclean. And [if] it holds anything at all, it is unclean.[35]

4:13 A. He who makes a band to beautify, and to tie around an animal's chest, and for the neck of a beast — it is clean.

B. [To place] beneath the belly of the ass — it is unclean.

C. Remnants of a band — four handbreadths, sufficient to place under the belly of an ass.

D. He who makes a band of any length — it is clean.

E. [But if one makes it] to strengthen sacking and packing-bags with it, to convey [something] with it from place to place — it is unclean.

32. M. Kel. 26:6.   33. *ibid.*   34. M. Kel. 26:8.
35. M. Kel. 26:6.

4:14   A. All cords for a beast are clean, and for a man, all are clean, except for those made of sacking and of cloth.

B. The sling whose receptacle is of flax ropes —

C. R. Dosa ben Harkinas declares clean.

D. And sages say, "[One of] three [fingerbreadths] is unclean, and [one of] two is clean."

E. [If] the middle one broke, it [the whole still] is unclean, and [if] the outer one [broke], it is clean.

F. [If] its thong-hold broke [and] a handbreadth remained on it, it is unclean.

G. All the rush mats, whether of bamboo or of sacking or of plaited rope —

H. R. Dosa says, "It is susceptible to corpse-uncleanness."

I. And sages say, "It is susceptible to *midras*-uncleanness."[36]

5:1   A. A shirt of fine linen — when does it receive uncleanness?

B. When its manufacture will have been completed.

C. And what is the completion of its manufacture?

D. When one will have opened the neck-hole.

E. And the one for the adult [is measured] in accord with his size, and the one for the child in accord with his size.

F. And when is its purification?

G. When it will have worn out and no longer will serve its former purpose.

H. [If] it wore out and most of it is left on top, it is still susceptible, [but if] most of it is low-down, it is clean.

I. And if it is torn from the neck-hole, it is clean.

5:2   A. A shirt made of paper — when does it receive uncleanness?

B. When its manufacture will have been completed.

C. And when is the completion of its manufacture?

D. When one will have opened its neck-hole, one for the adult in accord with his size, and one for the child in accord with his size.

E. And when is its purification?

F. When it will have worn out and no longer will serve its former purpose.

G. [If] it wore out and most of it is left on top, it is susceptible to uncleanness; [if] most of it is low-down, it is clean.

And if it tore at the neck-hole, it is clean.

5:3   A. He who makes a shirt from felt — if there is in it three-by-three [handbreadths], it is unclean, and if not, it is clean, for [one does] not [find] among felt cloaks [one of a size] less than three-by-three.

---

36. M. Ed. 3:4—5.

B. A shirt of felt which wore out, if it serves its former purpose, is unclean, and if not, is clean.

5:4   A. He who makes a shirt for a wrapper — even any size is unclean.

B. He who makes a wrap from felt — it is not going to receive uncleanness until its manufacture will have been completed.

C. [If] it wore out, if there is in it three-by-three [handbreadths], it is unclean, annd if not, it is clean.

5:5   A. A cup of paper which one fixed to gird his loins is unclean.

B. A cup of bast [of a palm tree] which one fixed to gird his loins is clean.

C. Two cups of bast which one sewed together and fixed to gird his loins are unclean.

5:6   A. Said R. Yosé, "Jonathan b. Ḥersha of Gennosar asked before the sages in Yavneh, 'Two soles of bast which one sewed together and fixed for girding his loins, what are they [clean or unclean]?'

B. "They said to him, 'Unclean.'

C. "[He further asked], 'Soft green dates [which appear to have been bitten by a serpent] at their roots — what is their status?'

D. "They said to him, 'Even the entire palm is prohibited.'

E. "The balance of the espaliers [on which no vine is trained] — what is its status as to rendering [the vine] forfeit?'

F. "They said to him, '[It renders forfeit] on the place to which the new [vine] can extend for that entire year.'"

5:7   A. He who makes a belt out of the side of a garment [or] the side of a sheet —

B. The House of Shammai declare unclean.

C. And the House of Hillel declare clean, until one will have made a hem.

D. [If one makes a belt] out of the middle of the garment and the middle of the sheet, and one hemmed (on) one side [only] —

E. The House of Shammai declare unclean.

F. The House of Hillel declare clean, until one will have hemmed (on) the second side.

5:8   A. R. Simeon b. Judah says in the name of R. Simeon, "The House of Shammai and the House of Hillel did not differ concerning him who makes a belt out of the middle of a garment or the middle of the sheet, and made a hem on one side, that it is clean until one will have made a hem on the sec ond side.

B. "Concerning what did they differ?

C. "Concerning him who makes a belt out of the side of a garment and the side of a sheet —

D. "For the House of Shammai declare unclean.

E. "And the House of Hillel declare clean, until one will have made a hem."[37]

5:9 A. Rabban Simeon b. Gamaliel says, "A belt the sides of which wore out but the center of which stands is susceptible because [it constitutes] the remnants of a belt."

B. A hem which one separated from a garment and which one arranged to gird his loins is unclean because it is like a girdle of network.[38]

5:10 A. An [unclean] cloak which one began to tear, until the greater part is torn — that which touches even that which is torn on one side or on the other is connected.

B. After the greater part is torn, that which touches even that which is attached [to the cloak] is not connected.[39]

5:11 A. And what are the thick [fabrics] and what are the thin [fabrics]?

B. For example, the birrus [a thick cloak] and the [same] and the travelling cloak and the thick blankets and the felts and the coarse woolen blankets — these are the thick fabrics.

C. The silk and the silk stuffs and the cissaros-blossoms and the felt cap of the head — these are the thin fabrics.

D. They are not subject to the rule of three-by-three [fingerbreadths], but they are subject to the rule of three-by-three [handbreadths].[40]

5:12 A. He who makes a shirt from the wine filter — if there is in it three-by-three [handbreadths], it is unclean, and if not, it is clean.

B. The wine-filter which wore out, if it serves its former purpose, is unclean, and if not, it is clean.

C. R. Eleazar b. R. Simeon says, "[If the filter is] of sacking and of cloth — its measure is with wine-lees. [If] of bamboo or of goat's hair or of ropes — their measure is with pomegranates."[41]

5:13 A. A funnel of the olive presses, even though it is made like a strainer, is unclean.

B. A thread which separated from a piece of cloth, even a hundred cubits, is entirely a single connector.

C. And that with which one sews — any part which is needed for the sewing is a connector, and any part which is not needed for the sewing is not a connector.

5:14 A. The shirt of whores, even though it is made like a net, is clean.

B. [If] one made for it a hem three fingers [in width], whether above or below or on the sides, it [the shirt] is unclean.

C. R. Eliezer b. Jacob says, "He who makes a cloth from a fishnet and from a trap and doubled it and sewed it, and his flesh does not show through from inside it — it is unclean."[42]

5:15 A. A head band of a net is unclean by itself, because one fixes it to

37. M. Kel. 28:7.   38. *ibid.*   39. M. Kel. 28:8.
40. *ibid.*   41. M. Kel. 28:9.   42. *ibid.*

another net.

B. And what is its measure?

C. Sufficient to encompass from one ear to the next.[43]

5:16   A. The foil and the coverings and the chains which are in it are clean.

B. But because of being connectors of the head-band, they are unclean.

C. The strings which are in it [the net], when sewn [to the head band], are a connector, and when tied [to the head band], are not a connector.

D. Others say, "A net of an old lady which tore, if one places it on a chair, and her flesh touches the chair, is clean [of *midras*], and if not, it is unclean."[44]

5:17   A. The remnants of the girdle — sufficient to gird the loins of a child.

B. The remnants of the arm-bands — sufficient to wrap around the little finger.[45]

6:1   A. He who makes a change in a leather utensil —

from a flat form to a flat form —

it is unclean.

B. From a flat form to a receptacle, from a receptacle to a flat form, from one [sort of] receptacle to another — it is clean.

C. And with respect to cloth, everything is unclean.

D. Said R. Judah, "My colleagues were saying to me, 'The sacking and the leather and the matting which one patched on to one another have not been annulled by one another."[46]

6:2   A. The sacking and the hide and the mat which were torn, if one places them on the seat and his flesh touches the seat, are clean, and if not, they are unclean.[47]

B. The sacking and the leather and the matting which one threw into the rubbish are unclean.

C. A patch which one patched on to a basket requires intention after its separation.

6:3   A. A cloak of a poor man which wore out, if most of its hems survive, even though there does not remain in it a cloth three-by-three [fingerbreadths], is susceptible to uncleanness.

B. [If] the larger part of its hems have not survived, if there is in it a piece of cloth three-by-three [fingerbreadths], it is susceptible to uncleanness, and if not, it is clean.

C. Rabban Simeon b. Gamaliel says, "If there is in it a piece of cloth three-by-three [fingerbreadths], it is unclean, and if not, it is clean."

D. [If] threads were protruding from it, any one which is opposite the

---

43. M. Kel. 28:10.   44. *ibid.*   45. M. Kel. 29:1.
46. M. Kel. 28:5.   47. *ibid.*

hem is a connector, and any which is not opposite the hem is not a connector.[48]

6:4   A. The goatskin which the priest opened so as to detach a loaf of heave-offering with it is clean.

B. [A piece of] leather which one made into a table to eat on it is unclean, and its measure is a handbreadth.

C. A sleeve and a border of a shirt, lo, these are measured double.

D. This is the general rule: That which comes doubled is measured doubled, and that which comes flat is measured flat.[49]

6:5   A. Said R. Yosé, "And with what *midras* did this have contact?"

B. R. Yosé agrees that if they were two, one on top of the other, they have not annulled one another.[50]

6:6   A. A cloth of three-by-three [fingerbreadths] which one found in the house, lo, this is unclean, for the whole house is regarded as well-guarded.

B. [If] one found it behind the door, or soiled, or [with] a *pondion* tied up in it, or [with] a needle stuck in it, or stuffed into a basket or in a pail, it is clean.

C. And [if found outside the house] it is never unclean until one will put it aside for a cloth.

D. R. Simeon says, "[If it was put aside] for a purpose which is susceptible to uncleanness, it is unclean, and [if put aside] for a purpose which is not susceptible to uncleanness, it is clean."[51]

6:7   A. A piece of cloth three-by-three [fingerbreadths] which was made up entirely of threads running alongside one another is unclean.

B. R. Yosé b. R. Judah says, "If it was entirely made up of threads running alongside one another, it is unclean, but if there was in it a border, it is clean."

6:8   A. [A piece of cloth] less than three-by-three [handbreadths] which one arranged to stop up a hole in the bath house, or to empty out the pot, or to wipe off the millstones —

B. "'[If] it is kept in readiness, it is unclean, and [if] it is not kept in readiness, it is clean,' the words of R. Eliezer.

"R. Joshua says, 'Whether or not kept in readiness, it is clean,' " the words of R. Meir.

C. R. Judah says, "R. Eliezer says, 'Whether it is kept in readiness or not kept in readiness, it is unclean.'

"R. Joshua says, 'Whether it is kept in readiness or not kept in readiness, it is clean.'

"R. 'Aqiva says, '[If] it is kept in readiness, it is unclean, and [if] it is not kept in readiness, it is clean.' "[52]

---

48. M. Kel. 28:8.   49. M. Kel. 27:6.   50. M. Kel. 27:9.
51. M. Kel. 27:11.   52. M. Kel. 28:2.

6:9 A. A piece of cloth three-by-three [fingerbreadths] which one made into a plaster, poultice, or compress is clean.

B. A piece of cloth three-by-three [handbreadths] which one made into a plaster, a poultice, or a compress is unclean.

C. Rabban Simeon b. Gamaliel says, "A plaster is clean, and a poultice or a compress is unclean."

D. And so did Rabban Simeon Gamaliel say, "He who makes a plaster from drugs — it is clean; and from herbs, it is unclean, because it dries off."

E. "And with leather: a plaster is clean, and a poultice and a compress are unclean."

F. R. Yosé and R. Simeon say, "The words of Rabban [Simeon b.] Gamaliel appear best in reference to wrappers of books, and with his rulings do we agree."

G. R. Judah says, "Also one for book-bags is like them."

H. R. Eleazar b. R. Ṣadoq says, "A reading desk of a scroll is clean, and its case is unclean. And the staff which is on it is a connector for uncleanness and for sprinkling."[53]

6:10 A. The head-wrap of an old lady which [was] unclean with *midras*-uncleanness and which one put on a scroll —

B. R. Meir declares clean.

C. And R. Yosé declares unclean.[54]

D. All utensils descend to their uncleanness with intention but do not ascend from their uncleanness except with some act which changes their character.

E. R. Judah says, "An act which changes their character for the worse."[55]

7:1 A. The threads of a girdle and their upper garment — any length at all.

B. The threads of the undergarment — ten.

C. And if they have a woven part [or, net] — any length.

D. Rabban Simeon b. Gamaliel says, "A woven part counts in the measure of three-by-three [handbreadths], but does not contribute to the measure of three-by-three [fingerbreadths]."

E. [When] it is broad, if one puts it on a chair and his flesh touches the chair, it is clean, and if not, it is unclean.

F. The threads of the birrus and the thick cloak and the felt cap, and the thick blankets and the felts and the coarse blankets and the bolsters and the mattresses — three fingerbreadths.[56]

7:2 A. The cord of the plummet — twelve.

53. M. Kel. 28:3.   54. M. Kel. 28:5.   55. M. Kel. 25:9/T. Kel. B.B. 3:13.
56. M. Kel. 29:1.

B. And of the carpenters — eighteen.

C. The cord of the nail of the builders and of the plasterers — fifty cubits.

D. Rabban Simeon b. Gamaliel says, "Also of the surveyors — fifty cubits."

E. The cord of the scales of metal dealers — two handbreadths, because he takes hold of it with his two hands and raises it up.[57]

7:3   A. The handle of a knife — a handbreadth.

B. And the remnants of the spindle — a handbreadth.

C. And the remnants of the brand — a handbreadth.

D. And the remnants of the baker's shovel — two handbreadths.

E. And the handle of the ax, from its back — three fingerbreadths. And R. Yosé says, "A handbreadth from its back is entirely clean."

F. A handle of the plane and the small plane — six.

G. The handle of the opener and the small opener — five [handbreadths].

H. The handle of the small slaughtering knife, five, and of the slaughtering knife — ten [handbreadths].[58]

7:4   A. The shaft of the trowel of house-holders —

B. The House of Shammai say, "Seven."

C. And the House of Hillel say, "Eight."

D. Of the plasterers —

E. The House of Shammai say, "Nine."

F. And the House of Hillel say, "Ten."

G. More than this is not a connector either for uncleanness or for sprinkling.

H. Under what circumstances?

I. When one is not going to cut [it] off.

J. "But when one is going to cut [it] off, it is a connector for uncleanness and not for sprinkling," the words of R. Meir.

K. R. Yosé says, "Also not for uncleanness."[59]

7:5   A. Said R. Yosé, "I say one thing and they said one thing. I say to them one thing: 'Do you not agree with me concerning the cord of the nail of the builders and of the plasterers — fifty cubits long; for [even] if one wants to keep more than this, it is clean?'

B. "And they said to me on another thing: 'Do you not agree concerning the fringes of the sheet and the handkerchief and the head-wrap and the felt-cap of the head — six fingerbreadths, and of fringes of the undergarment — ten; for if one wants to keep more than this, it is unclean?'

C. "And I prefer my words to their words, for I reply from a matter which is a connector for uncleanness and for sprinkling concerning a matter

---

57. M. Kel. 29:3.   58. M. Kel. 29:8.   59. *ibid.*

which is connected for uncleanness and for sprinkling, and they reply to me from a matter which is a connector for uncleanness and for sprinkling concerning a matter which, they agree, is not a connector for sprinkling."[60]

7:6   A. [Concerning] all those items to the remnants of the handles of which they have referred: [The handles have] their handles before them.

B. That which one grasps with one hand, for example the handle of the ax — a handbreadth; and that which one grasps with two hands, for example, the trowel, — two handbreadths.[61]

7:7   A. Glass utensils [are susceptible to uncleanness because of a decree] of the words of scribes.

B. And wooden utensils, and leather utensils, and bone utensils, and glass utensils — their uncleanness is equivalent:

C. When they are flat, they are clean, and when they are formed into receptacles, they are unclean.

D. The chest, box, and cupboard of glass which come in due measure are clean.

E. But all other glass utensils, even though they come in due measure, are unclean.

F. This [rule] is more strict concerning glass utensils than leather or wooden utensils.

G. Glass utensils do not receive uncleanness until their manufacture has been completed.

H. And Rabban Simeon b. Gamaliel says, "When they will have been taken from the forms."[62]

I. A tray which one made into a mirror, even though one makes use of it, is clean.

J. [If] it was unclean and one made it into a mirror, it remains unclean until one will have affixed it with a nail.[63]

7:8   A. A spoon of metal, whether it has a handle or not, whether it holds anything at all or does not hold anything at all, is unclean.

B. And [a spoon] of wood and of bone and of glass, [if] it holds anything at all, is unclean.

C. And [if] it does not hold anything at all, it is clean.

D. Or [if] it only drips and pours out [its contents] —

E. R. 'Aqiva declares unclean.

F. And R. Yoḥanan b. Nuri declares clean.[64]

7:9   A. A stone cup which was perforated and into which one poured lead

B. R. Yosé says in the name of R. Yoḥanan b. Nuri, "It is unclean because it is a metal utensil."

C. A cup of glass which was perforated and into which one poured lead

60. *ibid.*   61. M. Kel. 29:4.   62. M. Kel. 30:1.
63. M. Kel. 30:2.   64. *ibid.*

D. R. Yosé says in the name of R. Yoḥanan b. Nuri, "It is unclean as a metal utensil."

E. R. Simeon b. Gamaliel says, "Judah ben Shammuʻa declares unclean, in the name of R. Meir."

F. A large glass jug, the bottom of which has been removed, if it can set in its normal way —

G. Rabbi declares unclean.

H. And sages declare clean.

I. If to begin with one made it without a bottom, all agree that it is unclean.[65]

7:10　A. The [glass] cup and the flask which were perforated, whether above or below, are clean.

B. A tray and the bowl which were perforated above are unclean, and [those which were perforated] below are clean.

C. [If] they were cracked, [and] if they can hold hot water as cold, they are unclean, and if not, they are clean.

D. R. Eleazar b. R. Ṣadoq says, "The Sidonian cups which were chipped are clean, because they cut the mouth."

E. And sages declare unclean.[66]

7:11　A. A flask of wine and of oil, the neck of which was removed, if it is held in one hand, is unclean, and if in two hands, it is clean.[67]

B. A glass lantern which has a receptacle for oil is unclean. [If it has a receptacle] for the light, it is clean.

C. And unclean is only that part which serves a need.

7:12　A. The glass bed and chair and stool and armchair and crib and all glass utensils suitable for lying are unclean.

B. The glass pen-knife, and pen, and plummet, and weights, and pressing plates, and measuring rod, and measuring table are clean.

---

65. M. Kel. 30:3.　　66. *ibid.*　　67. M. Kel. 30:4.

AHILOT

1:1 A. One [and the same rule applies to] him who touches and who overshadows and who moves [a corpse] — all are counted [as made unclean] by the corpse.

B. You have only the man alone who is made unclean by bearing [the weight of] the corpse.

C. Foods and liquids and utensils are not made unclean by bearing [the weight of] the corpse.

D. Said R. Yosé, "In this manner you may state [the rule]: Whatever is made unclean by a corpse for uncleanness [that passes at] evening is clean [after contact with] the Zab in all respects."

1:2 A. How so a man with a man? Two with a corpse and one with a Zab.

B. Utensils with utensils? Three with a corpse and two with a Zab.

C. Utensils, man, and utensils? Four with a corpse and three with a Zab.

D. Under what circumstances? With reference to heave-offering and holy things.

E. But the Nazir shaves only [when made unclean] by a corpse alone. And they are obligated for making the Sanctuary and holy things unclean only because of [contact with] the corpse alone.[1]

1:3 A. Said R. 'Aqiva, "I have a fifth. The tent-peg stuck into the Tent, in which it is placed."

B. They said to him, "The Tent and the tent-peg come under one category."[2]

1:4 A. The gentile and the beast and one who is eight years old and a clay utensil and foods and liquids which touch the corpse — utensils which touch them are clean.

B. (And) just as the limb from the corpse and the limb from the living person which lack a bone, in respect to [touching] a man, [leave him] clean, so [if touched by] carrion and creeping things, he is clean.

C. A limb which does not have an appropriate amount of flesh, in respect to man, is unclean, and, in respect to carrion and creeping things, is clean.[3]

1:5 A. The bone-marrow, whether in man or beast, whether in a wild animal or fowl, and whether in carrion or torn things, and whether in abominable things or creeping things, is unclean, and they are liable on its account for *pigul, notar,* and *tammé.* And it renders unclean in an olive's bulk for carrying, and in a lentil's bulk for contact.

B. The sum of the matter is this: the marrow, lo, it is like flesh in every

---

1. M. Oh. 1:1−3.   2. M. Oh. 1:1.   3. M. Oh. 1:8.

respect.

1:6 A. Nine in the head — and the cheeks with them.

B. Five in the knee — two on one side and two on the other, and the protruding cartilege in the middle.[4]

1:7 A. Whatever has on it tendons and bones, lo, this is a limb, and whatever does not have on it tendons and bones is not a limb.

B. The extra [fingers] count in the number [of the limbs of the body].

C. One who lacks [the normal number of bones], who has in him only two hundred, and one who exceeds [the normal number of bones], who has on him two hundred eighty — they all join together [to be subjected to] the number of one hundred twenty-five.

D. The living person — to him does not apply [the specified] number nor [does] a quarter-*qab* of bones [apply to him].[5]

2:1 A. An Israelite who slaughtered an unclean animal for a gentile and slaughtered in it two or the greater part of two [organs of the throat], and it is still jerking — it contaminates with the uncleanness of foods but not with the uncleanness of carrion.

B. A limb which separates from it is as if it separated from the living creature, and flesh which separates from it is as if it separated from a living creature. And it is prohibited [for use] by the children of Noah, and even if the beast died. [If] one killed it by stabbing, it does not contaminate through the uncleanness of foods.

[If] he cut so much as renders it *ṭerefah,* there is no uncleanness pertaining to it at all.

C. And a gentile who slaughtered a clean beast for an Israelite and slaughtered in it two or the greater part of two [organs of the throat], and it is still jerking — it renders unclean as does food, but it does not render unclean as does carrion, and a limb which separates from it is as if it separates from a living creature. And flesh which separates from it is as if it separates from a living creature. And it is prohibited [for use] by the children of Noah, and even if the beast dies.

[If] he killed it by stabbing, it does not render unclean as foods convey uncleanness.

[If] he slaughtered in it one [organ of the throat] or the greater part of one, no uncleanness pertains to it at all.

[If] a gentile cut only so much as does not render *ṭerefah,* and an Israelite came and completed it [the slaughtering], it is permitted for eating.

D. [If] an Israelite slaughtered in it two or the greater part of two [organs of the throat] — the same rule applies to a gentile and to an Israelite: one chops flesh from it and waits until it dies, and it is permitted

4. *ibid.*   5. M. Oh. 2:1.

for eating.

2:2   A.   "A 'ladleful of corpse-mould' of which they spoke includes from the joint of his finger and above," the words of R. Meir.

B.   And sages say, "His handfuls."[6]

2:3   A.   And what is the [sort of] corpse which produces corpse-mould?

B.   That which is buried naked, in a stone sarcophagus, on a marble floor or table.

C.   But that which is buried in its shroud, and in a wooden coffin, on dirt does not produce corpse-mould.

D.   And he that takes dirt from under it — that is dirt of graves — "a ladleful and a bit more."

E.   A mixture which is found in the grave and the character of which one does not know, lo, this is a dirt of graves — "a ladleful and a bit more."[7]

2:4   R. Eleazar b. R. Ṣadoq explained, "One sifts out the pebbles and the chips which are certain[ly not corpse-matter]. One takes that which is certain [to be corpse-matter] and leaves that which is in doubt. And this is the dirt of graves — 'a ladleful and more.'"[8]

2:5   A.   A backbone which has been stripped of the greater part of its vertebrae, even though its outline stands, is clean.

B.   When it is in the grave, even if it is broken, and even if it is crushed, it is unclean, because the grave joins it together.[9]

2:6   A.   The skull which had in it a single long perforation, or in which were many perforations — they join together [to make up] the measure of the drill.

B.   Said R. Yosé b. Hameshulam, "M'ŚH: In 'Eyn Bul someone's skull was chopped open, and the physician patched a patch of gourd on it, and he lived."

C.   Said to him R. Simeon b. Eleazar, "Is there proof from that case? Even though he lived out the entire summer, when the rains came, the cold overtook him, and he died."[10]

2:7   A.   An olive's bulk of flesh which separates from a limb of a living person —

B.   R. Eliezer declares unclean.

C.   They answered R. Eliezer three answers:

D.   "No. If you have said so concerning corpse, to which apply the [laws concerning] the 'greater part,' the 'quarter-*qab*,' 'corpse-mould,' will you say so concerning a limb from a living person, to which 'greater part,' 'quarter-*qab*,' 'corpse-mould' do not apply?

E.   "Another matter: Which depends on which ? Does the limb depend upon the flesh, or does the flesh depend on the limb? The flesh depends on

---

6. *ibid.*   7. *ibid.*   8. M. Oh. 2:2.
9. M. Oh. 2:3.   10. *ibid.*

the limb.

F. "Is it possible that the flesh should render unclean through contact, carrying, and Tent, while the limb should be clean?"

G. Said R. Simeon, "I should be surprised if [under all circumstances] R. Eliezer declared it unclean. He declared it unclean only when there is on the limb appropriate flesh, so that this and this should render unclean through contact, carrying, and Tent."[11]

2:8   A. A bone the size of a barley-corn which separates from the limb of a living person —

B. R. Neḥunya declares unclean.

C. They answered R. Neḥunya three replies:

D. "No. If you have said so concerning the corpse, to which the 'greater part,' the 'quarter-qab,' 'corpse-matter' apply, will you say so concerning the limb from a living person, to which the 'greater part,' 'quarter-qab,' 'corpse-matter' do not apply?

E. "Another matter: Which depends on which? Does the limb depend upon the bone, or does the bone depend on the limb? The bone depends on the limb. Is it possible that the bone should render unclean through contact, and carrying, and that the limb should be clean?"

F. Said R. Simeon, "I should be surprised if [under all circumstances] R. Neḥunya declared [it] unclean.

G. "He declared [it] unclean only when there is on the limb a bone the size of a barley-corn, so that this and that should render unclean through contact and through carrying."

H. R. Joshua answered the opinions of both of them.

I. "If bone and flesh which separate from the living person, who has in him two hundred forty-eight limbs, are clean, a limb on which there are not two hundred and forty-eight [parts] — is it not logical that the bone and flesh which separate from it should be clean?"

J. Rabbi replied to the opinion of R. Joshua, "No. If you speak concerning those things which separate from the living person, which indeed have separated from something which is clean, will you say so concerning those things which separate from the limb, which indeed have separated from something unclean?"[12]

3:1   A. Said R. Judah, "R. 'Aqiva and sages did not differ concerning a [single] quarter-log of blood which exuded from two corpses, that it is clean.

"Concerning what did they differ?

"Concerning a quarter-log of blood which exuded from two quarter-logs from two corpses, for

"R. 'Aqiva declares unclean.

11. M. Ed. 6:2—3.   12. *ibid.*

"And sages declare clean."

B. R. Simeon b. Judah says in the name of R. Simeon, "R. 'Aqiva and sages did not differ concerning a quarter-*log* of blood which exuded from two quarter-*logs* from two corpses, that it is unclean.

"Concerning what did they differ?

"Concerning a quarter-*log* of blood which exuded from two quarter-*logs* from two corpses, for R. 'Aqiva declares unclean and sages declare clean."[13]

3:2 A. Abba Saul says, "A quarter-*log* is the beginning of the blood of a child."

B. The blood of a child, all of which has exuded and which does not add up to a quarter-*log* —

C. R. 'Aqiva says, "Any amount."

D. And sages say, "A quarter-*log*."

E. For R. 'Aqiva says, "Uncleanness [applies] to blood and uncleanness [applies] to bones. Just as bones, even though they do not add up to a quarter-*qab,* are unclean, so blood, even though it does not add up to quarter-*log,* is unclean."[14]

3:3 A. They answered R. 'Aqiva [with] three answers:

B. "No. If you have said so concerning bones, the larger number of which are unclean even when not a quarter-*qab,* will you say so concerning blood, which is unclean only in a quarter-*log?*

C. "Another matter: No. If you have said concerning bones —while the minority of the bones is unclean, a bone the size of a barley-corn which separates from them is unclean. Will you say so concerning blood, which is unclean only if it is a quarter-*log?*

D. "Another matter: No. If you have said so concerning bones concerning which it is known that all of them are before you, will you say so concerning blood? For we say that, if there remained of it a drop of any amount, it is clean."

E. He said to them, "I too have said so only [in a case in which we are sure that] all of it has exuded."

F. They said to him, "It is not possible to be sure of the matter."[15]

3:4 A. A quarter-*qab* of bones from most of the skeleton in volume, and bones from the greater part of the skeleton in number, even though they do not contain a quarter-*qab,* are unclean.

B. R. Judah says [the rule] in other language:

C. "The House of Shammai say, 'A quarter-*qab* of bones from the skeleton, from the greater part of the frame or from the greater part of the number,

D. "the greater part of the frame [of the skeleton] and the greater part of the number of a corpse, even though they do not add up to a quarter *qab*

13. M. Oh. 2:2.   14. *ibid.*   15. *ibid.*

"are unclean."

E. And what is its frame? The shoulders and the thighs and the ribs and the backbone.

F. And what is its number? Even the fingertips and toes, so long as there are in it one hundred twenty-five.[16]

3:5 A. Said R. Joshua, "I can make the words of the House of Shammai and the words of the House of Hillel one.

B. "From the shoulders and from the thighs there are found the greater part of its frame in volume.

C. "[And] half of the greater part of its frame and half of the greater part of its number [of bones] do not join together."[17]

3:6 A. Half an olive's bulk of flesh and half an olive's bulk of corpse-dregs join together.

B. But all other forms of uncleanness which pertain to the corpse do not join together, because their required measurements are not alike.[18]

3:7 A. The rolling stone and the buttressing stone render unclean through contact and through Tent but do not render unclean through carrying.

B. R. Eliezer says, "They do render unclean through carrying —

"by an argument a fortiori: if they render unclean through contact, which is minor, will they not render unclean through carrying, which is major?"

C. Said to him R. 'Aqiva, "If they render unclean through contact, which is commonplace, will they render unclean through carrying, which is not commonplace?"

D. Said to him R. Eliezer, "What is this, 'Aqiva? Is not the uncleanness of the Tent less common than either of them? And lo, they do render unclean by that means. Then, if they render unclean through Tent, which is uncommon, will they not render unclean through carrying, which is commonplace?"

E. R. 'Aqiva withdrew, and R. Joshua jumped into the argument.

He [Joshua] said to him [Eliezer], "The uncleanness of Tent is more common than the uncleanness of carrying, for he who overshadows a corpse in a *Sukkah* is unclean, but he who moves it [the *Sukkah*] is clean. He who makes his *Sukkah* at the door of a grave — he who overshadows it [the *Sukkah*] is unclean, but he who moves it is clean."[19]

3:8 A. Said R. Simeon, "But that is the very matter under discussion. If a *Sukkah,* which has a door, lo, it [the *Sukkah*] interposes on it [the corpse], a *Sukkah* which has no door — that is the rolling stone itself.

B. "But thus is it necessary to answer him: More common is the uncleanness of the Tent than the uncleanness of carrying, for all things may be

16. M. Oh. 2:1.   17. *ibid.*   18. M. Oh. 2:6.
19. M. Oh. 2:4.

made unclean by a Tent, and you have nothing which is made unclean by carrying except for man alone."[20]

3:9 A. M'ŚH: In Bet Daggan in Judah a person died on the eve of Passover, and they went to bury him.

B. And the women entered and tied the rope to the rolling stone. The men drew [on the rope] from the outside, and the women entered and buried him. And the men went and [in a state of cleanness] made their Paschal sacrifice in the evening.[21]

3:10 A. Two large stones of four by four handbreadths which one made a rolling stone for a grave —

B. he who overshadows both of them is susceptible to uncleanness.

C. [If] one of them was removed, he who overshadows the second is clean, because the uncleanness in such a circumstance has a way by which it may go forth.[22]

4:1 A. R. Yosé says, "A ladleful of corpse-mould renders unclean through contact, carrying, and Tent."

B. R. Simeon says, "Three forms of uncleanness exude from the corpse, each of which contaminates by two but not by the third.

C. "These are they: The rolling stone and buttressing stone [of the grave], and a bone the size of a barley-corn, and a ladleful of corpse-mould.

D. "The rolling stone and buttressing stone render unclean through contact and through airspace [should be: Tent] and do not render unclean through carrying.

E. "And how does carrying [apply to] them? [With] a bone the size of a barley-corn.

F. "A bone the size of a barley-corn renders unclean through contact and carrying and does not render unclean through Tent.

G. "And how does Tent [apply to] it? With a ladleful of corpse-mould.

H. "A ladleful of corpse-matter renders unclean through carrying and through Tent and does not render unclean through contact."

I. And so did R. Yosé say, "An olive's bulk of corpse which one divided even into ten parts renders unclean through carrying and through Tent and does not render unclean through contact."[23]

4:2 A. Said R. Judah, "Six matters did R. 'Aqiva declare unclean, and he then reversed himself.

B. "M'ŚH: They brought buckets of bones from Kefar Ṭabya, and they left them in the open air at the synagogue in Lud.

C. "Teodoros the physician came in, with all the physicians with him. They said, 'There is not present a backbone from a single corpse, nor a skull

20. *ibid.*   21. *ibid.*   22. *ibid.*
23. M. Oh. 2:1, 2:7.

from a single corpse.'

D. "They said, 'Since some present declare unclean and some present declare clean, let us arise for a vote.'

E. "They began from R. 'Aqiva, and he declared [them] clean.

F. "They said to him, 'Since you, who [in the past] declared unclean, have declared clean, let them be clean.'"

G. Said R. Simeon, "And until the day of R. 'Aqiva's death, he declared them unclean. Whether or not he reversed himself after he died, I do not know."[24]

4:3 A. Fat of the corpse which was whole and which one melted is unclean.

B. And if a man touched it when it is melted, he is unclean.

C. [If] it was in pieces and one melted it, it is clean,

D. for connection effected by man is no connection.

E. An *etrog* which burst and which one reassembled on a spindle or on a chip is not connected,

F. for connection effected by man is no connection.[25]

G. The vertebrae of the corpse which one made into a handle for a knife, lo, this is not connected,

H. for connection effected by man is no connection.

4:4 A. An olive's bulk of flesh from a corpse which was divided into two is unclean, and one does not take account of the possibility that it has been diminished. (And if after it was divided a man overshadowed it . . .)

B. An *etrog* which was divided into two parts is acceptable, and one does not take account of the possibility that it has been diminished.

C. A quarter-*log* of blood which was divided into two parts is unclean, and one does not take account of the possibility that it has been diminished.

D. A meal-offering which five priests have mixed is acceptable, and one does not take account of the possibility that it has been diminished. If one emptied it from one vessel to another, it is acceptable.

Rabban Simeon b. Gamaliel says, "If one was careless, lo, this is unfit.[26]

4:5 A. An olive's bulk of corpse-matter and an olive's bulk of corpse-dregs and a ladleful of corpse-mould from two corpses join together with one another.

B. A ladleful of corpse-mould when it has any amount of dirt in it is unclean.

C. And R. Joshua [Simeon] declares it clean, because it has been annulled.

D. "A quarter-*log* of blood which was absorbed in clothing" — How do they estimate it?

E. One brings water by measure and washes it [the garment] in it [the

24. M. Oh. 2:6.   25. M. Oh. 3:4.   26. M. Oh. 3:2.

water]. One brings another [supply of] water and puts in it a quarter-*log* of blood. If their appearance [= the two measures of water] is alike, lo, this [garment] is unclean. If not, lo, this is clean.[27]

4:6   A. R. Yosé says, "The earlier sages say, 'From the incline and inward, the house is unclean. From the incline and outward, the house is clean.'

B. "They reverted to rule, 'An incline, whether inward or outward — the house is clean.'"[28]

4:7   A. [If] the corpse is outside and his hair is inside, even though in the Tent is only any amount [of hair] at all, the house which overshadows it [the hair] is unclean.

B. The bone which has on it two half olive's bulks [of corpse-matter], one attached by man, and one attached by Heaven —

C. if one brought that which was attached by man into the house, the house is clean, for that which is connected to it does not join with it.

D. [If] one brought that which was attached by Heaven inside the house, it is unclean, for, lo, that which is connected to it joins with it.[29]

[Alternative reading, following *TR* III, p. 104: C. . . . the house is unclean, because its fellow joins with it. D. (If) one brought in that which is attached by Heaven, the house is clean, because its fellow (= the half-olive's bulk attached by man, outside the house) is not joined with it.]

4:8   A. Two bones and on them [at one end] are two half olive's bulks, and one brought their tips [at the other end] inside —

B. Judah b. Naqosa' says in the name of R. Jacob, "Even if both of them are attached by Heaven, the house is clean, for two bones do not join together to form two half-olive's-bulks."

C. [If] an olive's bulk of a corpse was lost inside the house, and they sought and did not find it, the house is clean.

D. When it will be found, the house renders unclean retroactively.[30]

4:9   A. All liquids which exude from the corpse are clean except for his blood.

B. But all those liquids in a corpse which look like blood, lo, these are unclean.[31]

4:10   A. And what is 'mixed blood'?

B. R. Eleazar ben Judah says, "One who was slain, from whom a quarter-*log* exuded [both] while he was alive and after he died —

"[if there is a] doubt [as to whether a full quarter-*log* exuded] while he was alive or [whether it exuded] after he died —

"this is 'mixed blood.'"

C. And sages say, "One who was slain, from whom a quarter-*log* of blood exuded while he was alive and after his death, and it still has not

27. *ibid.*   28. M. Oh. 3:3.   29. M. Oh. 3:4.
30. *ibid.*   31. M. Oh. 3:5.

ceased [to flow] —

"[if there is a] doubt concerning whether the greater part [exuded] in his life and the smaller part after he died, or whether the greater part [exuded] after he died and the smaller part in his life —

"this is mixed blood."[32]

4:11 A. R. Judah says, "One who was slain who was placed on a bier and his blood dripped out into the hole — it is unclean, because the drop of [blood of] death is mixed [up in the remainder]."

B. And sages declare clean, because each single drop is detached from the other.

C. R. Simeon says, "One who was crucified whose blood gushed forth, and under whom is found a quarter-*log* of blood — it is clean. But a corpse whose blood drips forth and under whom is found a quarter-*log* of blood — it is unclean."

D. And R. Judah declares [it] clean, "For I say that the final drop of death remained on the wood."[33]

4:12 A. There are three kinds of quarter-*logs*. How so?

B. [If] one was smitten to death and is writhing, and a quarter-*log* of blood exuded from him, and they moved him in the assumption that he is alive and brought him to another place, and a quarter-*log* [then] exuded from him —

the first is the blood of the life, the second is mixed blood, and the third is the blood of death.

C. And what is the difference between the blood of death and mixed blood?

(But) [as to] blood of death — the Nazir shaves on its account, and they are liable on its account for rendering the sanctuary and its holy things unclean.

[As to] mixed blood — the Nazir does not shave on its account, and they are not liable on its account for rendering the sanctuary and its holy things unclean.[34]

4:13 A. Said R. Eleazar, "At first the elders were divided. Some of them say, 'A quarter-*log* of blood and a quarter-*qab* of bones,' and some of them say, 'A half-*qab* of bones and half-*log* of blood [contaminate, etc.].'

B. "The court which followed them said, 'A quarter-*log* of blood and a quarter-*qab* of bones [suffice to contaminate] heave-offering and sacred meals, [but] a half-*qab* of bones and a half-*log* of blood [must be present to contaminate] the Nazir and the sanctuary.'"[35]

4:14 A. Said R. Eleazar, "When I went to Ardaqsis, I found R. Meir and Judah b. Patyrosh who were in session and reasoning about law.

32. *ibid.*   33. *ibid.*   34. *ibid.*
35. *ibid.*

B. "Judah b. Patyrosh says, '[As to] a quarter-*log* of blood — the Nazir does not shave on its account, and they are not liable on its account for rendering the sanctuary and its holy things unclean.'

C. "Said to him R. Meir, 'Should this be more lenient than the creeping thing? Just as the creeping thing, which is lenient — the Nazir shaves on its account, and [on its account] are they liable for making the sanctuary and its holy things unclean, a quarter-*log* of blood, which is stringent, is it not logical that the Nazir should shave on its account, and that they should be liable on its account for rendering the sanctuary and its holy things unclean?'

D. "Judah ben Patyrosh was silent.

E. "I advised R. Meir, 'Do not have contempt for him. He served as an expert for you concerning Joshua ben Mamal.'

F. "He said to me, 'Yes, and he was a master of laws.'

G. "I advised him in this language:

H. "He said to me in the name of R. Joshua, '[For] every form of corpse-uncleanness concerning which the Nazir shaves, they are liable for rendering the sanctuary and its holy things unclean, and for every form of corpse-uncleanness for which the Nazir does not shave, they are not liable for rendering the sanctuary and its holy things unclean.'"[36]

5:1   A. R. Ishmael the son of R. Yosé says in the name of R. Nathan, "A corpse which [in size] is less than four handbreadths — its opening is the equivalent of its size, and its roof is clean."

B. R. Simeon b. Eleazar says in the name of R. Meir, "A corpse which is larger than four handbreadths — its opening is equivalent to its size."[37]

5:2   A. R. Yosé says, "The backbone and skull are like a corpse."

B. Others say in the name of R. Nathan, "Everything unclean which exudes from the corpse is like the corpse, and its opening is four handbreadths."[38]

5:3   A. A rainspout which is arched under the house, four handbreadths wide, with its outlet, four handbreadths, and it [a corpse] fell into it —

B. the house is clean.

C. [If] it fell into the house —

D. what is in it is clean.

E. It is four handbreadths wide, but its outlet is not four handbreadths

F. [if a corpse] fell into it, the house is unclean.

G. [If] it fell into the house, what is in it is clean.

H. [If] there are neither in it nor in its exit four handbreadths —

I. [if a corpse] fell into it, the house is unclean.

J. [If a corpse] fell into the house, what is in it is unclean.

36. *ibid.*   37. M. Oh. 3:6.   38. *ibid.*

K. [If] it was broad [on the] inside [part of the spout] and narrow [on the] outside [part that projects] —

L. uncleanness is in the wide part —

M. the house is unclean.

N. [If uncleanness is] in the narrow part, it is judged half and half.

P. Uncleanness is in the house —

Q. utensils in the wide part are unclean, and those in the narrow part are clean.[39]

5:4 R. Judah agrees concerning clefts and overhanging rocks, that, even though they are not [made as] a Tent, they are regarded as equivalent to a Tent.[40]

5:5 A. A cupboard which stands, whether in the house or in the open air

B. uncleanness is in it —

C. utensils which are in its thick walls are clean.

D. Uncleanness is in its thick walls —

E. utensils which are in it are clean.

F. And R. Yosé says, "Half and half."

G. [If] it was standing in the midst of the house, and uncleanness is in it, the house is unclean.

H. Uncleanness is in the house —

I. what is in it is clean,

J. for it is the way of uncleanness to exude, and it is not its way to seep in.

K. Utensils which are between it and the ground, which are between it and the wall, which are between it and the roof-beams —

L. if there is there a cubic handbreadth, are unclean, and if not, they are clean.

M. Uncleanness is there —

N. the house is clean.

P. Utensils which are in the wall behind it and which are in the plaster above it are regarded half and half.

Q. Uncleanness is under its [the cupboard's] leg or on top of its leg, and it presses down —

R. uncleanness breaks forth upward and breaks forth downward.

S. To what is this [matter] likened?

To a pillar which stands in the midst of the house, and uncleanness is under it, and it presses down —

uncleanness breaks upward and breaks forth downward.

T. [If] it was set on its side and sealed, and uncleanness is under it, and it presses down —

uncleanness breaks forth upward and breaks forth downward.

---

39. M. Oh. 3:7.   40. *ibid.*

Utensils which are lying in the small cupboards which are in the cupboard on either side are clean.

U. [If] it was standing in the midst of the doorway, opening outward, and uncleanness is in it, the house is clean.

V. [If] uncleanness is in the house, what is in it is clean, for it is the way of uncleanness to exude, and it is not the way of uncleanness to seep in.[41]

5:6 Said R. Yosé, "Is this the law? Is the power of the utensil to interpose greater in the tightly sealed jar or in Tents? If it affords protection from the power of the tightly sealed jar with respect to a rolling stone [of the grave], all the more so by means of Tents [will protection be afforded]."[42]

5:7 A. [If] its base was drawn backward three fingerbreadths, and uncleanness was there opposite the beams, the house is clean.

B. For I regard the beams as though they descend and close off.

C. Another matter: Uncleanness does not enter the Tent and does not exude from it except through an opening of a square handbreadth.

D. Utensils which are opposite the olive's bulk —

E. Rabbi declares unclean.

F. And sages declare clean.

G. Said Rabbi, "I prefer their opinion to mine. Under what circumstances? When it is open. But when it is sealed, lo, this is like a closed grave and contaminates on all its sides."[43]

5:8 A. Said R. Yosé, "R. Yoḥanan b. Nuri came to R. Ḥalafta. He said to him, 'What do you rule concerning the eye of an oven?'

"He said to him, 'It is unclean.'

"He said to him, 'Also do I rule so, but 'Aqiva declares [it] clean.'"

B. An eye of an oven a handbreadth in height but not a handbreadth in breadth, [or] a handbreadth in breadth and not a handbreadth in height, is clean.

C. [If] one placed a board on it, uncleanness breaks forth through the board. It is made unclean and renders the oven unclean.[44]

5:9 A. A hatchway which is between the house and the upper room, and on which a pot, perforated so as to admit liquids, is placed —

R. 'Aqiva says, "It affords protection."

And sages say, "It does not afford protection."

B. [If] it is damaged so as to allow olives to fall out, it affords protection,

C. — up to [a perforation of] less than a handbreadth.

D. [If] one gathered into it purification-water and ashes [for] purification[-water], it affords protection for the purification-water but does not afford protection for heave-offering.

41. M. Oh. 4:1.   42. M. Oh. 4:3.   43. ibid.
44. M. Oh. 5:1.

E. When you find [occasion] you may rule: That which is clean affords protection for itself.

F. How so?

G. [If] there were there utensils, they are clean for purification-water and unclean for heave-offering. It comes out that that which is clean affords protection for itself.[45]

5:10 A flagon which is full of clean liquids and which one emptied into another flagon, if there are liquids in it, they are unclean.[46]

5:11 A. A woman who was kneading in one trough, and her hands were busy in the dough — so long as she is raising this and putting down this, raising this and putting down this, the woman and the trough are unclean with seven-days-uncleanness, but the dough is clean. [If] she removed her hand from it and returned it, it is unclean and makes the dough unclean.

B. Said R. Joshua, "I am ashamed by your words, House of Shammai. Is it possible that the woman and the trough are unclean for seven days, and the dough is clean? [And that] the flagon should contract seven days' uncleanness and the liquid should remain clean?"

C. After he stood up, a certain disciple among the disciples of the House of Shammai said before him, "Rabbi, may I say before you a reason that the House of Shammai say concerning it?"

D. He said to him, "Speak."

E. "The vessel of an 'am ha'ares, what is it [its status], unclean or clean?"

F. He said to him, "Unclean."

G. "And does something unclean afford protection? If so, let this thing protect the vessels of a *haber*.[47]

5:12 A. "Another matter: And if an 'am ha'ares says to you concerning his vessel that it is unclean, when we purified the food and liquid in it, we have purified [the food] for himself, but when we have purified the vessel, we have purified it for you and for him."

B. R. Joshua reverted to teach according to the words of the disciple.

C. R. Joshua said, "I bow to you, bones of the House of Shammai."[48]

6:1 A. R. Judah says in the name of R. Joshua, "Just as utensils afford protection with Tents which have sides, so they afford protection with Tents which do not have sides,

B. "both clean clay and wooden utensils.

C. "Under what circumstances?

D. "In the case of a utensil which forms a square [cubic] handbreadth.

E. "But a utensil which does not form a square [cubic] handbreadth

45. M. Oh. 5:2.   46. M. Oh. 5:4.   47. *ibid.*
48. *ibid.*

does not afford protection.

F. "Under what circumstances?

G. "When it is fixed tightly outside from one side and inside from both sides. But if it was fixed tightly about a half-handbreadth on one side and about half a handbreadth on another side, lo, it does not afford protection."[49]

6:2   A. A pot which is set alongside the wall of a tent on the outside —

B. uncleanness is under it —

C. and it presses down —

D. the uncleanness breaks forth upward and breaks forth downward.

E. It was a handbreadth high off the ground —

F. uncleanness is under it —

G. [space] underneath it is unclean.

H. Its inside and the part above are clean, because it affords protection with the wall of the Tent.

I. [If the uncleanness is] inside it or on top of it, the whole is unclean.[50]

6:3   A. [If] it was upside down —

uncleanness is under it, and it presses down —

uncleanness breaks forth upward and breaks forth downward.

B. [If] it was a handbreadth off the ground, and uncleanness is under it, [space] under it is unclean. Its inside and upper surfaces are clean, because it is adjudged like the sloping outer side of Tents.

C. Inside or on top of it, opposite up to the firmament is unclean.[51]

6:4   A. [If] it was placed on two pegs outside, protruding from it [the wall] a square handbreadth, it does not afford protection.

B. [If] less than a handbreadth —

C. R. 'Aqiva says, "It affords protection."

D. And sages say, "It does not afford protection."[52]

6:5   A. A wall, part of which serves the house and part of which serves the garden —

it was placed on the side which serves the house —

it affords protection.

On the side that serves the garden — it does not afford protection.

B. A beam which is placed from wall to wall, and a pot is with it, if there is not a square handbreadth between its mouth and the beam, lo, this affords protection. If there is between its mouth and the beam a square handbreadth, lo, this does not afford protection.

C. [If] it was fixed tightly on the ground and on the beam, if there is not between its mouth and the beam a handbreadth, lo, this affords protection.

D. If there is between its mouth and the beam a square handbreadth, lo,

49. M. Oh. 5:6.   50. M. Oh. 5:7.   51. *ibid.* Reading: *TR* III, pp. 110–111.
52. *ibid.*

this does not afford protection.[53]

6:6 A. [If] its mouth was above, attached to the beam, lo, this affords protection.

B. [If its mouth] protruded from it by a square handbreadth, it does not afford protection.

C. [If the mouth was] less than a handbreadth —

Abba Saul says, "In this there is a dispute:

"R. 'Aqiva says, 'It affords protection.'

"And sages say, 'It does not afford protection.'"

D. [If] one of its heads was placed on the wall of a house, and its other head was placed on the wall of a garden,

[if] it was on the side that serves the house, it affords protection.

[if] it was on the side that serves the garden, it does not afford protection.

E. Abba Saul says, "Even in this case there is a dispute."[54]

7:1 A. Four who were carrying the bier —

and the poles are not so thick as the ox-goad —

uncleanness is under it —

utensils which are on top of it are unclean.

B. Uncleanness is on top of it —

utensils which are under it are unclean.

C. R. Eliezer declares clean.

D. And so did R. Eliezer say, "[If] an olive's bulk of corpse-matter in the mouth of a raven overshadowed the bier, man and utensils which are under it are clean.

E. "[If] it overshadowed a new oven or double-stove, they are clean."

F. [If] it was placed on four utensils, even utensils of dung, stone, and clod, and they are not a cubic handbreadth in space —

uncleanness is under it —

utensils which are on it are unclean.

G. Uncleanness is on it —

utensils which are under it are clean.

H. And R. Eliezer declares [them] clean.

I. [If] it was set on four little chairs placed on four stones, and they are not a handbreadth in height —

uncleanness is under it —

utensils which are on it are unclean.

J. Uncleanness is on it —

utensils which are under it are clean.

K. And if the tops of the little chairs are visible, in either case they are

53. *ibid.*   54. *ibid.*

clean.[55]

7:2 A. A beam, one head of which is set on a stone and one head set on a bench —

B. they examine the beam:

C. if the bench should be removed, and it can stand by itself, it affords protection, and if not, it does not afford protection.

D. R. Yosé bar Judah says, "They examine the beam: if one should descend and sit under it, and there is under it a space of a cubic handbreadth, lo, this affords protection, because it is regarded as the sloping sides of Tents."

7:3 R. Judah says in the name of R. Eliezer, "Even though the door is open, the house is clean, because the key has not been made unclean."[56]

7:4 A. A house which one subdivided with clean jars, and their mouth is toward the clean side — they afford protection. [If their mouth is facing] the unclean side, they do not afford protection.

B. R. Simeon ben Judah says in the name of R. Simeon, "[Even if the mouth faces] the unclean [side], they afford protection, unless their mouth contains a handbreadth in space."

C. [If] one plastered them with plaster, whether on the inside or on the outside, if the plaster can stand by itself, it affords protection, and if not, it does not afford protection.[57]

7:5 A. A wall which is cracked, whether horizontally or vertically, and is made like a funnel,

wide on the inside and narrow on the outside —

uncleanness is in the wide part —

the house is unclean.

And [if uncleanness is] in the narrow part, it is adjudged half and half.

B. [If it is] wide on the outside [of the house] and narrow on the inside uncleanness is on the wide part —

the house is clean.

And [if uncleanness is] in the narrow part — it is adjudged half and half.

C. [If] it is cracked vertically and [the crack] opens outward in either direction, [and if it is] broad on the top and narrow on the bottom, and uncleanness is in either the wide part or the narrow part, the house is unclean.

D. [If] it is cracked horizontally, and [the crack] opens outward in either side,

[if the crack is] wide on one side and narrow on the other side —

uncleanness is on the wide part —

the house is unclean.

And [if uncleanness is] in the narrow part —

it is adjudged half and half.

55. M. Oh. 6:1.   56. M. Oh. 6:2.   57. *ibid.*

E. And how much should this crack be?

Rabbi says, "The size of the fist of Ben Baṭṭiah."[58]

7:6   A. A wall which is [composed] half of stone and half of [the wall of] a building is adjudged half and half.

B. [If material] is removed from it on the inside and added to it on the outside, and the uncleanness is found from the midpoint of the wall and outward, the house is unclean.

C. [If material] is removed from it from the outer side and added to it on the inner side, and uncleanness is found from the midpoint of the wall and outward, the house is clean.

D. [If] one [wall] was rock and one was building, that which is [constituted by] the building is adjudged half and half, and that [constituted by] the rock is adjudged like the garlic peel.

E. R. Yosé says, "[If] uncleanness is from the midpoint on the wall and outward, the house is clean.

F. "That which stands above it on top of the uncleanness is clean, for the uncleanness does not pass beyond the beams, and even though the beams are not in that direction."

G. R. Meir and R. Simeon say, "From the midpoint and outward, uncleanness breaks forth and goes upward, breaks forth and goes downward."[57]

7:7   Uncleanness which is placed on the wall, whether from its midpoint and inward or from its midpoint and outward — the house is clean.[60]

7:8   A. A wall which is between two houses, and uncleanness is in its midst — the house which is nearer to the uncleanness is unclean, and the one which is nearer to the clean [side] is clean.

B. Half and half — both of them are unclean.

C. R. Eliezer says, "They burn on their account heave-offering, but they are not liable on their account for rendering the sanctuary and its holy things unclean."[61]

7:9   A. Plaster which is facing the open air, and uncleanness is in it —

B. [if the uncleanness is] from its midpoint and downward, the house is unclean. And that which stands on top of it directly over the uncleanness is clean.

C. [If the uncleanness is located] from its midpoint and upward, the house is clean, and that which stands directly above the uncleanness is unclean.

D. Half and half — the house is unclean.

E. And that which stands above it directly over the uncleanness —

F. R. Meir declares unclean.

---

58. M. Oh. 6:4.   59. M. Oh. 6:3.   60. M. Oh. 6:4.
61. *ibid.*

G. And R. Simeon declares clean.[62]

7:10   A. R. Judah says, "The entire wall serves the house."

B. And so did R. Judah say, "The entire plaster-coating serves the upper room."

C. Sages agree with R. Judah in the case of two caverns, one on top of the other, and uncleanness is in the lower one —

the lower one and ground are unclean. The upper one and ground are clean.

Uncleanness is in the upper one —

the upper one and ground are unclean. The lower one and ground are clean.

D. Uncleanness is between them — the upper one is unclean, and the lower one is clean. And the roof of the upper one is clean.

E. So did R. Judah say, "A wall which is between two *kokhs* or between two caverns — up to six handbreadths is adjudged half and half. More than that is adjudged like the garlic peel."

F. So did R. Judah say, "A wall which is between two niches or between two caverns —

"[if the wall is thicker than six handbreadths, then] up to six handbreadths, it is adjudged half and half; [if it is thicker] than that, it is adjudged like the garlic peel."[63]

7:11   A. A pot which is placed on the side of the wall of a cavern does not afford protection. [If it is placed] on the side of the arch of a cavern, lo, this affords protection.

B. [If] it was set on the window which is between two houses, and uncleanness is in one of them, lo, this [other house] is clean, because it affords protection [together] with the wall of the second.

C. [If] uncleanness was in the pot which is between them, and there is in its space a cubic handbreadth, if there is not between its mouth and the lintel a space of a cubic handbreadth, lo, this affords protection.

D. If there is between its mouth and the lintel a cubic handbreadth, lo, this does not afford protection.[64]

7:12   A. "A pitcher of purification-water which is placed in the window, and there is in its place a cubic handbreadth, if there is not between its mouth and the lintel a space of a cubic handbreadth, lo, this affords protection, and if not, it does not afford protection," the words of R. Eliezer.

B. R. Joshua says, "It never affords protection, until there will be space, on its inside, of a cubic handbreadth."

7:13   A. A pillar which stands in the midst of the house, and uncleanness is under it, and it presses down —

uncleanness breaks forth and ascends, breaks forth and descends.

---

62. *ibid.*   63. M. Oh. 6:3.   64. M. Oh. 6:1, 5:5—6.

B. But if there is in the place of the uncleanness a cubic handbreadth, lo, this is like a closed grave and conveys uncleanness round about itself.

C. Utensils which are under the capital are clean.

D. And R. Yoḥanan b. Nuri declares unclean.[65]

7:14   A. A box which one made into a wall-cupboard, even though one makes use of it, is clean.

B. [It] was unclean and one made it into a wall-cupboard,

It is unclean until one will affix it with a nail.[66]

7:15   A. A wall cupboard which is open toward the house, and uncleanness is in it —

the house is unclean.

B. Uncleanness is in the house —

C. what is in it is clean, because it is the way of uncleanness to exude, and it is not its way to seep in.[67]

7:16   A. [If] uncleanness is in its ground, or in the wall which is inside of it

uncleanness breaks forth and ascends, breaks forth and descends.

B. And they regard the wall cupboard as if it is sealed, and it is adjudged half and half to introduce the uncleanness to the house.[68]

7:17   A. Three wall-cupboards, one on top of the other, and uncleanness is under them or on top of them —

uncleanness breaks forth and ascends, breaks forth and descends.

B. And they regard the wall-cupboards as if they were sealed, and they are adjudged half and half to bring the uncleanness into the house.

C. R. Judah says in the name of R. Joshua, "One leaned against it clean *Sukkot* to eat the paschal lambs in them."

8:1   A. [If] an olive's bulk of corpse-matter is under the part of the canvas which lies flat on the ground or on top of it —

uncleanness breaks forth and ascends, breaks forth and descends.

B. Uncleanness is on the inside —

he who touches it on the inside is unclean with seven days' uncleanness; [he who touches it] on the outside is unclean with the uncleanness which passes in the evening.

C. Uncleanness is on the outside —

he who touches it on the outside is unclean with seven days' uncleanness; [he who touches it] on the inside is unclean with the uncleanness which passes in the evening.

And he who enters it is clean.

D. A half-olive's bulk is on the inside and half on the outside —

he who touches it, whether on the inside or on the outside, is unclean

65. M. Oh. 6:6, 7.   66. M. Oh. 6:7.   67. *ibid.*
68. *ibid.*

with the uncleanness which passes in the evening.

E. And the Tent itself is unclean with a seven days' uncleanness.

F. Said R. Nathan, "If it affords protection for others, all the more so for itself."[69]

8:2 A. A Tent which was stretched out on four metal tent-pegs —

B. R. Jacob says, "It does not afford protection, because something which is unclean holds it up."

C. And R. Yosé says, "It affords protection."

D. [If] it was stretched out on fork-shaped reeds —

E. R. Yosé says, "It affords protection."

F. And R. Simeon says, "It does not afford protection until it is stretched out as the Tent is stretched out."[70]

8:3 A. A sheet which one sewed and placed on top of a crib, if there is not between it and the ground a cubic handbreadth, lo, this affords protection.

B. Under what circumstances?

When the sheet will stand if the crib is removed.

C. But if the crib is removed and the sheet falls, even though one sewed it, and even though it is removed from the earth only any small measure, lo, this does not afford protection.

D. And if it was a Tent of reed-matting, even though one did not sew it, and even though one did not give it thought, and there is not between it and the earth a cubic handbreadth, lo, this affords protection. And if there is between it and the ground a cubic handbreadth, it does not afford protection.

8:4 A. The corpse is in the house, and it has many doors — [if] all are locked, all are unclean.

B. [If] one of them is opened, even though one did not give thought to it, he has purified all of them.

C. [If] there were in it many windows, [if] all of them are locked, all of them are clean.

D. [If] they were open, they all are unclean, and they have not afforded protection for the doors.

E. A small door in the middle of a large door — he who overshadows both of them is unclean.

[If] one gave thought to remove it through the small [door], the small one has purified the large one.

F. [If] they were parallel to one another, he who overshadows both of them is unclean.

G. [If] one gave thought to remove it through one of them, lo, its fellow is clean.

H. [If] it had one door to the north and one door to the south, and one gave thought to remove it through the northern one, and afterward his brethren or relatives came and said that they [should] remove him only through the southern one, the southern one has purified the northern one. [And this is so] only on condition that one not practice deception. But if one has practiced deception, lo, these both are unclean.[71]

8:5   A. Houses which open out on the portico, and the corpse is in one of them,

if the way of the corpse is to go forth in the courtyard, the gate house and the houses are clean.

B. And if not, the gate house is unclean, and the houses are clean.[72]

8:6   A. [If] the room which is inside the house is locked, and uncleanness entered into the inner room through the window —

B. the outer room is clean, because the uncleanness goes forth by the way by which it entered.[73]

8:7   A. R. Judah says, "He who opens at the outset —

"The House of Shammai say, 'When he opens four handbreadths.'

"And the House of Hillel say, 'When he begins.'

B. "He who opens a blocked-up passage —

"The House of Shammai say, 'When he begins.'

"And the House of Hillel say, 'When he thinks [of doing it, it affords protection].'"[74]

8:8   A. The abortions do not have an opening of the womb until the head is rounded —

B. "like the spindle-top of the warp," the words of R. Meir.

C. R. Judah says, "Like the spindle-top of the woof."

D. R. Eliezer b. R. Ṣadoq says, "From the time the travailing has reached that stage when the ringlike formations at the mouth of the vagina are visible [indicating the passage of the embryo's head]."

E. Said R. Yosé, "I say one thing, and they said one thing. I say to them that the way of uncleanness — its way is to exude, and its way is not to seep in.

F. "And they said to me, 'The abortion is not unclean until it comes forth into the air of the world.'"[75]

9:1   A. R. Meir [alt.: Eliezer] says, "A Nazir and the corpse are under the belly of a camel —

"the Nazir does not shave on their account, and they are not liable on their account because of rendering the sanctuary and its Holy Things unclean."

B. Uncleanness which is placed in the wall, even half-and-half,

71. M. Oh. 7:3.   72. ibid.   73. ibid.
74. ibid.   75. M. Oh. 7:4.

C. and so a herd of cattle, wild beast, and fowl,

D. and so living [creatures] which were going one after another, even with the head of one between the legs of the next in succession —

E. the Nazir does not shave on their account, and they are not liable on their account for rendering the sanctuary and its Holy Things unclean.[76]

9:2 A. [If] one moved the mill-stones, in the midst of which is a gentile, or in the midst of which is a menstruating woman, his clothes are rendered unclean with *midras*-uncleanness.

B. What are the mill-stones? Any which one uproots and moves from its place.

C. In respect to corpse-uncleanness, his clothes are clean, until his clothes enter [the mill-stones] by a square handbreadth.[77]

9:3 A. What is the intertwined foliage? A tree which shades the ground.

B. R. Judah says, "They deem the lower ones as if they go upward and the upper ones as if they descend downward.

C. "And if they were touching one another by a square handbreadth, they bring [uncleanness through overshadowing] and interpose."[78]

9:4 A. What are the protruding thorns? A thorn which projects from the wall.

B. [If] they were set on the fence, they deem them as if stones were piled up on them.

C. [If] they became weak, they deem them as if they were tent-pegs of metal.

D. And if they were separated from one another —

E. "if they can take the soft plaster," the words of R. Meir.

F. And sages say, "Medium plaster."

G. R. Judah says, "If one introduces the thread on one side and it goes out the other side and touches, even though it is not exact, lo, this intervenes."[79]

9:5 A. R. Yosé says, "The ropes of the bed and the webbing of windows interpose between the house and the upper room, lest uncleanness pass to the second side."

B. [If] they were placed on top of the corpse in the open air, that which overshadows the perforation is unclean, and that which is not over the perforation is clean, because the uncleanness exudes by the way which it enters.

C. R. Judah says, "If they can[not] take medium plaster, they do not interpose.

"If they were placed in the house, lo, these interpose, for I regard the beams as though they descend and seal up."[80]

9:6 R. Yosé says, "A box which is full of utensils, and which one threw on

---

76. M. Oh. 8:1.   77. M. Oh. 8:3.   78. M. Oh. 8:2.
79. *ibid.*   80. M. Oh. 8:4.

top of an olive's bulk of corpse-matter — they are unclean, but if it [the box] were placed on top of the corpse in the open air, they [the utensils] would have been clean."[81]

9:7   A. A beam which floats on top of the water —

uncleanness is on this side —

utensils which are on the other side are clean.

B. R. Jacob says, "They regard the beam: if one went down and sat, and there is under it a space of a cubic handbreadth — [if] uncleanness is on one side, utensils which are on the second side are clean."

9:8   A. Three houses, one inside the other —

about half an olive's bulk is in the innermost or in the middle, and about an olive's bulk is in the outermost —

the outermost is unclean.

The innermost and the middle one are clean.

B. A half olive's bulk is in the innermost and a half olive's bulk is in the middle one —

the inner one is clean, and the outer and the middle ones are unclean.

C. Said R. Judah, "I say one thing and they said one thing. I say to them: 'R. Eliezer agrees with R. Joshua concerning two jars whose lips are toward the house, that the house is unclean.

"'Concerning what case did they differ?

"'Concerning two rooms of the house, for:

"'R. Eliezer declares clean, and R. Joshua declares unclean.'

"And they said to me, 'R. Joshua agrees with R. Eliezer concerning two rooms which are open toward the house, that the house is clean.

"Concerning what did they differ?

"'Concerning two jars, for:

"'R. Eliezer declares unclean, and R. Joshua declares clean.'"[82]

10:1   A. A hive which is in the midst of the house and a basket is placed over its mouth —

R. Judah says, "It affords protection."

And sages say, "It does not afford protection."

B. For R. Judah says, "Just as the board affords protection, so the basket affords protection."

C. [If] it was lying on its side with a square handbreadth, all agree that it does not afford protection.[83]

10:2   A. A column of pots which is standing in the midst of the house, from the ground to the beams, [with] the bottom of one over the mouth of another —

B. if there is not between the mouth of the upper one and the beams a

81. M. Oh. 8:1.   82. M. Oh. 8:6.   83. M. Oh. 9:5.

square handbreadth, or between the bottom of the nethermost one and the ground a square handbreadth —

[if] uncleanness is in it, the house is unclean.

[If] uncleanness is in the house, what is in it is unclean, for it is the way of uncleanness to exude, and it is not its way to seep in.

C. If there is between the mouth of the uppermost one and the beams a square handbreadth or between the bottom of the nethermost one and the ground a square handbreadth —

[if] uncleanness is in it, the house is unclean.

[If] uncleanness is in the house, what is in it is clean [Sens: unclean].

D. [If] one was unclean and placed in the middle, and there is in its place a cubic handbreadth —

uncleanness is in it —

the house is unclean.

Uncleanness is in the house — what is in it is unclean.

E. If there is not in its place a cubic handbreadth —

uncleanness is in it —

the house is unclean.

Uncleanness is in the house —

what is in it is clean.[84]

10:3 A. A large jar which stands in the midst of the house from the ground to the beams,

if there is not between its mouth and the beams a square handbreadth, or between its bottom and the ground a square handbreadth —

uncleanness is in it —

the house is unclean.

B. [If] uncleanness is in the house, what is in it is clean, for it is the way of uncleanness to exude, and it is not its way to seep in.

C. If there is between its mouth and the beams a square handbreadth, or between its bottom and the ground a square handbreadth —

uncleanness is in it —

the house is unclean.

Uncleanness is in the house —

what is in it is unclean.

D. [If] its mouth is narrow and there is not between its shoulder and the beams a square handbreadth, lo, this affords protection, and if not, it does not afford protection, until there will be (in) its shoulder a square handbreadth.

E. [If] its bottom was pointed and there is not between its bottom and the ground a square handbreadth, lo, this affords protection, and if not, it does not afford protection, until there will be at its bottom a square

84. M. Oh. 9:9—10.

handbreadth.[85]

10:4 A. [If] it was a hive, damaged and repaired with straw, even an *'ammah* above the ground, lo, this affords protection.

B. A hive which stands in the midst of the door, closing the entire doorway, if there is not between its mouth and the lintel a square handbreadth, and between its bottom and the earth a square handbreadth, and uncleanness is inside it, the house is clean.

Uncleanness is in the house —

what is inside it is unclean, for it is the way of uncleanness to exude, and it is not its way to seep in.

C. If there is between its mouth and the lintel a square handbreadth, and uncleanness is inside it, the house is unclean.

Uncleanness is in the house —

what is in it is unclean.

D. If there is not between its sides and the doorposts a square handbreadth, and [or] between its bottom and the earth a square handbreadth —

uncleanness is inside it —

the house is clean.

Uncleanness is in the house —

what is in it is clean.[86]

10:5 A. Two hives which are standing in the midst of the doorway and sealing the entire doorway —

if the bottom of this one is not on top of the bottom of the other,

if there is not between the upper one and the lintel a square handbreadth, or between the mouth of the bottom one and the ground a square handbreadth —

uncleanness is in them —

the house is unclean.

Uncleanness is in the house —

what is in them is clean, for it is the way of uncleanness to exude, and it is not its way to seep in.

B. If there is between the mouth of the upper one and the lintel a square handbreadth, or between the mouth of the bottom one and the ground a square handbreadth —

uncleanness is in them —

the house is unclean.

Uncleanness is in the house —

what is in them is unclean, and the utensils which are between them are clean.

C. If there is between their sides and the doorposts a square

85. *ibid.*   86. *ibid.*

handbreadth or between them and the earth a square handbreadth —

uncleanness is in them —

the house is clean.

Uncleanness is in the house —

what is in them is clean.

D. [If] one of them is made unclean, it is unclean, and the house and its fellow [hive] are clean.

E. And so [is the rule if] the mouth of this one is on top of the bottom of the other,

and so [is the rule if] the bottom of this one is on top of the bottom of the other.[87]

10:6 A. And what is 'loosely fitting'? Whatever has a handbreadth on its four sides, and on its three sides, and on its two sides, opposite one another.

B. What is tightly fitting? Whatever does not have a handbreadth in any one direction.[88]

C. R. Eleazar and R. Simeon agree concerning uncleanness under the stopper —

uncleanness breaks forth and ascends, breaks forth and descends.

D. [If] it was setting on its bottom in the open air —

(with) uncleanness inside it, and it renders unclean —

E. "That which touches it from any direction is unclean," the words of R. Meir.

And sages say, "Unclean is only what is opposite its cover alone."

F. [If] it was turned upside down on its mouth — that which touches it from any side is unclean.[89]

10:7 A. A tomb which is carved out of the rock and covered —

he who touches it any place is clean.

And unclean is only that which is opposite its cover alone.

To what is it comparable? To a large pit filled with corpses, with a large stone on its mouth, in which case unclean is only that which is opposite its open space alone.

B. [If] it was built into the wall of a sepulchre, if it protruded in any amount at all into the midst of the sepulchre,

that which enters into it is unclean.

And if not, unclean is only that which is opposite its cover alone.

C. [If] one built a sepulchre on top of it, lo, it is like a sealed grave and renders unclean round about it.[90]

10:8 A. That which is made like a case — he who touches it on any place is clean.

B. He who touches its upper part [Š'WH; Albeck, p. 543: M'LH] —

87. *ibid.*   88. M. Oh. 9:3.   89. M. Oh. 9:14.
90. M. Oh. 9:15.

C. R. Eliezer declares unclean.

D. And R. Joshua says, "From a handbreadth and downward — he is clean. From a handbreadth and upward — he is unclean,

E. "for the upper part is only that which is a handbreadth above the ground."[91]

10:9   A. A jar which is setting on its bottom in the open air and about a half-olive's bulk of corpse-matter is placed under it directly beneath its bottom —

uncleanness breaks forth and ascends, breaks forth and descends,

and [what is in] the jar is unclean.

B. About an olive's bulk of corpse-matter —

part of it is placed under its side, and part of it is placed under its bottom

whatever is opposite the uncleanness, whether above or below, is unclean, and whatever is not opposite the uncleanness, whether above or below, is clean.

C. And if there is in its side a square handbreadth, all is unclean.

D. Two half olive's bulks —

one of them is placed under its side, and one of them is placed under its bottom —

whatever is opposite the uncleanness, whether above or below, is unclean. And whatever is not opposite the uncleanness, whether above or below, is clean.

E. [If] that which is set under its side protruded toward its bottom, it is as if the whole is opposite its bottom.

And [if] that which is placed under its bottom protruded under its side, it is as if the whole is under its side.

10:10   A. [If] it was turned over on its mouth, and there is in its side a square handbreadth, and in its rim is not a square handbreadth,

[or if] there is in its rim a square handbreadth, and there is not in its side a square handbreadth,

whatever is opposite the uncleanness, whether above or below, is unclean, and whatever is not opposite the uncleanness, whether above or below, is clean.

B. And if there is in its side and rim a square handbreadth, everything is unclean.[92]

10:11   A. [If] it was full of foods and liquids and sealed with a tightly-stoppered cover and placed on top of the corpse in the open air, utensils which are above it and which are below it are unclean, and foods and liquids which are in it are clean.

B. [If] it was lying on its side in the open air, lo, it is like a hive in every respect.[93]

91. *ibid.*   92. M. Oh. 9:16.   93. *ibid.*

11:1 A. A pot which is placed at the side of the threshold, so that, if it is raised up. [and] its lips are drawn back from the lintel in any measure at all uncleanness breaks forth and ascends, breaks forth and descends.

B. [If] it was a handbreadth above the ground and uncleanness is under it, inside it, or on top of it, everything is unclean, and the house is clean.

C. [If it is] in the house, unclean is only the house.

D. [If it is so situated] that if it is raised up [and] its side will touch the lintel in any measure at all —

[if] uncleanness is under it, and it presses down, —

uncleanness breaks forth and ascends, breaks forth and descends.

E. [If] it was a handbreadth above the ground, and uncleanness is under it, [space] under it is unclean.

F. [If uncleanness is] inside it or on top of it, the house is clean, because it is afforded protection with the side of the Tent.

G. [If the uncleanness is] inside it or on top of it, everything is unclean, and the house is clean.

H. [If it is] in the house, unclean is only the house.

I. [If it is so situated] that, if it is raised, [and] its lips will touch the lintel [for a space of] a square handbreadth, [if] uncleanness is under it and it presses down —

uncleanness breaks forth and ascends, breaks forth and descends.[94]

11:2 A. [If] it was a handbreadth off the ground —

[if] uncleanness is under it or in the house, [space] under it and the house are unclean. [If uncleanness is] inside it or on top of it, it is clean.

B. [If] uncleanness is inside it or on top of it, everything is unclean.

C. [If it is so situated] that, if it is raised, [and] its lips cover the lintel in any amount at all, [if] uncleanness is under it and it presses down —

uncleanness breaks forth and ascends, breaks forth and descends.[95]

11:3 A. [If] it was a handbreadth above the ground, if there is in its side a square handbreadth, and uncleanness is under it, or in the house, or inside it, or on top of it, everything is unclean.

B. [If] there is not a square handbreadth on its side, uncleanness is under it —

under it is unclean.

C. [Space] inside it and on top of it and the house are clean, because of being afforded protection with the side of the Tent.

D. [If uncleanness is] inside it or on top of it, everything is unclean, and the house is clean.

E. [If uncleanness is] in the house, it alone is unclean.[96]

11:4-5 A. [If] it [the pot] was set under a hatchway so that, if it is raised up, (and) its lips will touch the beam in any degree at all —

94. M. Oh. 10:6—7.   95. *ibid.*   96. *ibid.*

uncleanness is under it, and it presses down —

uncleanness breaks forth and ascends, breaks forth and descends.

B. [If] it was a handbreadth above the ground and uncleanness is under it, or in the house, or inside it, or on top of it —

everything is unclean.

C. [If it is so situated] that if it is raised up, it goes up and sets on the hatchway and fits tightly on all sides of the hatchway,

and uncleanness is under it and it presses down,

uncleanness breaks forth and ascends, breaks forth and descends.

D. [If] it was a handbreadth off the ground, [and if] uncleanness is under it or in the house, [space] under it and in the house is unclean. Inside it and on top of it [space] is clean.

[If uncleanness is] inside it or on top of it, [space] opposite it up to the firmament is unclean.

E. [If it is so situated that] if it goes up, it goes up and goes through the hatchway, and there is not a handbreadth of space between it and the hatchway, and uncleanness is under it and it presses down, uncleanness breaks forth and ascends, breaks forth and descends.

F. [If it was] a handbreadth off the ground and uncleanness is under it, [space] underneath it is unclean. [Space] inside it and on top of it and the house is clean, because it is afforded protection with the side of the Tent.

G. [If uncleanness is] inside it or on top of it, everything is unclean.

H. [If it is so situated] that if it goes up, it goes up and goes through the hatchway, and there is between it and the hatchway an opening of a handbreadth, and uncleanness is under it, and it presses down, uncleanness breaks forth and ascends, breaks forth and descends.

I. [If] it was a handbreadth off the ground,

uncleanness is beneath it,

[space] beneath it is unclean.

[But] inside it and on top of it and the house, [space] is clean, because it is adjudged like the sloping sides of Tents.

J. [If] it is inside it or on top of it, everything is unclean, and the house is clean.

K. [If it is] in the house, unclean is only the house.[97]

11:6 A. A hatchway which is [open] to the air, and there is not in it a square handbreadth, and an olive's bulk of corpse-matter is placed under it, and one placed something which is susceptible to uncleanness —

B. if there is there a handbreadth square,

C. everything is unclean, and if not, unclean is only that which is directly above the olive's bulk of corpse-matter alone.[98]

11:7 A. A hatchway which is open to the air, and there is not in it a

---

97. *ibid.*   98. M. Oh. 10:2.

square handbreadth, and an olive's bulk of corpse-matter is placed under it

B. "the house is unclean, and he who overshadows it is unclean," the words of R. Meir.

C. R. Judah says, "He who overshadows it is clean."

D. R. Simeon says, "If uncleanness was there before his foot, the house is unclean and the person who overshadows it is unclean, and if not, the house is unclean, but the person who overshadows it is clean."

E. [If] part of the uncleanness is in the house and part is directly below the hatchway,

F. "the house is unclean and the one who overshadows the hatchway is unclean," the words of R. Meir.

G. R. Judah and R. Simeon say, "The person who overshadows the hatchway is clean."

H. R. Yosé says, "If there is not sufficient bulk in the uncleanness to be divided, for example, an olive's bulk of corpse-matter, the backbone, and the skull, [then] the house is unclean, and the one who overshadows it is clean, and if not, the house is unclean, and the one who overshadows it is unclean."[99]

11:8 A. Two half olive's bulks, one placed in the house and one placed directly under the hatchway —

he who overshadows [the hatchway] is clean.

B. [If] the one which is placed in the house protruded directly under the hatchway, it is as if the whole were directly under the hatchway.

C. [If] about an olive's bulk of corpse-matter was in the mouth of the raven, and it overshadowed the hatchway in which there is not a square handbreadth, the house is unclean.

D. R. Yosé declares clean, until the uncleanness will be the size of a square handbreadth.[100]

11:9 A. A jar of purification-water which was placed in the hatchway —

if it is hung down, it is unclean, and if it is not, it is clean.

B. Under what circumstances?

C. In the case of a hatchway which is not a square handbreadth. But in the case of a hatchway which is a square handbreadth, whether or not it is hung down, it is unclean.

D. Under what circumstances? In the case of a jar of clay. But if it was of stone, whether or not the hatchway was a square handbreadth, and whether or not it hung down, it is clean.

11:10 A. A hatchway which is between the house and the upper room, and there is not in it a square handbreadth —

uncleanness is in the house —

utensils which are in the upper room are clean.

99. M. Oh. 10:3.   100. *ibid.*

Uncleanness is in the upper room —
utensils which are in the house are clean.

B. For I regard the beams as if they descend and seal off.

C. Another matter: Uncleanness does not enter a Tent and does not leave it except in a space of a square handbreadth.

D. Utensils which are directly above the olive's bulk —
Rabbi [Yosé] declares unclean.
And sages declare clean.
Said Rabbi, "I prefer their opinion to mine."[101]

11:11 A. Hatchways, one on top of the other, and there is in them a square handbreadth —
and something which is susceptible to uncleanness is set —
if there is there a square handbreadth —
everything is unclean.
And if not, unclean is only that which is opposite the lower one alone.

B. [If] they are wide above and narrow at the bottom, from the narrow part and downward is unclean, from the narrow part and above it is clean.

C. If they were broad at the bottom and narrow at the top, unclean is only that which is directly above the narrow part alone.[102]

12:1 A. And how much should this crack be?

B. The House of Hillel say, "Any amount:

C. "The breadth of the plumbline."

D. And R. Yosé says in the name of the House of Hillel, "A square handbreadth."

E. Said Rabbi, "I should be surprised if R. Yosé said a square handbreadth. He spoke about only as much as an olive's bulk of corpse-matter alone."

F. Uncleanness is inside, and utensils are outside, even though there is in the crack no more than any small amount — the breadth of plumbline — lo, this interposes.[103]

12:2 A. A se'ah-measure overturned on its mouth, a jar overturned on its mouth, two baskets, one on top the other, with a stone on top of the baskets [to keep them in place] bring the uncleanness.

B. A se'ah setting in its normal way, and a jar setting in its normal way, and a blown-up skin, and a pillow full of straw, and a bolster full of down, and a bolster full of handkerchieves, two stones, one on top of the other, and a basket on top of a stone do not bring the uncleanness.[104]

12:3 A. A dog which ate flesh of the corpse and entered the house —
the house is clean, for whatever is swallowed by man or beast or wild

101. M. Oh. 10:2.   102. M. Oh. 10:4.   103. M. Oh. 11:1.
104. M. Oh. 11:2.

animal or birds is clean.

B. [If] he vomited it up, the house is unclean.

C. [If] he died, if it had not remained in his intestines while he was still alive for three full days, the house is unclean, and in the case of birds and fish, forthwith.

D. R. Judah b. Betera says, "In the case of fish, forthwith, and in the case of birds, twenty-four hours."

R. Eleazar says in the name of R. Judah b. Betera, "In both cases, twenty-four hours."[105]

12:4 A. The cellar which is in the house, and the candlestick is in it, and its cup projected, and a basket is set on it —

B. Under what circumstances?

C. One of metal, but [in the case of] one of wood, lo, this interposes.

D. R. Eleazar b. R. Yosé says, "Under what circumstances? One of wood. But one of metal is susceptible to becoming unclean, and an unclean utensil cannot interpose."[106]

12:5 A. A board which is placed over the mouth of the cistern, and uncleanness is under it or on top of it —

utensils which are directly below the overhanging part on either side are unclean.

B. [If] it was a basket, and it has a rim of a handbreadth, and uncleanness is under it

utensils which are directly below the overhanging part on either side are unclean.

C. If it was smooth, lo, it is like a board.

D. Utensils which are directly below the overhanging part on either side are unclean.[107]

12:6 A. The walls of the house and the walls of the cistern which are equal to one another, and uncleanness is either in the house or in the cistern —

B. utensils which are in the walls of the house and which are in the walls of the cistern are adjudged half and half.

C. And if the walls of the house are wider than those of the cistern, and uncleanness is in the house, utensils which are in the walls of the cistern are unclean, and those in the walls of the house are adjudged half and half.

D. If the walls of the cistern were wider than the walls of the house, and uncleanness was in the house, utensils which are in the walls of the cistern are clean, and those which are in the walls of the house are adjudged half and half.[108]

13:1 A. A board which is placed over the mouth of an old oven, and

105. M. Oh. 11:7.   106. M. Oh. 11:8.   107. M. Oh. 11:8—9.
108. *ibid.*

uncleanness is under it or on top of it —

everything is unclean, and the oven is unclean.

B. And R. Yoḥanan b. Nuri declares the oven clean.

C. [If] the head of one was placed over the mouth of a new oven, and the head of one was placed on the mouth of an old oven —

or [if] they were two old ones, one on one side, one on the other, and a new one in the middle —

R. Yoḥanan b. Nuri declares clean in the case of the oven.[109]

13:2 A. A board which is placed on the mouth of an oven and sealed with a tightly-sealed stopper —

and uncleanness is under it or on top of it —

everything is unclean, but directly above the airspace of the oven it is clean.

B. Uncleanness is over the airspace of the oven — directly above it up to the firmament is unclean.[110]

13:3 A. A grating which is placed over the mouth of an oven and protrudes in any measure at all and has a rim of a handbreadth —

uncleanness is under it —

utensils which are on top of it are clean.

B. Uncleanness is on top of it —

utensils which are under it are clean.

C. And if it was flat, lo, it is like a board and requires a square handbreadth.[111]

D. And R. Eliezer agrees concerning a window-sill which one made in the first place, that it brings uncleanness.[112]

13:4 A. A sandal of a cradle which [one deliberately made by] chipping away the plaster — its measure is a square handbreadth.

B. [If] the house was chipped away on its own, its measure is the width of a fist.

C. [If] plaster flowed under it in any amount —

and [the sandal is located] from the half-way point of the plaster and upward, whether there is the requisite measure or whether there is not the requisite measure,

the house is clean.

D. [If the sandal is located] from the half-way point of the plaster and downward, if there is in it the requisite measure, the house is unclean, and if not, they reckon [removes of] uncleanness as they reckon [removes of] uncleanness [in the case] of the corpse.[113]

13:5 A. A bed-frame which is dressed with the tufts — the child is unclean with uncleanness which lasts for seven days.

109. M. Oh. 12:1.   110. M. Oh. 12:2.   111. *ibid.*
112. M. Oh. 12:3.   113. M. Oh. 12:4.

[If] it [the bed-frame] is woven with ropes, the child is unclean with uncleanness which passes in the evening.

B. The board of the reeds which is woven with ropes and plastered with plaster —

a loaf kneaded in fruit juice is placed on it —

lo, this brings [uncleanness] and interposes.

C. R. Yohanan b. Nuri says, "All round things are clean.

"Nothing brings uncleanness except for the round cakes of figs, because they sit under them in coils."[114]

13:6 A. A camel which is standing in the open air —

uncleanness is under it —

utensils which are on it are clean.

Uncleanness is on it —

utensils which are under it are clean.

B. [If] it was crouching —

uncleanness is [compressed] under it —

directly below it to the nethermost deep is unclean, and above it up to the firmament is unclean.

C. Uncleanness is under its foot or on top of its foot, and it is pressing down —

uncleanness breaks forth and ascends, breaks forth and descends.

D. [If] one placed a board on top of it,

uncleanness is on this side —

utensils which are on the second side are unclean.

13:7 A. The beams of the house and the upper room, of which the upper ones were directly above the lower ones —

uncleanness is under them —

[space] under them is unclean.

[Uncleanness is located] between them — between them [space] is unclean.

And on top of them it is clean.

[Uncleanness is] on top of them —

[space] directly above it up to the firmament is unclean, and under them it is clean.

B. Under what circumstances?

When they have a square handbreadth.

And [if] they do not have a square handbreadth, uncleanness breaks forth and ascends, breaks forth and descends.

C. [If] the upper ones protruded, closing the space between the lower ones —

uncleanness is under them —

114. *ibid.*

[space] under them and between them is unclean.

Between them —

[space] between them and under them is unclean.

[Space] on top of them is clean.

[If uncleanness is] on top of them, space directly above it up to the firmament is unclean, and [space] under them and between them is clean.

D. Under what circumstances?

When they have a square handbreadth and there is a square handbreadth [of empty space] between them.

E. [If] there is not between them a square handbreadth, and uncleanness is under them —

[space] under them is unclean. Between them and on top of them it is clean.

[If uncleanness is] between them or on top of them, [space] even directly above them up to the firmament is unclean, and under them it is clean.

F. Under what circumstances?

G. When there is in them [the lower ones] a square handbreadth.

H. And [if] there is not in them a square handbreadth — uncleanness breaks forth and ascends, breaks forth and descends.

I. [TR III, p. 134 adds:] If they were laid out at right angles [Lit.: warp and woof] — [if] uncleanness is under one of them —

J. [space] under all of them is unclean, and on top of them is clean.

K. [Uncleanness is] on top of them — directly above it up to the firmament it is unclean, and below them it is clean.

L. Under what circumstances? When they are a square handbreadth. If not, then uncleanness breaks forth, etc.[115]

13:8 A. A *se'ah*-measure which is lying on its side in the open air does not bring uncleanness under its entire [surface] until there will be in its circumference four-and-a-half handbreadths.

B. If it was a half-handbreadth high, [it does not function as a Tent] until there will be in its circumference three handbreadths.[116]

13:9 A. A column which is set in the open air does not bring uncleanness under its side until there will be in its circumference twenty-four handbreadths.

B. R. Yosé says, "Twenty-five."

C. For R. Yosé would rule, "You do not have twenty-five [handbreadths] of which the earth does not consume a handbreadth."

D. And so he would say, "(At the end of the book of Jeremiah)

E. "'And there were ninety-six pomegranates on the side,' and it says, 'All the pomegranates were one hundred' [Jer. 52:23]. It is not possible to say a hundred, for already have ninety-six been mentioned, and it is not pos-

115. M. Oh. 12:5.   116. M. Oh. 12:7.

sible to say ninety-six, for a hundred have already been mentioned. On this basis one must rule, Four are swallowed up in the wall and ninety-six appear outside."

F. And its narrow side is adjudged like the sloping sides of Tents.[117]

13:10   A. "An olive's bulk of the corpse cleaved onto the threshold —

B. "R. Eliezer declares the house unclean.

C. "And R. Joshua declares [it] clean.

D. "[If] it lay below the threshhold, [the thickness of the threshhold] is deemed to be divided into halves to make the house unclean," the words of R. Jacob.

E. R. Simeon said, "R. Eliezer and R. Joshua did not differ about that which was placed under the threshhold, that the house is clean.

"Concerning what did they dispute?

"Concerning that which cleaved onto the threshhold, for R. Eliezer declares the house unclean, and R. Joshua declares it clean."

F. [If] it cleaved to the lintel, the house is unclean.

G. R. Yosé declares clean until there will be in the uncleanness an area of a square handbreadth.[118]

13:11   A. Two projections, one on top of the other, and uncleanness is in the wall which is between them —

B. if it protruded in any measure at all into the midst of [either] one of them, it [that one] is unclean and its fellow is clean, and if not, it is adjudged half and half.[119]

13:12   A. "The bearers of the corpse who were passing in the public way — their Tent is joined with the Tent of the window to render the house unclean," the words of R. Eliezer.

B. And R. Joshua says, "They do not raise up that which is low to join Tent to Tent."[120]

14:1   A. A door which one made for light — its measure is the size of the drill.

B. [If] one closed it for light, its measure is a square handbreadth.

C. Two windows, one inside the other, the outer one of which is made for light —

its measure is the size of a drill.

D. [If] one removed the stopper of the glass, its measure is the size of a fist.

E. And what are the remnants of the light hole?

F. A window which was stopped up, and [one] did not have plaster with which to complete the work, or one's fellow called him, or the darkness of

117. *ibid.*   118. M. Oh. 12:8.   119. *ibid.*
120. *ibid.*

Sabbath night fell.

G. And what are the remnants of the light hole?

H. a height of two fingers with a breadth of the thumb.[121]

14:2   A. A window which is between two houses — its measure is a square handbreadth.

B. [If] one tore down the outer one, even though one did not give thought to it, its measure is the thickness of a drill.

C. [If] one placed the [roof] beam in the middle of the window, the bottom part['s measure is] with a square handbreadth, and the top [part's measure is] with the thickness of a drill.[122]

14:3   A. What are the gratings? Those of the granaries.

B. [What are] the lattice-works? Those of the huts.

C. Rabban Simeon b. Gamaliel says, "Windows which are in the villages — their measure is with a square handbreadth, for they are made only for strengthening, to bring the board [or: breeze] in through them."[123]

14:4   A. R. Judah says three rules concerning them, in the name of R. 'Aqiva: "He who makes [a hole] for listening, and for guarding, and for a peephole — in any measure;

"for bringing in utensils and for taking out utensils and for use and for the lamp — its measure is a square handbreadth."

B. For a reed and for the weaver's stave —

The House of Shammai say, "With its own measure."

And the House of Hillel say, "A square handbreadth."[124]

C. R. Judah says, "Even the thigh-bone of 'Og, lo, this diminishes the handbreadth."

14:5   A. And so Rabbi said, "Less than an olive's bulk of flesh is diminished by means of a quarter-qab of bones. Less than a bone the size of a barley corn is diminished by about an olive's bulk of flesh."

B. And about an olive's bulk of carrion and about a lentil of a creeping thing do not diminish.

C. And R. Judah says, "They do diminish."

D. "This is the general rule," said Rabbi, "Any uncleanness which is not from the corpse, or which is from the corpse but is not joined with that uncleanness, lo, this does diminish."[125]

14:6   A. Grass which one uprooted and left in the window, or which grew up by itself, and the bird which made a nest in the window, and a rag which is less than three-by-three fingerbreadths, and fowl, and the gentile, and the cattle, and a child born at the eighth month, and clay utensils, and foods and liquids, and a Scroll of the Torah, and the salt — lo, these do diminish.

B. But the snow, and the frost, and the ice, and the water do not

121. M. Oh. 13:1.   122. M. Oh. 13:2   123. M. Oh. 13:1.
124. M. Oh. 13:4.   125. M. Oh. 13:5—6.

diminish.[126]

14:7 A. A wall-projection which is above the remnants of the light hole — its measure is the height of two fingers over the breadth of the the thumb.

B. That which is over a hole the size of a drill — [its measure is] any amount at all.

C. And R. Yosé says, "With its own breadth."

D. A projection which is over the door — its measure is any amount at all.

E. [If] one closed it up, its measure is a square handbreadth.

F. [If] one opened it, its measure is any amount.[127]

14:8 A. Two wall projections, one on top of the other, and the door is below them —

the lower one['s measure is] any amount at all.

And the upper one, even [if it is] inside three courses which are twelve handbreadths — its measure is a square handbreadth.

B. [If] one tore down the lower one, or [if] it [the upper one] projected over it — its measure is any amount.

C. Two doors, one on top of the other, and the projection is above them

for the upper one, any amount [suffices], and for the lower one, even if it is within three courses which are twelve handbreadths, its measure is a square handbreadth.

[If] one tore down the upper one, or [if] it overhung the lower one by a handbreadth on either side, its measure is any amount at all.[128]

14:9 A. When have they said, "A wall projection brings uncleanness whatever its depth"?

For that which projects.

But not for a rounded moulding until it forms a square handbreadth.

B. And what is a rounded molding?

Any which is girded [to the wall] on both sides and left [without support] in the middle.[129]

14:10 A. R. Yosé b. R. Judah says, "The cornices and the carvings and the reliefs bring uncleanness."

B. Rabbi says, "They ruled more stringently in the case of the reed than in that of the wall-projection, for the reed is carried about, and the wall-projection is immovable."

C. The wall projection which goes forth from the wall and has a square handbreadth, and uncleanness is under it, and utensils are in the wall, and over them is about a garlic-peel's thickness [of plaster] — they [the utensils] are clean.

D. [If] uncleanness is in the wall and utensils are under it, and on them

126. *ibid.*   127. M. Oh. 14:2.   128. M. Oh. 14:1.
129. *ibid.*

is a garlic peel's thickness of plaster — they are clean.[130]

15:1 A. Flat tablets of marble, placed one on top of the other —
uncleanness is under one of them —
and even though they are a cubit above the earth —
uncleanness breaks forth and ascends, breaks forth and descends.

B. Tablets touching one another and tables touching one another —
they reckon [removes of uncleanness] concerning them the way they
reckon [removes of uncleanness] concerning the corpse.

C. A tablet which is placed on the side of the leg of a table and uncleanness is under the tablet — he who touches either the tablet or the table is unclean with the seven days' uncleanness.

D. [If] uncleanness is under the table, he who touches the table is unclean with uncleanness which lasts for seven days, and [he who touches the
tablet] is unclean with uncleanness which passes in the evening.[131]

15:2 A. He who overshadows directly above the square is unclean. [He
who overshadows the area] not directly above the square is clean.

B. R. Menaḥem b. R. Yosé says, "One way or the other, he is unclean,
since it is adjudged like the corner of a tablet."

C. Utensils which are directly above the square are unclean. Those
which are not directly above the square are clean.

D. R. Menaḥem b. R. Yosé says, "One way or the other they are unclean, because they are adjudged like the corner of a tray."[132]

15:3 A. Jars which are lying on their sides in the open air, the shoulder of
this one on the side of the other, and the shoulder of this one on the side of
the other,
a handbreadth above the ground,
and in the shoulders is a square handbreadth [of shared surface] —
uncleanness is under them —
[space] under [all of] them (and on top of them) is unclean.

B. [Uncleanness is] on top of them —
[space] on top of them (and under them) is unclean.
But inside of them it is clean.

C. [If] they are a handbreadth above the ground, but there is not a
square handbreadth in the shoulders, and uncleanness is under one of them
under it and on top of it [space] is unclean.
On top of it —
on top of it and under it is unclean.
And its inside is clean.

D. Under what circumstances?
In the case of clean ones.

130. M. Oh. 14:3.   131. M. Oh. 15:1.   132. M. Oh. 15:2.

E. But if they were unclean and a handbreadth above the ground — uncleanness is under one of them —

they are all unclean.[133]

15:4 A. A house which one divided with boards or with hangings from the sides or from the beams, and uncleanness is in the wall —

utensils which are in the partition[ed part] are unclean.

B. And those which are in the wall on its outer side and which are in the plaster on top of it are adjudged half and half.

C. And if there are there four handbreadths, [the effect of] the wall is annulled.

D. Rabbi says, "He who says 'a handbreadth' also says 'four handbreadths,' and he who says 'four handbreadths' will not say 'a handbreadth.'"

E. [If] one partitioned it off from the ground and uncleanness is in the partion[ed-off part] —

utensils which are in the house are unclean.

F. Uncleanness is in the house —

utensils which are in the partioned[ed-off part] —

G. if there is in their place a cubic handbreadth, are clean, and if not, they are unclean.

H. And those in the ground are unclean.

I. Uncleanness is in the ground —

J. utensils which are in the partition[ed-off part] are clean and those which are in the house are unclean.[134]

15:5 A. A house which is full of straw, and there is between it and the beams a square handbreadth.

and uncleanness is inside —

whatever is directly opposite the exit of the uncleanness through the whole breadth of the door is unclean.

And in the portico, unclean is only that which is directly opposite the uncleanness from the beams and outward.

B. R. Yosé says, "Straw which is one is not destined to remove, lo, it is like dirt, and dirt which one is destined to remove, lo, it is like straw.[135]

15:6 A. A heap of pebbles, and so a sheaf of grain, and uncleanness is in it —

uncleanness breaks forth and ascends, breaks forth and descends.

B. And if there is in the place of the uncleanness a cubic handbreadth, lo, it is like a sealed grave and contaminates on all sides.[136]

15:7 A. And what is the courtyard of the tomb? That is the floor to the midst of which the caves open.

---

133. *ibid.*   134. M. Oh. 15:4—5.   135. M. Oh. 15:6.
136. M. Oh. 15:7.

B. If there is in it the appropriate measure, he who enters it is unclean.

C. Under what circumstances?

D. When it is not open to the air.

E. But if it is open to the air, even if one is only any small amount distant from the lintel, he is clean, on condition that he not touch the lintel.[137]

15:8   A. "A pile of pebbles which one made into a rolling stone for a grave — he who touches it up to four handbreadths is unclean," the words of R. Judah.

B. And sages say, "Unclean is only the inner row, needed for the grave."

C. Said Rabbi, "The words of R. Judah appear to be correct when one is not destined to cut it off, and the words of the sages, when one is destined to cut it off."[138]

15:9   A. A jar which is full of clean liquids, sealed with a tightly stopped-up cover, which one made into a rolling stone for a grave —

B. Said R. Eleazar b. R. Simeon, "In this case —

"The House of Shammai declare unclean.

"And the House of Hillel declare clean.

C. "Said the House of Shammai to the House of Hillel, 'And which is more likely to receive uncleanness, man or liquids?'

"They said to them, 'Liquids.'

"They said to them, 'And since man, who is not likely to receive uncleanness, if he touches it, is made unclean, liquids which are in it, is it not logical that they [too] should be unclean?'

D. "The House of Hillel said to them, 'Do you not agree concerning someone who was clean who swallowed a clean ring and entered the Tent of the corpse, that even though he is made unclean with the uncleanness that lasts for seven days, the ring is clean?'

"The House of Shammai said to them, 'No. If you have said so concerning a ring, which is not made unclean through the carrying of a Zab, will you say so concerning liquids, which are made unclean through the carrying of the Zab?'

"The House of Hillel said to them, 'We compare seven days' uncleanness to seven days' uncleanness, and you compare seven days' uncleanness to the uncleanness which passes in the evening. It is better to compare the uncleanness which lasts for seven days to that which lasts for seven days than to compare the uncleanness which lasts for seven days to the uncleanness which passes in the evening.[139]

15:10   A. "'Another matter: A man who touches the corpse renders utensils unclean, and utensils which touch a corpse render man unclean.

"'A man who touches a corpse renders a clay utensil unclean, but a clay utensil which touches the corpse does not make the man unclean.

137. M. Oh. 15:8.   138. *ibid.*   139. M. Oh. 15:9.

B. "'And is it not an argument *a fortiori?* Just as man who is made unclean both by a corpse and by something which touches a corpse [is so contaminated as] to render something which touches him unclean, [but nonetheless] affords protection for what is inside him — a clay utensil, which is not made unclean [from its outer side] by a corpse and by something which touches a corpse so as to render unclean that which touches it — is it not logical that it should afford protection for what is in it?'"[140]

15:11   A. Said R. Simeon, "We do not require to press matters thus.

B. "From the place from which man is made unclean, from there liquids are made unclean, and from the place in which liquids afford protection, from there is man afforded protection.

C. "Where the man is made unclean in the open, so liquids are made unclean in the open [outside].

D. "Where liquids are afforded protection, on the inside, also a man whom one placed in a large jar which one sealed with a tightly sealed cover and made into a rolling stone for a grave is clean."[141]

15:12   A. All movables bring the uncleanness if they are as thick as an ox-goad.

B. Said R. Ṭarfon, "May I bury my sons, that this law is distorted. I do not know what is the nature of the case. But the one who heard it heard but erred."

C. And M'ŚH B: One was passing and an ox-goad was on his shoulder. And one side overshadowed the grave, and they declared him unclean on account of the fact that utensils overshadowed the corpse.

D. And the one who heard heard but erred.[142]

15:13   A. Said R. Judah, M'ŚH B: "One was ploughing and shook the plough, and it came out that a [whole] skull of a corpse was cleaving to the plough, and they declared him unclean because he overshadowed the corpse.

B. "And the person who heard about it heard but erred."

C. Said R. Judah, M'ŚH B: "One was ploughing and shook the plough and it turned out that the skull of a corpse was cleaving to the plough, and they declared him unclean because he moved the corpse, and the person who heard heard but erred."[143]

15:14   A. The ox-goad which one placed on the ox, and one head was placed on a corpse, and one was placed on a man,
    or one head was placed on the corpse, and one was placed on utensils,
    — it is clean.

B. They spoke only concerning a man who was carrying [the ox-goad] alone.[144]

140. *ibid.*   141. *ibid.*   142. M. Oh. 16:1.
143. *ibid.*   144. *ibid.*

16:1 A. Mounds which are near, whether near a city or a road, whether new or old, are unclean,

B. because women bury their abortions there, and lepers, their limbs.

C. But those which are distant — new ones are clean, and old ones are unclean,

D. for I say, "Perhaps there was there a road or a city."

E. And what is a mound? This is a mound of dirt which is on the pit.

F. He who overshadows part of it is unclean, and one need not say, the entire thing.

G. Its dirt is unclean because it is dirt of a mound.

H. [If] one dug dirt from it and piled it against it, it is not subject to the rule of dirt of mounds.

I. The mound which was unclean and declared clean, lo, this is clean, and one does not take account of the possibility that it has become unclean.[145]

16:2 A. It is all the same whether one finds three corpses, or finds three *kokhs,* or finds a *kokh* in a cave or a vault, or found ten [corpses] and there are not four cubits to eight between them —

B. "they all are [subject to the rule of] contaminated soil and are [subject to the rule of] a graveyard," the words of R. Simeon.

C. And sages say, "We regard the middle ones as if they were not [present], and the outer ones join together from four cubits up to eight."

D. [If] one found the head alongside his knees, it is not subject to the law of contaminated soil, and it is not a graveyard.

E. [If one found] the head of this one alongside the knees of the next, and the head of the other alongside the knees of the next, they are subject to the rule of contaminated soil, and they are not subject to the rule of the graveyard.

F. And that which lacks [limbs] is not subject to the rule of contaminated soil and subject to the rule of the graveyard.

G. And what is the meaning of lacking?

Rabbi says, "Something which, if taken from a living person, would cause his death."

H. [If] one found two at first and then one, it is known that they are subject to the rule of contaminated soil, but they are not subject to the rule of the graveyard.[146]

16:3 A. M'ŚH B: R. Yeshebab was examining [soil] and found two at first, and one was [already] known. He removed the soil and marked them off as a graveyard.

B. When he came to R. 'Aqiva, he said to him, "All your labor has been in vain. You also would have to search out all the known graves of the Land

145. M. Oh. 16:2.   146. M. Oh. 16:3.

of Israel.

C. "But they have said only, 'He who finds three in the first instance.'"[147]

16:4   A. [If] one found one on this side of the public way and two on the other side of the public way, he searches on either side but omits the public way.

B. [If one found] two on one side of a fence and two on the other side of the fence, he does not have to search out the place of the fence, for so is the way of the builder, to examine [the place in which he builds] until he reaches stone or virgin soil.[148]

16:5   A. What is virgin soil? Any in which there is no mark, and the dirt of which is not loose.

B. [If] one examined [the soil] and reached water, lo, this is like virgin soil.

C. [If] one examined [the soil] and found a sherd, lo, this is like virgin soil.[149]

16:6   A. He who searches —

B. "The House of Shammai say, 'He searches two and leaves a cubit.'

"And the House of Hillel say, 'He searches a cubit and leaves a cubit,'" the words of R. Jacob.

C. And sages say, "The House of Shammai say, 'He searches a cubit and leaves a cubit.'

"And the House of Hillel say, 'He searches a cubit and leaves two.'"[150]

16:7   A. He who brings out dirt from a place of the uncleanness eats his heave-offering.

B. R. Judah says, "He piles up the dirt of this on top of the dirt of that."

C. And our rabbis have said, "Its dirt is clean."[151]

16:8   D. He who searches eats his heave-offering.

E. He who clears away the ruin does not eat his heave-offering.

F. His disciples asked Rabban Yoḥanan b. Zakkai, "He who searches — may eat [heave-offering]?"

He said to them, "He does not eat."

They said to him, "You have taught us that he should eat."

He said to them, "Well have you spoken. A deed which my own hands have done and my own eyes have seen, yet I forgot [the law], but when my ears have heard [the law], how much the more so [should I remember it]!"

And it was not that he did not know, but that he wanted to stimulate the disciples.

G. And some say it was Hillel the Elder whom they asked, and it was not that he did not know, but that he wanted to stimulate the disciples.

H. R. Joshua says, "He who repeats a tradition but does not work [on

147. *ibid.*   148. M. Oh. 16:5.   149. M. Oh. 16:4.
150. *ibid.*   151. *ibid.*

it] is like a man who sows seed but does not harvest, and he who learns Torah and forgets it is like a woman who bears and buries."

I. R. 'Aqiva says, "A song is in me, a song always."[152]

16:9 A. It comes out that one may say, There are three kinds of graves.

B. A grave which is discovered — they empty it out. Once one has emptied it out, its place is clean, and it is prohibited for benefit.

C. A grave which inconveniences the public — they empty it out. Once one has emptied it out, its place is unclean, and it is prohibited for benefit.

D. A grave which is known — they do not empty it out. [If] one has emptied it out, it is clean, and it is permitted for benefit.[153]

16:10 A. A field in which a grave is lost — he who enters it is unclean. [If] one examined [the soil] and found a grave in it, he who enters it is clean,

for I say that the grave that was lost is the grave that one found.

B. [If] one examined the soil and in it found three graves — he that enters it is clean. And we do not take account of the possibility that they form a graveyard.[154]

16:11 A. He who empties out his grave into the public way and [some else] walked there —

he empties it out bone by bone, and everything is clean.

B. He into whose field a grave opened gathers bone by bone, and all is clean.

C. M'ŚH B: Judah and Hillel, sons of Rabban Gamaliel, were walking along the border of 'Oni. A man found them, whose graveyard opened into his field.

D. They said to him, "One gathers bone by bone, and all is clean."[155]

16:12 A. A pit into which they toss people slain in battle — one gathers bone by bone, and all is clean.

B. And he who is buried without permission — [the ground in which he is buried] has no contaminated soil, and [the ground] does not fall under the law of a graveyard.

C. Rabban Simeon b. Gamaliel says, "Abortions do not acquire a grave and are not subject to the law of contaminated soil, but one who is buried without permission — [the ground in which he is buried] is subject to the law of contaminated soil."[156]

16:13 A. R. Judah says, "A cistern into which they toss abortions is clean."

Said R. Judah, M'ŚH B, "The servant-girl of one olive-farmer in Damin threw an abortion into a cistern. A priest came and looked to see what she threw in. The matter came before the sages, and they declared him clean, because the weasel and panther drag it away forthwith."[157]

---

152. *ibid.*   153. M. Oh. 16:5.   154. M. Oh. 18:2—3, 17:1.
155. M. Oh. 16:5.   156. *ibid.*   157. *ibid.*

16:14 A. A grave, the door of which one has closed, does not render unclean on all sides.

B. [If] one breaks down its door frame again and closed it off, it contaminates on all sides.

C. [If] an opening of four handbreadths was broken into it, whether above or below, unclean is only the space directly opposite the breach alone.

D. If it had a door facing north and one opened in it another door to the south, the southern door has rendered the northern door clean.[158]

17:1 A. He who ploughs up the grave, lo, he makes a hundred cubits in all directions [into a grave-area].

B. He who ploughs on top of the grave, and so he who ploughs on top of the coffin, even covered over with boards and with stones, and even [if he ploughs] on top of them by two heights [of a person], lo, this makes a grave-area.[159]

17:2 A. He who ploughs up something of the body of a corpse does not make a grave-area.

B. You have no one who makes a grave-area except one who ploughs up a grave only.

C. And R. Eliezer b. Jacob says, "Also the pool."

D. Said R. Yosé, "Under what circumstances? With ground sloping downward, but with ground sloping upward, one does not make a grave-area [at all]."[160]

17:3 A. The three vetch-plants of which they spoke [are the ones] set in their normal fashion,

B. in a dry place of the fence, but not in a wet place.

C. And he who ploughs in a field of hills and in a field of a declivity, lo, he makes a grave-area.

D. He who builds [on top of it] is clean. And he who sows on top of it is clean.

E. R. Meir says, "He who ploughs a pit filled with bones, lo, this makes a grave-area."[161]

17:4 A. Partners and sharecroppers and guardians do not make a grave-area.

B. He who ploughs in his own property and in his fellow's — his own does he make a grave-area, and that of his fellow he does not make a grave-area.

C. But it [that of the fellow] enters into the measure of the grave-area.

D. The presumption of tomb-markers which are in the Land of Israel is that they are clean, except for those that are marked off.[162]

---

158. M. Oh. 17:5.   159. M. Oh. 17:1.   160. *ibid.*
161. *ibid.*   162. M. Oh. 17:3.

17:5 A. A field which is assumed to be a grave-area, even if it is a space of four *kors,* and even if it is contiguous to the place of the [soft] wet [mud], and even if a clean [field] surrounds it on all four sides, lo, this remains in the assumption of being a grave-area.

B. Two fields designated as grave-areas, one above the other —
and the rains overflowed three handbreadths between the lower and the upper —
both of them are unclean.[163]

C. R. Yosé says, "Even though the opening of the upper one is not directly above the opening of the house, the upper room is clean."[164]

17:6 A. A grave-area which they have declared clean, lo, this is clean, and two disciples of sages have to supervise the process.

B. Said R. Judah, "R. Eliezer and sages did not differ concerning dirt from a grave-area which comes with vegetables, that it is clean until there will be a single place sufficient dirt to seal packing bags.

"Concerning what did they differ?

"Concerning dirt which comes from abroad in vegetables, for:

"R. Eliezer says, 'It joins together.'

"And sages say, 'It does not join together until there will be in one place sufficient dirt for sealing letters.'"[165]

17:7 A. He who brings coffins, and ovens, and basins, and clay utensils from abroad to the Land, [if] it is before they have been heated, they are unclean because of deriving from the land of the gentiles and clean as clay utensils. And [if they are brought] after they have been heated, they are unclean because they are clay utensils and clean because of coming from the land of the gentiles.

B. It comes out that one rules: When they are unclean because of the land of the gentiles, they are clean because of clay utensils, and when they are unclean because of being clay utensils, they are clean because of the land of the gentiles.

C. [If] one brought dirt from a place of uncleanness and kneaded it in a place of cleanness, or from a place of cleanness and kneaded it in a place of uncleanness, it is unclean. [If] one kneaded it [unclean dirt] on the rock, even in a place of cleanness, it is clean.

D. He who makes bricks of [dirt found in] the grave area, [if he does so] in the place of uncleanness, it is unclean, and [if] in the place of cleanness, it is clean.

E. R. Simeon says, "Even if the brick is from the grave-area, from the place of the uncleanness, it is clean, for they have spoken of a clod [as unclean] only as it is in its original condition."

F. Dirt of the grave-area with which they plaster roofs and ovens is

163. M. Oh. 17:4.   164. M. Oh. 17:5.   165. *ibid.*

clean because it is annulled.

17:8   A. A grave-area in which one made a rubbish heap ten handbreadths high, [if] one can move it, is clean. [If] one moved it from its place, it is unclean.

B. R. Simeon b. Gamaliel declares clean.

C. A grave-area which one floored with boards and stones, if one cannot move them, is clean.

D. If one uprooted them from their place, it is unclean.

E. R. Simeon b. Gamaliel declares clean.[166]

17:9   A. R. Eliezer b. Jacob says, "A grave-area which they filled with large clods of dirt which one cannot move is unclean."

B. R. Simeon b. Judah says in the name of R. Simeon, "[If] one broke the ground, you have no greater examination than that."

C. [If] one walked in a grave-area lower than three handbreadths and one took dirt from there, he is clean. [If] one walked in this grave-area, he does not walk in another grave-area, and if he walked in it, he is clean.

D. [If] one gathered grapes in this grave-area, let him not gather in another grave-area, and if he gathered, he is unclean.[167]

17:10   A. These are the words of the House of Hillel:

B. "He who burns the stubble and stalks burns them in their place."

R. Judah says, "They burn them outside."

C. And so did R. Judah say, "A field in which a tomb is lost — no tree is planted there, and no seed is sown there, and they dig up vegetables in it, and they do not keep an oak in it, and they do not plant in it cucumbers and pumpkins, so that people will not get used to walking there."[168]

17:11   A. A field in which a grave is lost, and it is a field of *kokhs* — it is a field of *kokhs* in which a grave is lost.

B. And what is a field of *kokhs*?

Any in which one ploughs the ground and turns up *kokhs* on the sides.[169]

17:12   A. [If] one found a field which is marked off [as having corpse-matter in its midst], and its nature is not known — if there is a tree in it, one may be sure that a grave was ploughed up in it.

B. [If] there is no tree in it, one may be sure that a grave has been lost in it.

C. Said R. Judah, "Under what circumstances? When there is there a sage or a disciple, for not everyone is expert in this matter."[170]

17:13   A. R. Yosé says, "The assumption concerning bones which are covered up, lo, it is that they are of man, until it will be known for sure that they come from cattle.

B. "[If] they are lying in the open, lo, they are assumed to be of cattle,

166. M. Oh. 18:5.   167. *ibid.*   168. M. Oh. 18:2—4.
169. *ibid.*   170. *ibid.*

until it will be made known that they are of man."

C. The House of Shammai agree with the House of Hillel that they do not examine [the soil] in connection with heave-offering, but it should be burned.[171]

18:1 A. The rule applying to the land of the gentiles is more strict than that applying to the grave-area, and that applying to the grave-area is more strict than that applying to the land of the gentiles.

B. For the land of the gentiles — [even] its virgin soil is unclean, and renders unclean when one enters it, and cannot be purified from its uncleanness — rules which do not apply to the grave-area.

C. More strict is the rule concerning the grave-area, for even though clean soil surrounds it on four sides, lo, it remains in the assumption of being a grave-area.

18:2 A. The land of the gentiles — if one can enter it in cleanness, he is clean.

B. And how near it must it be so that one may be able to enter in cleanness?

C. Rabban Simeon b. Gamaliel says, "Even a single furrow, lo, this intervenes."

D. Said R. Simeon, "I can make it possible for priests to eat clean food in the tannery which is in Sidon and which is in the villages of Lebanon,

"because they are near the sea or the river."

E. They said to him, "Lo, the fish-pool intervenes."[172]

18:3 A. The assumption concerning roads taken by immigrants from Babylonia, even though they are surrounded by the land of the gentiles, is that they are clean.

B. R. Simeon b. Gamaliel says, "Up to the place at which a man turns right and left and is not ashamed."

18:4 A. Cities surrounded by the Land of Israel, for example, Sisit and the villages around it, Ashkelon and the villages around it, even though they are free of tithe and of the rule of the sabbatical year, are not subject to the law governing the land of the gentiles.

18:5 A. He who enters the land of the gentiles in an ark, box, or cupboard is clean.

[He who enters] in a carriage, a wagon, a boat, or on a raft, is unclean.

B. He who puts the greater part of his head and of his body into the land of the gentiles is unclean.

C. A clay utensil, the air-space of which one put inside the land of the gentiles, is unclean.

D. Chairs and thrones, the greater part of which one put inside the land

171. *ibid.*   172. M. Oh. 18:7.

of the gentiles, are unclean.

18:6   A. All make [a house subject to the law of] a dwelling of the gentiles: even a slave, even a servant-girl, even a eunuch, even a child of nine years and one day;

B. a gentile married to a Samaritan woman, and a Samaritan married to a gentile woman, a gentile whose slaves are Samaritans, and a Samaritan whose slaves are gentiles.

C. Samaritans are subject to the law of the dwelling of the gentiles.

18:7   A. On account of a dwelling of the gentiles do they suspend [the status of holy things].

B. R. Yosé b. R. Judah says, "They even burn [heave-offering]."

C. And how long should [a gentile] remain inside it so that it requires examination?

D. Testified Abba Yudan of Sidon in the name of R. Eliezer, "Forty days, even though a woman is not there with him." And the law is in accord with his opinion.

E. [If] one entered, and one left and did not stay there forty days, it is clean, and if he stayed there forty days, it is unclean.[173]

18:8   A. [If] he who guards it died, if he [the gentile] stayed there forty days, it is unclean.

B. When one enters and leaves, even though he stayed there forty days, it is clean, because it is presumed to be guarded.

C. All are believed concerning it, to guard it, and even a slave, and even a woman, and even a child of nine years and one day.[174]

18:9   A. Sewer pipes which emerge from the land of the gentiles to the Land of Israel — they make for them webs, and so diminish their size to less than a handbreadth.

18:10   A. How do they examine a dwelling of gentiles? An Israelite enters first and afterward a priest.

B. If a priest enters first, even though he found it paved in marble or with a mosaic, he is unclean.

18:11   A. A store is not subject to the law of the dwelling of the gentiles, unless one [actually] lives therein.

B. A colonnade is not subject to the law of the dwelling of gentiles, unless one lives therein.

C. A dwelling of gentiles, even though it is destroyed, lo, it is unclean.

D. And [the laws of] the dwelling of gentiles and [of] the grave-area do not apply abroad [where the rabbis' authority does not extend].[175]

18:12   A. The feed-sheds, and granaries, and the bath, and the water-house, and the gate-house, and the airspace of the courtyard, the fruit shelters, and the way-stations for travellers, and the field-huts and the

173. *ibid.*   174. M. Oh. 18:10.   175. *ibid.*

hedged-in-place, and the huts and the tents are not subject to the law of the dwelling of the gentiles.

B. Fortifications and legion-camps —

Rabbi declares unclean.

And sages declare clean.

C. The armory- and the weapons-hut —

R. Judah declares unclean.

And R. Yosé declares clean.

D. The gate-house and the airspace of the courtyard, when joined with the dwelling of gentiles, are unclean on account of the law of the dwelling of the gentiles. If they are not joined with the dwelling of the gentiles, they are not subject to the law governing the dwelling of the gentiles.

E. The summer-houses, even though they are joined with the dwelling of the gentiles, are not subject to the law governing the dwelling of the gentiles.[175]

18:13 A. What is east of Qisri? From directly opposite its Mansion-house towards its winepress.

B. Testified Judah the Baker concerning the eastern side that it is clean [of graves].

C. And the whole remainder is unclean because of the land of the gentiles.[176]

18:14 A. He who goes from Akko to Kezib, on his right, to the east — the road is insusceptible on account of the law governing the land of the peoples and is liable for tithes and the law of the seventh year until it is clarified that it is free of those obligations. On the left, westward, the road is unclean on account of the land of the peoples, and it is free of tithes and of the law governing the seventh year until it will be made certain that it is liable —

B. up to Kezib.

C. R. Ishmael b. R. Yosé says in the name of his father, "Up to Lebanon."

18:15 A. At first they used to say, "The surrounding borders of Ashkelon from the great tomb to Yagud and to the Negev and to Tar'in were unclean. The sages voted concerning them and declared them clean.

18:16 A. Testified Judah b. Jacob of Bet Guvrin and Jacob b. Isaac of Bet Gufnin concerning Qisri that they possessed it from ancient times and declared it free without a vote.

B. Said R. Ḥanin, "That year was the seventh year, and gentiles went to their circuses and left the market full of fruits, and Israelites came and swiped them, and when they came back, they said, 'Come, let us go to sages, lest they permit them pigs also.'"

18:17 A. Said R. Zeriqa, "On the fifth of Second Adar twenty-four elders

176. M. Oh. 18:9.

voted concerning it and declared it free, for all were entering it [and it was clean, not regarded as gentile land]."

18:18 A. M'ŚH B: Rabbi and R. Ishmael the son of R. Yosé and R. Eliezer Haqappar spent the Sabbath in the stall of Pazzi in Lud, and R. Pinḥas b. Ya'ir was sitting before them.

B. They said to him, "Ashkelon — What do you [rule] concerning it?"

C. He said to them, "They sell wheat in their basilicas, and they bathe and [forthwith] eat their Passovers in the evening."

D. They said to him, "What is the rule about remaining in it, in respect to the land of the peoples?"

E. He said to them, "When one [gentile] has remained in it [the basilica] forty days, [it is unclean]."

F. They said to him, "If so, come and let us vote [formally] concerning it to free it from tithes."

G. And R. Ishmael the son of R. Yosé did not vote with them.

H. When he went out, Rabbi said, "Why did you not vote with us?"

I. He said to him, "Concerning uncleanness which I [formerly] declared unclean, I have [now] declared clean. But not in respect to tithes.

J. "I was afraid of the High Court, lest they remove my head."

NEGAIM

1:1 A. Said R. Yosé, "Joshua, the son of R. 'Aqiva, asked R. 'Aqiva, saying to him, 'Why have they said, 'Appearances of plagues are two which are four?'

"He said to him, 'If not, what should they say?'

B. "He said to him, 'Let them say, '[Any shade of white] from the skin of an egg and above [brighter] is unclean.'

"He said to him, '[They used the cited language] to teach that they join together.'

C. "He said to him, 'Let them say, '[A shade of white] from the skin of an egg and above is unclean, and they join together with one another.'

"He said to him, 'To teach you that if one is not an expert in them and in their names, he should not examine the plagues.' "[1]

1:2 A. R. Eliezer b. Jacob said in the name of R. Hananiah b. Kina'i, who said in the name of R. 'Aqiva, "How do you know that a priest who is an expert in plagues and not in itches, in itches and not in bald spots, in man and not in clothing, in clothing and not in houses, in the primary appearance [color] and not in the secondary appearance [color], in the secondary appearance and not in the tertiary appearance, should not examine the plagues, until he is an expert in them and in their names?

B. "Scripture states, 'This is the Torah for every plague of leprosy: for the itch, and for leprosy of the garment and in the house, and for the swelling and for the eruption, and for the spot and to teach [when it is unclean and when it is clean. This is the law for leprosy] [Lev. 14:54].' "[2]

1:3 A. Said R. Nathan, "Not that R. 'Aqiva rules [that reddishness] of the lime is dimmer than it.

B. "But [that reddishness] of the swelling is dimmer than it."[3]

C. For it is not possible for a swelling to render unclean in the first instance.

D. But it is possible for the spreading to render unclean when it is one day old.

E. How so?

A bright spot —

and in it are tokens of uncleanness —

and one certified him —

and the tokens of uncleanness went away —

and he came to a priest —

and he declared him clear —

and afterward spreading appeared on it —

---

1. M. Neg. 1:1   2. *ibid.*   3. M. Neg. 1:2.

This is spreading which can render unclean on its first day.[4]

1:4 A. [There are] four appearances through which the flesh of the skin is rendered unclean.

B. And by them the boil and the burning and the bald head and the bald forehead [Lev. 13:41—44] are rendered unclean:

C. The spreading renders unclean, even though it is not of the very same appearance [color] but of another appearance [color], and on condition that it is one of the four appearances [colors].

D. The quick raw flesh renders unclean in any appearance, and even white on black or black on white.

E. And white hair renders unclean in any appearance of white, and even the appearance [color] of old age, but the hair [must be] white.

F. And scalls render unclean in any appearance [color], and even white on black and black on white.

G. And they are signified as unclean with thin golden hair, the appearance of which is like an image of gold.[5]

1:5 A. Garments and skins are rendered unclean by the greenest of the green and the reddest of the red.

B. What is the greenest of the green shades?

C. R. Eliezer says, "Like wax and like a green gourd."

D. Sumkhos says, "Like the wing of a peacock and like the branches of a palm tree."

E. What is the reddest of the red?

F. Like the finest crimson which is in the sea.

G. Their spreading is like them [in the same shade], and to them does not apply the color of variegation.

H. The highest color in their group is like the appearance of the shadow in the sun.

I. And the deepest color among them is like the appearance of the sun in the shade.[6]

1:6 A. R. Ishmael says, "The appearances of plagues are twelve."

B. R. Hananiah, the Prefect of the Priests, says, "The appearances of plagues are sixteen."

C. R. Dosa b. Harkinas says, "The appearances of plagues are thirty-six."

D. 'Aqavya b. Mehallel says, "The appearances of plagues are seventy-two."[7]

1:7 A. A person who is blind in one of his eyes is not permitted to judge, as it is said, "In accord with the entire vision of the eyes of the priest [Lev.

4. M. Neg. 1:3.   5. *ibid.*   6. M. Neg. 11:4.
7. M. Neg. 1:4.

13:12]."

And it also says, "And by their word every dispute and every plague shall be [decided] [Deut. 21:5]."

B. Scripture links disputes to plagues. Just as plagues [are decided in accord with] the entire vision of the eyes of the priest, so too disputes [are settled in accord with] the entire vision of the eyes of the priest.[8]

1:8 A. As to a dark house the windows of which are closed, they open those windows and examine its plague.

B. A sheet which is folded over — they smooth out its folds and examine its plague.

C. [If] the plague appears in holes or in slits, one is not subjected to it. [If] one removed it [from these places], lo, this is like what is folded which is spread out and like the hidden places of the body which are revealed.

D. "Like one who weaves at a standing loom:
"for the armpit," the words of R. Meir.

E. R. Judah says, "Like one who spins flax:
"for the left hand."

F. Said Rabbi, "The words of R. Meir seem to me correct for the right hand and the words of R. Judah for the left."[9]

1:9 A. Just as one is examined for his plague, so is he examined for his shaving, as it is said, "Then he shall shave himself [Lev. 13:33]." And it is said, "And on the seventh day he shall shave all his hair off his head; he shall shave off his beard and his eyebrows, all his hair. . . [Lev. 14:9]."

B. Just as his eyebrows [are shaved] externally, excluding the concealed place, so all his hair which appears [is shaved], excluding that which is concealed.[10]

1:10 A. "A man examines all plagues except for his own plagues," the words of R. Meir.

B. And sages say, "Also not the plagues of his [own] house [and] his [own] clothing and that of his relatives."

C. All vows does a man release except for his own vows.

D. R. Judah says, "Also not the vows of his wife."

E. And sages say, "One has to say, 'Those between him and her.' "
And are they not his own vows?
But: those between her and other people.

F. And one examines his own holy things and his own tithes and is consulted in regard to his own purities and impurities.[11]

1:11 A. They do not judge two suits as at one time, and even an adulterer and an adulteress. But they judge the first, and afterward they judge the second.

---

8. M. Neg. 2:3.   9. *ibid.*   10. M. Neg. 2:4.
11. M. Neg. 2:5.

B. And they do not vote concerning two matters at one time, and they do not deal with two questions at one time. But they vote concerning the first, and afterward they vote concerning the second. And they accept a question concerning the first, and afterward they accept a question concerning the second.

1:12 A. They do not administer the bitter water to two suspected adulteresses at one time, so that one may not hold contempt for the other.

B. And R. Judah says, "This is not the reason. But because it is said 'And the priest shall bring her near [Num. 5:16].' One woman does he bring near, and he does not bring near two."

1:13 A. They do not burn two red heifers at one time. Once one is made into ashes, one brings another and burns [the second] in succession and does not doubt [the correctness of the matter].

B. And they do not break the neck of two heifers at one time.

And R. Eliezer says, "If the measure is exactly between two villages, the two of them bring two heifers."

C. And they do not wipe out three apostate villages in the Land of Israel so as not to destroy the villages of Israel. But they carry out the law for one or two.

D. The people of the apostate village — they do not judge two of them at one time, but they judge the first, and afterward they judge the second.

1:14 A. Under no circumstances is the priest permitted to declare him unclean until his eyes are upon it and upon the skin of the flesh which is outside it.

B. [If] while he is still declaring him shut up or clear, another plague is born in him, lo, this one is subject to it.

C. And, if after he shut him up, another plague is born in him, he is not subject to it for uncleanness and for cleanness, except at the end of the week.

D. [If] his plague went away, even after three years, lo, he is subject to its uncleanness until a priest says to him, "Clean."

E. The priest is believed to say, "This plague has spread, this plague has not spread," [whether] the bright spot came before the white hair, or the white hair came before the bright spot.[12]

F. And he is believed concerning his own plagues.

1:15 A. A priest who examined him in the first instance is subject to him at the end of the first week. [If] he examined him at the end of the first week, he is subject to him at the end of the second week. [If] he is subject to him at the end of the second week, he is subject to him at the end of the third week.

B. [If] he died or fell ill, another priest is subject to him, and he may not say to him, "Go and come back." But he is subject to him forthwith.[13]

1:16 A. A priest who declared a clean person to be unclean or declared

12. M. Neg. 3:1.   13. *ibid.*

the unclean person to be clean, and [the spot] is subject to him at the end of the first week, even though he declared the unclean to be unclean and declared the clean to be clean, has done nothing at all.

B. In respect to the uncleanness, it says, "He is unclean, and the priest has declared him unclean," and in respect to cleanness it says, "He is clean, and the priest declares him clean [Lev. 13:37]."

C. This is one of the things concerning which Hillel came up from Babylonia.

2:1   A. There is [a strict rule applying] to white hair which does not [apply] to golden hair, and there is [a strict rule applying] to golden hair which does not [apply] to white hair.

B. White hair does not afford protection for another hair from its power, which is not the case with golden hair.

C. And there is [a strict rule applying] to golden hair, for golden hair is sufficiently powerful in its place to render unclean in any appearance [color], which is not the case with white hair.[14]

2:2   A. [If] there were two [white] hairs in the plague and they protruded outside of it, he is unclean.

[If] they were outside it and protruded into it, he is clean.

B. Said R. Meir, "So that people will not imagine that by ignoramuses are they adjudged: if he saw white hair, he is unclean, and the white is not clean."[15]

2:3   A. His disciples asked R. Yosé, "A bright spot, and in it is black hair — do they take account of the possibility that it has perhaps reduced the place of the bright spot to less than a split bean?"

B. He said to them, "A bright spot, and in it is white hair — do we take into account the possibility that its place has reduced the bright spot to less than a split bean?"

C. They said to him, "No. If you have said so concerning white hair, which is a token of uncleanness, will you say so concerning black hair, which is not a token of uncleanness?"

D. He said to them, "Lo, even if there are ten white hairs on him — are not only two [of them] tokens of uncleanness?

E. "Do I take account of the possibility concerning the addition[al hair] that perhaps it has diminished the place of the bright spot to less than a split bean?"

F. They said to him, "No. If you have said so concerning white hair, which is a kind of uncleanness, will you say so concerning black hair, which is not a kind of uncleanness?"

G. He said to him, "Also black hair — ultimately the bright spot will

14. M. Neg. 4:1-3.   15. M. Neg. 4:4.

turn it [white], so it is a kind of uncleanness."[16]

2:4   A. A bright spot, and a streak goes forth from it —

B. two bright spots, and a streak goes forth from this one to that one —

C. if there is in it the breadth of two hairs, it subjects them to uncleanness with white hair and with spreading.

D. But as to quick flesh, it does not join them together until it [the streak] is of the breadth of a split bean.

E. R. Eleazar b. R. Simeon says, "Just as it does not join them together to render unclean with quick flesh until it is as wide as a split bean, so they are not made subject to uncleanness with white hair and spreading until there will be in it the breadth of a split bean."[17]

2:5   A. Two bright spots —

B. and a streak of quick flesh is between them —

C. [if] on one side a place of [the size of] one hair broke out, and on the other side a place of [a size of] one hair,

D. it is subject to uncleanness because of spreading, and insusceptible because of quick flesh.

E. [If] on one side a place of two hairs broke out, and on the other side a place of two hairs, it is subject to uncleanness because of spreading and subject to uncleanness because of quick flesh.

F. A bright spot which has been declared clear after certification —

quick flesh and white hair are in the spreading—

or [he has been declared clean] after quarantine —

it does not serve to impose quarantine from now on.

G. But they go to his account to be declared unclean because of white hair and spreading which come after the plague.[18]

2:6   A. A bright spot after the clearance —

B. it contracted and spread, or spread and contracted —

C. it changed in appearance from snow-white to lime-white and [or] from lime-white to snow-white —

D. lo, this is just as it was.

E. A bright spot the size of a split bean, and it spread to the extent of a half a split bean further, and from the primary sign about a half split bean disappeared —

F. R. 'Aqiva says, "Let it be inspected as at the outset."

G. And sages declare clean.

H. A bright spot the size of a split bean, and it spread to the extent of a split bean and more —

I. [if] about a half a split bean disappeared from the primary sign,

J. R. 'Aqiva declares unclean.

K. And sages say, "Let it be inspected as at the outset."[19]

16. *ibid.*   17. M. Neg. 4:5.   18. *ibid.*   19. M. Neg. 4:7—9.

2:7 A. A bright spot the size of about a half split bean —

and in it are two hairs —

B. there was born in the bright spot about a half split bean —

and in it are two hairs —

C. lo, this is to be certified.

D. [If] one erred and did not know whether it [the spot] turned it [the hair white], and whether it [the spot] came first, he is clean.

E. And if after he certified him unclean, he erred, and it is not known whether it turned it white, and whether it came first, he is unclean.

F. [If] two disappeared on him, he is unclean; and [if] three, he is clean.

G. R. Eleazar b. R. Simeon says, "If there is doubt whether the bright spot came before the white hair, or whether the white hair came before the bright spot, since a doubt in matters of plagues produces a lenient ruling, he is clean."[20]

2:8 A. A bright spot —

B. and in it is quick flesh less than the size of a lentil —

C. R. Meir says, "Let him be shut up."

D. And sages say, "They are not subjected to it."

E. [If] the bright spot grew larger, it is shut up.

F. [If] it diminished, it is clean.

G. [If] the quick flesh grew larger, it is unclean.

H. [If] it grew smaller,

I. R. Meir declares unclean,

J. for the plague spreads into its own midst.

K. And sages declare clean,

L. for the plague does not spread into its own midst.[21]

2:9 A. A bright spot the size of a split bean —

B. and quick flesh the size of a lentil encompasses it —

C. and outside of the quick flesh is a bright spot —

D. and this quick flesh diminishes, and it becomes a bright spot —

E. R. Gamaliel says, "If it grew small on the inside, the inside is to be certified, and the outside is clean.

"[If] it is on the outside, the inside is to be shut up, and the outside is clean."

F. R. 'Aqiva says, "One way or the other,

"the inside is to be shut up, and the outside is clean.

G. "If it is because of spreading, they do not take account of the inside, for the plague does not spread into the midst of the plague.

"If it is because of spreading [quick flesh], they do not take account of the outside, for the bright spot is in the midst of it."[22]

2:10 A. R. Simeon said, "When [do] the words of R. 'Aqiva [apply]?

20. M. Neg. 4:11.   21. M. Neg. 6:3.   22. M. Neg. 6:5.

B. "When it is the size of a lentil exactly.

C. "[If] it was greater than a lentil,

D. "and this additional amount of quick flesh grew smaller, and was made into a bright spot,

E. "if it is on the inside,

F. "the inside is diminished on account of the spreading, and the outside [is diminished] on account of its quick flesh.

G. "[If] it is on account of the quick flesh on the outside, the inner side is to be shut up, and the outside is to be certified."[23]

2:11 A. Said R. Yosé, "These are the words of R. Ḥanina b. Gamaliel, but I say concerning both of them that the outside is clean, for I regard the bright spot as if the boil is in the place of the quick flesh."[24]

2:12 A. Twenty-four tips of limbs are in man, and they are not made unclean because of quick flesh.

B. And if their place has a flat space the size of a split bean, lo, they are made unclean through plagues.

C. R. Leazar says, "The corns and the wens and the warts are not made unclean because of quick flesh. But if their place has a flat space the size of a split bean, lo, they are subject to uncleanness through plagues."

D. R. Yosé b. R. Judah says, "[If] a bright spot was near the head, the eye, and the ear, and the nose, and the mouth, it is clean, as it is said, 'And the priest shall see the plague on the flesh of the skin [Lev. 13:3]' — meaning that it must be wholly on the surface of the skin of the flesh and susceptible to spreading."

E. [A bright spot even the requisite the size of] a split bean on the tip of this nose, spreading down this way and that —

F. one about the size of a split bean on the tip of his finger, spreading this way and that —

G. it is clean, as it is said, 'And he shall see it' — the whole of it at one instant.[25]

2:13 A. A bright spot is on [covers] all of him, but on his head is living flesh —

B. a bright spot is on his foot, but over all of him is living flesh —

C. or there was on him a bright spot running above to below like a belt of living flesh, encompassing him about in the center —

D. he is clean, as it is said, 'And there is quick raw flesh in the swelling [Lev. 13:10]' —

E. until the quick flesh is encompassed in the midst of the swelling.

F. The red skin which is on the lips is adjudged like the private parts.

G. And the fold of flesh which is spread open, lo, it is like the skin of the flesh in every respect.[26]

---

23. M. Neg. 6:6.   24. *ibid.*   25. M. Neg. 6:7.   26. M. Neg. 6:8.

2:14   A. A bright spot —

B. on a gentile before he converted, and afterward he converted —

C. on the head before it grew hair, and it grew hair, and after it grew hair, it became bald —

D. on a beard before it grew hair, and it grew hair, and after it grew hair, it became a hairless scab —

E. and on the flesh before it produced a boil, and it produced a boil, and after it produced a boil, it produced a scab —

F. the skin of the flesh before it produced a burning, and it produced a burning, and after it produced a burning, it produced a scab —

— is clean.[27]

2:15   A. R. Liezer b. Jacob says, "Since its beginning and its end is unclean, it is unclean."

B. And sages say, "One examines it as in the first instance."

C. [If] there was a bright spot [on a gentile] before he converted, and after he converted, another bright spot was joined to it,

D. the first does not subject it [the bright spot] to uncleanness on account of the tokens of white hair and spreading, and does not hinder the spreading.

E. [If there was] a half split bean before he converted, and a half split bean [developed, completing the requisite measure] after he converted, he is clean.[28]

3:1   A. He who uproots the tokens of uncleanness from his plague,

B. whether he uprooted it in its entirety or whether he uprooted part of it,

C. whether [he did so] before he came to a priest, or whether [he did so] after he came before a priest,

D. whether [he did so] while he was certified unclean, or whether [he did so] during quarantine, or whether [he did so] after he was declared clear —

E. lo, such a one is smitten with forty stripes.[29]

3:2   A. He who tears a plague out of a garment,

B. and he who scrapes a plague off the wall of the house,

C. lo, this one is smitten with forty stripes, as it is said, "Take heed, in an attack of leprosy, to be very careful to do according to all that the Levitical priests shall direct you [Deut. 24:8]."

D. But he carries the beam on his shoulder and [walks] with the bast on his foot, (and) if it [the bright spot] goes away, it goes away.

E. [If] there were two hairs on him —

F. he removed one and the other fell out —

27. M. Neg. 7:1.   28. *ibid.*   29. M. Neg. 7:4.

G. he is clean.

H. There were three —

I. he removed one and two fell out —

J. he is clean.

K. [There were three and he removed] two, and one fell out — he is unclean.

M. [If] his bright spot grew less than a split bean, one way or the other, he is clean.

N. [If] it spread over his entire body, one way or the other, he is clean.[30]

3:3   A. [If] there was on him quick flesh the size of a lentil —

B. he cauterized half of it, and half of it disappeared — he is clean.

C. [If] there was more than a lentil —

D. he cauterized the excess,

.   E. and that part about the size of a lentil disappeared [on its own] —

F. he is clean.

G. [If he cauterized the] lentil, and the excess went away, he is unclean.

H. [If] his bright spot diminished in size to less than a split bean, one way or the other, he is clean.

I. [If] it spread over his whole body, one way or the other, he is unclean.[31]

3:4   A. Said R. Yosé, "Under what circumstances? When a bright spot appears on this excess [of quick flesh].

B. "And if this excess became a boil, it is clean.

C. "For even if the bright spot was the size of a *sela,* and a boil was joined to it, it is clean"

D. I began bringing proofs to them:

E. "On what account is he clean before he comes to the priest? Is it not because the priest has not seen the tokens of uncleanness which are on him? Also [if he does so] while he is quarantined, let him be clean, until the priest sees the tokens of uncleanness which are on him."

F. They said to him, "Well have you spoken."[32]

3:5   A. [If] one cut it off intentionally,

B. R. Liezer says, "When another plague will be born on him, and he will be purified from it, [he will be clean]."

C. And sages say, "This one cannot ever be purified."

D. Said R. Judah, "R. Eliezer and sages did not dispute concerning one who cut it off and cut off with it living flesh, that such a one never will have purification.

E. "Nor do they differ concerning one who cut it off and left any amount whatever of it, for, if it spreads over his entire body, lo, he is clean.

30. *ibid.*   31. *ibid.*   32. *ibid.*

F. "Concerning what did they disagree? Concerning one who cut it off exactly.

G. "For R. Eliezer says, 'He has no purification until another plague will be born on him, and he will be purified from it.'

H. "And sages say, 'If it spread over part of him, he is unclean. If it spread over the whole of his body, he is clean.' "[33]

3:6 A. A leper who has been quarantined may circumcise himself, and he is free of the sacrifice.

B. And one who has been certified unclean may circumcise himself, but he is liable for the sacrifice.

C. [If] there was a bright spot the size of a bean, and about half a split bean was removed by the circumcision, and at the end of the week it became as large as a *sela* —

D. he is to be inspected as if at the beginning.[34]

3:7 A. A bright spot the size of a split bean —

B. and in it is quick flesh the size of a lentil —

C. it broke forth over his entire body —

D. and left the quick flesh in its place —

E. he is unclean.

F. The tips of the limbs reappeared in him —

G. he is unclean,

H. until the bright spot the size of a split bean will diminish.

I. And how much is the reappearance of the tips of the limbs?

J. R. Meir says, "Any amount at all."

K. R. Yosé says, "The size of a lentil."

L. Said R. Meir, "And is it because of quick flesh that they are unclean? And is it not so that quick flesh does not render unclean in the tips of limbs?

M. "But it is the decree of the King: Even any amount at all. '[35]

3:8 A. Said R. Yosé, "And is it because of the tips of the limbs that they are unclean? And is it not so that if part of his body in the middle reappears, he is unclean? But it is said, 'Living flesh' [Lev. 13:14], and it is said, 'Living flesh' [Lev. 13:10].

B. "Just as in the latter Scripture the meaning is, 'Living flesh the size of a lentil,' so living flesh said here means, 'The size of a lentil.' "[36]

3:9 A. White hair which reappears after the breaking forth from certification [of cleanness has produced a decree of cleanness],

B. [or after] quick flesh, white hair, or spreading after the quarantine [has produced a certification of cleanness],

is clean [and the breaking forth is not hindered by the white hair].

C. And R. Joshua declares unclean.

---

33. *ibid.*   34. *ibid.*   35. M. Neg. 8:2—3.
36. *ibid.*

D. Said R. Joshua, "White hair is a sign of uncleanness, and quick flesh is a sign of uncleanness. Just as quick flesh which reappears renders unclean, so white hair returns and renders unclean."

E. Said to him R. 'Aqiva, "The particular [contaminating] quality of quick flesh which reappears and renders unclean is that it renders unclean whether in reverse order or not in reverse order. Will you say so of white hair, which renders unclean only in reverse order?

F. "And furthermore, it is said, 'Flesh' [Lev. 13:14] —

"Living flesh which reappears renders unclean, and white hair which returns does not render unclean."[37]

3:10 A. [If] it spread over his entire body but not over about half a lentil of space near the head, the beard, the boil, the burning, and the blister which are festering —

B. the head and the beard reappeared, having grown bald —

C. and the boil and the burning formed a scab and grew quick —

D. and their place was filled by a bright spot —

E. R. Jacob says, "Since a sign of cleanness is located near a sign of cleanness, he is clean."

F. And sages say, "Let him be inspected as at the outset."[38]

3:11 A. Two bright spots —

B. one unclean and one clean —

C. it broke forth from this to this —

D. into this one from the skin of the flesh, and into this one from the skin of the flesh —

from the skin of the flesh into them —

E. he is clean.

F. And R. Nehemiah says, "If in the first place it broke forth from the unclean one to the clean one, he is clean.

"And if from the unclean to the unclean, he is unclean."

G. He who comes [to the priest] entirely white —

and in it is round or elongated quick flesh —

lo, this one is shut up.

H. If the limbs reappeared on him, lo, they are as they were [and he is to be shut up].

I. And sages say, "If it spread over part of him, he is unclean; if it spread over all of him and over the quick flesh, he is clean."[39]

3:12 A. Two bright spots,

B. one is quarantined, and one is certified [unclean],

C. one is quarantined and one is to be quarantined,

D. one is to be quarantined, and one is to be certified,

E. one is quarantined, and one is certified,

37. *ibid.*   38. M. Neg. 8:5.   39. M. Neg. 8:6.

F. one is quarantined, and one is clean,

G. [if] one erred and does not know which is first and which is second —

H. he is clean.

I. Two bright spots —

J. one is certified, and one is to be certified,

K. one is to be certified, and one is to be shut up,

L. one is certified, and one is shut up,

M. one is certified, and one is clean —

N. if one erred and does not know which is first and which is second —

O. he is unclean.[40]

3:13 A. The boil and the burning — both of them are a single sign, and both of them are [a sign of] a single uncleanness.

B. And why have they been distinguished from one another?

C. Because they do not join together.

D. About a half split bean of a boil and about a half split bean of a burning do not join together.

E. [if] a boil became a burning, the burning has nullified the boil.

F. And [if] a burning became a boil, the boil has nullified the burning.

G. Lo, [if] these are before you, [however,] and it is not known whether it is a burning or whether it is a boil — he is clean.[41]

3:14 A. The boil and burning and the scalls,

B. and the boil and the burning and the bald spot on the head and the bald spot on the temple,

C. and the boil and the burning and the skin of the flesh

D. do not join together with one another and do not spread from one to the other.

E. [If] one shut him up because of a boil, and at the end of the week it had become like the skin of the flesh,

F. [or if one shut him up] because of [the bright spot on] the skin of the flesh, and at the end of the week it had produced a boil,

G. let him be examined afresh.[42]

4:1 A. R.'Aqiva says, "The long golden hair is clean, but it affords protection from the power of thin [short] golden hair and the spreading which comes after [the appearance of] the scall."

B. What is its sign?

C. R. Leazar b. R. Simeon says, "That which is unclean in white hair is clean in golden hair.

D. "[That which is] clean in white hair is unclean in golden hair."[43]

E. There were on him two [black] hairs growing —

40. M. Neg. 5:4—5.   41. M. Neg. 9:2.   42. *ibid.*

43. M. Neg. 10:1.

F. lo, these afford protection,

G. gathered together and dispersed,

H. encompassed and not encompassed.

I. But those [black ones] which remain [from before the scall's appearance] do not afford protection unless they are encompassed.

J. There were on him two hairs —

K. one growing [a black hair grew up after the scall appeared] —

L. and one encompassed —

M. lo, these afford protection

N. when dispersed.

O. There were on him two hairs,

P. one golden,

Q. and one growing [after the scall appeared, the black hair grew up] —

R. one golden,

S. and one [black one] remaining [from before the scall's appearance] —

T. a mate appeared for the golden hair —

U. he is unclean.

V. [If a mate appeared] for the one that is growing, and for the one that remains —

W. he is clean.

X. And if he shaves the scall: even a Nazir, lo, this one shaves.

Y. His shaving is by any man, and his shaving is by any thing.

Z. [If] he shut him up and did not shave him, lo, this one is shut up.[44]

4:2   A. A scall, and a streak goes forth from it —

B. two scalls, and a streak goes from one to the other —

C. if it is two hairs wide, they subject him to be unclean through thin golden hair and spreading,

D. [and] to enjoy protection from that [black hair] which is growing.

E. But as to that [black hair] which remains, it does not afford protection until it [the streak] will be as broad as a split bean.

F. R. Leazar b. R. Simeon says, "Just as it does not afford protection for what remains until it will be as wide as a split bean, so they do not subject him to uncleanness through thin golden hair and spreading [or] afford protection with the growing [hair] until it will be as wide as a split bean."[45]

4:3   A. A scall inside of a scall causes the inner to be shut up and clears the outer.

B. Judah b. Neqosa' says in the name of R. Simeon, "Every scall which one certified [unclean] on the basis of thin golden hair and spreading,

"and they went away —

"it is not going to serve [as a sign of] uncleanness forever."[46]

4:4   A. A scall the size of a split bean is on his head and [or] on his beard

44. M. Neg. 10:3.   45. M. Neg. 10:6.   46. M. Neg. 10:7.

B. let him be shut up.

C. [If] it remained on him the first week, one gives him a second week.

D. [If] it remained on him the second week, he is cleared.

E. After [the clearance], thin golden hair and spreading appear on him

F. he is unclean.

G. Black hair appeared on him, or black hair gathered together on the side —

H. he is clean.

I. Black hair went away and left behind golden hair in its place —

J. he is clean.

K. And not only is he clean, but it affords protection from the power of thin golden hair and spreading which come after the scall.[47]

4:5   A. A scall the size of a split bean is on his head and on his beard —

B. at the end of the first week, and at the end of the second week

C. and thin golden hair and spreading appear on it —

D. he is unclean.

E. [And] black hair appeared on it or gathered together on the side —

F. he is clean.

G. Black hair went away and left golden hair in its place —

H. he is clean.

I. And not only is he clean but it affords protection from the power of thin golden hair and spreading which come after the scall.[48]

4:6   A. A scall the size of a split bean is on his head and on his beard —

B. at the end of the first week,

C. and at the end of the second week

D. black hair comes together on the side —

E. he is clean.

F. It went and produced a scall —

G. it is unclean because of spreading.

H. A scall the size of a split bean is on his head and on his beard —

I. he is shut up.

J. His head and his beard became entirely covered by a scall all at once

K. whether during certification, or during quarantine, or during the clearance —

L. he is clear, because it broke forth.

M. [If his head or beard became entirely covered by a scall all at once] after the clearance —

N. he is unclean,

O. because of spreading.[49]

4:7   A. He who comes with his head and beard entirely covered by scalls is shut up.

---

47. M. Neg. 10:8.   48. *ibid.*   49. *ibid.*

B. [If] it remained on him one week, they give him a second week.

C. [If] it remained on him two weeks, he is declared clear.

D. [If] after the clearance, thin golden hair appears on him, he is unclean.

E. [If] black hair was born on him, whether in the middle or on the side, he is clean.

F. Black hair went away, and left golden hair —

G. he is clean.

H. And not only is he clean, but it affords protection for thin golden hair which comes after the scall.

I. He who comes [to the priest] entirely covered by a scall is shut up,

J. at the end of the first week,

K. and at the end of the second week, thin golden hair appears on him,

L. he is unclean.

M. [If] black hair appeared on him, whether in the middle or on the side

N. he is clean.

O. [If] the black hair went away and left golden hair in its place,

P. he is clean.

Q. And not only is he clean, but it affords protection from the power of thin golden hair which comes after the scall.[50]

4:8   A. He who comes entirely covered with a scall is shut up

B. at the end of the first week,

C. and at the end of the second week, black hair appears on it on the side,

D. he is clean.

E. [If] the scall returned, he is unclean because of spreading.

F. He who comes entirely covered by a scall on his head and on his beard —

G. he is shut up.

H. Two hairs grow,

I. one on the head and one on the beard,

J. they do not join together.[51]

4:9   A. Scalp-baldness and forehead-baldness — the two of them are subject to a single sign, and the two of them are a single uncleanness.

B. And why are they distinguished from one another?

C. Because they do not join together with one another.

D. And what is scalp-baldness, and what is forehead-baldness?

E. From the crown and sloping backwards is scalp-baldness, from the forehead and toward the front is forehead-baldness.[52]

4:10   A. The hairless places which are in the head or in the beard [are regarded as equivalent to the beard].

---

50. M. Neg. 10:9.   51. *ibid.*   52. M. Neg. 10:10.

B. A beard of the woman or a beard of the eunuch which did not produce hair — lo, they are like the skin of the flesh in every respect.

C. Once they have put forth hair, lo, they are like the beard in every respect.[53]

4:11 A. Scalp-baldness and forehead-baldness and scalls,

B. and the boil, and the burning

C. do not join together with one another,

D. and do not spread from one to the other.

E. You find, therefore:

F. the head is made unclean through five [separate] kinds of plagues:

(1) before it produces hair, it is susceptible to uncleanness because of the [bright spot which appears on] the skin of the flesh;

(2) if it put forth hair and became bald, it is unclean because of scalp-baldness;

(3) a scall [on the head] is unclean because of scalls;

(4) if it [the head] produces a boil, it is unclean because of a boil;

(5) if it [the head] produces a burning, it is unclean because of a burning.[54]

4:12 A. What is the head, and what is the beard?

B. From the cheek bone and upward, this is the head.

C. From the cheek bone and downward, this is the beard.

D. From the front, one stretches the thread from ear to ear,

E. for from the thread and upward, this is the head;

F. from the thread and downward, this is the beard.

G. As to the back of the head: from the protruding cartilege of the neck and upward, this is the head; from the protruding cartilege and downward, even though it produces the hair, lo, this is like the skin of the flesh in every respect.

H. In front of him: from the knob of the windpipe upward, this is the beard; from the knob of the windpipe downward, even though it produces hair, lo, this is like the skin of the flesh in every respect.

I. These are the signs of the head and the beard, for susceptibility through plagues, and for susceptibility to uncleanness through scalls, and for susceptibility to uncleanness through boils, and a burning, and a baldspot of the scalp and a baldspot of the forehead;

J. and because of [violating the rule that] a razor shall not pass across his head [Num. 6:5]. But for the beard one is liable only for pointed ends of the beard of the chin alone.[55]

5:1 A. Felted stuffs, and skin, and the tents, lo, they are subject to uncleanness through plagues.

---

53. *ibid.*   54. M. Neg. 10:9.   55. *ibid.*

B. Camel's hair and sheep's wool which one hackled together —

C. R. Simeon b. Judah says in the name of R. Simeon, "Since doubt in matters of plagues is resolved in favor of a lenient decision, a mixture of half and half is clean."[56]

5:2 A. "All garments, whether colored by man or colored naturally, are not susceptible to uncleanness through plagues.

"The hides and [thread spun for] the warp and the woof are like them," the words of R. Meir.

B. R. Judah says, "All garments, whether colored by man or colored naturally, are not susceptible to uncleanness through plagues.

"And all houses, whether colored by man or colored naturally, are susceptible to uncleanness through plagues."[57]

5:3 A. R. Simeon says concerning them three principles in the name of R. 'Aqiva:

B. "All garments, whether colored by man or colored naturally, are not susceptible to uncleanness through plagues.

C. "And all houses, whether colored by man or colored naturally, are susceptible to uncleanness through plagues.

D. "And hides colored naturally are susceptible to uncleanness, and those [colored] by man are not susceptible."[58]

5:4 A. A garment whose warp is colored and whose woof is white —

B. whose woof is colored and whose warp is white —

C. everything follows [the color of] the woof.

D. And in the case of pillows and bolsters, after the warp.

E. And this and that follow the status of that which can be seen.[59]

5:5 A. A garment whose warp is silk and whose woof is wool —

B. whose woof is silk and whose warp is wool —

C. they are not susceptible to uncleanness through plagues.

D. [If] one shut it [a garment] up on account of a half split-bean of red, and at the end of the week one came and found it the size of a split-bean of green,

E. or [if] one shut it up on account of a split-bean of green, or on account of a split-bean of red, and at the end of the week one came and found it a half split-bean of green and a half split-bean of red —

F. one gives it a second week [of quarantine].

G. And R. Judah says, "Let it be inspected afresh."

H. [If] one shut it up on account of a split-bean of green or on account of a split-bean of red, and at the end of the week one came and found it the size of a *sela'* of green, and about the size of a *sela'* of red, lo, this is to be burned.

56. M. Neg. 11:2.   57. M. Neg. 11:3.   58. *ibid.*
59. M. Neg. 11:4.

I. R. Judah says, "Let it be examined afresh."[60]

5:6 A. That [garment] which comes [before the priest] entirely covered by a plague is shut up.

B. [If] it remained on it for one week, one gives it a second week.

(C. [If] it remained on it two weeks —

to clear after —

let it be cleared.)

D. [If] it remained on it for two weeks, or [if] it contracted and spread at the end of a week,

lo, this one should be entirely burned.

E. A plague —

F. and at the end of the week it broke forth over all of it —

G. lo, this one should be entirely burned.

H. [If] it was dimmer in the first instance than the third [shade] [light red, light green] —

let it be washed, and shut up.

I. [If it is dimmer than] the second color [red or green] —

J. R. Ishmael [or: Simeon] says, "Let it be washed and shut up."

K. And sages say, "This is not subject to the priest."

L. And at the end of the first week [if it is dimmer] than the second color, let it be washed and shut up.

M. At the end of the second week [if it is dimmer] than the second color [in the first week it did not change, and in the second week it grew dim] —

N. one tears it and it requires a patch.

O. And R. Neḥemiah says, "It does not require a patch."

P. [If] it goes back to a fainter color, it is clean.

Q. [If] it goes back to a plague, whether it is its color or whether it is not its color,

R. lo, this is to be burned.

S. And the patch itself is to be burned.

T. [If] it [the faint spot] spreads at the end of the first week, and [or] at the end of the second week, and [or] at the end of the third week,

U. one washes it, and it is clean.

V. [If] it returns to a fainter color, it is clean.

W. [If] it [then] returns to a plague, whether it is its color or whether it is not its color —

X. let it be examined afresh.[61]

5:7 A. He who fixes a patch from something which is clean onto that which has been shut up, and a plague appears on the [quarantined] garment

B. one saves the patch.

C. [If] it spread from the garment to the patch, this and that are to be

---

60. *ibid.*   61. M. Neg. 11:5.

burned.

D. [If] it appears on the patch, as to the first garment, one burns the garment.[62]

E. And the patch serves itself through the signs.

5:8 A. He who affixes a patch from that which is shut up onto that which is clean —

B. and a plague appears on the garment —

C. one burns the patch.

D. [If] it spread from the garment [on which the patch was added] to the patch, this and that are to be burned.

E. [If] it appears on the patch,

F. the first garment is to be burned,

G. and the patch serves itself through signs,

H. and requires burning at the end.[63]

5:9 A. Two garments which have been shut up,

B. from one of which one took a patch, which one patched onto the other,

C. [and from one of which one took] a patch, which one patched on that

D. and a plague appeared on one of them —

E. it and its patch are to be burned.

F. [If] it appeared on one of the patches —

G. they all are to be burned.[64]

5:10 A. A summer garment on which are white and colored checks —

B. they spread from one to the other.

C. R. Neḥemiah says, "It never is susceptible to uncleanness through plagues until there will be on its white patch three-by-three fingerbreadths."

D. The yarn in the coil joins together, and there is spreading from one to the other.[65]

5:11 A. Two wings of a shirt join together and spread from one to the other.

B. Said R. Neḥemiah, "Under what circumstances? When it is on the row of slips [in the loom to which the threads of the warp are attached].

C. "But [if] one split them and sewed them together and made them one, they do not join together, and they do not spread from one to the other."

D. The loom which is spread out, lo, [the two parts of] this [loom] join together.

E. R. Simeon says, "If it was doubled and lying, or it was closely ordered with pillows and bolsters, it joins together, and if not, it does not join together."[66]

---

62. M. Neg. 11:6.　　63. *ibid.*　　64. *ibid.*

65. M. Neg. 11:7.　　66. M. Neg. 11:9.

5:12   A. The warp, so long as it is going to be woven, is connected to that which is woven.

B. [If] one completed weaving, it is unclean only up to the point at which it is going to be split off.[67]

5:13   A. A garment on which a plague appeared, and one made it into a warp —

B. a warp and one made it a garment —

C. it is examined afresh.

D. [If] a plague appeared on the threads,

E. the sheet is clean.

F. [If] it spread from threads to threads,

G. the sheet is unclean.

H. [If it spread from the threads] to the sheet,

I. they [the threads] are clean.

J. But [if] one burns the garment, one burns the threads with it.[68]

K. This is the summary-principle of the matter:

L. Whatever is susceptible to be made unclean through the corpse is susceptible to be made unclean through plagues.

M. More stringent is the rule of corpse-uncleanness than the rule of the uncleanness of plagues:

N. For everything is made unclean by the corpse, and not everything is made unclean through plagues.

1. Connection applies to corpse-uncleanness and connection does not apply to uncleanness of plagues.

O. More strict is the rule concerning plagues.

P. For plagues render unclean in wood and in stones and in dirt and in the warp and in the woof, which is not the case with corpse-uncleanness.[69]

5:14   A. A garment on one head of which a plague has appeared —

and at the end of a week it appears on the [other] side —

B. the second [head] is unclean because of spreading.

C. And in hides it spreads from this to that side.

D. R. Ishmael son of R. Yoḥanan b. Beroqa' says, "A wine-skin and a shepherd's wallet on which a plague has appeared —

"one sets them in their ordinary position and examines their plague."

E. R. Liezer b. Jacob says, "The birrus and the Brundisian cloaks, the knee-britches and the thick blankets and the thick felt and the mattresses and the pillows and the bolsters are not made unclean through plagues until they will be examined in the web and in the soft surface wool."[70]

5:15   A. A quarantined garment which one colored or which one sold to a gentile is clean.

---

67. M. Neg. 11:10.   68. *ibid.*   69. M. Neg. 11:11.
70. *ibid.*

B. R. Leazar b. R. Simeon says, "Lo, it is still regarded as shut up."

C. A garment which has been shut up, which one cut up and made patches which are less than three fingerbreadths-by-three-fingerbreadths, and there was among them one which was three-fingerbreadths-by-three-fingerbreadths, and a plague appeared in this one which is three-fingerbreadths-by-three-fingerbreadths — it alone is unclean.

D. R. Leazar b. R. Simeon says, "They all are to be burned."[71]

6:1 A. A diseased house has never come into existence and is never going to come into existence.

And why was it written?

To tell you, 'Expound and receive a reward.'

B. And R. Leazar b. R. Simeon says, "A place was on the border of Gaza, and they called it, 'A Quarantined Ruin.' "

C. R. Simeon b. Judah of Kefar 'Akkum said, "A place was in Galilee which they marked off, for they said, 'Diseased stones were in it.' "

D. And Jerusalem is not made unclean through plagues.[72]

E. Said R. Judah, "I heard only the Sanctuary alone."

6:2 A. They do not measure from it [Jerusalem] toward the corpse;

B. they do not bring [on its account] the calf whose neck is broken [Deut. 21:18].

C. And it [Jerusalem] is not made a 'destroyed city.'

D. R. Nathan says, "Also the law concerning the rebellious son does not apply to it, as it is said, 'And they shall bring him to the elders of his town and to the gate of his place [Deut. 21:19]' — excluding Jerusalem, which belongs to [all] Israel."

E. They do not keep the corpse in it overnight.

F. And they do not carry the bones of a man through it.

G. And they do not rent houses in it.

H. And in it they do not provide a place for a resident alien.

I. And they do not set up graves in it, except for the graves of the house of David and the grave of Huldah the prophetess, which were there from the days of the former prophets.

J. And it is not planted, and it is not sown, and it is not ploughed, and they do not raise trees in it, except for rose gardens, which were there from the times of the former prophets.

K. And they do not raise dung-heaps in it, because of the uncleanness.

L. And they do not build from [houses in] it projections and balconies to the public domain, because of thereby making a Tent for the transmission of uncleanness.

6:3 A. A synagogue and a woman's house and a house shared by partners

71. M. Neg. 11:12.   72. M. Neg. 12:4.

lo, these are susceptible to uncleanness through plagues.

B. A round house, which is made like a dove-cot, is not susceptible to uncleanness through plagues.

C. Two-cornered houses, three-cornered houses, five-cornered houses are not susceptible to uncleanness through plagues.[73]

6:4 A. A house which was built on four beams is not susceptible to uncleanness through plagues.

B. One built on four pillars is susceptible to uncleanness through plagues.

C. A house built at the bottom in living rock and at the top out of building materials, a building made at the bottom of building materials and at the top of bricks, is susceptible to uncleanness through plagues.

D. The house which is in the sea is not susceptible to uncleanness through plagues.

E. A house, one side of which is owned by a gentile and the other side by a Israelite, one side in the [holy] Land and the other side outside of the Land, is not made unclean through plagues.

F. And the house which is on the ship is not susceptible to uncleanness through plagues.[74]

6:5 A. Wood — sufficient to place under the lintel.

B. R. Judah says, "Sufficient to make a sandal for the outer side of the lintel."

C. Dirt — sufficient to place between one row and its fellow,

D. and between one stone and the next.

E. And how much is the measure of stones?

F. "A load of two," the words of Rabbi.

G. R. Simeon b. Leazar says, "The extension and the crib for cattle and the wheat-bin are not susceptible to uncleanness through plagues, and do not join together with plagues, and the plague does not spread into them, and when one pulls down the house, they are not pulled down with it."[75]

6:6 A. The wood and the stones and the dirt are made unclean through plagues,

B. and join together with the plagues;

C. and the plague spreads into them;

D. and when they pull down the house, they pull them down with it.[76]

6:7 A. How is the appearance [examination] of the plague?

B. [There may be] doubt [as to] whether there is in it a plague-sign the size of two split beans, or whether there is not.

C. [There may be] doubt [as to] whether it is the greenest of green shades [or] the reddest of the red shades.

73. M. Neg. 12:1.   74. *ibid.*   75. M. Neg. 12:4.
76. M. Neg. 12:2.

D. He would come to the priest, and the priest says to him, "My son, Go and examine yourself and return [from your evil ways].

E. "For plagues come only because of gossip, and leprosy comes only to those who are arrogant.

F. "And the Omnipresent judges man only in mercy."

G. Lo, they [plagues] come on his house:

[if] he repents, it requires dismantling; and if not, it requires demolishing.

H. Lo, they appear on his clothing:

[if] he repents, it requires tearing; and if not, it requires burning.

I. Lo, they appear on his body:

[if] he repents, he repents; and if not, "Solitary shall he dwell; outside of the camp is his dwelling [Lev. 13:46]."

J. R. Simeon b. Leazar says in the name of R. Meir, "Even on the arrogant do plagues come, for so we find concerning Uzziah [II Chron. 26:16].'"[77]

6:8   A. One would scrape the dirt which is between one stone and the next, and it would show through in the midst of the house.

B. R. Yosé b. R. Judah says, "In the ground of the house he would remove the dirt to a depth of three fingers, as it is said, 'And he shall cause the inside of the house to be scraped about [Lev. 14:41].'"

C. And so did R. Yosé b. R. Judah say in the name of R. Liezer, "That which grows dim in the second week and disappears — one scrapes it, and it requires birds."[78]

6:9   A. A house in which a plague-spot appeared in its eastern side —

B. one [then] divided it [the house] —

C. and it appeared on its western side —

D. it is adjudged as a single house.

E. [If] one [first] divided it [the house], and it [the plague then] appeared in its [the house's] eastern side, and [then] went and appeared in its western side —

F. it is judged like two houses.

G. [If] a plague-mark appeared between a plank and the wall, and [or] between a hanging and the beams — it is not subject to it.

H. [If] one removed it, lo, it is like a folded piece of flesh which is uncreased and like the private places which have been revealed.[79]

6:10   A. There is a more strict rule applying to dismantling than to tearing down, and to tearing down than to dismantling.

B. As to dismantling :

C. A stone which is in the corner, when one removes it, he removes the entire thing.

---

77. M. Neg. 12:5.   78. M. Neg. 13:1.   79. ibid.

·

D. When he tears down [the house], he tears down his [stone] and leaves his fellow's.

E. As to tearing down:

F. One tears down stones which exhibit a plague-mark and stones which do not exhibit a plague-mark.

G. But when dismantling, one dismantles only stones which have plague-marks.

H. Since, lo, there is [a strict rule] concerning dismantling which does not apply to tearing down, and there is a [strict rule] concerning tearing down which does not apply to dismantling, one has to state [the rule] concerning dismantling, and one has to state [the rule] concerning tearing down.[80]

6:11 A. These and those render unclean through contact and render unclean through carrying and do not render unclean on top of a stone to the nethermost deep.

B. And they are sent forth outside of every town to an unclean place.

C. And even though there is no unclean place there, its place is unclean.

6:12 A. A house which is shut up, from which stones fell off — they are clean.

B. Two houses which are shut up, from one of which one took a stone (and) which one built into the other —

C. and the plague appeared in one of them —

D. it alone is unclean.

E. And R. Leazar b. R. Simeon says, "Stones are like the patch."[81]

7:1 A. That [house] which comes [under the priest's examination] wholly covered by a plague is shut up.

B. [If] it [the plague] stood on it [the house] for one week, one gives it a second week.

C. [If] it stood on it two weeks, or [if] it contracted and [then] spread at the end of a week, lo, one removes all of them.

D. [If] a [primary] plague at the end of a week broke out over all of it — lo, this one dismantles all of them.

E. [But] they do not require him to reconstruct another in its place.

F. And not only so, but even if a plague-mark appeared in it on one side [wall], lo, this one takes down that side.

G. And they do not require him to build another in its place.

H. [If] he built it, and afterward a plague appeared, it is examined afresh.

I. The house is not torn down except when it [the plague] returns after the dismantling only.[82]

80. M. Neg. 13:2.   81. M. Neg. 13:5.   82. M. Neg. 13:1.

7:2 A. A house which is torn down — one saves the wood and the stones and the dirt which he brought to it once it was [originally] built.

B. But one does not save either the wood or the stones or the dirt with which one built it.

C. R. Judah says, "A frame which is built on top of it is torn down with it."

D. Its stones, wood, and dirt render unclean in the amount in which [the bulk of] a dead creeping thing renders unclean.

E. R. Leazar Ḥisma says, "In any quantity whatever."

F. Their ashes render unclean through entry.

G. And R. Simeon declares clean.[83]

7:3 A. He whose hands overshadow a stone, whether above or below, is clean.

B. R. Simeon declares unclean.[84]

C. A loaf of heave-offering wrapped in bast or in paper placed over a stone afflicted with plague, whether above or below, is clean.

D. R. Simeon declares unclean.

E. He who puts his hand into a house afflicted with plague and touched it on the inside —

F. Rabbi declares unclean.

G. And R. Leazar b. R. Simeon declares clean, until he puts in his head and the greater part of his body.

H. And so did R. Joshua b. Qorḥa declare clean, in the name of R. Leazar b. 'Azariah.[85]

7:4 A. A house which is shut up renders unclean on its inside, and the one certified unclean [does so] on its inside and on its outside.

B. This and that render unclean through entry.

C. And stones which have a plague render unclean from their outer sides.[86]

D. A house which surrounds a house afflicted with plague,

E. and so, a tree which shades a house afflicted with plague —

F. he who enters the outer [house] is clean.

G. R. Leazar says, "An olive's bulk of it renders unclean through entry. The whole [house] logically should render unclean through entry."[87]

7:5 A. The unclean person passes under the tree, and the clean one stands [there] —

B. he is clean.

C. He [the unclean person] stands under the tree and the clean person passes —

D. he is unclean.

83. M. Neg. 13:3.   84. *ibid.*   85. M. Neg. 13:4.
86. *ibid.*   87. M. Neg. 13:6.

E. And if he stood [still], he is unclean.

F. A stone afflicted with plague —

G. he is clean.

H. Stones afflicted with plague returned under the tree —

I. he is clean.

J. And [if] they were unbound, he is unclean.

K. As it is said, "His dwelling place" —

L. his dwelling place is unclean.[88]

7:6   A. An unclean cloak of a size of three-by-three-fingerbreadths, but not [of a volume of] an olive's bulk —

B. one put the larger part of it into a clean house —

C. it has made it unclean.

D. And R. Neḥemiah declares clean until one will put the whole thing in[to the house].

E. And a clean [cloak], of which one put three-by-three-fingerbreadths into an unclean house, is made unclean.

F. And R. Neḥemiah declares clean until one will put in the larger part of it.

G. And an unclean [cloak], of which one put even as much as an olive's bulk into a clean house, has made it unclean.[89]

7:7   A. He who puts his head and the greater part of his body into a house afflicted with plague is unclean.

B. A clay utensil, the airspace of which one put into a house afflicted with plague, is unclean.

C. Benches and chairs, the larger part of which one put inside a house afflicted with plague, are unclean.[90]

7:8   A. He who entered a house afflicted with plague with his garments folded up and lying on his shoulder, and his sandals and his ring in the palm of his hand —

B. he and they are unclean forthwith.

C. But if he were dressed in them, they [would have been] clean until he remained a sufficient time to eat a piece of bread.[91]

7:9   A. [If] one was standing inside and stretched his hand outside, and his fellow gave him his sandals and his rings in the palm of his hand, he and they are unclean forthwith.

B. But if he had been dressed in them, he would have been clean until he had remained long enough to eat a piece of bread.

C. [If] he was standing outside, with his sandals on his feet,

D. and he stretched [his hand] inside,

E. with his ring on his finger,

88. M. Neg. 13:7.   89. M. Neg. 13:8.   90. ibid.
91. M. Neg. 13:9.

F. and he stretched them [it] inside —

G. R. Judah declares unclean forthwith.

H. And sages say, "Until he will remain there [for an interval] sufficient for eating a piece of bread."

I. They said to R. Judah, "When his entire body is unclean, he does not render what is on him unclean until he remains for a sufficient time to eat a piece of bread. So when his entire body is not unclean, should he (not) render unclean what is on him before he remains for a time sufficient to eat a piece of bread?"

J. Said to them R. Judah, "The reason is that the power of that which is capable of becoming unclean is stronger to afford protection than is the power of the clean to afford protection.

K. "Israelites receive uncleanness and afford protection for clothing in the house afflicted with plague. But the gentile and the beast do not receive uncleanness and do not afford protection for clothing in the house afflicted with plague."[92]

7:10 A. And how much is a piece of bread? A half-loaf of wheat purchased at three to a *qab*, and three for barley.

R. Simeon would say concerning it, "Two thirds is food for two meals."

For the sages said with respect *'eruvé tehumin*, a fourth is called a half-piece of bread to render the body unfit, half of it is called a piece of bread to eat in the house afflicted with plague.

B. One reclines and eats it with condiment —

C. measured according to the average man.[93]

7:11 A. A leper who entered a house —

B. all the utensils which are there, lo, they are unclean.

C. Said R. Judah, "Under what circumstances? When he entered with permission.

"[If] he did not enter with permission, all the utensils which are there, lo, they are clean until he will remain for a time sufficient to light the candle."

D. [If] he enters a synagogue,

E. they make for him a partition.

F. He enters first and leaves last.[94]

7:12 A. Utensils which are hanging on the wall —

"above ten handbreadths are clean," the words of R. Judah [Meir].

B. And R. Simeon says, "Above four cubits."

C. And R. Yosé b. R. Judah says, "Utensils which are buried in the ground of the house below three fingerbreadths are clean."

D. Rabbi says, "The chest, box, and cupboard which are in the house afflicted with plague, even though utensils are covered in them, they [the utensils] are unclean.

"The well and the cistern which are in the house afflicted with plague,

---

92. M. Neg. 13:10.   93. M. Neg. 13:9.   94. M. Neg. 13:11.

even though they are uncovered — utensils which are in them are clean."[95]

7:13 A. "Whatever affords protection with a tightly sealed cover in the Tent of the corpse affords protection with a tightly sealed cover in the house afflicted with plague.

B. "Whatever affords protection when covered up in the Tent of the corpse affords protection when covered up in the house afflicted with plague.

C. "And the house afflicted with plague is like the Tent of the corpse,"

D. the words of R. Meir.

E. And R. Yosé says, "Whatever affords protection with a tightly sealed cover in the Tent of the corpse affords protection when covered up in the house afflicted by plague.

(F. "And whatever affords protection merely covered up in the Tent of the corpse affords protection when covered up in the house afflicted with plague.)

G. "And whatever affords protection when covered up in the Tent of the corpse even uncovered in the house afflicted by plague is clean."

H. R. Simeon says, "Whatever affords protection with a tightly sealed cover in the Tent of the corpse affords protection with a tightly sealed cover in the house afflicted with plague, and whatever affords protection when covered up in the Tent of the corpse affords protection when covered up in the house afflicted by plague."[96]

7:14 A. A more strict rule applies to man than applies to garments, and to garments than applies to man:

B. In respect to man:

C. A token of uncleanness renders unclean at the first inspection [with a bright spot and quick flesh];

D. he can be made unclean through quick flesh;

E. he can be made unclean through a variegation;

F. he can be made unclean through four appearances [colors] one brighter than the other [while clothing requires the brightest only];

G. and he is liable to bring an offering, and requires birds —

H. none of which applies to clothing.

I. More strict is the rule concerning clothing:

J. That which stands [unchanged] for two weeks in clothing is regarded as unclean;

K. and spreading far [from the original token] in clothing is unclean;

L. and that which breaks over all of the clothing is unclean;

M. and it is sent out of every city, but a man is sent out only of cities encompassed by a wall;

N. and they cannot be purified from their uncleanness;

95. M. Neg. 13:12.   96. *ibid.*

O. and he who purchases a garment from a gentile — it is inspected afresh —

P. which is not the case in man [in whom the spot is completely ignored].

7:15 A. There is a strict ruling applying to man that does not apply to houses, and to houses that does not apply to man.

B. For in respect to a man:

C. a token of uncleanness renders unclean forthwith;

D. and he is made unclean through quick flesh;

E. and he is made unclean through variegation;

F. and he is made unclean through four appearances, one brighter than the other;

G. and he is made unclean through clothing;

H. and he is made unclean in the Land and abroad —

I. which is not the case for houses.

J. More strict is the rule concerning houses:

K. for that which remains for three weeks in houses is unclean;

L. and the spreading which is far [from the original primary sign of uncleanness] in houses is unclean;

M. and that which breaks forth [over the entire house] in houses is unclean;

N. and "it is sent forth" applies to every city, but a man is sent forth only from cities encompassed by a wall;

O. and they cannot be purified from their uncleanness;

P. and he who purchases a house from a gentile—it is examined afresh—

Q. which is not the case in man.

7:16 A. A more strict rule applies to clothing than applies to houses, and to houses than applies to clothing:

B. for that which stands unchanged for two weeks in clothing is unclean;

C. and that which spreads in clothing is burned forthwith;

D. and [clothing] is made unclean in the warp and woof —

E. which is not the case in houses.

F. A more strict rule applies to houses:

G. for houses are subject to uncleanness over an inspection process lasting three weeks;

H. and they are susceptible to uncleanness when colored;

I. and they require birds —

J. which is not the case for clothing.

8:1 A. A leper [who is a priest] does not purify another leper.

B. But he is consulted concerning purities and impurities of his own.

C. And all are fit to declare the leper clean,
even the Zab,

and even an unclean person,

and even a person unclean with corpse-uncleanness.

D. And just as it is a duty to declare them clean, so it is a duty to declare them unclean.

E. And a priest who declared [someone] unclean — it is his duty to declare [the same person] clean, as it is said,

F. "To declare him clean or to declare him unclean" [Lev. 13:59]

G. — inside the Land and abroad.

8:2 A. A hyssop which is fit for the purification-rite is fit for the leper.

B. [If] one sprinkled with it for the purification-rite, it is fit for the leper.

C. R. Eleazar says, "Cedar-wood and hyssop and a red thread which are mentioned in the Torah are [to be articles] with which work has not been done [which have never been used]."[97]

D. Said R. Judah, "I was spending the Sabbath and I went to R. Ṭarfon's house.

"He said to me, 'Judah, my son, give me my sandal,' and I gave him [his sandal].

"He put his hand out the window, and he took a staff from there.

"He said to me, 'My son, with this [staff] I have purified three lepers.'

"And I learned from it [the staff] seven laws:

"That it is of cypress-wood.

"And its head is smooth and planed.

"Its length is a cubit.

"And its breadth is a fourth of the thickness of the leg of a bed, divided one into two, and then two into four.

"They sprinkle, they repeat, and they do it a third time [with the same piece of wood].

"And they purify both while the House is standing and not while the House is standing.

"And they purify in the provinces."

8:3 A. He would bring two undomesticated birds. And what are they?

B. Those that dwell in town.

C. R. Simeon b. Leazar says, "They are *Qibla'ot*."

D. He slaughtered one of them into a clay utensil over living water.

E. He dug a hole and buried it before him,

F. and it is prohibited for use.

G. One immersed [his finger] and sprinkled seven times on the back of the hand of the leper.

H. And some say, "On his forehead."

I. And if he sprinkled blood on him in any place, he has carried out the obligation.

97. M. Neg. 14:6.

J. And thus would he sprinkle on the lintel of the house outside.

K. And if he sprinkled blood on it in any place, he has carried out his obligation.

L. [If] he sent it forth and it returned, even five times [he continues to do so].

M. It is permitted for food and fit for purifying another leper therewith.[98]

8:4 A. R. Yosé the Galilean says, "His eyelids do not require shaving."

B. [If] one shaved and left behind two hairs in his first shaving and went and shaved him a second time [after the week between shavings], only the first shave goes to his credit alone.[99]

8:5 A. The shave of the leper, his immersion, and his sprinkling hinder [the purification-process]. But all the other actions do not hinder [the purification process].

B. The slaughtering of his birds, his sprinkling, and his shaving are in day time, and the rest of his actions are either in day time or in night time.

C. These [three] apply to men, and all the other actions apply to both men and women.

D. These are to be done by priests, and all the other actions may be done either by priests or by Levites.

8:6 A. A leper may engage in sexual relations during the days when he is completely unclean and is prohibited during the days of his counting.[100]

B. R. Yosé b. R. Judah says, "If he is prohibited during the days of his counting, all the more so is he to be prohibited during the days when he is completely unclean."

C. Said R. Ḥiyya, "I said before Rabbi, 'You have taught us, Our Rabbi, that Jotham was born to Uzziah [II Kings 15:5] only during the days of his certification.' "

D. "He said to him, 'Indeed, thus did I state.' "

8:7 A. The two birds of a leper, one of which died, or one of which fled, or one of which turned out to be *ṭerefah* —

B. let him purchase a mate for the second.

C. [If] he slaughtered one of them, but the second turned out to be domesticated, or turned out to be *ṭerefah*,

D. both of them are permitted,

E. and let him bring [new birds] afresh.

F. [If] he slaughtered it,
and its fellow died,
or turned out to be *ṭerefah*,

G. both of them are prohibited,

H. and he should bring two [new birds] afresh.[101]

---

98. M. Neg. 14:1.   99. M. Neg. 14:4.   100. M. Neg. 14:2.   101. M. Neg. 14:5.

8:8 A. If one slaughtered it without the cedarwood and hyssop and crimson thread —

B. R. Jacob says, "Since it was slaughtered not in proper order, it is permitted for eating."

C. R. Simeon says, "Since its slaughter was not in accord with its requirement, it is prohibited for use."[102]

8:9 A. A leper immerses in the court of the lepers.

B. He comes and stands in Nicanor's gate.

C. And R. Judah says, "He did not require immersion,

D. "for he had already immersed on the preceding day."

E. They said to him, "This [which you have said] is not part of the law.

"But whoever enters the courtyard through Nicanor's gate would immerse in that same courtyard."[103]

F. And he would bring his guilt-offering and its *log* [of oil] in his hand and set it up by Nicanor's gate.

G. And the priest stands on the inside and the leper on the outside. And the leper places his hand under the hoof of the beast. And the priest places his hand on the hand of the leper and brings [waves] it from one side to the other and up and down, and places his two hands on it and goes in and slaughters it at the northern side of the altar.

8:10 A. All layings-on of hands which take place in the Sanctuary [require that] forthwith after the laying on of hands come the slaughtering,

B. except for this one, which was at the gate of Nicanor.

C. And all the layings on of hands which are in the Sanctuary took place in the northern side of the altar,

D. except for this one, which was at Nicanor's gate.

E. For he cannot enter the courtyard until some of the blood of his sin-offering and guilt-offering is sprinkled on him.[104]

F. Whether his sin-offering took precedence over his whole-offering or his whole-offering over his sin-offering, what is done is done.

G. [If] his whole-offering took precedence over his guilt-offering, they are offered on the altar and require drink offerings, but they have not completed the fulfillment of their owner's obligation.

H. [If] the sin-offering took precedence over the guilt-offering, it is left to pasture until its visage is disfigured and then goes out to the place of burning.

9:1 A. The guilt-offering of a leper which one slaughtered not for its purpose [his name], or the blood of which one did not place on the thumbs goes to the credit of the altar and requires drink offerings.

B. But it has not completed the fulfillment of the obligation of the

102. *ibid.*   103. M. Neg. 14:8.   104. M. Neg. 14:9.

owner.

C. And he has to bring another guilt-offering to render himself fit.

9:2   A. If one slaughtered it outside of its proper time and outside of its proper place, it is left to rot until its visage is disfigured and then goes out to the place of the burning.

B. And two priests received its blood, one with a utensil and one by hand.

C. The one who received the blood in a utensil receives the blood first, and the one who receives the blood by hand receives it after him, and if he changed [the order], it is fit.

D. This one who received the blood with a utensil received it in his right hand. And this one who received it by hand receives it in the left. And if he changed [the hand for receiving the blood], it is unfit.

E. This one who received in a utensil comes and sprinkles it on the altar. And this one who received by hand comes to the leper. And if they changed [the matter], it is unfit.

F. [If] that which is in the hand is poured out, he should not place [on the leper, blood] from the utensil. And if the blood in the utensil is poured out, he should not place blood on the altar from the blood in the hand.

G. And if there is blood of the soul in another cup, let him go back and receive [blood again].[105]

9:3   A. [If] one gave precedence to the placing of blood on the large limbs in wrong order, let him go back and place blood on the large limbs in the right order.

B. The remnants of the blood which are in the hand would he discard into the sewer.

C. He would empty it out from the *log* and bring it to the leper.

D. Wherever he put the blood, there he puts the oil, as it is said, "On the place of the blood of the guilt-offering [Lev. 14:28]."

E. And even though the blood was changed, one puts it [the oil] on its place [on which the blood had been put], and it is fit.[106]

9:4   A. And up to what point do the laws of sacrilege apply [to the oil]?

B. Until he will place his placing [of blood].

C. R. Simeon says, "Until he will carry out his sprinklings [of blood on the altar]."

D. [If] one gave precedence to the placing of the oil over that of the blood, let him fill it up [the *log* of oil] and go and place oil after applying the blood.

E. [If] one gave precedence to the placing of the blood on the limbs over the seven, and the *log* is poured out, he brings another *log*, and begins from the beginning on the thumb and big toe, after the seven [sprinklings have

105. M. Neg. 14:10.   106. *ibid.*

been done]. [If] the placing of the blood on the limbs was in the wrong order of precedence, let him go and put them on the limbs in the right order.[107]

9:5   A. The remainder of the oil in the *log* is consumed by the males of the priesthood;

B. and that of the hand:

C. one puts it on the head of the one who is purified for atonement.

D. "[If] the *log* is found lacking before the oil is poured out, let him go and fill it up.

E. "[If it is found lacking] after the oil is poured out, let him bring other [oil] afresh," the words of R. Jacob.

F. R. Simeon says, "Even after the oil was poured out, let him fill it up."

G. But if the *log* is found lacking after the blood is sprinkled, all agree that one should bring another afresh.[108]

9:6   A. [If] one had already placed part of the placings inside, and the *log* [of oil] was poured out, let him bring another and begin afresh inside.

B. R. Leazar and R. Simeon say, "Let him begin from the place at which he stopped."

C. [If] he completed the placings inside and put part of the placings on the thumb and big toe, and it was poured out, let him bring another and begin from the beginning on the limbs.

D. And R. Leazar and R. Simeon say, "[Let him begin] from the place at which he left off."

E. And in all cases they are not eaten, outside of the last, which is eaten.

F. And R. Leazar b. R. Simeon says, "They all were eaten."[109]

9:7   A. A leper who was afflicted with plague and went and again was afflicted with plague brings one sacrifice for all.

B. [If] he brought his birds and was afflicted,

C. "Let him bring a sacrifice for each one," the words of R. Eleazar.

D. And sages say, "One sacrifice for all, until he will bring his guilt-offering."

E. [If] he brought his guilt-offering, and was afflicted, brings his guilt-offering and was afflicted,

he brings a sacrifice for each one.

F. R. Simeon says, "One sacrifice for all, until he will bring his sin-offering."

G. If he brought his sin-offering and was afflicted, brought his sin-offering and was afflicted —

H. he brings a sacrifice for each one.[110]

9:8   A. A leper who brought his sacrifice while he was poor and became rich finishes the process in the status of a poor man.

---

107. *ibid.*   108. *ibid.*   109. *ibid.*
110. M. Neg. 14:11.

B. The rich man who became poor completes his purification in the status of a rich man.

C. "Everything follows the man's status at the time of the sin-offering," the words of R. Simeon.

D. R. Judah says, "(After) the man's status at the time of the guilt-offering."

E. But a woman after childbirth who brought her offering while poor and grew rich completes the process in the status of a rich woman, for she does not bring her sin-offering from the same variety from which she brings her whole-offering.[111]

9:9 A. Two lepers whose clay flasks were mixed together — this one gives his to that one, and this one gives his to that one.

B. [If] their birds were mixed up, this one gives his to that one, and this one gives his to that one.

C. [If] their *logs* were mixed up, this one gives his to that one, and this one gives his to that one.

D. And if he sprinkled from both of them for one of them, he has fulfilled his obligation.

E. [If] their guilt-offerings were mixed up, this one is slaughtered for the sake of one of them, and this one is slaughtered for the sake of one of them, and he sprinkles from this one for both of them.

F. [If] their sin-offerings were mixed up, this one is slaughtered for the sake of one of them, and this one is slaughtered for the sake of one of them.

G. [If] one of the sin-offerings died, let them bring a sin-offering in partnership, and one makes a condition concerning it, and it is eaten.

H. [If] one of the lepers died, both of them [the animals] die, and the [survivor] brings two afresh.

I. [If] the blood of one of them was sprinkled, and one of the lepers died

J. this is what the men of Alexandria asked R. Joshua.

K. He said to them, "He cannot bring a sin-offering of a beast, for the sin-offering of a beast does not come in a case if doubt.

L. "And a sin-offering of fowl he cannot bring, for a rich man who brought the sacrifice of a poor man has not carried out his obligation.

M. "Lo, how does he behave?

N. "Let him write his property over to someone else and bring the sacrifice of a poor man.

O. "And it comes out that the poor man brings the sin-offering of fowl."

P. R. Joshua said to them, "Now you have asked something of sagacity."[112]

---

111. *ibid.*   112. M. Neg. 14:13.

PARAH

1:1 A. A bullock twenty-four months and one day old — lo, this is a fully grown bullock.

B. And R. Leazar says, "They give it thirty days after the twenty-four months.

C. "For every place in which, 'A bullock of the herd' is said, [the reference is to one which is] two years old.

D. "[But] bullock plain [without further explanation] is three years to five years old."

E. R. Yosé the Galilean says, "Bullocks are two years old, as it is said, 'A (bullock) two [years old] bullock of the herd will you take for purification-offering' [Num. 8:8]."

F. They said to him, "It does not say 'two' [years old], but 'second' [in ordinal relationship] to the first.

G. "Just as the first is not eaten, so the second is not eaten."

H. Said R. Simeon, "To what is a purification-[offering] likened? To a paraclete, who enters in to appease [the judge]. Once the paraclete has accomplished appeasement, then the gift is brought in."[1]

1:2 A. Rabbi says, "Why does Scripture say, 'A two [year old] bullock of the herd will you take for a purification-offering' [Num. 8:8]?

B. "If it is to teach that they are two [bullocks], lo, it already has been said, 'And he will prepare the one as a purification-offering and the one as a whole-offering' [Num. 8:12].

C. "Might one think that the purification-offering takes precedence over the whole-offering in every aspect of the rite?

D. "Scripture says, 'And a second bullock of the herd will you take for the purification-offering.'

E. "Or, 'A second bullock of the herd will you take for a purification-offering' —

F. "Might one think that the whole-offering should take precedence over the purification-offering in every aspect of the rite?

G. "Scripture says, 'And he will prepare the one as a purification-offering and the one as a whole-offering to the Lord' [Num. 8:12].

H. "How so? The blood of the purification-offering takes precedence over the blood of the whole-offering, because it appeases [the Lord]. The limbs of the whole-offering take precedence over the pieces of the purification-offering, because they are wholly burned up in the fire."

1:3 A. R. Simeon says, "Why does Scripture say, 'And a second bullock

---

1. M. Par. 1:2.

171

of the herd will you take for the purification-offering' [Num. 8:8]?

B. "If it is to teach that they are two, lo, it already has been said, 'And he will prepare the one as a purification-offering and the one as a whole-offering to the Lord' [Num. 8:12]. If so, why is it said, 'And a second bullock of the herd will you take for a purification-offering' [Num. 8:8]?

C. "Might one think, the purification-offering is consumed by the Levites?

D. "Scripture says, 'Second.'

E. "Second to the whole-offering.

F. "Just as the whole-offering is not consumed, so the purification-offering is not· consumed."

1:4 A. In like manner:

B. Said R. Yosé, "'They that had come from the captives of exile offered up whole-offerings to the God of Israel, twelve-bullocks for all Israel, ninety-nine rams, seventy-seven lambs, and, as a purification-offering, twelve he-goats — all this is a burnt-offering for the Lord' [Ezra 8:35].

C. "Is it possible that the purification-offering is a burnt-offering?

D. "But just as the burnt-offering is not eaten, so the purification-offering is not eaten."

E. And so did R. Judah say [that] they brought them on account of idolatry.

1:5 A. R. Simeon says, "In every place in the Torah in which heifer is mentioned without further specification, it means one year old, and a heifer and a lamb [are also to be] one year old [Lev. 9:3]. Of the herd — two years old, as it is said, 'Take for yourself a heifer of the herd for a purification-offering and a ram for a burnt-offering' [Lev. 9:2].[2]

B. "Perfect — in respect to years.

"And perfect — free of every sort of blemish."

C. R. Yosé says, "Three atonement-offerings [come] from the bullocks, and three from the rams, and three from the goats.

D. "Three [come] from the bullocks: A bullock which comes with the unleavened bread.

"And the bullock of the Day of Atonement.

"And the heifer whose neck is broken.

E. "Three [come] from the rams:

"A guilt-offering because of a certain sin,

"And a suspensive guilt-offering.

"And a female sheep of the individual.

F. "Three [come] from the goats:

"The goats of the festivals.

"And the goat of the Day of Atonement.

2. *ibid.*

"And the goat of the prince."

1:6   A. "Lambs a year old which are mentioned in the Torah are three hundred and sixty-five [days old], one for each of the days of the solar year," the words of Rabbi.

B. And sages say, "From the first of Nisan to the first of Nisan, from the ninth of Ab to the Ninth of Ab. [If it] is a leap year, it is a leap year for it."

1:7   A. A year which is stated with reference to the houses of cities encompassed by a wall, and years said with reference to the field of possession, and the six [years] spoken of with reference to the Hebrew slave, and all other references to years with respect to the son and daughter — all are from [birth] day to [birth] day.

B. Required whole-offerings of the individual are suitable from the thirtieth day and onward, and even on the thirtieth day.

C. And if they offered them up on the eighth day, they are suitable.

1:8   A. R. Eleazar says, "The Passover is suitable only from the thirtieth day of its birth and onward."

B. This is the general principle which R. Eleazar stated:

C. "Any animal concerning which 'a year old' is said is acceptable from the thirtieth day and onward.

D. "But if one offered it up on the eighth day, it is suitable."

E. With reference to a firstling on which, at the moment of birth, a blemish appeared, one may slaughter and eat it even on the very day on which it is born.[3]

2:1   A. R. Eliezer says, "It is not purchased from the gentiles."

B. They said to him, M'ŚH W, "They purchased it from gentiles in Sidon, and it was called Romah."

C. R. Judah says, "They guard it with care that one not do with it any sort of labor at all."

D. Said they to him, "If so, the matter has no limit. But it is presumed to be suitable."[4]

E. R. Meir says, "A cow whose eyeballs are black, if there is no other cow which is like it, is unfit."[5]

2:2   A. [If] its horns and hoofs were removed and the marrow with them, it is unfit.

B. One [born by Caesarean section] from the side is unfit.

C. And R. Simeon declares fit.

D. The hire [of the harlot] and the price [of a dog] are unfit.

E. R. Eliezer declares fit.

F. Since it is said, "You will not bring the harlot and the price of the dog

3. M. Par. 1:4.   4. M. Par. 2:1.   5. M. Par. 2:2.

to the house of the Lord your God" [Deut. 23:18] —

.G. this one does not come to the house.[6]

2:3 A. Any sort of labor on account of which they are liable in connection with Holy Things renders unfit in the case of the cow.

B. [If] one brought it in to the [threshing] team [to suck], and it [accidentally] threshed with its mother, it is fit.

C. And if it is so that it will [both] suck and thresh, it is unfit.

D. This is the general principle: Whatever is for its own necessity is suitable, and for some other necessity [than its own] is unfit.[7]

2:4 A. And the yoke renders unfit whether it is used for actual work or not for actual work.

B. It may be redeemed for any blemish whatsoever.

C. [If] it died, it may be redeemed.

D. [If] one slaughtered it, it may be redeemed.

E. [If] one found another more beautiful than it, it may be redeemed.

F. [If] one [already] had slaughtered it on its wood-pile, it may not ever be redeemed.

G. If its price comes from the heave-offering [appropriation] of the chamber [of the Temple treasury], [if the beast is redeemed, the funds] go to the heave-offering of the chamber [of the Temple treasury].

2:5 A. A more strict rule applies to the cow than to Holy Things and to Holy Things which does not apply to the cow.

B. [Supply, following Sens to M. Parah 1:1 and *TR* III, p. 214:] For the cow is suitable only when red, and any sort of labor renders it unfit, which is not the case with Holy Things. And more strict is the rule applying to Holy Things, for Holy Things are redeemed only on account of a permanent blemish, and do not go forth for secular use, [for example] to be sheared, and to be worked, and the person who shears them or who does work with them incurs forty stripes, which is not the case with the cow. More strict is the rule concerning the heifer [whose neck is to be broken] than that which applies to Holy Things, and [more strict is the rule applying to] Holy Things than that applying to the heifer.

C. For as to a heifer, age renders [it] unfit,

D. and labor renders it unfit,

E. which is not the case with Holy Things.

F. For Holy Things are redeemed only for a permanent blemish, and never go forth for ordinary use, to be sheared, and to be worked.

G. And the one who shears and the one who works them, lo, this one is smitten with forty stripes, which is not the case with the heifer.

2:6 A. [More strict is the rule] concerning the cow than applies to the heifer, and [more strict is the rule] concerning the heifer than applies to the

6. *ibid.*   7. M. Par. 2:3.

cow.

    B. For the cow is suitable only if it is red,

    C. and blemishes render it unfit,

    D. And [if] one did work with it, it is unfit,

    E. which is not the case with the heifer.

    F. More strict is the rule applying to the heifer.

    G. For as to the heifer, age renders it unfit,

    H. which is not the case with the cow.

2:7   A. [If] there were on it two black hairs or white ones in one follicle, it is unfit. In two follicles — it is fit.

    B. R. Judah says, "Even in two follicles, and they are opposite [adjacent to] one another, it is unfit."

    C. [If] there were on it two hairs —

    D. their root is red, and their head black —

    E. R. Yosé ben Hammeshulam says, "One shaves the top and does not reckon with the possibility that he is liable on account of shearing."[8]

3:1   A. What is the difference between the priest who burns the cow and the priest of the Day of Atonement?

    B. The priest of the Day of Atonement — his separation is in a state [or, for the sake] of sanctity, and his brothers, the priests, touch him.

    C. The priest who burns the cow — his separation is in a state [for the sake] of cleanness, and his brothers, the priests, do not touch him,

    D. except for those who help him,

    E. because he sprinkles.[9]

3:2   A. Courtyards were in Jerusalem, built on top of stone, and under them was a hollow, because of the grave in the depths.

    B. They bring pregnant women, who give birth there and raise their sons there,

    C. until they are seven or eight years old.

    D. And they bring oxen,

    E. and on top of them are doors.

    F. And the children sit on top of them.

    G. R. Judah says, "Oxen with broad bellies, so that the feet of the youngsters should not protrude and become unclean by reason of the grave in the depths."

    H. And all agree that the youngsters require immersion.[10]

3:3   A. They said before R. 'Aqiva in the name of R. Ishmael, "Stone cups were suspended from the horns of the oxen. When the oxen kneeled down to drink, the cups were filled up."

    B. He said to them, "Do not give the *Minim* a chance to cavil after you."[11]

8. M. Par. 2:5.   9. M. Par. 3:1.   10. M. Par. 3:2.   11. *ibid.*

3:4 A. They came to the gate which opens out from the court of the women to the rampart.

B. And stone flasks were set up along the wall of the stairs of the woman's court, and [with] their covers of stone visible to the rampart,

C. and in them were ashes of every cow which they had burned,

D. as it is said, "And it will be for a testimony of the children of Israel" [Num. 19:9].[12]

3:5 A. One hits the male and it starts backward.

B. And ash was poured out.

C. He takes and mixes from that which is poured out.

D. "These rites they did when they came up from the exile," the words of R. Judah.

E. R. Simeon says, "Their ashes went down with them to Babylonia and came up with them."

F. They said to him, "Was it not made unclean in the land of the gentiles?"

G. He said to them, "They decreed uncleanness on the land of the gentiles only after they came up from the Exile."[13]

3:6 A. Ishmael b. Phiabi — two, one in the status of one who had immersed on the selfsame day, and one in the status of one upon whom the sun has set [and who therefore is completely clean].

B. About this one which has done in the status of one who had immersed on the selfsame day, they engaged in argument with him.

C. He said to him [them], "Tithe is eaten by one who had immersed on the same day, but heave-offering by one upon whom the sun has set.

D. "Tithe, which is eaten by one who had immersed on the same day— all the more so do they add a degree of sanctity to it.

E. "Most Holy Things are eaten inside the veils, and lesser Holy Things are eaten outside the veils.

F. "Lesser Holy Things, which are eaten outside the veils — all the more so do they add to them a degree of sanctity.

G. "Most Holy Things are eaten on one day, and Lesser Holy Things are eaten over a period of two days.

H. "Lesser Holy Things, which are eaten over a period of two days—all the more so do they add to them a degree of sanctity."

I. They said to him, "If we preserve them [the ashes prepared by you in perfect cleanness], we give a bad name to the former generations, for they will say that they [who used ashes of the rite done by a *ṭebul yom*] are unclean."

J. They decreed concerning it and poured it out, and he went and did another in the status of one who had immersed on the same day.[14]

---

12. M. Par. 3:3.   13. *ibid.*   14. M. Par. 3:5.

3:7 A. They would make a causeway from the Temple Mount to the Mount of Olives, arches upon arches, an arch directly above each pier, because of the grave in the depths.

B. R. Eliezer says, "There was there no causeway, but pillars of marble were set up there, and planks of cedar on top of them."

C. And the cow did not need to go out on the causeway [being insusceptible anyhow].[15]

D. And they made the priest who burns the cow unclean,

E. because of the Sadducees, so that they should not say that it is done by someone upon whom the sun has set for the completion of his purification.[16]

3:8 A. WM'ŚH B: A certain Sadducee had awaited sunset [for purification] and [then] came to burn the cow.

B. And Rabban Yoḥanan ben Zakkai became cognizant of his intention, and he came and placed his two hands on him and said to him, "My lord, High Priest. How fitting are you to be high priest! Now go down and immerse one time."

C. He went down and immersed and emerged. After he came up, he [Yoḥanan] tore (on) his ear [rendering him unfit to serve].

D. He said to him, "Ben Zakkai — when I have time for you."

E. He said to him, "When you have time."

F. Not three days passed before they put him in his grave.

G. His father came to Rabban Yoḥanan ben Zakkai and said to him, "Ben Zakkai, my son did not have time."[17]

3:9 A. [The spaces beneath] the place of its pit and its woodpile and the house of immersion were hollow, because of a grave in the depths.

B. They bound it with a rope of bast and put it onto the wood pile.

C. And some say, "It went up with a contraption."

D. R. Eliezer b. Jacob says, "They made a causeway on which it ascended."

E. Its head was to the south and its face to the west.[18]

3:10 A. How does he carry out the rite?

B. He slaughters with his right hand and receives the blood with [the palm of] his left hand,

C. And sprinkles with his right finger.

D. And if he changed [hands], it is unfit.

E. R. Judah says, "He would slaughter with his right hand and [then] put the knife [down] before him or [give it] to this one who stands at his side,

F. "and he receives the blood with [the palm of] his right hand,

15. M. Par. 3:6.   16. M. Par. 3:7.   17. *ibid.*
18. M. Par. 3:9.

"and puts it into his left hand,

"and sprinkles with his right finger,

"and if he changed [hands], it is unfit."

G. [If] it splashed from his hand when he sprinkles, whether outside its pit or outside its wood-pile, it is unfit.

H. R. Eliezer b. Jacob says, "Outside its pit — it is unfit.

I. "Outside its wood-pile — he should not bring it back.

J. "And if he brought it back, it is fit.

K. "And if he brought the blood which is in his hand outside and [then] put it back, it is fit."[19]

3:11 A. [If] some of its skin, its flesh, or its hair burst outside its pit — let him put it back.

B. And if he did not put it back, it is unfit.

C. [If it burst] outside its wood-pile,

D. lo, this one adds wood to it and burns it in its place.

E. R. Eleazar [Sens: b. R. Simeon] says, "An olive's bulk [of skin, flesh, or hair] spoils [the rite]; less than an olive's bulk does not spoil [the rite and need not be put back]."[20]

3:12 A. [If] its horn or its hoof or its excrement burst, one does not have to restore it,

B. for something which does not spoil the cow when it is alive does not spoil it when it is being burned.

C. And R. Leazar b. R. Simeon adds, "Shall I throw? Shall I throw? And shall I throw?"

D. And they say to him, "Yes, and yes, and yes" —

E. three times for each thing

F. Whether one tore it open by hand, or whether he tore it open with a knife, or whether it was torn by itself,

G. [or] whether one threw [the wool, hyssop, and wool] into its body, or whether one threw [them] into its pyre,

H. (or) whether one threw the three things all at once, or whether one threw the three of them one after the other,

I. it is suitable.

J. [If] one threw them in before the flame had caught most of it, or after it had been made into ashes, it is unfit.[21]

3:13 A. [If] one took a bone or a black cinder and mixed [the purification-water] with it, lo, this one has done nothing.

B. If there is on it dirt of any amount from its body, one crushes it and mixes, and it is suitable.[22]

3:14 A. And they divided it into three parts.

---

19. *ibid.*   20. M. Par. 3:11.   21. *ibid.*
22. *ibid.*

B. One part one places on the Rampart.

C. And one part is placed on the Mount of Olives.

D. And one part is divided among all the watches.

E. [From] this which is divided among all the watches did Israelites sprinkle.

F. [With] this which was put on the Mount of Olives did the priests mix [the purification-water].

G. And this one which was placed on the Rampart did they keep, as it is said, "And it shall be for a testimony of the children of Israel. It is for water for purification of impurity" [Num. 19:9].[23]

4:1   A. A cow is not made unsuitable if it is left overnight.

B. And even if one slaughtered it one day and burned it the next day, lo, this is suitable.

C. [If] one sprinkled by night, his sprinkling is unfit.

D. And even if all of them [but one] were by day, and one was by night, his sprinkling is unfit.

E. [If] one sprinkled with a utensil [instead of with his index finger], his sprinkling is unfit.

F. And even if all of them [but one] were by hand, and one of them was with a utensil, his sprinkling is unfit.

G. [If] one sprinkled with his left hand, his sprinkling is unfit.

H. And even if all of them [but one] were with the right [index finger], and one was with the left, his sprinkling is unfit.

4:2   A. [If] seven priests sprinkled at once, their sprinkling is unfit.

B. [If they did so] one after the other, their sprinkling is suitable.

C. Sprinklings with reference to the cow which one sprinkled not for their own name, or which were not properly directed [to the door of the Holy of Holies], or one of which was lacking, or [if] one dipped [his finger] one time and sprinkled twice, [or dipped] two times and sprinkled once, lo, these are unfit.[24]

4:3   A. Eight from seven — if it is a priest who did [other] work with it, it is unfit.

B. But if another priest [did it], it is fit.

C. [If] a mourner before the kin's burial [or] one who was lacking in atonement burned it, it is suitable.

D. Joseph the Babylonian says, "A mourner before the kin's burial is suitable. One who lacks atonement is unsuitable."[25]

4:4   A. [If] one whose hands and feet were not washed burned it, it is unsuitable.

B. And R. Eleazar b. R. Simeon declares fit,

23. *ibid.*   24. M. Par. 4:1—2.   25. M. Par. 4:2.

C. as it is said, "When they come to the Tent of Meeting, they will wash in water and not die" [Ex. 30:20] — lo, the washing of the hands applies only inside [the Temple court, and not on the Mount of Olives].[26]

4:5   A. R. Yosé the Galilean says, "The sacrifices which our fathers offered on Mount Sinai did not require flaying and cutting up, for flaying and cutting up apply only from the time of the giving of the Torah and thereafter."

4:6   A. The burning of the cow and its sprinklings [are done] by the high priest, and all of the other aspects of its rite [are done] by an ordinary priest.

B. "It is said, 'And you will give it to Eleazar the Priest' [Num. 19:3] — it [is burned by] Eleazar, who is prefect, but all other cows [in the future are burned] by an·ordinary priest,'" the words of R. Meir.

C. R. Yosé b. R. Judah and R. Simeon and R. Eliezer b. Jacob say, "It [is done] by Eleazar, who is prefect, and all other cows [are offered up] even by the high priest."

D. Its requirement is with the four white garments of an ordinary priest [even if the high priest does it].

E. [If] one did it in the golden garments or in the secular garments, it is unfit.[27]

4:7   A. His disciples asked Rabban Yoḥanan b. Zakkai, "A cow — in [what garments] is the rite carried out?"

B. He said to them, "In golden garments [of the high priest]."

C. They said to him, "You have taught us, 'In white garments.'"

D. He said to them, "Well have you spoken. And a deed which my own hands did, and my own eyes witnessed — and I forgot [the rule] — when my ears hear [the rule], all the more so [should I remember it]."

E. Not that he did not know, but he wanted to stimulate the disciples.

F. And there are those who say they asked Hillel the Elder.

G. Not that he did not know, but that he wanted to stimulate the disciples.

H. For R. Joshua says, "He who repeats but does not work [at remembering the tradition] is like a man who sows and does not harvest.

I. "And one who learns Torah and forgets is like a woman who bears and buries."

J. R. 'Aqiva says, "A song is me, always a song."[28]

4:8   A. They do not burn two cows in one pit.

B. After the ashes are formed, one may bring another and burn on top of it and need not be concerned.

C. [If] one burned it in two halves, one after the other —

D. said Rabbi, "I say in this case that it is suitable."[29]

26. M. Par. 4:1.   27. ibid.   28. ibid.
29. M. Par. 4:2.

4:9   A. A cow to which an invalidity happened, before it was made invalid, renders clothing unclean. After it was made invalid, it does not make clothing unclean.

B. R. Simeon says, "Whether before or after it was made unsuitable, it does not render clothing unclean, because it is adjudged in accord with its ultimate disposition."

C. Said R. Simeon, "Hananiah b. Gamaliel happened to find me [or, I found] in Sidon, and he said, 'If a matter of unsuitability happened to it, what is the law?'

D. "I said to him, 'Before it is made unsuitable, it renders clothing unclean. After it is made unsuitable, it does not make clothing unclean.'

E. "He said to me, 'And is it not so that, in your name, R. Leazar said to me, 'Whether it is before, or whether it is after it is made unsuitable, it [supply: does not] make clothing unclean, because it is adjudged in accord with its ultimate disposition'?

F. "And I said to him, 'That is not what I said. But whether I said it or whether I did not say it, the matters thus appear to me [to be sound].'"[30]

4:10   A. At all times do they add wood to it.

B. Said R. Judah, "Even when they would add [wood], they would add only bundles of hyssop, whose ashes are good and abundant."[31]

4:11   A. Every aspect of the rite of the cow is by day,

B. except for the gathering of the ashes and the drawing [of water] and the mixing [of the ashes and the water].

C. Every aspect of the rite is done by priests [or: by men],

D. except for gathering the ashes and drawing [of water] and mixing.

E. The sprinkling is done by day only.

F. They do not draw [water] and do not mix and do not sprinkle from it before the ashes are formed [or: except with a utensil].

G. All aspects of its rite does work [for some other purpose] render unfit,

H. except for gathering its ashes and sprinkling its water.[32]

4:12   A. There are six distinctive traits [which apply] to the purification [water].

B. They fill and mix the purification-water anywhere [with any sort of utensil (*TR* III, p. 229)].

C. They sprinkle purification-water and purification-ashes anywhere [with any sort of utensil (*TR* III, p. 229)].

D. An 'am ha'areṣ who said, "I am clean so far as purification-water is concerned" — they accept [that statement] from him.

E. [If he said], "These utensils are clean for purification-water" — they accept [that statement] from him.

30. M. Par. 4:4.   31. *ibid.*   32. *ibid.*

F. [If] one immersed in order to sprinkle but did not sprinkle, he eats heave-offering in the evening [after sunset].

G. [If] they saw in his hands purification-water and purification-ashes [not mixed], they prepare clean things with him [or] (on) his garments or (on) his sandals.

4:13 A. An 'am ha'areṣ who brought utensils for his purification — a ḥaber may take [purchase these same utensils] from him for his purification- and for his heave-offering.

B. [If] he brought them for his heave-offering, a ḥaber does not take [purchase] them from him for his purification- and for his heave-offering.

C. [If] a ḥaber said to an 'am ha'areṣ, "Bring utensils for my purification" — the ḥaber accepts them from him for his purification- and for his heave-offering.

D. [If] he brought them for his heave-offering, the ḥaber does not accept them from him for his purification- and for his heave-offering.

E. [If] he brought them for the purification- and for the heave-offering [of a ḥaber], for the purification-offering of a ḥaber he takes them from him, whether they are for him or for someone else, on condition that he not practice deception [needing only the one for heave-offering]. But if he practices deception, lo, these are unclean.

F. And as to utensils for heave-offering, a ḥaber does not take them from him for his purification- and for his heave-offering.

4:14 A. An 'am ha'areṣ who said, "These utensils have I brought for my purification, and I changed my mind concerning them and decided to use them for my heave-offering" — since they were designated [for a baser purpose] in the possession of the 'am ha'areṣ [even] for one moment, lo, these are unclean.

5:1 A. He who brings a clay utensil for the purification [rite] immersed and spent the night with the oven.

B. [If] he spent the night before immersing —

C. Rabbi declares unclean.

D. R. Yosé b. R. Judah says, "[If] he spent the night and afterward immersed, if it was not in the presumption of being guarded, it is unclean."

E. As to heave-offering, one opens the oven and takes [the utensil].

F. [If] one found it open or one of them opened it —

G. R. Simeon says, "From the second row."

H. R. Yosé says, "From the third row."

I. R. Simeon ben Judah says in the name of R. Simeon, "The House of Shammai say, 'From the third row.'

J. "And the House of Hillel say, 'From the second row.'"

K. And this is the first Mishnah.

L. Our rabbis have said, "One [an 'am ha'areṣ] opens and takes and is not held back.

M. "And the *ḥaber* comes even after three days and takes [a pot out]."[33]
5:2   A. [If] one *['am ha'areṣ]* removed the cover and [a *ḥaber*] found dirt on the utensils, lo, this one [the *ḥaber*] takes [a utensil].

B. [If however] one of them was [already] taken out, they all are in the possession [domain] of an *'am ha'areṣ*.

C. [In] a place in which they plaster over the half-burned [utensils] with white mud, the *ḥaber* stands and supervises their plastering.

D. The column [of pots] which he supervises is not unclean — but that row only [is clean].
5:3   A. The *ḥaber* stands above and the *'am ha'areṣ* stands below.

B. He pulls [out a utensil with something insusceptible to uncleanness, but does not touch the utensil himself] and gives [it] to him.

C. The *'am ha'areṣ* is believed to say, "I did not make it unclean," because [in any event] he is in the presumption of being guarded.
5:4   A. [If] one filled the bucket to drink [from it] and changed his mind concerning it, [if he changed his mind] before it [the bucket] touched the water and he emptied it out, he needs to wipe it off.

B. [And if] after it touched the water he changed his mind concerning it, he empties it and does not have to dry it off.

C. Rabban Simeon b. Gamaliel says, "He does not even have to pour it out."[34]
5:5   A. [If] one let down the bucket to draw water with it, and the rope slipped from his hand, if before it touched the water he changed his mind concerning it, he empties it out and needs to dry it off.

B. [If] it is still in the water and he changed his mind concerning it, he empties it out and does not have to dry it off.

C. Rabban Simeon says, "He does not even have to empty it out."[35]
5:6   A. A reed which one cut off for [use in collecting the ashes of] the purification [rite] —

B. R. Eliezer says, "He immerses it and does not have to make it unclean."

C. And R. Joshua says, "He makes it unclean and immerses it."

D. [If] one gathered into it purification-water and purification-ashes—

E. [if he did so] before he immersed it, they are unclean.

F. And R. Simeon declares clean.

G. WM'ŚH B: One person cut off his reed in Bet She'arim, and R. Simeon did declare it clean, and sages unclean.[36]
5:7   A. All are suitable for mixing, except for a deaf-mute, idiot, and child.

B. And R. Judah declares fit in the case of the child.

33. M. Par. 5:1.   34. M. Par. 5:2.   35. *ibid.*
36. M. Par. 5:4.

C. R. Ishmael b. R. Yoḥanan b. Beroqah says, "A deaf-mute, idiot, and child who mixed, and others are supervising them — their mixing is valid."

D. A *ṭumṭum* [one whose sex is not known] — his mixing is unfit, because he is in the status of one who might need to be circumcised, and the uncircumcised person is unfit for mixing.

E. An androgyne — his mixing is valid.

F. R. Judah declares unfit, because it is a matter of doubt whether he might be a woman, and the woman is unfit for mixing.[37]

5:8 A. The [broken] sides of wooden utensils, bone utensils, and glass utensils — they do not mix in them.

B. [If] one planed and smoothed them and made them into utensils, they do mix in them.

C. A stopper which one shaped into a utensil is suitable for mixing.

D. The egg of the ostrich is suitable for mixing.[38]

E. Whether one hews [a hole] in the water channel or whether [he hews a] receptacle,

F. even though the water uprooted it and attached it —

G. they do not draw with it, and they do not mix in it, and they do not sprinkle from it, and it does not require a tightly sealed stopper, and it does not render the immersion-ritual pool unclean.

H. [If] one [deliberately] uprooted it and then affixed it to the ground and gave thought to it after its being uprooted —

I. they do draw with it and mix with it and sprinkle from it, and it requires a tightly sealed stopper, and it renders the immersion-ritual pool unfit.[39]

5:9 A. A spring which flows down to a basin, and one wishes to mix in it [the basin] —

B. one stops it [the water] up, and lets it [the basin] dry off, and goes and then leads the water channel [to it] and mixes in it.

C. A trough which is encompassed by holes, if they were mixed [by a connecting channel as wide as] the stopper of a leather skin,

D. one mixing serves all of them,

E. and if not, they require mixing for each one separately.

F. R. Judah says in the name of R. Leazar, "[If] one made for it a brim of mud to lead the water,

G. "whether it may be moved with it, or whether it may not be moved with it, it is suitable."

H. The trough which is in the mud, if it is moved with it, it [the water in the mud trough] is suitable, and if not, it [the water in the mud trough] is unsuitable.

5:10 A. Two stones which one placed near one another and made into a

37. *ibid.*   38. M. Par. 5:5—6.   39. M. Par. 5:7.

trough,

B. and so two kneading troughs,

C. and so the trough which was divided —

D. Said R. Yosé, "In this case, I besought the law before R. 'Aqiva.

E. "I said in his presence, 'The two of them are not mixed, for the water which is in the crack is not gathered together in a utensil.'"[40]

F. And if one touched the sponge which is outside the water, it is unfit.

G. And if it fell into water which was mixed,

H. one takes it and rings it out,

I. and the water is suitable.[41]

6:1   A. He who goes to mix [ashes and water], lo, this one takes a key and opens [a door, if need be], or a spade and digs, or a ladder and moves it from one place to another, and it [the mixing] is acceptable,

B. because he is occupied with the mixing.

C. But if, after he took the ash out, he closed the door behind him, it [the water] is unfit,

D. because he is thus carrying out an [extrinsic] act of labor along with it [the mixing process].

E. [If] he cuts off olive leaves, if so that it [the ash] will enter the reed, it is fit.

F. If [he does so] so that it will hold a large quantity of ash, it is unfit.

G. [If] he stuck it into the ground or gave it to those standing by his side,

H. if there are there watchmen, it is suitable.

I. If there are no watchmen there, it is unfit.[42]

6:2   A. [If] one took the ash and saw that it is excessive and put it back [in the reed], it is suitable.

B. [If] he put the ash [into the water] and saw that it is excessive, he takes part of it out and goes and mixes [it] in some other place [another quantity of water].

C. [If] the wind blew the ash and thereby put it on to the water, he dries it off and mixes with it, and it is suitable.

D. [If] one put it into the mixture —

E. R. Simeon and R. Meir say, "He dries it off and mixes therewith."

F. And sages say, "Whatever has touched the water — they do not mix with it [in some other mixture]."[43]

6:3   A. [If] one splashed water with his hand and with his feet and with the clay sherds, not with a trough [a utensil] — it is unsuitable, because the water was not drawn with a utensil.

40. M. Par. 5:9.   41. M. Par. 6:3.   42. M. Par. 6:1.
43. M. Par. 6:2.

B. But if the jar broke and one splashed it out with his hands, feet, and clay sherds, not with a trough, it is suitable, because it was [originally] drawn with a utensil.

C. [If] he put in the ash and afterward put in the water, it is unfit.

D. And R. Simeon declares fit.

E. R. Simeon agrees that if he put in the water and afterward put in the ash and saw it, that it is excessive, and then added other water to it, that it needs a second mixing [of ashes].

F. For purification-water does not produce purification-water.

G. But only the putting in of the ashes produces purification-water.[44]

6:4   A. [If] one was standing and mixing and trembled or got tired,

or his fellow pushed him, or the wind pushed him, or another came and mixed [in his place] —

B. lo, this is unfit,

C. as it is said, "And for the unclean they take of the ashes" [Num. 19:17] —

D. until they [explicitly] intend [to do the work] for drawing and for mixing and for sprinkling.[45]

E. If one [simultaneously] drew for himself with one hand and did work with the other hand —[46]

F. and mixed for himself with one and [simultaneously] did work with the other hand —

G. and mixed for himself with one hand and did work with the other hand —

H. drew and mixed —

I. mixed and drew —

J. for himself with both hands as one [simultaneously] —

K. in all cases it is unfit.

L. If one drew for another person with one hand and did work with the other hand —

M. mixed for another person with one hand and did work with the other hand —

N. drew and mixed —

O. mixed and drew —

P. for another person with both hands at once —

Q. if it is for himself, it is fit.

R. And if it is for someone else, it is unfit.

6:5   A. Said R. Simeon, "When [does this rule apply]? When there are guards there.

"[If] there are no guards there, [if] he mixed for others, it is as if he mixed for himself."

---

44. M. Par. 6:5.   45. M. Par. 6:1.   46. T. Par. 6:4B-8, 7:1−3 serve M. Par. 7:1−4.

B. [If] he drew for himself with his two hands at once, for a single mixture, it is unfit.

C. In the case of two mixtures, it is fit.

D. [If] one mixed for himself with his two hands at once,

E. in a single mixture, it is suitable;

F. in two mixtures, it is unfit.

G. [If] one drew and mixed,

H. mixed and drew,

I. with his two hands at once —

J. they are both unfit.

K. [If] one drew for another person with his two hands at once in respect to a single mixture, it is fit.

In respect to two mixtures, it is unfit.

L. [If] one mixed for someone else with his two hands at once, whether this is in connection with a single mixture or whether it involves two mixtures, it is fit.

M. [If] one drew and mixed —

mixed and drew —

with his two hands at once —

the mixture is fit [the owner has done no work], and the drawing [of water] is unfit.

N. This is the principle: Any sort of work with which there is drawing, whether it is for oneself or for someone else, — it [the water] is unfit.

And any sort of work with which there is no drawing of water —

work done for himself — [the water] is unfit;

and for someone else — it is fit.

6:6   A. Whatever is in one's hand and one did work, whether there are guards there or there are no guards there — it is unfit.

B. Anything which is in one's hand and one did not work — if there are guards there — it is unfit.

C. [If] there are no guards there, it is unfit.

D. [If] one drew for himself and for someone else with his two hands at once —

E. they all are unfit.

F. [If] one mixed for himself and mixed for someone else with his two hands at once —

G. that for himself is unfit, and that [mixture done] for someone else is fit.

H. [If] one drew for himself and mixed for someone else —

I. with his two hands at once —

J. they both are unfit.

6:7   A. [If] one drew for himself with his two hands, one after the other [in succession], the first [mixing] is unfit, and the second is fit.

B. [If] one mixed for himself with his two hands, one after the other, the first is fit, and the second is unfit.

C. [If] one drew and mixed for himself with his two hands, one after the other, they both are unfit.

D. [If] one mixed and drew for himself with his two hands one after the other, they are both fit.

E. [If] one drew for someone else with his two hands, one after the other

F. [if] one mixed for someone else with his two hands, one after the other —

G. [if] he drew and mixed —

H. mixed and drew —

I. for someone else with his two hands, one after the other —

J. they all are fit.

6:8 A. [If] one drew for himself and for someone else with his two hands, one after the other,

B. his own is unfit, and his fellow's is fit.

C. [If] one mixed for himself and for someone else with his two hands, one after the other,

D. his own is fit, and that of the other is unfit.

E. [If] one drew for himself and mixed for another with his two hands, one after the other, both are unfit.

F. [If] one mixed for himself and drew for someone else with his two hands, one after the other —

G. they both are fit.

H. [If someone said], "Draw for me, and [then] draw for yourself,"

I. "Mix for me, and mix for yourself" —

J. they are all suitable.

K. "Draw them for me and mix them for me, and I shall draw them for you and I shall mix them for you" —

L. they are all unfit.

M. "Draw for me and draw for yourself, mix for me and mix for yourself" —

N. the first and the last are unfit,

O. and the one in the middle is fit.

P. "Draw for me and I shall draw for you, mix for me and I shall mix for you" — the first and the last are fit and the middle ones are unfit.

Q. And if there are guards there, they are all fit.

7:1 A. An individual who drew five jars of water to mix a single mixture

B. he would take each one out and pour —

C. even though he closed the door behind him,

D. it is fit,

E. because he is occupied with the mixing.

F. And if after he took out the last, he closed the door behind him, it [all] is unfit,

G. because he did [extraneous] work with it [along with the rite].

H. And if there are guards there, he has rendered unfit only that which is in his hand alone [but not what is already mixed].

7:2 A. [Supply: An individual who drew five jars of water]

B. to mix [with them] five mixtures —

C. he would bring out each one and pour it —

D. if there are guards there,

E. this one with [the exit of] which he closed the door is fit.

F. This one with [the exit of] which he did not close the door is unfit.

G. [If] his jar was lying before him, and his fellow said to him, "Give it to me," and he gave it to him, they are both unfit.

H. And if he said to him, "Take it for yourself" — his own is unfit, and that of the other is fit.

I. [If] there were two jars before him, and his fellow said to him, "Give them to me," and he gave them to him —

J. his own is unfit, and that of his fellow is fit.

K. If he said to him, "Take it for yourself" — they are both fit.

7:3 A. He who draws water for his own use and for the purification-rite draws his own first and ties it to the carrying yoke, and afterward he draws the water of the purification-rite.

B. [If] he was drawing water to drink, and it was not possible to have [arrange] them other than both on a single yoke,

C. whether he drew his own first and afterward drew that of the purification-rite, or whether he drew the water of the purification-rite first and afterward drew his own,

D. he places his own behind him and the purification-water before him. And if he placed the water of the purification-rite behind him, it is unfit.

7:4 A. He who brings the rope to the owner —

B. [if] it is on his way, it is fit.

C. [If] it is not on his way, it is unfit.

D. [For] this law did the men of Asya come up on three festivals to Yavneh.

E. On the third festival they declared it fit for them, as a special dispensation [an instruction of the interim].

F. Said R. Yosé, "Not [concerning] this did they give [a dispensation], but concerning one who brings up the rope and goes and arranges it at the end of the process.

G. "They taught him [who asked] that it is suitable in the past and unfit in the future."[47]

47. M. Par. 7:6—7.

7:5 A. He who was, he and his water, in the Tent of a corpse,

B. and his water was in a jar which was tightly sealed with a stopper —

C. just as he is unclean, so it is unclean.

D. [If] he is inside and the water is outside, just as he is unclean, so his water is unclean.

E. [If] he is outside and his water is inside, just as he is clean, so his water is clean.

F. Said R. Simeon, "To such a one as this they say, 'Keep yourself [clean] so that your water should be clean as well.'"[48]

7:6 A. He whose water was on his shoulder —

B. and a minor declared her unwillingness to remain wed, in his presence,

C. and [another] performed the rite of ḥaliṣah, in his presence,

D. and he put aside a stone for someone,

E. and he showed the way to someone,

F. if he stood still [in order to do so], it [the water] is unfit, and if he did not stand still [in order to do so], it is fit.

G. Said R. Judah, "This is the principle: something which is on account of work, whether he stood still or did not stand still — it is unfit.

"Something which is not on account of work, if he stood still — it is unfit; and if he did not stand still — it is fit."[49]

7:7 A. R. Eliezer says, "He who gives his water over to one who is unclean, and the owner did work — it is unfit."

B. R. Judah says in his name, "[If] the unclean person did work, the water is fit, since it remains in the possession of the owner.

C. "[If] the owner did work, it is unfit, since it is in the possession of the unclean person."[50]

D. R. Yosé says, "He who breaks down in order to make a fence and one made a condition with him—

E. "even though he made a fence, it is fit."

F. And so did R. Yosé say, "He who eats on condition of storing up [dates in the harvest], and one made a condition with him — even though he actually did store [dates], it is fit."[51]

7:8 A. He who burns the cow and [he who burns] bullocks and the one who sends out the goat render clothing unclean.

B. "A cow and bullocks and the goat which is sent forth themselves do not render clothing unclean. But they render food and liquid unclean," the words of R. Meir.

C. And sages say, "A cow and bullocks which are burned render food and liquid unclean. A goat which is sent forth does not render food and li-

48. M. Par. 7:10.   49. M. Par. 7:9.   50. M. Par. 7:10.
51. M. Par. 7:12.

quid unclean,

"because it is alive, and that which is alive does not render food and liquid unclean."[52]

7:9 A. R. Simeon says, "A cow which was fit for one moment [at the very least] renders food and liquid unclean.

B. "Bullocks which are burned and goats which are burned which were not fit a single moment [at the very least] do not render food and liquid unclean."

C. R. Judah says, "A cow, once it has been slaughtered, renders unclean through carriage, as do its ashes."

8:1 A. There is thus that which says, "Those things which made you unclean could not have made me unclean, but you [delete: did not] made me unclean."

B. How so?

C. A defective vessel which is full of clean liquid, with an unclean defective vessel overturned on its mouth —

the liquid flowed from the lower one and was made unclean in the airspace of the upper one and went back, rendering the lower one unclean.

D. Lo, this one says, "That which made you unclean did not make me unclean, but you made me unclean."[53]

8:2 A. A Zab who sat on an immovable stone — the food and liquid which are under it are clean.

B. Something on which to lie or on which to sit which is under it is unclean.

C. Lo, this [food, liquid] says, "That which made you [something for lying etc.] unclean could not have made me unclean, but you made me unclean."

D. R. Judah says, "There is thus that which says, 'The things which make the things unclean which make you unclean cannot make me unclean, but you made me unclean.'

E. "How so?

F. "A bowl which is full of clean liquid, and its outer side is unclean. And it is placed on top of a table, and a loaf of [bread of] heave-offering, wrapped up, is on top of the table. [If] the liquid flowed from inside it [the bowl] and touched its outer part, it [the liquid] is made unclean and renders the table unclean, and the table goes and renders the loaf unclean.

G. "Lo, this says, 'That which could make the things unclean which made you unclean could not have made me unclean, but you made me unclean.'"

8:3 A. There is thus that which says, "He made me unclean, and I made

52. M. Par. 8:3.   53. M. Par. 8:6.

him unclean."

B. How so?

C. A *ṭebul yom* who had in his hand flour of heave-offering and unconsecrated liquid which is clean, and he mixed this with that —

D. they are unclean.

E. Lo, this one says, "He made me unclean, and I made him unclean."

F. A pot which is full of clean liquid, and unclean lupines of a size smaller than an egg are placed inside it. [If] they swell up and so are made into the size of an egg, they are unclean.

G. Lo, this one says, "He made me unclean, and I made him unclean."

H. A clean person on the head and greater part of whom fell three *logs* of drawn water, even if he is clean, and they are clean, is made unclean and makes them unclean.

I. Lo, this one says, "He made me unclean, and I made him unclean."

8:4   A. There is thus that which says, "He made me unclean, and I made him clean."

B. How so?

C. An [unclean] patch which one patched on the basket renders unclean at one remove and renders unfit at one remove. [If] one separated it from the basket, the basket renders unclean at one remove and renders unfit at one remove, and the patch is clean.

D. Lo, this one says, "He made me unclean, and I made him clean."

8:5   A. There is thus that which says, "I made him clean, and I made him unclean" [Better: he made me . . .].

B. How so?

C. A pool which contains exactly forty *se'ahs* of water —

one went down and immersed in it —

he is clean.

And the pool is unclean [= unfit].

D. Lo, this one says, "I made him clean, and he made me unclean."

8:6   A. There is thus a case in which he says, "He made me clean, and I made him clean."

B. How so?

C. A box which is unclean with corpse uncleanness, and one brought a nail which is unclean and fastened it [the box] with it [the nail, onto a wall]

D. The box is clean, and the nail is clean.

E. Lo, this one says, "He made me clean, and I made him clean."

F. A clean person who sprinkled the unclean person — the one who sprinkles is clean, and the unclean person is clean.

G. Lo, this one says, "He made me clean, and I made him clean."

H. Three pools — in this one are twenty [*se'ahs* of water], and in this one are twenty [of valid water], and in this one are twenty *se'ahs* of drawn water —

and that holding drawn water was at the side —

I. [if] three people went down and immersed in them, and they [the three pools] were mixed together —

J. the pools are clean, and those that immerse in them are clean.

K. Lo, this one says, "I purified him, and he purified me."

9:1   A. [Water from] all rivers is unfit for mixing the purification-water.

B. R. Judah agrees concerning a spring which wells forth from two separate locations and goes back and is mixed together in a single place, [that it is] suitable.

C. And so did R. Judah say, "A man draws a jar from this spring and a jar from that spring and pours them into a single trough and mixes."[54]

9:2   A. And so did R. Judah say, "A man draws a flask from this jar and a flask [of water] from that jar and puts them into a single trough and mixes."

B. And so did R. Judah say, "The sources of Ṣalmon are prohibited because it ceases to flow in time of war."

C. They said to him, "And were not all the waters of Creation interrupted in the time of war? Siloam — an ant would walk in it [in time of war]."

D. But a spring which emerges on one side in one year and on the other side in the next year, or which flows abundantly during the rainy season and diminishes in the dry season is fit.[55]

9:3   A. All agree concerning a well into which a freshet of rain ran down, that one has to wait until the water returns to its former condition.

B. "A spring which emerges for the first time — one has to investigate [its status]," the words of R. Judah.

C. And sages say, "One does not have [to examine it]."[56]

D. [If] his jug was lying before him, and into it flowed a freshet of rainwater — it is unfit.

E. [If] dew descended into it, it is unfit.

F. [If] dew descended into it by night —

G. R. Eliezer says, "Let him leave it in the sun, and the dew will evaporate."

H. And sages say, "Dew evaporates only ʿ n [the surface of] fruit alone."[57]

9:4   A. Purification-water into which fell spring-water and pool-water and fruit-juice —

B. if the greater part is purification-water, it renders unclean through carriage.

C. And if the greater part is fruit-juice, it does not render unclean

54. M. Par. 8;10.   55. *ibid.*   56. M. Par. 8:11.
57. M. Par. 9:1.

through carriage.

D. Half and half [if the mixture is exactly half purification-water and half fruit-juice] — it renders unclean in carriage.

E. One way or the other, it is unfit for sprinkling.[58]

9:5 A. Said Rabbi, "If [the law is in accord with] the words of R. Eliezer, [then] sprinkling of any amount at all [of purification-water] is acceptable."

B. [If] half of it is from suitable water and half of it is from unsuitable water, then sprinkling renders clean in any amount at all.[59]

9:6 A. [If] there fell into it a kind of spider, an [other sort of] spider, an [other sort of] spider, a fish, a frog —

B. and they burst open, and its color [that of the water] changed — it is unfit.

C. [If] they did not burst open and [if] its color did not change, it is fit.

D. R. Judah says, "Even though they did not burst and its color did not change, it is unfit, because they run."

E. And all agree concerning the locust [which falls into the purification-water] that it [the water] is unfit, because it runs.

F. And all agree that [if] it bursts, it does not render unfit [since it is dry].[60]

G. R. Eliezer and R. Simeon say, "The opinion of Rabban Gamaliel appears [to us to be correct] in the case of the snake, and with his opinion do we agree."[61]

H. Said R. Yosé, "And is it not so that the rulings of R. Eliezer in matters concerning the cow are entirely directed toward leniency?

I. "For R. Eliezer says, 'When he will [actually] turn it up [to drink, but not merely think about doing so].'

J. "And R. Joshua says, 'When he will [actually] drink,

K. "'on account of the liquid of his mouth.

L. "'And if he poured it directly into his throat, it is suitable.'"[62]

9:7 A. Purification-water, the color of which changed on account of itself [naturally], is suitable.

B. [If] it changed on account of soot,

C. or there fell into it a plant producing blue dye, dyer's madder — it is unfit.

D. This is the general rule: Whatever renders unfit through a change of color in a spring renders unfit in the case of purification-water in a flask.[63]

9:8 A. The ash of purification, the color of which changed on account of itself [naturally] and on account of soot, is fit.

B. [If] it changed on account of stove-ash, or there fell into it lime or gypsum, it is unfit.

58. M. Par. 9:7.   59. M. Par. 9:1.   60. M. Par. 9:2.
61. M. Par. 9:3.   62. M. Par. 9:4.   63. M. Par. 8:11.

C. Purification-water which froze over and then went and melted is fit.

D. [If] one made them melt in [by the] fire, it is unfit.

E. [But if he did so] in the sun, it is fit.

F. Said R. Eleazar b. R. Ṣadoq, "[If it is] something in which one keeps something warm on the Sabbath, it is fit.

G. "And [if it is] something in which one does not keep something warm on the Sabbath, it is unfit for the purification-rite."

H. The water which is drained off and which is drawn off is unfit.

9:9 A. A man should not take purification-water and purification-ash and ride on a cow or on his fellow in a situation in which his feet do not touch the ground.

B. But he brings them over on a bridge.[64]

C. All the same is the Jordan and all other rivers.

D. R. Ḥananiah b. 'Aqavya says, "They spoke only concerning the Jordan alone."

10:1 A. Purification-water and purification-ash which are mixed, whether they are unclean or whether they are clean, render the person who is clean for heave-offering unclean through contact and through carrying.

B. R. Yoḥanan b. Nuri says, "Purification-water which has been made unclean — lo, it is like the ash of the hearth."

C. Ash which is unfit which one placed in the water, whether it [the water] is suitable for mixing, or whether it is not suitable for mixing, renders the hands of the person who is clean for heave-offering unclean through contact and through carrying.

D. R. Yoḥanan b. Nuri says, "Ash of the purification-rite which was made unclean, lo, it is like the ash of the hearth."[65]

10:2 A. "Whatever is suitable to become unclean through corpse-uncleanness, even if it is [in fact] unclean, is not regarded as [unclean with] maddaf-uncleanness, and whatever is not [unclean with] maddaf-uncleanness in respect to heave-offering is not [regarded as unclean with] maddaf-uncleanness with respect to the purification-rite. And they did not innovate uncleanness in respect to the purification-rite," the words of R. Eliezer.

B. Said R. Eliezer, "(M'ŚH) [Shema'iah] a man of the village of 'Otenai had in his hand a jar full of purification-water, and he pushed against the door, from which the key, unclean with corpse-uncleanness, was suspended.

"And he came and asked Rabban Yoḥanan ben Zakkai. And he said to him, 'Shema'iah, go and sprinkle your water' [despite shifting the key]."

C. And R. Joshua says, "Even that which is clean — it is subject to maddaf-uncleanness."[66]

64. M. Par. 9:6.   65. M. Par. 9:8—9.   66. M. Par. 10:1.

10:3 A. M'ŚH B: R. Ishmael was following after R. Joshua. He [Ishmael] said to him, "He who is clean for the purification-rite who moved the key which is clean for the heave-offering — what is the rule? Is he unclean or clean?"

B. Said he [Joshua] to him, "He is unclean."

C. He said to him, "And why?"

D. He said to him, "Perhaps there was in its [the key's] hand [power] a former uncleanness.

E. "Or perhaps [if permitted to move something clean] he may forget and move the unclean thing."

F. He said to him, "But even if not, [he is not unclean even if] he most certainly moved it, [for the key does not convey uncleanness if it is moved]."

G. "But your words appear correct in a matter which is susceptible to become unclean with *midras*-uncleanness [in which case:]

H. "Or perhaps there was in its hand a former uncleanness.

I. "Or perhaps he may forget and move the unclean thing."

J. He [Joshua] moved him on to another matter:

K. Said he to him, "Ishmael, How do you pronounce the passage, 'For your love *[dodekha]* is better than wine,' or, 'For your breasts *[dadekha]* are better than wine' [Song of Songs 1:2]?"

L. He said to him, "'For your breasts are better than wine.'"

M. He said to him, "Thus [indeed] is the matter, for lo, its fellow teaches concerning it [proves by analogy how it is to be read], 'Your anointing oils are fragrant' [Song 1:3]."

N. And sages say, "That which is unclean is unclean with *maddaf*-uncleanness, and that which is clean is not subject to *maddaf*-uncleanness."

O. The unclean person of whom they spoke is one unclean with corpse-uncleanness and not one unclean with *maddaf*-uncleanness.

10:4 A. Rabbi says, "One who is clean for the purification-rite who moved the spittle or the urine of one who is clean for the heave-offering rite is unclean.

B. "[If] he moved his blood, lo, he is clean."

C. [If] he moved the insect and the carrion and semen —

D. R. Eliezer declares clean.

E. And R. Joshua declares unclean.[67]

10:5 A. A jar of purification-water which one placed on top of a dead creeping thing —

B. R. Eliezer declares clean.

C. And sages declare unclean.

D. Under what circumstances?

E. In a situation in which, if one removed the dead creeping thing, the

67. *ibid.*

jar would move.

F. But in a situation in which, if one removed the dead creeping thing, the jar would stand [unmoved],

G. and even if a corpse or carrion were touching it on its outer side,

H. it is clean.

I. [If] one set it on top of something on which one sits or lies, or on top of an unclean clay utensil, it is unclean.

J. [If] one placed it on top of food and liquid and on top of a scroll of the Torah —

K. R. Yosé declares clean.

L. And R. Meir [Sens: sages] declares unclean.[68]

M. If one passed it over an oven or over [TR III, p. 249: a clay utensil or over] carrion or over a dead creeping thing —

N. R. 'Aqiva declares unclean.[69]

10:6 A. R. 'Aqiva agrees that if one passed it, in a case of sprinkling, on top of something on which one lies and sits, and on top of an unclean clay utensil, that it is clean.

B. For nothing renders unclean above and below except an olive's bulk of corpse-matter and things which defile through overshadowing.[70]

10:7 A. A jar of purification-water and a jar of heave-offering which touched one another —

B. they are both clean.

C. [If he carries them] with his two hands [simultaneously], they are both unclean.

D. [If they were wrapped] in two pieces of paper, they are both clean.

E. R. Joshua says, "That containing the purification-water is unclean."

F. A jar of purification-water and a pitcher of heave-offering which touched one another — they are both clean.

G. [If one wrapped them up] in two pieces of paper, they are clean.

H. R. Joshua says, "That containing the purification-water is unclean."

I. Under what circumstances?

J. When it is of stone.

K. But if it is of clay [Sens deletes: all agree that the jar of purification-water is clean].[71]

10:8 A. A pitcher of purification-water and a pitcher of heave-offering which touched one another — they are both clean.

B. [If they were wrapped in] two pieces of paper, they are both clean.

C. R. Joshua says, "That containing the purification-water is unclean."

D. This is the general principle which R. Joshua laid down: "Whatever renders purification-water unclean in contact renders it unclean in carrying,

68. M. Par. 10:3.   69. M. Par. 10:5.   70. *ibid.*
71. M. Par. 10:6.

and whatever does not render purification-water unclean [supply: in contact] does not render it unclean in carrying."[72]

11:1   A. Hyssop which is susceptible to uncleanness and utensils which are clean for the purification-rite are afforded protection by a tightly sealed cover.[73]

B. Any matter of doubt which is clean for heave-offering is clean for the purification-rite —

C. except for the hands, since they are a matter of doubt which pertains to the body.

D. A matter of doubt concerning QWPṢYN [?] is clean for heave-offering [and] unclean for the purification-rite, since it is a matter of doubt about that which is unfit.

E. Lattice work is clean for holy things and for heave-offering and for purification-rite.

F. And R. Eleazar says, "The lattice work is unclean for the purification-rite and clean for holy things and heave-offering."[74]

11:2   Said R. Judah, "I too have said thus, but my associates have decreed for me that I should agree with them in a matter of cleanness."[75]

11:3   A. A ring of pressed figs of heave-offering which fell into purification-water, which one removed and ate, even though it is the size of an egg's bulk, whether it is unclean or clean —

B. if so, cleanness does not apply to the purification-rite,

C. for I say, "The one who sprinkles is made unclean, and the one who sprinkles goes and makes the water unclean;

D. "the hyssop is made unclean by the water, and the hyssop goes and makes the water unclean."[76]

11:4   A. Said R. Meir, "Under what circumstances? When he drew it out with a spindle or with a chip. But if he removed it with his hand, he is made unclean and makes the purification-water unclean."

B. R. Yosé and R. Simeon say, "The person who is clean for heave-offering does not make the purification-water unclean."[77]

11:5   A. Whoever requires immersion in water, whether on account of the rulings of the Torah or on account of the rules of the scribes, before his immersion in water renders purification-water and purification-ash and the one who sprinkles purification-water unclean through contact and through carriage.

B. R. Leazar says in the name of R. Tarfon, "The one who is unclean on account of corpse-uncleanness takes utensils which are clean for the purification-rite on a yoke on his shoulder and does not fear [that he renders

72. *ibid.*   73. M. Par. 11:1.   74. M. Par. 11:2.
75. *ibid.*   76. M. Par. 11:3.   77. *ibid.*

them unclean]."[78]

11:6 A. A hyssop taken from an *ashera* and from an idol and an apostate city is unfit.

B. And that which is taken from clean [heave-offering] —

he should not sprinkle with it.

But if he sprinkled with it, it is suitable.

C. They do not sprinkle either with the young shoots or with the berries.

D. And if one sprinkled with the young shoots and entered the sanctuary, he is free.

E. With young shoots [better: berries], and he entered the sanctuary, he is free.

F. With the young shoots and he entered the sanctuary, he is liable.[79]

11:7 A. What are the young shoots?

B. "Calyxes which have not ripened, whereas leafage refers to what has not sprouted," the words of R. Meir.

C. Sages say, "Leafage refers to calyxes which have not ripened, whereas sprigs designate what has not sprouted at all."[80]

11:8 A. They did not disagree about law but about language, for:

B. R. Eliezer says, "They burn heave-offering on their account, but they are not liable on their account for rendering the sanctuary and its holy things unclean."[81]

C. "That which is gathered for purification-water is as if it were gathered for food," the words of R. Meir.

D. R. Judah and R. Yosé and R. Simeon say, "It is as if it were gathered for wood."[82]

12:1 A. Hyssop — when is it suitable for sprinkling?

B. When it has begun to sprout.

C. [If] one sprinkled with it before it has begun to sprout —

D. Rabbi declares unfit.

E. R. Leazar b. R. Simeon declares fit.

F. R. Yosé agrees concerning hyssop that, if in the first instance it has two [stalks], and its remnant one, (that) it is unfit.[83]

12:2 A. The remnants of hyssop are suitable, and the remnants of *sisit* are suitable.

B. One descended and immersed and came up —

C. if there is on him a rivulet of rain water, and he sprinkled,

D. his sprinkling is unfit.

E. And if there is on him dripping moisture, and he sprinkled,

F. his sprinkling is fit.

---

78. M. Par. 11:6.   79. M. Par. 11:7.   80. *ibid.*

81. *ibid.*   82. M. Par. 11:8.   83. M. Par. 11:9.

G. And R. Judah says, "If there are on him liquid-pearls, and he sprinkled, his sprinkling is unfit."[84]

12:3 A. A hyssop, the wood of which one dipped with the young shoots,

B. even though he sprinkles and the water drips from the wood of the young shoot,

C. it is fit.

D. He sprinkles in the normal way and does not scruple lest it [the water] goes forth from the wood.[85]

12:4 A. A hyssop only part of which one dipped —

B. R. Judah declares fit.

C. For R. Judah says, "One dips part of it and goes back and adds to it until he dips the whole thing."

D. [If] one dipped the whole thing, he should not sprinkle a second sprinkling from it, except after he dries it off.[86]

12:5 A. "A flask the mouth of which is narrow — they sprinkle from it a second sprinkling, but not the first sprinkling,

B. "because the water is wrung out," the words of R. Judah.[87]

12:6 A. Three rules did R. Simeon b. Gamaliel state in the name of R. Simeon b. Kahana:

B. "In the times of the priests they did not refrain from sprinkling with a hyssop that was immersed in a flask with a narrow mouth.

C. "And they crack nuts of heave-offering with unclean hands and did not scruple on account of uncleanness."[88]

12:7 A. He who says to his fellow, "Sprinkle on me and I shall sprinkle on you" —

B. R. 'Aqiva declares unclean.

C. And sages declare clean.

D. He who watches over purification-water, even for ten days, lo, he is confirmed in his assumed status [of cleanness] and does not require immersion.

12:8 A. All are fit to sprinkle, except for a deaf-mute, an idiot, and a minor.

B. R. Judah declares fit in the case of a minor.

C. R. Ishmael b. R. Yoḥanan b. Beroqah says, "A deaf-mute, an idiot, and a minor who sprinkled, and others oversee them — their sprinkling is fit."[89]

12:9 A. [If] one intended to sprinkle before him and sprinkled behind him

B. behind him, and the sprinkling went before him —

C. his sprinkling is unfit.

D. [If one intended to sprinkle] before him, and he sprinkled to the sides

---

84. *ibid.*   85. M. Par. 12:1.   86. M. Par. 12:2.
87. *ibid.*   88. *ibid.*   89. M. Par. 12:10.

E. behind him, and he sprinkled to the sides behind him —

F. his sprinkling is fit.[90]

12:10   A. They sprinkle on a man and upon things connected to him, whether he is awake or asleep,

B. and on utensils, whether on the inside or on the outside,

C. except for the fender of the kettle of those that boil olives,

D. for it renders the sprinkling unclean in its airspace opposite the fender,

E. in which case they sprinkle on its outer parts [first].[91]

12:11   A. If one dipped the hyssop for the sake of [sprinkling] something which is suitable for sprinkling and then sprinkled something which is suitable for sprinkling,

B. water which drips is unclean, and suitable for sprinkling [something else].

C. And if there is [more water] on the hyssop, one may repeat [the sprinkling].

D. [If one immersed the hyssop] for the sake of something which is suitable for sprinkling, and sprinkled on something which is not suitable for sprinkling —

1. (and) on the gentile,

2. and on the cow,

3. on a trough of stone,

E. the water which drips is clean,

F. and unfit for sprinkling.

G. And if there is [more water] on the hyssop, he should not repeat [the sprinkling, since the water is unfit].

H. [If one dipped the hyssop] for the sake of something which is not fit for sprinkling, since at the beginning of its dipping it was unfit, so its sprinkling is unfit.[92]

12:12   A. And so did Rabban Simeon b. Gamaliel [Sens: Gamaliel] say to one who sprinkles, "Step back, lest you be made unclean."

B. They said to him, "And did they not slip in front of a window in the public place, trampling there, and they did not refrain, because they said, 'Purification-water which has carried out its purpose does not render unclean.'"[93]

12:13   A. And how much must be in the water['s volume] so that there should be enough for sprinkling?

B. Enough for him to dip the tips of the buds and sprinkle,

C. except for that which the hyssop absorbs.

D. R. Judah says, "They regard them as if they were on a hyssop of

90. M. Par. 12:2.   91. *ibid.*   92. M. Par. 12:3.
93. M. Par. 12:4.

brass,

E. "which does not absorb [water]."[94]

12:14 A. One who is clean for the purification-rite, the hands of whom were made unclean —

B. his body is made unclean.

C. He makes his fellow unclean, and his fellow, his fellow.[95]

D. And as to the outer part of a pitcher:

E. A pitcher of purification-water, the outer side of which is made unclean — its inside is made unclean.

F. It renders its fellow unclean, and its fellow, its fellow,

G. and also the one who sprinkles.[96]

12:15 A. They do not say in connection with the purification-rite, "This is first and this is last." But they are all [in the] first [remove of uncleanness].

B. For they do not count [removes of uncleanness] with reference to sprinkling the purification-water.

C. A piece of dough which is prepared in connection with the purification-rite,

and the dead creeping thing touched one of them,

even if they are a hundred,

they are all first.

D. For they do not count [removes of uncleanness] with reference to the purification-rite.[97]

12:16 A. An Arbelite spindle is a connector for uncleanness and for sprinkling.

B. And one used for spinning flax and of a wick —

C. lo, one should not sprinkle on it.

D. And if one sprinkled, it is sprinkled.[98]

12:17 A. [*TR* III, p. 255, supplies:] All handles of utensils which come from [are attached at] the factory, for example, the handle of the sickle and the handle of the knife, are connected for uncleanness and for sprinkling.

B. All handles of the utensils which are drilled are connected.

C. And R. Yoḥanan b. Nuri says, "Even that which is wedged."

D. "Excrement which is on the toilet-seat is connected for sprinkling, but it is not connected for uncleanness," the words of R. Yosé the Galilean.

E. R. 'Aqiva says, "Whatever is connected for sprinkling is connected for uncleanness, but there is something which is connected for uncleanness and not connected for sprinkling."[99]

12:18 A. The [small] kettle is connected for uncleanness and for sprinkling.

B. The cover of the kettle which is connected by a chain —

---

94. M. Par. 12:5.   95. M. Par. 12:7.   96. M. Par. 12:8.
97. M. Par. 12:6−7.   98. M. Par. 12:8.   99. M. Par. 12:10.

C. The House of Shammai say, "It is all one connector."

D. And the House of Hillel say, "If one sprinkled on the kettle, he has sprinkled on the cover.

"If one has sprinkled on the cover, he has not sprinkled on the kettle."

E. Said R. Yosé, "These are the words of the House of Shammai.

F. "The House of Hillel say, 'It is all one connector.'"[100]

12:19 A. [If] one dipped the hyssop at night — [it is unfit].

B. Not that the water is unfit.

C. But one has to dip a second time.

D. [If] one dipped [the hyssop] at night, his sprinkling is unfit.

E. And the water is unclean because of [being suitable] purification-water.[101]

100. *ibid.*   101. M. Par. 12:11.

NIDDAH

1:1 A. How does a period of twenty-four hours diminish the period from one examination to the next examination?

B. [If] she examined herself after the Sabbath and found herself clean and spent Monday and Tuesday and did not examine herself, and on Wednesday she examined herself and found herself unclean — lo, this one imparts uncleanness in the preceding twenty-four hour period and not from one examination to the next.[1]

1:2 A. How does the period from one examination to the next examination diminish the period of twenty-four hours?

B. [If] she examined herself in the morning and found herself clean and spent the second hour and the third hour, not examining herself, and then at the fourth hour examined herself and found herself unclean — lo, this renders unclean from examination to examination and not in a given twenty-four hour period.

C. And this is that to which they referred, saying, The period of twenty-four hours is diminished by the period from one examination to the next examination, and the period from one examination to the next examination is diminished by the period of twenty-four hours.[2]

1:3 A. A *ṭumṭum* [one whose sex is unknown] and an androgyne who saw [a drop of blood] — sufficient for them is their time.

B. "A female proselyte who saw a drop of blood for the first time, sufficient for her is the time [at which she saw the drop of blood]," the words of R. Judah.

C. R. Yosé says, "Lo, she is like all other women. She renders unclean for the preceding twenty-four hours and for the period from examination to examination."[3]

D. And she who sees a drop of blood [caused] abnormally —sufficient for her is her time.[4]

1:4 A. What is a case of seeing a drop of blood caused abnormally?

1. [If] she was sick and saw a drop of blood —

2. [if] she jumped and saw a drop of blood —

3. [if] her husband hit her and she saw a drop of blood —

4. [if] she was bearing a heavy burden and saw a drop of blood —

B. — this is a matter of an abnormal cause.

C. And what is the sort of case for which her time is sufficient?

D. [If] she sat down on a bed and on a chair and on a bench and was engaged in preparing things requiring cleanness and had intercourse and

1. M. Nid. 1:1.   2. *ibid.*   3. M. Nid. 1:2.
4. M. Nid. 1:6.

205

then got up and saw a drop of blood — he [the husband] is clean, and the things requiring cleanness are clean.[5]

1:5 A. R. Eliezer says, "Four women — sufficient for them is their time: a virgin, a pregnant woman, a nursing mother, and an old woman."

B. Said R. Joshua, "I heard only the virgin."

C. Said to him R. Eliezer, "They do not say, 'He who has not seen the new [moon] should come and give testimony,' but he who has seen it.

"You have not heard, but we have heard.

"You have heard one, but we have heard four."

D. All the days of R. Eliezer the people followed the rule laid down by him. After R. Eliezer died, R. Joshua restored the matter to its former status.

E. And the law is in accord with R. Eliezer.[6]

1:6 A. Who is a virgin?

B. Any girl who has never seen a drop of blood in her life,

C. and even if she is married and had children, I call her a virgin until she will see the first drop of menstrual blood.

D. It comes out that they did not refer to virgin in respect to the tokens of virginity but a virgin in respect to menstrual blood.[7]

1:7 A. Who is a pregnant woman?

B. Once the presence of the foetus is recognized —

C. [Zuckermandel, p. 642, 1. 1, Lieberman, *TR* III, p. 257: Said Sumkhos in the name of R. Meir:]

"Three months, as it is said, 'And it came to pass at the end of three months' [Gen. 38:24]."

D. [If] she was in the presumption of being pregnant and saw a drop of blood and afterward she miscarried something which is not a human foetus — sufficient for her is her time.

E. And even though there is no Scriptural proof of the matter, there is a Scriptural allusion to the matter: "We were with child, we writhed, we have as it were brought forth wind" [Is. 26:18].[8]

1:8 A. A girl who did not reach her time for seeing blood and who saw a drop of blood —

B. at the first and at the second appearance of the blood, sufficient for her is her time.

C. [But when she sees] the third [drop of blood], she imparts uncleanness [to what she touched] during the preceding twenty-four hour period.

D. [If] she missed her flow for three periods and then saw a drop of blood, sufficient for her is her time.

E. And once [a girl] has reached her time for seeing blood, and she saw a

5. *ibid.*   6. M. Nid. 1:3.   7. M. Nid. 1:4.
8. *ibid.*

first drop, sufficient for her is her time, and [after she saw] a second, she imparts uncleanness during the preceding twenty-four hour period.

F. And at the third [period] — sufficient for her is her time.[9]

G. [If] she missed three periods and then she saw a drop of blood, she imparts uncleanness during the preceding twenty-four hour period.[10]

1:9   A. And from what time is a girl likely to see a drop of blood?

B. From the time that she will produce two pubic hairs.

C. Said R. Eleazar, M'ŚH B: "[There was] a young girl in Haitalu whose time had come to see blood and who missed three periods, and the case came before the sages, and they said, 'Sufficient for her is her time.' "

D. They said to him, "It was an interim ruling."[11]

1:10   A. R. Yosé and R. Simeon say, "A pregnant woman and a nursing mother — her time is not sufficient for her until she will miss three periods.

B. "And the days of her pregnancy join together with the days of her nursing."[12]

1:11   A. [If] an old lady missed three periods and then saw a drop of blood — sufficient for her is her time.

B. [If] she [again] missed three periods and saw a drop of blood, [still] sufficient for her is her time.

C. [If] she [again] missed three periods and saw a drop of blood, lo, she is equivalent to all other women. She imparts uncleanness for the preceding twenty-four hours or from one examination to the next.

D. Not [only] that she has settled on a fixed period, but even if she has diminished, [or] she has added to it.

E. [If] she missed three of them and saw a drop of blood, sufficient for her is her time.

F. [If] she [again] missed the three of them and saw a drop of blood, sufficient for her is her time.

G. [If] she [again] missed the three of them and saw a drop of blood, lo, she is like all other women and conveys uncleanness for the preceding twenty-four hour period or from one examination to the next.

H. But that she has established a period for herself.[13]

1:12   A. The four women concerning whom they have said, Sufficient for them is their time — how so?

B. [If] she saw a blood stain and afterward saw a drop of blood — sufficient for her is her time.

C. [If] she missed three periods between one appearance and another appearance of blood and did not see a drop of blood and afterward saw a drop of blood — sufficient for her is her time.

D. [If] she missed three periods during the days of her purifying and did

9. M. Nid. 1:3.   10. M. Nid. 1:5.   11. ibid.
12. ibid.   13. ibid.

not see a drop of blood, and afterward saw a drop of blood, sufficient for her is her time.[14]

2:1 A: "A nursing mother whose infant died during the twenty-four months of nursing imparts uncleanness within the preceding twenty-four hour period.

B. "Therefore if she goes on and nurses her infant, even during a period of five years, sufficient for her is her time," the words of R. Meir.

C. R. Judah and R. Yosé and R. Simeon say, "Sufficient for her is her time only during the twenty-four months in which it is normal to nurse the infant.

D. "Therefore if she goes on and nurses her infant even for five years, only the twenty-four months apply to her, [during which she falls under the rule of] the nursing mother."[15]

2:2 A. "[A nursing mother] whose husband died — lo, she should not be betrothed nor should she be wed until twenty-four months have been completed," the words of R. Meir.

B. And R. Judah says, "Eighteen months."

C. And R. Jonathan b. Joseph says, "The House of Shammai say, 'Twenty-four months,' and the House of Hillel say, 'Eighteen months.' "

D. Said Rabban Simeon b. Gamaliel, "In accord with the opinion of the one who says, 'Twenty-four months,' she is permitted to be wed in twenty-one months. In accord with the opinion of the one who says, 'Eighteen months,' she may be wed in fifteen months, for the milk deteriorates only after three months [of conception]."

2:3 A. "An infant continues to suckle all twenty-four months. From that point onward, he is like one who sucks from an abomination," the words of R. Eliezer.

B. And R. Joshua says, "The infant continues to suck even for five years. If he separated [from the nipple] and returned after twenty-four months, lo, this is one who is like one that sucks from an abomination."

2:4 A. A woman is obligated to care for her child for twenty-four months. The same rule applies both to her child and to one that is given her as a son to suckle.

B. The woman to whom a son is given to suckle should not do [additional] work [while caring] for him and should not suckle another child with him.

2:5 A. An infant who recognizes his mother — they do not give him to a wet-nurse because of the danger to life.

B. An infant sucks from the gentile woman and from the unclean cow, and from any of them does he suck, and even on the Sabbath. [If] he was

14. M. Nid. 1:3.   15. M. Nid. 1:4.

weaned, it is prohibited.

C. Abba Saul says, "We would suck from a clean animal on the festival."

2:6 A. Three kinds of women have intercourse with a contraceptive device: a girl under age, a pregnant woman, and a nursing mother.

B. A girl under age — lest she become pregnant and die.

C. What is a girl under age? From eleven years and one day until twelve years and one day.

D. One younger than that or older than that — one has intercourse in the normal way.

E. Therefore one has intercourse in the normal way and does not scruple.

F. A pregnant woman — lest she make the foetus into a sandal.

G. A nursing mother — lest she kill her infant.

H. For R. Meir did say, "The entire period of twenty-four months one winnows inside and scatters [seed] outside."

I. And sages say, "One has intercourse in the normal way, and the Omnipresent will look out for him, as it is said, 'The Lord guards the innocent' [Ps. 116:6]."

2:7 A. A man should not marry a woman made pregnant by his fellow or one who is nursing the child of his fellow,

B. as it is said, "Do not remove an ancient landmark or enter the fields of the fatherless" [Prov. 23:10].

2:8 A. Any hand which makes many examinations — in the case of women is to be praised; in the case of men is to be cut off.

B. And R. Tarfon says, "It should be cut off [while lying] on his bellybutton."[16]

C. They said to him, "Lo, his belly will be split open."

D. He said to them, "Indeed, I intended exactly that."

E. They drew a parable: To what is the matter compared?

F. To one who puts his finger in his eye, for all the time that he exerts pressure, he brings forth an abundance of tears.

G. Under what circumstances?

H. With reference to seminal emission,

I. But if it is with reference to flux —

J. Any hand which makes many examinations, lo, it is to be praised.

2:9 A. An imbecile [male] — they dunk him and feed him with heave-offering [food] in the evening.

B. And they watch him as to sleeping, and if he went to sleep and got up, he is forthwith unclean.

C. R. Eleazar b. R. Ṣadoq says, "They make him a leather bag, and they

16. M. Nid. 2:1.

put it on him and inspect its contents. If inside it semen is found, he is unclean, and if not, he is clean."

D. They said to him, "You turn out to remove him from a situation of doubt and to place him into a situation of certain [uncleanness], because he ends up being heated by the bag."

E. He said to them, "Yes. Is it not so that in accord with your opinion he is unclean [anyhow]?"

F. They said to him, "You say, 'If semen is found [in the bag] he is unclean, if not, he is clean,' and we say, 'A drop in any amount exuded from him and was absorbed by the bag.' "

3:1   A. "All the women concerning whom sages have said, 'Their time suffices' —

B. "their blood stain [causes them to] impart uncleanness retroactively,

C. "except for the minor who is not apt to see [a drop of blood], for to her the matter of blood stains does not apply," the words of R. Meir.

D. And sages say, "All the women concerning whom sages have said, 'Sufficient for them is their time' —

E. "their blood stain is like their appearance [of blood],

F. "and a minor who is apt to see blood is subject to the rule of blood stains."[17]

3:2   A. Every woman who has a fixed period — her blood stain imparts uncleanness retroactively.

B. For if she sees [blood] not at the time of her fixed period, it imparts uncleanness to objects she touched during the preceding twenty-four hours.

C. Rabbi says, "They ruled more strictly in the matter of the blood stain than in the matter of the appearance of blood.

D. "For the blood stain imparts uncleanness retroactively, and the appearance of blood imparts uncleanness only during the preceding twenty-four-hour period."[18]

3:3   A. "[If] she saw a blood stain and afterward she saw blood, lo, this one takes account of the possibility of flux," the words of R. Meir.

B. And sages say, "She does not take account of the possibility of flux."

C. "She who sees a blood stain — if there is in it sufficient [blood] for it to be divided into three drops for three days, lo, this one takes account of the possibility that it is flux, and if not, she does not take account of the possibility that it is flux," the words of R. Meir.

D. R. Judah b. Agra says in the name of R. Yosé, "One way or the other, she takes account of that possibility."[19]

3:4   A. Said Rabbi, "The opinion of R. Judah b. Agra appears to me sound when she did not examine herself, and the opinion of R. Meir appears

17. M. Nid. 2:3.   18. *ibid.*   19. M. Nid. 6:13.

to me sound when she examined herself."

B. R. Ḥananiah b. Antigonos says, "One way or the other, she does not take account of the possibility [that it is flux].

C. "Should she blame her blood stain on others? It is logical that she should blame her blood stain on herself."[20]

3:5   A. Sometimes blood stains do put a woman into the category of one afflicted with flux,

B. How so?

C. [If] she puts on herself five shirts which had been examined by her,

D. if she saw on them three drops [of blood] on three days,

E. or [if] she saw a blood stain and afterward she saw two unclean days

F. lo, this one takes account of the possibility of flux.[21]

G. [As to the meaning of] "forthwith" they drew an analogy. To what is the matter compared?

H. To the attendant and the witness who stood behind the lintel.

I. Once the attendant went out, the witness forthwith entered.

J. This is "forthwith."[22]

3:6   A. After a time of which they spoke —

B. after the time sufficient for drying, and not after the time sufficient for examination.

C. And what is the meaning of after a time?

D. After sufficient time for the woman to get off the bed and wash her face.

E. R. Eleazar b. R. Ṣadoq explained, "Sufficient time for her to put out her hand and take the lamp [or: test-rag] from under the bolster or from under the chest."[23]

3:7   A. During this period, they are unclean as a matter of doubt and free of the obligation of a sacrifice [sin-offering] but liable for the suspensive guilt-offering.[24]

B. After this time —

C. R. Judah the son of Rabban Yoḥanan b. Zakkai says, "The one who has intercourse with her is free to enter and burn incense in the Temple."

3:8   A. A pregnant woman and a nursing mother — the one who has intercourse with them is clean, and [so in the case of] any woman who has a fixed period.

B. And all other women are unclean in respect to contact, and clean in respect to intercourse.[25]

C. Under what circumstances?

D. When he left her clean.

E. But if he left her unclean, lo, she remains in the presumption of being

20. *ibid.*   21. *ibid.*   22. M. Nid. 2:2.
23. M. Nid. 2:3.   24. M. Nid. 2:2.   25. M. Nid. 2:3.

unclean,

F. until she shall tell him, "I am clean for you."[26]

3:9   A. Blood which is found in the front-hall —

B. they burn heave-offering on its account and are liable on its account for contamination of the sanctuary and its holy things.

C. That which exudes from the room — if it is known that it is blood caused by a blow, it is clean, and if not, it is unclean.

D. [If] it is in doubt whether it is blood of the room or blood caused by a blow, it is unclean.

E. R. Simeon b. Leazar says in the name of R. Meir, "Blood which exudes from the room, even though it is known that it is blood caused by a blow, is unclean."

F. And our rabbis said, "Blood caused by a blow is clean."[27]

3:10   A. It comes out that one rules,

B. there are three matters of doubt concerning a woman.

C. As to [a blood stain on] her flesh, if it is in doubt whether it is clean or unclean, it is unclean.

D. And as to [a blood stain on] her clothing, if it is a matter of doubt whether it is unclean or clean, it is clean.

E. And as to matters of contact and shifting, they follow the majority.[28]

3:11   A. Black as ink sediment — [if] it is deeper than this, it is unclean; [if] it is lighter than this, even like stibium, it is clean.

B. Not that from the beginning of its formation it [black blood] was black, but when it was discharged, it turned black.

C. To what is the matter comparable?

D. To the blood caused by a blow.

E. [For] once it begins to flow, it turns black.

F. Bright crocus color —

G. Like the bright color which is on top, and not on the bottom, on a wet one, and not on a dry one; as one examines it in the shade, and not as one examines it in sunlight.

H. Like earth-water — how so?

I. "One brings dirt from the valley of Bet Kerem and floats water over it," the words of R. Meir.

J. And R. Judah says, "From the valley of Sikni."

K. And R. José says, "From the valley of Jotapata."

L. R. Simeon b. Eleazar says in the name of R. Meir, "Also: from the valley of Gennosar."

M. [As to dirt] which is like them: They examine them when they are turbid, and they do not examine them when they are clear.

N. [If] they became clear, they do not go and make them turbid a sec-

---

26. M. Nid. 2:4.   27. M. Nid. 2:5.   28. *ibid.*

ond time,

O. for there is no limit to water and dirt.

P. Like water mixed with wine: Two parts water, and one part wine, from the wine of the Sharon —

Q. Similar to that of the Carmel,

R. new and not old.[29]

4:1   A. She who produces a piece [a shapeless object] —

B. Sumkhos says in the name of R. Meir, and so did R. Simeon b. Leazar say in accord with his opinion, "They cut it open. If there is blood inside it, lo, this one is a menstruant. If not, she is not a menstruant."[30]

4:2   A. She who produces [an abortion] like a rind, like a hair, like dust, like red flies —

B. Rabban Simeon b. Gamaliel says, "They crush it, together with spit, on the fingernail. If it dissolves, lo, this one is a menstruant, and if not, she is not deemed a menstruant."[31]

4:3   A. Said R. Eleazar b. R. Ṣadoq, "Two cases did father bring from Ṭiv'in to Yavneh.

B. "M'ŚH B: A woman did produce an abortion like red rinds [scabs], and they came and asked R. Ṣadoq about it, and R. Ṣadoq went and asked sages. And sages sent and called physicians, and they [the physicians] said, 'The woman has a wound inside [her body] and therefore she produces [from its crust] abortions like red rinds.'[32]

4:4   A. "ŚWB M'ŚH B: A woman who had an abortion like red hairs, and they came and asked R. Ṣadoq, and R. Ṣadoq went and asked sages, and they went and called physicians, and they said, 'She has a wart in her intestines. Therefore she produces abortions of red hairs.' "[33]

4:5   A. "She who produces an abortion like a beast, wild animal, or bird
. . . ,

B. the words of R. Meir.

C. And sages say, "[She is not unclean] unless it bears human form."

D. Said R. Ḥananiah b. Gamaliel, "The opinion of R. Meir appears preferable in the case of a beast, because the eyeballs of a beast are similar to the eyeballs of man, and the opinion of sages in respect to the fowl, which in no way bear the form of man."[34]

4:6   A. M'ŚH B: A woman in Sidon three times produced an abortion shaped like a raven, and the matter came before sages, and they said, "Anything which does not bear human form is not deemed a foetus."[35]

4:7   A. The facial features of which they spoke may be any one of the

29. M. Nid. 2:7.   30. M. Nid. 3:1.   31. M. Nid. 3:2.
32. ibid.   33. ibid.   34. ibid.
35. ibid.

features of the face except for the ears.

B. The sandal of which they spoke is similar to the sandal, a fish in the sea.

C. Rabban Simeon b. Gamaliel says, "It is like the tongue of the ox."

D. Our rabbis said, "[It is not deemed unclean] unless it bears human form."[36]

4:8 A. And why did they say, A sandal? Is it not so that there is no sandal with which there also is not a bit of embryo?

B. [But they have so ruled because of the] possibility that she will produce with it a male and so be in disarray in respect to a female.

C. Or [because of the] possibility that she will produce two, one [a female child] before sunset and one [the sandal] after sunset, and it will turn out that she counts the beginning of her period of menstruation in accordance with the first and the beginning of her period of menstruation in accordance with the second.[37]

4:9 A. The placenta of which they spoke — in its first stage it is like the thread of the warp, and its head is like a lupine, and it is hollow like a trumpet.

B. And there is no placenta less in size than a handbreadth.

C. Rabban Simeon b. Gamaliel says, "It is like the craw of a hen."

D. And why did they refer to a placenta? And is it not so that there is no placenta without a bit of the child with it?[38]

4:10 A. The umbilical cord is a connector in man, up to handbreadth, to receive uncleanness and to impart uncleanness.

B. But in a beast, it is [TR III, p. 265: *not*] a connector.

C. A caul which goes forth over the skin of the flesh of man, whether alive or dead, lo, this is clean and permitted for enjoyment.

D. And what is a sac, the limbs of which are formed?

E. Abba Saul did say, "At the beginning of its creation it is like a *rashon*-locust.

F. "Its two eyes are like two drippings of a fly.

G. "Its mouth is narrow as a stretched hair.

H. "And his sexual organ is like a lentil.

I. "And if it was female, her sexual organ is like the longitudinal split of a barley-grain. It has no developed hands and feet.

J. "And concerning such a thing it is explained in tradition, 'Hast thou not poured me out as milk and curdled me like cheese? Thou has clothed me with skin and flesh and knit me together with bones and sinew. Thou hast granted me life and favor and thy providence has preserved my spirit' [Job 10:10-12]."

4:11 A. They do not estimate it [the foetus] with water, because the water

36. M. Nid. 3:4.   37. *ibid*.   38. *ibid*.

is hard and disturbs its shape.

B. And they estimate it only in oil, because the oil is soft and makes it clear.

C. And they examine it only in sunlight.

4:12 A. She who produces an abortion which was not formed —

B. R. Joshua says, "It is a valid birth."

C. And sages say, "It is not a valid birth."

D. R. Ishmael b. R. Yosé says in the name of his father, "They cut it up. If there is blood in it, lo, this one is deemed to be a menstruant, and [as to] the flesh, lo, it is a valid birth."[39]

4:13 A. "[If] the placenta is in the house, the house is unclean," the words of R. Meir.

B. R. Judah and R. Yosé and R. Simeon say, "The house is clean."

C. They said to R. Meir, "Do you not agree that if she brought it out in a bowl to the outer house, that it is clean?"

D. He said to them, "Because it [has been mashed in water and] is annulled in the outer house."

E. They said to him, "Just as it is annulled in the outer house, so in the inner one it is not a valid birth."[40]

4:14 A. [If] it came out in pieces or feet foremost, it is not deemed a foetus, until the greater part of it will emerge.

B. And R. Yosé says, "Until it will emerge in the normal way."

C. If it emerged in the normal way before its greater part emerged. . .

D. And R. Yosé says, "Until the greater part of its head will emerge."

E. And what is the greater part of its head?

F. This is its forehead.[41]

4:15 A. She who aborts a creature with a body which is not shaped or a creature with a head which is not shaped —

B. it is not a viable birth.

C. [If it has] a hand which is shaped or a foot which is shaped, lo, this is a viable birth.

D. [If it has] a hand which is unshaped or a foot which is unshaped, it is not a viable birth.

E. [If it has] a body which is unshaped, it is not a viable birth.

F. What is a body which is unshaped?

G. [One lacking a part] that one may take from the living person and he would survive —

H. lo, this is a viable birth.

I. [One lacking a part that one may take] from the living person and he would die — lo, this is not a viable birth.

4:16 A. She who aborts and it is not known what it is [male or female] —

39. M. Nid. 3:3.   40. M. Nid. 3:4.   41. M. Nid. 3:5.

B. let her sit out [the days of uncleanness and cleanness] for a male and for a female and for menstruation.

C. And why have they said [that she should be unclean] as a menstruating woman?

D. That if she should see blood on the thirty-fourth day, [and if] she should go back and see it on the forty-first day,

E. she should turn out to count the beginning of her menstrual period from the first and the beginning of her menstrual cycle from the last [such appearance].

F. And why did they say a [she should sit out the days of uncleanness and cleanness of a] female?

G. That if she should see blood on the seventy-fourth day and she should see blood on the eighty-first day, she should turn out to count the beginning of her menstrual period from the first and the beginning of her menstrual period from the last [such appearance].[42]

4:17 A. Said R. Ishmael, 'M'ŚH B: Cleopatra, the queen of the Alexandrians, brought her maidservant who was sentenced to death to the king, and he cut her up, and found that the male child was complete on the forty-first day and the female on the eighty-first day."

B. They said to him, "They do not bring proof from here.

C. "And from what source do they bring proof?

D. "From [an Israelite] who came to her husband [first],

E. "or from one whose husband had come back from abroad."[43]

5:1 A. Samaritan women from their cradle are deemed menstruants.

B. And Samaritans convey uncleanness to a [couch] beneath as to [a cover] above, because they have intercourse with menstruating women,

C. for (ŚHN) they [Samaritan women] continue unclean [for seven days] for any sort of blood —

D. a day on which she is clean, she counts among the seven.[44]

5:2 A. Sadducean women, when they are accustomed to follow in the ways of their fathers, lo, they are like Samaritans.

B. [If] they left [those ways to walk] in the ways of Israel, lo, they are like Israel[ites].[45]

5:3 A. M'ŚH B: A Sadducean chatted with a high priest, and spit spurted from his mouth and fell on the garments of the high priest, and the face of the high priest blanched.

B. Then he came and asked his [the Sadducee's] wife, and she said, "My lord priest: Even though we are Sadducean women, they [we] all bring their inquiries to a sage."

42. M. Nid. 3:6.   43. M. Nid. 3:7.   44. M. Nid. 4:1.
45. M. Nid. 4:2.

C. Said R. Yosé, "We are more expert in the Sadducean women than anyone. For they all bring their questions to a sage, except for one who was among them, and she died."[46]

5:4 A. Israelite girls, when they are minors, before they have reached the age of puberty, lo, they are assumed to be clean, and the women do not examine them.

B. When they have reached the age of puberty, lo, they are assumed to be clean, but the women do examine them.

C. R. Judah says, "Even after they have reached the age of puberty, the women do not examine them, lest they spoil it with their hands.

D. "But they put on oil and dry it off on the outside, and they thus are examined on their own."

5:5 A. "The blood of a gentile woman and the blood of purifying of a woman with ṣara'at —

B. "The House of Shammai say, 'Lo, it is like the blood of her wound.'

C. "The blood of a woman after childbirth who has not immersed imparts uncleanness when it is wet, and it does not impart uncleanness when it is dry," the words of R. Meir.

D. R. Judah says, "It imparts uncleanness wet and dry."[47]

5:6 A. R. Eliezer says "[This is one] of the lenient rulings of the House of Shammai and of the strict rulings of the House of Hillel:

B. [TR III, p. 269:] "The blood of one who has given birth but not immersed —

C. "The House of Shammai say, 'It imparts uncleanness when it is wet, and it does not impart uncleanness when it is dry.'

D. "And the House of Hillel say, 'It imparts uncleanness when it is wet and when it is dry.'

E. "The House of Hillel said to the House of Shammai, 'Do you not agree concerning the menstruating woman, that, if her time to immerse came and she did not immerse, she is [still] unclean?'

F. "The House of Shammai said to them, 'No. If you have said so concerning a menstruating woman, who, if she immerses today and sees a drop of blood tomorrow, is unclean, will you say so concerning a woman who has given birth, who, if she immerses today and sees a drop of blood tomorrow, is nonetheless deemed clean?'

G. "The House of Hillel said to them, 'One who gives birth while in the status of a Zabah will prove the matter.'

H. "The House of Shammai said to them, 'If you bring evidence from the one who has given birth while with a flux, that is the law and the very answer [to your claim].' "

I. The one who gives birth as a Zabah — the days in which she is a

---

46. *ibid.*   47. M. Nid. 4:3.

Zabah count for her in respect to the days of her purifying, and they do not count for her in respect to the days of her childbirth.[48]

5:7 A. A woman in protracted labor — for how long should she have respite [so that blood appearing thereafter indicates that] she is a Zabah?

B. R. Eleazar [Eliezer] says, "Twenty-four hours."

And the law is in accord with his opinion.

C. R. Simeon b. Judah says in the name of R. Simeon, "The House of Shammai say, 'Three days.'

"And the House of Hillel say, 'Twenty-four hours.' "[49]

5:8 A. She who is in labor before giving birth, lo, she is deemed a menstruant.

B. [If] during the eleven days [of Zibah] she was in hard labor and had respite for one day,

labor for one day and respite for two days,

respite for one day and hard labor for one day and respite for one day — she gives birth in the status of a Zabah.

C. [If] she had respite for two days and was in labor for one day,

respite for one day and labor for two days,

labor for one day and respite for one day, and labor for one day — she has not given birth as a Zabah.

D. This is the general rule: [When] the respite comes immediately before the childbirth, she gives birth as a Zabah. [If] the labor is immediately before the childbirth, she does not give birth as a Zabah.

E. [If] she had labor for two days and had respite for one, even though she went and had hard labor afterward, she gives birth as a Zabah.[50]

5:9 A. How long should the labor be protracted so that [blood which she sees should be] assumed [to be caused] by the child?

B. "Even forty and fifty days," the words of R. Meir.

C. And R. Judah says in the name of R. Tarfon, "Sufficient for her is her month."

D. How so?

E. [If she had labor] two [days] of the eighth month and [one day] of the ninth, she has not given birth while a Zabah.

F. Three of the eighth month and [one] of the ninth — she has given birth as a Zabah.

G. R. Yosé and R. Simeon say, "Fourteen days,

H. "like one who has given birth to a female child.

I. "Therefore if she was in labor seventeen days [before giving birth], the first three are fitting for flux and she has [in consequence] given birth as a Zabah."[51]

48. *ibid.*   49. M. Nid. 4:4−5.   50. *ibid.*
51. *ibid.*

5:10 A. There can be a case in which a woman is in hard labor for twenty-five days and not be a Zabah.

B. How so?

C. Two not at her time, and seven of menstruation, and two after her [menstrual] period,

D. fourteen days which giving birth to a female child [causes to be clean].

E. But it is not possible for her to be in labor twenty-six days.

F. Where there is no child, she gives birth as a Zabah.[52]

5:11 A. There can be a case of a woman who sees blood on a hundred days and is not deemed a Zabah on their account:

B. Two not at her time, and seven during her menstrual period, and two after her menstrual period, and eighty after having given birth to a female, and seven during her menstrual cycle and two after her menstrual period.

C. And R. Meir says, "One hundred and fifty:

D. "Two not at her time, and seven during her menstrual cycle, and two after her menstrual cycle, and eighty days of purifying of a female and seven of her menstrual cycle, and two after her menstrual cycle, and fifty which are attributed to the child."

E. They said to him, "In accord with your view, she can be in labor her entire life and never be a Zabah during them."[53]

5:12 A. [If] she was in labor for three days, one after another, she is prohibited to her house [to have intercourse] and forbidden to eat heave-offering.

B. [If] one was in the assumption of being pregnant and went into labor and afterward aborted something which is not a viable birth, she has given birth as a Zabah.[54]

C. She who went into hard labor, and it [the baby] went forth by way of her side, has given birth in the status of a Zabah.

D. And R. Simeon says, "She has not given birth in the status of a Zabah."

E. The blood which goes forth from there is unclean.

F. R. Simeon declares it clean.[55]

5:13 A. She who ejects semen — [if it is] on the inside — it [the semen] is unclean.

B. And R. Simeon says, "It is sufficient for her to be like the one who has had intercourse with her.

C. "Just as the one who has had intercourse with her is not unclean inside and outside, so also she should not be deemed unclean inside as outside."[56]

---

52. *ibid.*   53. *ibid.*   54. *ibid.*
55. M. Nid. 5:1–2.   56. *ibid.*

5:14 A. A girl one day old may be a menstruant.

B. M'ŚH B: [Such a child was born in] 'En Bul, and they immersed her before [immersing] her mother.[57]

C. "At the age of three years," the words of R. Meir.

D. And sages say, "At the age of three years and one day."[58]

5:15 A. During the period in which the son and daughter are interrogated, even though [better: if] they said, "[We know] to Whom we have taken a vow, and to Whom we have sanctified an object," their vows are vows, and [things subject to] their acts of sanctification are deemed sanctified.

B. M'ŚH. B: The father of R. Ḥananiah b. Ḥananiah set upon him the vow of the Nazir, and then his father brought him before Rabban Gamaliel.

C. And Rabban Gamaliel was examining him [to determine] whether he had come to the age of producing tokens of maturity.

(D. And R. Yosé b. R. Judah says, "Whether he has come to the age of making vows.")

E. He said to him, "Why are you so troubled? If I am subject to the authority of father, lo, the authority of father is upon me, and lo, I am a Nazir. And if I am subject to my own authority, lo, I am a Nazir from this point forward."

F. He stood and kissed upon his head. He said, "I am certain concerning this one that he will not die before he has taught instruction(s)." And he did not die before he taught instruction in Israel.[59]

5:16 A. M'ŚH B: A boy sanctified his spade to Heaven, and his father brought him before R. 'Aqiva.

B. And R. 'Aqiva interrogated him.

C. He said to him, "My son, to what did you sanctify it? Perhaps it was to the sun or to the moon or the stars and the planets, because they are pretty?"

D. He said to him, "I sanctified it only to Him to whom iron belongs, blessed be He."

E. R. 'Aqiva said, "This one has been interrogated and found in good order."[60]

5:17 A. ŚWB MŚHB: a certain child.

B. They were traveling on a ship, and a sea-storm rose against them, and they were crying to their god, as it is said, "And the sailors feared and cried, each to his god" [Jonah 1:5].

C. That child said to them, "How long are you going to act foolishly? Cry out to him who created the sea!". . .

D. And the case came before the sages and they said, "This one has been

---

57. M. Nid. 5:3.   58. M. Nid. 5:4.   59. M. Nid. 5:6.
60. *ibid.*

interrogated and found in good order."[61]

6:1 A. An Ammonite, Moabite, Egyptian, Edomite, Samaritan, Netin, or Mamzer, [all] at the age of nine years and one day, who had intercourse with the daughter of a priest, Levite, and Israelite has rendered her unfit for marriage to the priesthood.

B. R. Yosé says, "Any one whose seed is fit — she is fit. And any whose seed is unfit — she is unfit."

C. Rabban Simeon b. Gamaliel says, "Any whose daughter you are permitted to marry — his widow are you permitted to marry. Any whose daughter you are not permitted to marry — you are not permitted to marry his widow."[62]

6:2 A. A boy nine years and one day old who produced two hairs — it is a mole.

B. A boy nine years and one day old and up to twelve years and one day old who produced two pubic hairs — it is a mole.

C. R. Yosé b. R. Judah says, "It is a token [of maturity]."

D. [A boy] from twelve years and one day old and up to thirteen years and one day old who produced two pubic hairs, lo, he is equivalent to a man in every respect.

E. A boy fourteen years and fifteen years old who has not produced two pubic hairs, lo, he is like a boy nine years and one day old in every respect.

F. A boy twenty years old who has not produced two pubic hairs, even though he produces them thereafter, lo, he is like a eunuch in every respect.

G. A girl twenty years old who has not produced two pubic hairs, even though she produced them thereafter, lo, she is treated as sterile in all respects.[63]

6:3 A. R. Yosé b. Kippar said in the name of R. Eleazar, "When thirty days of the twentieth year have passed, they count it as a complete year."

B. Rabbi taught in Lud concerning a girl who had entered thirty days of the eighteenth year, that she is like a girl eighteen years and one day old in every respect.[64]

6:4 A. What are the tokens of maturity?

B. R. Eleazar b. R. Ṣadoq says, "Once her breasts are firm."

C. R. Yoḥanan b. Beroqa' says, "Once the head of the nose turns white."

D. R. Yosé says, "When a ring forms around the nipple."

E. R. Simeon says, "When the *mons venera* grows lower."

F. And so did R. Simeon say, "Just as they listed three tokens on top, so they listed three top tokens on the bottom.

61. *ibid.*   62. M. Nid. 5:5.   63. M. Nid. 5:9.
64. *ibid.*

G. "If she is an unripe fig on the top, she has not brought tokens below at all.

H. "If she is a ripening fig on top, she has brought tokens on the bottom.

I. "If she is a fully ripe fig on the top, the *mons veneris* has grown lower."[65]

6:5   A. Until what time may a girl exercise the right of refusal?

B. "Until she will produce two pubic hairs," the words of R. Meir.

C. And R. Judah says, "Until the black will multiply over the white."

D. R. Yosé says, "Until a ring is formed around the nipple."

E. R. Simeon says, "Until the crest of the genitals begins to flatten."

F. Ben Shelaqit says, "Until she will have a full crown of hair around the pudenda."[66]

6:6   A. Said R. Simeon, "Hananiah b. Hakhinai found me in Sidon. He said to me, 'When you go to R. 'Aqiva, say to him, 'Until what time does a girl exercise the right of refusal?'

B. "If he says to you, 'Until she will produce two pubic hairs,' say to him, 'And before all of you did not Ben Shelaqit give testimony in Yavneh, 'Until she will have a full crown of hair around the pudenda?'

C. "And when I came and laid the matters before R. 'Aqiva, he said to me, 'I do not know Ben Shelaqit, and I know only, 'Until she will bring two pubic hairs.' "[67]

6:7   A. The two pubic hairs of which they spoke [establish puberty] even [if] one is on the hand and one on the foot,

B. one in the armpit and one in the loin,

C. even two between two joints of his fingers —

D. lo, these join together.[68]

6:8   A. All those who are inspected are inspected only by women.

B. So did R. Eliezer give over to his wife [girls who had to be inspected for the appearance of pubic hairs], and R. Ishmael gave them over to his mother.

C. R. Judah says, "Before the period [eleven years and one day] and after the period [twelve years and one day] women inspect them.

"Because on the testimony of women they do not permit to marry girls whose status may be in doubt."

D. R. Simeon says, "Even during the period itself."

E. A woman is permitted to testify in such wise as to impose a stringent ruling but not to impose a lenient ruling.

F. A woman is permitted to testify, "She is a minor," so that she should not carry out the rite of *ḥaliṣah*. And "she is an adult," so that she should

65. M. Nid. 5:8.   66. M. Nid. 6:11.   67. *ibid.*
68. *ibid.*

not exercise the right of refusal.

G. But she is not permitted to testify, saying, "She is a minor," so that the girl may exercise the right of refusal, or, "She is an adult," so that she may carry out the rite of *haliṣah*.[69]

6:9   A. Said R. Eleazar b. R. Ṣadoq, "When the court would carry out an inspection in Yavneh, once they found the upper token, they did not pay attention to the matter of the lower one."

B. R. Simeon says, "The girls of the cities — the lower one appears first, because of the baths.

C. "The girls of the villages — the upper one appears first, because they work at the grindstone and carry jars on their sides."[70]

6:10   A. Whatever imparts uncleanness in the Tent imparts uncleanness lasting seven days, but there is that which imparts uncleanness which lasts for seven days but does not impart uncleanness in the Tent.

B. Whatever has horns has hooves, and there is that which has hooves and does not have horns.

C. Whoever has the right to take charity has the right to take the tithe of the poor, and there is that one who takes the tithe of the poor and does not take charity.[71]

6:11   A. The blood of a menstruating woman and the flesh of the corpse

B. all these which became mouldy — lo, they are clean.

C. In the name of R. Nathan did they state, "Any piece of bread which became mouldy does not become unclean by reason of the uncleanness pertaining to food, and they burn it in its place."

D. And how much is its soaking in lukewarm water?

E. Judah b. Naqosa' says, "Until it will be [in] lukewarm water for twenty-four hours."[72]

6:12   A. Said R. Judah, "Why did they say concerning the creeping thing, Until the time of cleaning?

B. "For if one did not clean, it imparts uncleanness retroactively.

C. "And on what account did they say of the blood stain, Up to the time of washing?

D. "For it is the way of the Israelite women that they examine their blood stains when they wash them.

E. "If she did not examine her blood stain, it imparts uncleanness retroactively."[73]

6:13   A. R. Aḥa says, "Let her launder it. If it grows dim, it imparts uncleanness retroactively.

"If it does not grow dim, it does not impart uncleanness retroactively."

B. Rabbi says, "The blood stain before washing is not like the blood

69. *ibid.*   70. M. Nid. 6:1.   71. M. Nid. 6:9.
72. M. Nid. 7:1.   73. M. Nid. 7:2.

stain after washing. That before washing penetrates, and that after washing remains clotted [on the surface]."[74]

6:14 A. A spade which was stolen from the house — it [the house] is unclean retroactively, until one will state, "I inspected this place, and it was here."

B. R. Simeon b. Gamaliel declares clean,

C. "for I say, 'Perhaps one lent it to someone else and he forgot it, or perhaps he left it in the corner and it was stolen.'"[75]

6:15 A. Others say in the name of R. Neḥemiah, "All the blood stains which are found in the bathhouses of women are unclean."

B. If they are found in the bathhouse of Samaritans, it imparts uncleanness through overshadowing, because they bury their abortions there.

C. And R. Judah declares clean, because the weasel and the leopard drag them away forthwith.[76]

6:16 A. The Samaritan is believed to say, "A grave which was ploughed up by me is not a grave,"

B. for he testifies solely about the grave itself.

C. And [he is believed if he says of] a tree which overshadows [the grave], "There is not a grave [beneath it],"

D. for he testifies only about the grave itself.[77]

6:17 A. She blames [the bloodstain] on anything on which she can blame it.

B. M'ŚH W: R. Meir blamed it on collyrium.

C. And Rabbi blamed it on the sap of a sycamore.

D. [If there is a matter of doubt whether or not she has passed through the market of the butchers, lo, this one does not blame [it on the blood of slaughtered animals].

E. [If] she passed through, [but] it is a matter of doubt whether [blood] spurted on her or did not spurt on her, lo, this one blames [it on blood's spurting on her].

F. [If] she was handling things which are red, she does not blame [on these things] a stain which is black.

G. [If] she was handling a small quantity [of blood], she does not blame on it a large quantity.

H. She who blames it on a gentile —

I. R. Meir says, "She may do so only if it is a gentile suitable to produce blood."[78]

6:18 A. Rabban Simeon b. Gamaliel says, "She may blame a minor [uncleanness] on a major one.

B. "How?

74. *ibid.*   75. *ibid.*   76. M. Nid. 7:4.
77. M. Nid. 7:5.   78. M. Nid. 8:2.

C. "She blames her stain on a woman [to whom she had previously lent the garment] who was awaiting a day for a day, and [this is the case] if it was the latter's second day, and to a woman who counted seven days before performing immersion.

D. "Therefore this one is in good estate, [though the other] is in disarray."

E. Rabbi says, "She does not blame [her blood stain on the other, to whom she lent the garment].

F. "Therefore they are both in disarray."

G. All agree that she blames it on a woman [to whom she lent the garment] who is watching day against day on the first day, or to a woman who is sitting out the blood of cleanness, or to a virgin, whose blood is clean.

H. [If] it was found on her son, while he is sitting by her side, lo, this one is unclean, because he turns this way and that.

I. And not on her son alone did they so state, but in respect to any man.

J. But sages spoke in language applicable to current conditions.[79]

6:19 A. [If] it is found on her ribbons, lo, this one is unclean, because when she lets it loose, it touches the pudenda.

B. And if there was a wound on her neck, and it is found on her shoulder, lo, this one blames it [on the neck-wound].

C. [If] it [the wound] is found on her thigh, lo, this one blames it [on the blood on the thigh].

D. And they do not take account of the possibility that her hand brought it down there.

E. [If] it is found on her hand, she is unclean, because the hands are always busy.[80]

6:20 A. [If] there were on her two blood stains, one above and one below,

B. even if the one below is large and the one above is small, she blames the lower one [on the upper one],

C. up to the size of a split bean,

D. for I say, "From the place from which the upper one came, the lower one came also."

E. [If] there were two blood stains on her breast, one above and one below, even though the lower one is large and the upper one is small, she blames the lower one [on the upper one],

F. up to the size of a split bean,

G. for I say, "From the place from which the upper one came, the lower one came."[81]

7:1 A. [If] it was found on the sleeve of her tunic, if it reaches to opposite the pudenda, she is unclean, and if not she is clean.

---

79. *ibid.*   80. M.Nid. 8:1.   81. *ibid.*

B. Said R. Eleazar b. R. Yosé, "This law did I teach in Rome, declaring her unclean, and when I came to my colleagues, they said to me, 'You taught well.' "[82]

7:2 A. [If] she put on five garments which were examined for her, and [if] it was found on the innermost one,

B. lo, this one blames it on an external source.

C. And if she cannot blame it,

D. she does not blame it.[83]

7:3 A. A short girl who put on the garment of a tall girl, and a tall girl who put on the garment of a short girl —

B. [if] it is found near the pudenda of the tall girl, they are both unclean.

C. [If] it is found near the pudenda of the short girl, she is unclean, but the tall girl is clean.

D. Two of them [who] were grinding with a handmill, and it [blood] was found on the foot of the inner one —

E. they are both unclean.

F. [If] it is found on the foot of the outer one, she is unclean and her girl-friend is clean.

G. [If] it is found between them [b. Nid. 60b: both are unclean] —

H. this was a case:

I. (and) It was found on the edge of a bath,

J. and on an olive leaf with which she was lighting the oven —

K. And the case came before sages, and they declared them unclean.[84]

7:4 A. R. Neḥemiah says, "[If it is] on that which is susceptible to uncleanness, it is unclean, and [if it is on] that which is not susceptible to uncleanness, it is clean."

B. Rabban Simeon b. Gamaliel says, "If she killed [a louse], she blames [a bloodstain on it], but if [she did] not [kill a louse], she does not blame [it on it]."

[C. (b. Nid. 58b supplies:) And sages say, "In either case she blames it on it."][85]

7:5 A. Said Rabban Simeon b. Gamaliel, "I say one thing, and they say one thing. In accord with my opinion there is no limit to the matter, and in accord with their opinion there is no limit to the matter.

B. "In accord with my opinion, there is no woman who is not clean, for there is no bed on which there is no louse. And in accord with their opinion, there is no limit, for there is no bed which is not unclean, for there is no sheet on which there are not found drops of blood.

C. "But," he said, "I accept the view of R. Ḥanina b. Gamaliel more than my opinion and their opinion alike.

82. *ibid.*   83. M. Nid. 8:2.   84. M. Nid. 8:1.
85. M. Nid. 8:2.

D. "For he says, 'One blames it on the louse if it is the size of a split bean. Even though she did not kill it, one blames it on her son and on her husband.'

E. "And in accord with his opinion do we agree."[86]

7:6   A. A long blood stain is combined.

B. That which is made in drops is not combined.

C. R. Eleazar says, "The testing rag which is placed under the pillow, and blood is found on it, if it is round, lo, this is clean, because it is the blood of a louse, and if it is elongated, lo, this is unclean, because it is the blood which has been dried off."[87]

7:7   A. The woman who is doing her needs and saw blood —

B. "if she is standing she is unclean, and if she is sitting, she attributes [the blood to a sore in the bladder and is clean]," the words of R. Meir.

C. And R. Yosé says, "One way or the other, she attributes [it to a clean source and is clean]."

D. And R. Simeon says, "One way or the other, she does not attribute [it to a clean source and is unclean]."[88]

7:8   A. A man and a woman who made into the pot, and the blood was found in the pot —

B. R. Meir and R. Yosé say, "She does not attribute [it to a clean source and is unclean]."[89]

7:9   A. Blood which comes out with the excrement is clean.

B. Blood which drips out, whether before the water or after the water, is unclean.

C. A bloodstain which is attributed [to a clean source] is clean.

D. And that which concerns contacts and shiftings — they follow the majority.[90]

8:1   A. Lo, [if a woman] was married and saw blood during intercourse, she has intercourse one time, and a second and a third. Thereafter, she may not have intercourse, but she is to be divorced and married to someone else.

B. [If] she was married [to another man] and saw blood during intercourse, she has intercourse one time, and a second, and third. Thereafter she should not have sexual relations. But she should be divorced and married to some other.[91]

8:2   A. And how many times is she permitted to remarry? Up to three times. Thereafter she should not be married unless she examines herself with a reed.

B. How do they examine her?

C. One brings a reed and puts inside it a painting stick and brings an ab-

86. *ibid.*   87. M. Nid. 8:4.   88. M. Nid. 9:1.
89. M. Nid. 9:2.   90. *ibid.*   91. M. Nid. 10:1.

sorbent and puts it on the head of the painting stick.

D. [If] it [blood] is found on its head, lo, this is unclean, because it is blood of uterus [menstrual blood].

E. And [if it is found] on the sides, lo, [there is no flow from the uterus and] this one is clean, because it is blood rubbed off [from a wound on the sides of the vagina].

F. If she has a fixed period, lo, this one takes account of her fixed period.

G. If she has a wound, lo, she attributes it to it.

H. But if blood of her menstrual period was different from blood of her wound, lo, this one does not attribute it to it.[92]

8:3 A. "A woman is believed to state, 'A wound is in me on the source,' and 'A wound is not in me on the source,' " the words of Rabbi.

B. R. Simeon b. Eleazar says in the name of R. Meir, "Blood which exudes from the room, even though it is known that it is blood of a wound, lo, it is unclean."

C. And our rabbis have said, "The blood of the wound is clean."[93]

8:4 A. [If] she was examining herself with the right [hand] and it is unclean, with the left [hand] and it is clean, she should examine only with the left.

B. [If she was examining herself] in the courtyard and it is clean, in the antechamber and it is unclean, she should examine only in the courtyard.

C. [If she examined] herself, and she is unclean, [if she was examined] by her girl-friend and she was clean, she should be examined only by her girl-friend.[94]

8:5 A. All pregnant women are one and nursing mothers one, and they do not attribute it to one another.

B. A pregnant woman, a nursing mother, and an old woman — they do not attribute the blood to one another.

C. Said R. Meir, M'ŚH B: "A sycamore was in Kefar Saba, under which people took for granted uncleanness was located. They searched it out and found nothing under it. One time the wind came and blew it down from the roots, and the skull of a corpse was found cleaving to the roots."[95]

8:6 A. Said R. Yosé, M'ŚH B: "A cave was in Sheḥin in which people took for granted uncleanness was located. They examined it until the ground was smooth as a fingernail.

B. "One time they the workers went into it because of the rain, and when they were chopping with their spades in their hands, they found a mortar full of bones."[96]

8:7 A. Said R. Yosé, M'ŚH B: "A rock [clod] was in Bet Ḥoron, in which

---

92. *ibid.*   93. *ibid.*   94. *ibid.*
95. M. Nid. 9:4.   96. *ibid.*

they took for granted was uncleanness, but they were unable to inspect it.

B. "A certain elder said to them, 'Bring me a sheet.' They brought one to him, and they soaked it in water and spread it over it [the clod], and it turned out that at the sides it was wet, and at the center it was dry. They examined it and found there was a large cistern full of corpses."[97]

8:8   A. What is tasteless spit?

B. [Spit of] anyone who has tasted nothing since the preceding evening, even the entire day.

C. [If] one slept for the entire day, he does not produce tasteless spit.

D. [If] he was awake all night, he does produce tasteless spit.[98]

8:9   A. Water from boiled grits? — a paste made of grits of peeled beans.

B. Urine? — urine which has fermented.

C. And how much must they have fermented? For three days.[99]

8:10   A. Nitre — this is Alexandrian nitre.

B. Soap, Cimolian earth, and lion's leaf — from any place.

C. One rinses and does not have to dry.

D. [If] one passed them over not in their [given] order, the former are not counted, but the latter are counted.[100]

8:11   A. [If] one passed the seven substances on it, and it did not pass away, and one did it a second time and [then] it did pass away,

B. [and if he prepared] things requiring cleanness, they are deemed clean.

C. [If he passed over it] the six substances, and it did not go away, and one cleaned it with soap, and it went away, things requiring cleanness are suspended, for if he had passed soap over it in the first place, it would have gone away.[101]

8:12   A. As to blood which certainly is menstrual blood, one does not pass over it the seven substances.

B. A dyed garment is not made unclean through blood stains.

C. And R. Jonathan b. Joseph says, "It is made unclean through blood stains."[102]

8:13   A. A garment in which a blood stain has been lost — one passes over it the seven substances.

B. And R. Simeon b. Eleazar says, "One examines it in small sections.

C. "[If] semen was lost in it, if it was new, one examines it with a needle, and [if it was] worn out, one examines it in the sun."[103]

9:1   A. [If] she habitually saw blood at the beginning of the period, all the things requiring cleanness which she prepared at the beginning of the period

97. *ibid.*   98. M. Nid. 9:6—7.   99. *ibid.*
100. *ibid.*   101. *ibid.*   102. *ibid.*
103. *ibid.*

and at the middle of the period and at the end of the period are unclean.

B. [If she usually saw blood] at the middle of the period, all the things requiring cleanness which she prepared at the beginning of the period are clean. All the things requiring cleanness at the middle of the period are unclean.

C. At the end of the period — all the things requiring cleanness which she prepared at the beginning of the period and at the middle of the period are clean.

D. And all things requiring cleanness at the end of the period are unclean.

E. And R. Yosé says, "Days and hours also are fixed periods."[104]

9:2 A. How so?

B. "[If] she usually saw blood from the twentieth day to the twentieth day and from the sixth hour to the sixth hour,

C. "[if] the twentieth day came and she did not see [blood], she is prohibited to have intercourse all day long," the words of R. Judah.

D. And R. Yosé permits up to the sixth hour.

E. "[If] the sixth hour passed, and she did not see blood, she is prohibited to have intercourse all day long," the words of R. Judah.

F. And R. Yosé permits from the sixth hour and thereafter.

G. And they do not require her to have her hand in her eye all day long, but she examines herself twice [at the time of] her period.[105]

9:3 A. [If] she habitually saw blood on the fifteenth day, and she changed her pattern to the seventeenth day, this and that are prohibited. [If] she changed to the sixteenth day, the fifteenth day and the seventeenth day are unclean. The sixteenth day is clean.[106]

9:4 A. [If] she changed to the eighteenth day, the three of them are clean, and unclean is only the eighteenth day alone.

B. [If] she usually saw blood on the twentieth day and changed to the thirtieth day, this one and that one are prohibited, but she is permitted to have intercourse from the twentieth day to the thirtieth day.

C. And if she saw blood on the twentieth day, she is permitted to have intercourse on the thirtieth day,

D. because her period comes in good order.

E. [If] she did not see on the twentieth day, she is prohibited to have intercourse on the thirtieth day.[107]

9:5 A. She who sees blood imparts uncleanness [to objects which she touched] during the preceding twenty-four hours.

B. And to what does she impart uncleanness? Food and drink and objects used for lying and sitting and clay utensils which are tightly sealed.

104. M. Nid. 9:9—10.   105. *ibid.*   106. *ibid.*
107. *ibid.*

C. And she is in disarray [as to her fixed period].

D. And she does not impart uncleanness to the one who has intercourse with her.

E. And R. 'Aqiva says, "She does impart uncleanness to the one who has intercourse with her."

F. And she does not count seven days from its appearance but from the time that she saw blood.[108]

9:6 A. She who sees a blood stain imparts uncleanness retroactively.

B. And to what does she impart uncleanness? Food and drink and objects used for lying and sitting and open clay utensils.

C. And she is in disarray [as to her fixed period].

D. And she imparts uncleanness to the one who has intercourse with her.

E. But she does not count seven days from its appearance but from the time that she saw [blood].

F. And in any case [the uncleanness] is held in suspense and [consecrated food] is not burned.[109]

9:7 A. A girl whose time for seeing [blood] had not arrived and who was married —

B. the House of Shammai say, "They give her four nights" —

C. interruptedly, and even over a period of four months.

D. And the House of Hillel say, "All the time that she is wounded."

E. Under what circumstances?

F. When she did not stop [bleeding when having intercourse].

G. But [if] she stopped, and she [then] saw blood on account of intercourse, lo, this one is unclean as a menstruant.

H. They give her [all the time] until the wound is healed.

I. [If] the color of the blood changed [from that consequent upon the first act of intercourse], and she saw blood, lo, this one is unclean as a menstruant.[110]

9:8 A. [And the girl] whose time for seeing blood has come [and she was married] —

B. if she interrupted and saw blood not on account of sexual relations [and then produced blood], lo, this one is unclean as a menstruant.

C. They give her the first night only.

D. [If] the color of the blood changed and she saw [blood], lo, this one is unclean as a menstruant.

E. In connection with this one did the House of Hillel say, "The entire night is hers."

F. Rabban Simeon b. Gamaliel says, "They give her a whole 'onah, half a day and night."[111]

108. *ibid.*   109. *ibid.*   110. M. Nid. 10:1.   111. *ibid.*

9:9   A. And all of them who have seen [blood] —

B. they examine them with a reed,

C. except for the virgin, for her blood is clean, because it is hymeneal blood.

D. And in the case of all of them did R. Meir rule in accord with the opinion of the House of Shammai.

E. And in regard to all other appearances of blood, all is in accord with the nature of the blood,

F. R. Meir would say, "Various sorts of blood are different from one another."[112]

9:10   A. "The blood of menstruation is red. Hymeneal blood is dim.

B. "Blood of menstruation is turbid. Hymeneal blood is not turbid.

C. "Blood of menstruation is from the source. Hymeneal blood is from the sides."[113]

9:11   A. "If she saw a blood stain and afterward saw blood, lo, this one attributes her blood stain to her stain for a period of twenty-four hours," the words of Rabbi.

B. R. Simeon b. Eleazar says, "For the same day."

C. Said Rabbi, "I prefer the words of R. Simeon b. Leazar."

9:12   A. [If] she examined herself and her garment and lent it to her girl-friend and afterward blood is found on it, she is clean and her girl-friend attributes it to her.

B. Said R. Simeon to R. Judah, "Even you, if you had said, 'Let her hand be in her eyes all day long,' you would have stated a good rule.

C. "But what difference does it make to me whether she marked the separation to cleanness from afternoon and thereafter, or whether she marked her separation to cleanness on the first day, in which case she is clean?"[114]

9:13   A. Said R. Eliezer to R. Joshua, "How can you say that the first day and the seventh day are clean, but the intervening days are unclean?"

B. He said to him, "You also agree that one counts with interruptions in the case of the Nazir who sits underneath overhanging branches, or in the case of [a Zab] who sees a seminal emission during the days of his counting, that they do count with interruptions."

C. R. Yosé and R. Simeon say, "The opinion of R. Eliezer seems to us better than the opinion of R. Joshua and the opinion of R. 'Aqiva is better than the opinions of both of them.

D. "But the law follows R. Eliezer."[115]

9:14   A. The Zab and the Zabah and the menstruating woman and the woman who has given birth and the *mesora'* who died impart uncleanness

112. *ibid.*   113. *ibid.*   114. M. Nid. 10:2.
115. M. Nid. 10:3.

when they are carried — until the flesh will rot.

B. And they impart uncleanness only [if one carries] their larger part.

C. And they impart uncleanness only by decree of the scribes.

D. R. Simeon says, "They burn heave-offering on their account, but they are not liable on their account for making the sanctuary and its holy things unclean, for their uncleanness derives only from the opinion of scribes."

E. And so did R. Simeon say, "A gentile who died is clean in respect to imparting uncleanness to the one who carries him, for his uncleanness derives only from the opinion of scribes."[116]

9:15 A. And R. Judah agrees concerning the one who sits on the travailing stool and dies in childbirth and from whom a quarter-*log* of blood exuded,

B. that it imparts uncleanness by reason of a blood stain.

C. Said R. Yosé, "Therefore it does not impart uncleanness through overshadowing."[117]

9:16 A. At first they would immerse objects on account of [contact with] women who had died while in their menstrual period.

B. They reverted to immerse because of every one of them [whether they died menstruating or not], because of the respect due to women.

C. And first they would bring out incense before those who had [died of] intestinal illness.

D. They reverted to bring out incense before everyone, because of the honor owing to the dead.

E. At first they would bring out the rich on a bed and poor in a box.

F. They reverted to bring them out, whether on a bed or in a box, because of the respect owing to the poor.

9:17 A. At first they would bring [food] to the house of mourning of the poor in a colored glass utensil and to the rich in white glass.

B. They reverted to carry either in colored or in white glass because of the honor owing to the poor.

C. At first whoever had a corpse found that the deceased's expenses were more difficult to bear than the death of the person. Everyone began leaving their dead and running away.

D. Rabban Gamaliel behaved toward himself. . . Everyone behaved as did Rabban Gamaliel.

9:18 A. At first meat eaten for desire was regarded as insusceptible to uncleanness.

B. They reverted to decree concerning it that it should be subject to uncleanness of the hands.

C. They reverted and decreed concerning it that it should be subject to

116. M. Nid. 10:4.   117. M. Nid. 10:5.

uncleanness through contact.

D. They reverted and decreed concerning it that it should be like carrion itself and impart uncleanness through carrying.

E. They reverted and said every olive-pressing made in connection with meat of desire is unclean for Holy Things but clean for heave-offering.

F. They reverted and ruled that this applies to a beast and not to fowl.

G. R. Eleazar ben Judah of Kefar 'Ublin said, "Even if it was made in connection with one fowl or in connection with one chicken, it is unclean for Holy Things and clean for heave-offering."

9:19 A. The one whom the House of Hillel did call gluttonous, R. Judah did call, "One who has intercourse with a menstruating woman."

B. Said the House of Shammai to the House of Hillel, "Do you not agree concerning the one who sees blood during the eleven days, who immersed in the evening and had sexual relations, that she imparts uncleanness to objects used for sitting and lying and is liable for a sacrifice?

"Also she who sees a drop of blood on the eleventh day should be liable for a sacrifice."

C. The House of Hillel said to them, "No. If you say so concerning the one who sees blood during the eleven days, in which case the day after it joins with it for the imposition of uncleanness due to Zibah, will you say so in the case of the one who sees a drop of blood on the eleventh day, in which case the day afterward does not join together with that same day in regard to Zibah-uncleanness?"

D. The House of Shammai said to them, "If so, she [also] should not impart uncleanness to objects used for sitting and lying [since she is in no way unclean by reason of Zibah]."

E. The House of Hillel said to them, "If we have broadened the rule in respect to uncleanness imparted to objects used for lying and sitting, which is a stringency [imposed by us], shall we remove from him the obligation of bringing the sacrifice, which would be a leniency?"[118]

118. M. Nid. 10:8.

MIQVAOT

1:1 A. Said R. Neḥemiah, "Why have they said, 'If he did not rinse, it is clean?'

B. "For the water which is in the pond is not going to receive uncleanness until it is detached.

C. "[Even when] one has lifted it up, the clean predominates over the unclean.[1]

1:2 A. "And why have they said, 'If he rinsed, [it is unclean]?' The water which is on his hands is rendered susceptible to uncleanness and made unclean, and it makes the loaf unclean."

B. R. Simeon says, "Whether he rinsed or whether he did not rinse, it is unclean —

C. "For I say that in the end the flow of unclean water touches the loaf."[2]

1:3 A. A pond into which wine, honey, or milk has fallen — they follow the majority.

B. [If] olive-oil fell into it, even though it congealed, lo, this [pool] is unclean, because it is not possible for it to be freed from the particles of oil.

1:4 A. Wine of heave-offering which fell on fruit — one should rinse them off, and they are permitted.

B. And so olive-oil of heave-offering which fell into pieces of fruit — one should rinse them off, and they are permitted.

C. Olive-oil of heave-offering which fell on wine — one should skim it off, and the wine is permitted.

D. That which fell on brine — one should skim it off so that he annuls the taste of the olive-oil which is in it.

1:5 A. The assumption concerning mud and puddles which are by the doors of shops in the public domain during the rainy-season —

B. all are clean.

C. [When] the rain ceased, lo, they are like dirty water which is in the market-places —

D. they follow the majority.

1:6 A. Dirty water and rain-water which got mixed together —

B. whether in utensils or on the ground —

C. it is unclean.

D. R. Judah and R. Simeon say, "[If] it is in utensils, it is unclean. [If] it is on the ground, it is clean."[3]

E. [When] the rain ceased, those which are near the village and the road are unclean.

---

1. M. Miq. 1:1−4   2. *ibid.*   3. M. Toh. 4:8.

F. Those which are distant are clean until the larger number of people will walk there.

G. Under what circumstances?

H. In the case of a pool from which it is not possible to drink without one's footprints being discerned.

I. But a pool from which it is possible to drink without one's footprints being discerned —

J. [if] one found there the footprints of man [or] footprints of large cattle,

K. it is unclean.

L. [If one found there] footprints of small cattle, it is clean.[4]

1:7   A. A pool which does not contain forty *seahs* of water, and into which less than three *logs* of drawn water fell —

B. it is suitable for unconsecrated food, for *hallah,* and for heave-offering, and for washing the hands therewith.

C. And it is fit to be added to.

D. [If] rain fell —

E. [if] they formed the greater part and overflowed,

F. in accordance with the words of the House of Shammai — [if] they formed the greater part, even though they did not overflow —

G. and in accord with the words of R. Simeon, [if] they overflowed even though they did not form the greater part —

H. they are suitable for *hallah* and for heave-offering and for washing the hands therewith.

I. And it is fit to be added to.

J. And how [is a case in which] they formed the greater part, even though they did not overflow, in accord with the words of the House of Hillel?[5]

1:8   A. An immersion-pool which holds forty *se'ahs* and in it are nineteen *se'ahs,*

B. and less than three *logs* of drawn water fell therein —

C. once twenty-one *se'ahs* of rain-water have fallen in,

D. it is clean because they [rain-water] have formed the greater part.

E. What [is the case in which] they overflowed, even though they did not form the greater part, in accord with the words of R. Simeon?[6]

1:9   A. An immersion-pool which holds twenty *se'ahs,* and in it are nineteen *se'ahs,* and less than three *logs* of drawn water fell therein —
it is unclean.

B. Once one *se'ah* of rain-water has fallen therein, it is clean, because [now] it has overflowed.

C. And how much must it overflow?

4. M. Miq. 1:4—5.   5. *ibid.*   6. *ibid.*

D. Any amount at all.

E. [If] there fell into three *logs* of unclean drawn water —

F. it is unfit for *ḥallah* and for heave-offering and for washing the hands therewith.

G. And it is unfit to be added to.

H. [If] the rain fell —

I. until there will go forth from it its fullness and a bit more.[7]

1:10   A. [If] rain fell —

B. [if] it formed the greater part and overflowed, in accord with the words of the House of Shammai —

C. And in accord with the words of the House of Hillel, [if] it formed the greater part, even though it did not overflow —

D. and in accord with R. Simeon, [if] it overflowed, even though it did not form the greater part —

E. it is suitable for *ḥallah* and for heave-offering and for washing the hands therewith.

F. And it is unfit to be added to,

G. until there will go forth from it its fullness and a bit more.[8]

1:11   A. And how much is *and more?* Its fullness and more.

B. An immersion-pool which holds twenty *se'ahs,* and in it are nineteen *se'ahs* —

C. three *logs* of unclean water fell into it —

D. and rain fell,

E. and it was filled up —

F. it [the water] always remains in [its] unfitness,

G. until there will go forth from it its fullness and a bit more —

H. some small amount more to remove the three *logs.*[9]

1:12   A. An immersion-pool which contains forty *se'ahs* less a *qartob*

B. and three *logs* of unclean drawn water fell therein —

C. they are unfit for *ḥallah* and for heave-offering and for washing the hands therewith.

D. And unfit to be added to.

E. [If] less than three *logs* [fell in],

F. even if they are all unfit [or: unclean],

G. once a single *qartob* of rain-water fell therein —

H. they are clean.[10]

1:13   A. And just as they are clean for immersion, so they are clean for everything.

B. Above them:

Rain-drippings which have not ceased —

7. *ibid.*   8. *ibid.*   9. *ibid.*
10. *ibid.*

C. For they immerse [unclean] water in them.

D. And they do not immerse in them man and hands and utensils.

E. This is the general rule:

F. Any place in which man immerses, hands and utensils immerse.

G. [If] a man does not immerse, hands and utensils do not immerse.

H. And what are rain-drippings?

I. So long as the rains fall, and the mountains trickle [with water],

J. lo, they are like the water of a spring.

K. [If] they ceased to trickle,

L. lo, they are like the water of pools.[11]

1:14   A. He who digs at the side of the ocean and at the side of the river, in a swampy place —

B. lo, it [the water] counts as water in rain ponds.

C. He who digs at the side of the spring —

D. for so long as it [water] comes on account of the spring —

E. even though it stops and starts seeping again,

F. lo, it is like spring-water.

G. [If] it again ceases to flow,

H. lo, it is like the water of pools.

1:15   A. A spring, the waters of which are sparse, and it [drawn water] formed the greater part and expanded —

B. it cleanses when it is standing water.

C. And it does not cleanse when it is flowing,

D. except to the place to which it can reach in the first place.[12]

1:16   A. An immersion-pool which was measured and found lacking — all the acts requiring cleanness which were carried out depending upon it

B. whether this immersion-pool is in the private domain, or whether this immersion-pool is in the public domain — [Supply: are unclean.]

C. R. Simeon says, "In the private domain, it is unclean. In the public domain, it is clean."[13]

1:17   A. Said R. Simeon, "M'ŚH B: The water-reservoir of Disqus in Yavneh was measured and found lacking.

B. "And R. Ṭarfon did declare clean, and R. 'Aqiva unclean.

C. "Said R. Ṭarfon, 'Since this immersion-pool is in the assumption of being clean, it remains perpetually in this presumption of cleanness until it will be known for sure that it is made unclean.'

D. "Said R. 'Aqiva, 'Since this immersion-pool is in the assumption of being unclean, it perpetually remains in the presumption of uncleanness until it will be known for sure that it is clean.'

1:18   A. "Said R. Ṭarfon, 'To what is the matter to be likened? To one who was standing and offering [a sacrifice] at the altar, and it became

11. M. Miq. 1:6.   12. M. Miq. 1:7.   13. M. Miq. 2:1.

known that he is a son of a divorcee or the son of a *ḥaluṣah* —

"'for his service is valid.'

B. "Said R. 'Aqiva, 'To what is the matter to be likened?

"'To one who was standing and offering [a sacrifice] at the altar, and it became known that he is disqualified by reason of a blemish —

"'for his service is invalid.'"

1:19 A. "Said R. Ṭarfon to him, 'You draw an analogy to one who is blemished. I draw an analogy to the son of a divorcee or to the son of a *ḥaluṣah*.

B. "'Let us now see to what the matter is appropriately likened.

C. "'If it is analogous to a blemished priest, let us learn the law from the case of the blemished priest. If it is analogous to the son of a divorcée or to the son of a *ḥaluṣah,* let us learn the law from the case of the son of the divorcee or the son of a *ḥaluṣah.*'

1:20 A. "R. 'Aqiva says, 'The unfitness affecting an immersion-pool affects the immersion-pool itself, and the unfit aspect of the blemished priest affects the blemished priest himself.

B. "'But let not the case of the son of a divorcee or the son of a *ḥaluṣah* prove the matter, for his matter of unfitness depends upon others.

C. "'A ritual pool's unfitness [depends] on one only, and the unfitness of a blemished priest [depends] on an individual only, but let not the son of a divorcee or the son of a *ḥaluṣah* prove the matter, for the unfitness of this one depends upon ancestry.'

D. "They took a vote concerning the case and declared it unclean.

E. "Said R. Ṭarfon to R. 'Aqiva, 'He who departs from you is like one who perishes.'"

2:1 A. An immersion-pool which one left empty and came and found full is fit,

B. because it involves a matter of doubt concerning drawn waters in an immersion-pool,

C. and the assumption concerning immersion-pools is that they are fit.[14]

2:2 A. A water-duct which is pouring water into an immersion-pool, and a mortar is set at its [the duct's] side —

B. and it is a matter of doubt whether it [water] is [pouring] from the water-duct to the immersion-pool, or whether it is [pouring] from the mortar into the immersion-pool —

C. it is unfit, because the matter of unfitness is demonstrable.

D. And if the greater part [of water] in the immersion-pool is fit,

E. [Supply: it is fit] because this is a matter of doubt concerning drawn water in connection with an immersion-pool.[15]

14. M. Miq. 2:3.   15. *ibid.*

2:3 A. Two immersion-pools which do not contain forty *se'ahs* [of rain-water],

B. and three *logs* of drawn water fell [into one of them],

C. and it is known into which of them it has fallen,

D. and afterward, a second [volume, three further *logs* of drawn water] fell,

E. but it is not known into which of them they have fallen —

F. lo, I am able to attribute [the matter], saying,

G. "To the place into which the first [three *logs* of drawn water] have fallen, there have the second ones fallen [as well]."[16]

2:4 A. Three *logs* [of drawn water] fell into one of them, and it is not known into which of them they fell,

B. and afterward a second [volume of *logs* of drawn water] fell, and it is known into which of them they fell —

C. one cannot attribute [the matter], saying,

D. "Into the place into which the second ones have fallen, there did the first ones fall [as well]."

E. In one [of the immersion-pools] there are forty *se'ahs* [of rain-water], and in one of them there are not [forty *se'ahs* of rain-water] —

F. lo, I declare, "Into the one containing forty *se'ahs* of rain-water have they fallen."

G. [If] one is drawn water and one is fit water — lo, I declare, "They have fallen into the drawn water."[17]

2:5 A. Two immersion-pools which do not contain forty *se'ahs* [of rain-water],

B. and three *logs* [of drawn water] have fallen into one of them, and it is not known into which of them they have fallen —

C. and afterward rain came, and they [the two pools] were filled up [with suitable water] —

D. R. Yosé says, "They say to him that he should not immerse in [either] one of them.

E. "But if he did immerse in one of them and prepared things requiring cleanness,

F. "because this is a matter of doubt concerning drawn water in respect to an immersion-pool [supply: they are deemed clean].

G. "To what is the matter likened?

H. "To a person, one of whose hands has been made unclean, and it is not known which of them [is unclean].

I. "They say to him that he should not prepare things requiring cleanness with either one of them.

J. "But if he did prepare things requiring cleanness with one of them,

16. *ibid.*   17. *ibid.*

K. "they are clean, because it is a matter of doubt involving the hands."[18]

2:6   A. Two immersion-pools —

one containing forty *se'ahs* [of rain-water] and one not containing [forty *se'ahs* of rain-water] —

B. one immersed in one of them on account of a condition of uncleanness deriving from a major source of uncleanness and prepared clean things,

C. [he immersed] in the first and prepared [things requiring cleanness],

D. [he immersed] in the second and prepared [things requiring cleanness],

E. [if] these and those are lying [before him] —

F. the first are held in a state of suspense, and the second are clean.

G. Under what circumstances?

H. When [we deal with] a condition of uncleanness deriving from a major source of uncleanness.

I. But [if we deal with] a condition of uncleanness deriving from a minor source of uncleanness, these and those are clean.[19]

2:7   A. [If] he immersed in one of them on account of a condition of uncleanness deriving from a minor source of uncleanness and prepared things requiring cleanness —

B. they are clean.

C. [If] between times he was made unclean by a major source of uncleanness, and he immersed in the second [pool] and prepared [things requiring conditions of cleanness] —

D. these and those are lying [before him] —

E. lo, these prove [the condition of one another and both are kept in a state of suspense].

F. [If] the first were eaten, and [or] made [definitely] unclean, or perished before the second were prepared —

G. the second are deemed clean.

H. [If this took place] after the second were prepared, the second are held in a state of suspense.[20]

2:8   A. [If] he immersed in one of them on account of a condition of uncleanness deriving from a major source of uncleanness and prepared things requiring cleanness, they are suspended.[1]

B. [If] he was made unclean in the meantime by a minor source of uncleanness,

C. and he immersed in the second [pool] and prepared things requiring cleanness —

D. they are deemed clean.

E. [And if] these touched the others,

F. the first are held in a state of suspense, and the second are burned.

G. [If] he immersed in one of them on account of a condition of uncleanness deriving from a minor source of uncleanness,

H. and prepared clean things,

I. they are deemed clean.

J. [If] he was made unclean in the meantime by a major source of uncleanness and immersed and prepared things requiring cleanness,

K. they are held in a state of suspense,

L. [And if] these touched those,

M. the second are held in a state of suspense and the first are burned.[21]

2:9 A. Two immersion-pools of forty *se'ahs* each,

B. one containing drawn [water], and one containing suitable [water] —

C. and one immersed in one of them on account of a condition of uncleanness deriving from a major source of uncleanness and prepared things requiring cleanness —

D. they are held in a state of suspense.

E. [If he immersed] in the second and prepared things requiring cleanness — [following Sens] they are clean.

F. [If he immersed] in the first and did not prepare things requiring cleanness, then immersed in the second and prepared things requiring cleanness — they are clean.

G. [If he immersed] in the first and prepared [things requiring cleanness], [then immersed] in the second and prepared [things requiring cleanness] —

H. [if] these and those are lying [before him] —

I. the first are suspended, and the second are clean.

J. Under what circumstances?

K. In the case of a condition of uncleanness deriving from a major source of uncleanness.

L. But in the case of a condition of uncleanness deriving from a minor source of uncleanness, these and those are held in a state of suspense.

2:10 A. [If] two people went down and immersed in the two of them,

B. one unclean with a condition of uncleanness deriving from a major source of uncleanness, and one unclean on account of a minor source of uncleanness —

C. he who immerses on account of a major source of uncleanness is unclean.

D. And the one who immerses on account of uncleanness deriving from a minor source of uncleanness is clean.

E. One who is unclean with uncleanness deriving from a major source of uncleanness and one who immerses to cool himself —

F. he who immerses on account of uncleanness deriving from a major source of uncleanness is unclean, and the one who immerses to cool himself

21. *ibid.*

is clean.

G. One is unclean with uncleanness deriving from a minor source of uncleanness, and one immerses to cool himself —

H. both of them are kept in a state of suspense.

I. To what is the matter likened?

J. To two paths, one unclean and one clean, and there were two who went in the two of them and prepared things requiring cleanness.

K. In the case of one there is sufficient intelligence for interrogation, and in the case of the other there is not sufficient intelligence for interrogation —

L. in the case of the private domain, both of them are kept in a state of suspense.

M. In the case of public domain, the one who has intelligence for interrogation in a matter of doubt is deemed to be unclean.

N. And the one who does not have intelligence for interrogation in a matter of doubt is deemed clean.

2:11 A. Two immersion-pools, each containing twenty *se'ahs,*

B. one with drawn water, and one with suitable water —

C. one immersed to cool himself in one of them and prepared things requiring cleanness — they are clean.

D. [If he then immersed] in the second, and prepared things requiring cleanness — they are burned.

E. [If one immersed] in the first and did not prepare [things requiring cleanness], [and then immersed] in the second and prepared [things requiring cleanness] — they are burned.

F. [If one immersed] in the first and prepared things requiring cleanness, and [then immersed] in the second [and prepared things requiring cleanness] —

G. if these and those are lying before him —

H. the first are deemed clean,

I. and the second are to be burned.

2:12 A. Two women who engaged in preparing a bird which is suitable to produce [only] one] *sela'* of blood,

B. after a while, on this one a *sela'* of blood is found,

C. and a *sela'* of blood is found on the other —

D. both of them are in disarray.

3:1 A. A potsherd which is sunk down into the ground of a cistern of a press —

B. and rain fell, and it was filled up —

C. lo, it [the water] is unfit, because it has been guided by means of a utensil.

D. And R. Eliezer declares fit,

E. for the water is not [regarded as] drawn and does not render the immersion-pool unfit until it will actually fall into it [the pool, as drawn water].

3:2   A. [If] there were [poured] on one's head three *logs* of drawn water, and one went down and immersed in an immersion-pool which contains [exactly] forty *se'ahs* —

B. it is fit.

C. [If] one squeezed it out into it,

D. it is unfit.

E. [If] one dunked a thick [wet] blanket into it, and three *logs* [of drawn water] exuded from it into the immersion-pool,

F. it is fit.

G. [If] one squeezed it [water] from it [the blanket],

H. it is unfit.

I. And R. Simeon declares fit,

J. until one will actually intend [to pour drawn water into the immersion-pool by] detaching the water.[22]

K. And R. Joshua says, "One way or the other, he breaks."

L. R. Yosé says in the name of R. Joshua, "He may even tip it over and on condition that he not take and turn over [the jar]."

M. And so did R. Yosé say, "[If] one splashes with his hands and feet three *logs* [of drawn water] into an immersion-pool [lacking in forty *se'ahs*], it is unfit. [If] he leads them [or: if they follow] the course of the ground, it is fit."[23]

3:3   A. A legion which is passing from place to place,

B. and so a caravan [or: a cow] which is passing from place to place and they splashed with their hands or their feet (and) three *logs* into the immersion-pool — it is fit.

C. And not only so, but even if they made an immersion-pool in the first place, it is fit.

3:4   A. And what is mud which is measured with the water?

B. R. Yoḥanan b. Beroqah says, "That which is measured in a *log*."

C. R. Yosé says, "That which goes forth in a funnel."

D. And what is the measuring rod?

E. This is the shuttle containing the spool.

F. The mud which is on the sides counts in the measure of forty *se'ahs*, but they do not immerse in it.[24]

G. Three holes [containing water] in a gulch —

H. the lowest and the uppermost are of twenty *se'ahs* each,

I. and the middle one is of forty *se'ahs* —

J. the rivulet of rain-water enters into them and goes out of them —

22. M. Miq. 2:6.   23. M. Miq. 2:7—9.   24. M. Miq. 2:10.

K. R. Judah says, "R. Meir would say, 'They dunk in the uppermost one.' And I say, In the lowest one."

L. And sages say, "One way or the other,

M. "they immerse only in the middle one, in which forty *se'ahs* have come to a standstill."

3:5   A. Two pools of [exactly] forty *se'ahs* [of fit water] in each —

B. this one on top of that one —

C. and three *logs* fell into the upper one, and they were diverted and came into the lower one —

D. it is suitable, for I say, "The forty *se'ahs* were complete before three *logs* came down."

3:6   A. Two immersion-pools, each containing twenty *se'ahs* —

B. and this is beside that one —

C. and three *logs* of drawn water fell into one of them, and they were diverted and came into its fellow —

D. it is suitable.

E. R. Yosé says, "If the partition was removed, it is unfit.

F. "But," he said, "I accept the opinion of R. Joshua in the case of an immersion-pool which contains forty *se'ahs* of fit water, and three *logs* of drawn water fell into it,

G. "and they were divided into two,

H. "that this one is fit to be added to, and this one is fit to be added to."[25]

3:7   A. Two immersion-pools, each containing twenty *se'ahs*,

B. one with drawn water, and one with fit water —

C. two went down and brought the two into contact and immersed in them —

D. even if it [water] was red and turned white, or white and turned red —

E. the immersion-pools remain as they were, and the ones who immersed remain as they were.[26]

3:8   A. Three *logs* [which fell] into an immersion-pool —

B. and one who had an emission of semen who was ill, upon whom nine *qabs* of water have fallen —

C. a clean person on whose head and the greater part of whose body three *logs* of drawn water have fallen —

D. Abba Yosé b. Ḥanan says, "[If it is] from one utensil, from two, or from three, they join together.

E. "[And if it fell] from four, they do not join together."[27]

3:9   A. He who enters drawn water except for his finger-tips —

B. R. Eliezer declares unclean.

C. And sages say, "Even if only his head and the greater part of his body

25. M. Miq. 3:1.   26. M. Miq. 6:3.   27. M. Miq. 3:4.

entered into drawn water, he is unclean."

D. [If] there entered drawn water on his head but not the greater part of his body,

E. or the greater part of his body but not his head,

F. or his head and the greater part of his body, whether from the top or from the side came [into drawn water] —

G. he is clean,

H. until his head [and greater part of his body] will enter into drawn water in accord with the normal way [of doing so].

3:10 A. [If] part of it [the water] is drawn water and part of it is not drawn water —

B. [or if it is drawn water] into which wine, honey, or milk has fallen —

C. he is clean —

D. until it will be wholly drawn water.

E. Even if he is clean, and it [the drawn water] is clean, he is made unclean and renders it unclean.

F. Lo, this one says, "He made me unclean, and I made him unclean."

3:11 A. A clean person on whose head and the greater part of whose body three *logs* of drawn water have fallen is unclean.

B. [If] they fell on his head but not on the greater part of his body,

C. on the greater part of his body but not on his head,

D. [if] they fell on his head and on the greater part of his body whether from above or whether from the side —

E. he is clean —

F. until they fall on his head and the greater part of his body in the usual way.

3:12 A. [If] part of it was drawn water and part of it was not drawn water

B. [if] there fell into it wine, honey, or milk —

C. he is clean,

D. until it will be entirely drawn water.

E. And even if he is clean, and it is clean,

F. he is made unclean, and renders it unclean.

G. Lo, this one says, "He made me unclean, and I made him unclean."

3:13 A. R. Ishmael says, "[If] they [the three *logs* of drawn water] are clean, he remains clean, on account of the following argument *a fortiori:*

B. "And if when the rule concerning other liquids mixed with water is that they render the body unfit if one drinks a quarter-*qab,* the rule is not that the clean is like the unclean,

C. "in a situation in which liquids mixed with water do not render the body unfit,

D. "when three *logs* fall, is it not logical that we should not regard the clean as equivalent to the unclean?"

3:14 A. An immersion-pool will prove the matter:

B. For it is not the rule that other liquids which fall into it are treated as water.

C. And [here the law] treats the clean as equivalent to the unclean.

D. Rabbi answered the opinion of Abba Joseph HaḤorani:

E. "No. If you have stated the matter in the case of the immersion-pool, in which case the 'birds' [= bubbles] are not treated [as equivalent to water], will you say so in the case of the body, in which case the 'birds' [bubbles] are treated [as equivalent to water ?]"

4:1 A. A tray which one put beneath the water-spout to rinse [it].

B. and so too: utensils which one placed under the water-spout to rinse them —

C. the first drops of water [as they fall onto the tray or utensil] are susceptible to receive uncleanness.

D. [If] the requisite volume of forty *se'ahs* of rain water is completed, lo, these are fit.

E. A water-spout which one hewed out and afterward affixed spoils the immersion-pool.[28]

4:2 A. Water which is drawn on its own in buckets from the ocean and from the river,

B. and that which goes up on the water-pump

C. spoil the immersion-pool.

D. Rabban Simeon b. Gamaliel says, "That which goes up on the chain-works for drawing water does not spoil the immersion-pool, because it is not detached."

4:3 A. R. Eliezer b. Jacob says, "A roof on top of which there are twenty-one *se'ahs* of rain-water — one draws water and carries it on the shoulder and puts in it nineteen *se'ahs*,

B. "opens [a sluice], and mingles them in the courtyard."[29]

4:4 A. [If] there were forty *se'ahs* [on the roof], and it [the roof] was broken through,

B. and they [the forty *se'ahs* of rain-water] came [flowed] into the house

C. it [the water] is fit.

D. But [as they are flowing into the house] they do not dunk [utensils] in them,

E. for they do not dunk in air.

F. [If] one of its ends [the water-stream from the roof] reaches the ground,

G. they do immerse in it.

H. But they do not immerse in air.

---

28. M. Miq. 4:2.   29. M. Miq. 5:6.

4:5 A. A wave [of water] which was detached from the sea or from the river —

B. they do not immerse in it,

C. for they do not immerse in air.

D. If the two ends [of the wave] touched the ground,

E. they do immerse in it,

F. but they do not immerse in the crest [of the wave].[30]

4:6 A. A reservoir which distributes water [in pipes] among the villages,

B. if it was perforated by a hole the size of the stopper of a water-skin,

C. does not spoil the immersion-pool,

D. and if not, it spoils the immersion-pool.

E. This law did the people of Assya bring up three festival seasons to Yavneh, and at the third season, they declared it fit —

F. even if it was perforated by a hole the size of a needle.

4:7 A. Said R. Eleazar b. R. Yosé, "This law did I teach in Rome, [declaring the matter] clean.

B. "And when I came to my colleagues, they said to me, 'Rightly did you teach.'"

C. Under what circumstances?

D. When [it is perforated] from the side.

E. But [if it is perforated] from the bottom, it does not spoil the immersion-pool [even at less than the requisite hole of a stopper].

F. And if it was able to serve as a receptacle from the perforation and downward, [holding] any amount at all [of water], it spoils the immersion-pool.

G. [If] one stopped it up with plaster or with building materials,

H. it does not spoil the immersion-pool.

I. [If one stopped it up] with plaster and with gypsum, it does spoil the immersion-pool.

J. [If one put it] on the ground [thereby stuffing up the hole] or on plaster and gypsum,

K. or [if] one plastered it with mud on the sides,

L. it does not spoil the immersion-pool.

4:8 A. A spring which flows to the bidet, and from the bidet to the pool—

B. the first drops, as they flow — lo, they are unfit, because they are drawn water.

C. What should one do?

D. One should perforate it at the "eye of the beard" in any amount at all.

E. And it will come out that the small part of the water cleans the larger part.

30. M. Miq. 5:3.

F. "One stops up the flow by a corpse," the words of R. Judah.

G. Water which flows over the furrows and the indentation —

H. one dunks [utensils] in them [if the waters are] at a height of the thickness of a garlic peel and the breadth of the stopper of the waterskin.

4:9　A. A spring which is drawn out like a centipede —

B. and it [drawn water] formed the greater part over it [spring-water] —

C. and made it [the channel] wider —

D. it renders clean in a hollow [like an immersion-pool].

E. And it does not purify when it is flowing,

F. except up to the place to which it was able to reach in the first place.[31]

4:10　A. What is the rain-stream?

B. Rain-water which comes down an incline.

C. "They inspect it:

D. "If there is from its beginning to its end a [complete] intermingling,

E. "and there are forty *se'ahs* of rain-water [contained therein] —

F. "they dunk in it.

G. "And if not, they do not dunk in it," the words of the House of Shammai.

H. The House of Hillel say, "They do not dunk in it unless there will be before it a circle containing forty *se'ahs*."

I. WM'ŚH B: A family of laundrymen was in Jerusalem, who would make a dam with utensils and dunk in [the rain-stream dammed up by] them.

J. And all agree that utensils with which one made a dam have not been immersed.[31]

5:1　A. Holes on the rim of the immersion-pool,

B. and so tracks of the hooves of cattle —

C. if [the water in these] is joined together [with water in an immersion-pool] by a hole the size of the stopper of the waterskin —

D. they dunk therein.

E. And if not, they do not dunk therein.

F. And R. Judah says, "Lo, they are like the pit of the cavern."

G. The projections which are in the immersion-pool —

H. they dunk therein,

I. and on condition that they are mingled together through a hole the size of the stopper of the waterskin.[32]

5:2　A. A trough which is full of utensils —

B. and one brought it[s water] into touch with an immersion-pool —

C. it requires [mingling of water through] a hole the size of the spout of the waterskin.

31. M. Miq. 5:6.　　　32. M. Miq. 6:1.

D. But a spring [suffices] with [an intermingling] of any amount at all.[33]

E. R. Judah says in the name of the House of Shammai, "In regard to a large utensil [we require a hole the size of] four handbreadths.

F. "[And in the case of a small one], its greater part."[34]

5:3   A. A kettle which is full of utensils,

B. and one brought it into touch with [the water of] an immersion-pool

C. even though its mouth is narrow, in any amount at all,

D. the utensils which are in it are clean.

E. [If] one tipped it on its side, [the water in the kettle and that in the immersion-pool are not intermingled] until there will be a hole in its mouth the size of the spout of a waterskin.[35]

5:4   A. A spring which emerges through the oven, and one immersed in it a radish and a gourd [in order to rinse them off] —

B. if the water overflowed on top of it to their full [bulk],

C. lo, they are clean.[36]

D. The two fingers of which they have spoken — [they are in accord with the] average man.

E. And not [in accord with] the four which are in the handbreadth.[37]

F. An olive's bulk of carrion, a lentil's bulk of the insect —

G. [if] there is a doubt whether they form the requisite bulk or do not form the requisite bulk —

H. it is unclean.

I. For any matter the principle [of contamination] of which derives from the Torah, but the requisite measure of which derives from the words of Scribes —

J. its matter of doubt is deemed unclean.

5:5   A. They clean the immersion-pools,

B. the upper by the lower,

C. and the distant by that which is near —

D. how so?

E. One brings a pipe of wood or of bone or of glass

F. and places his hand(s) [under] the lower [end of the pipe]

G. until it will be filled with water,

H. and conveys it, and touches it [the water of the pool to the water of the pipe].

I. Even if it is [touching] by as little as a hair's breadth, it suffices.

J. And if the pipe is bent in any measure at all, it is unfit.

K. Under what circumstances?

L. When they were on top of the other.

M. But if they were side by side,

33. ibid.   34. M. Miq. 6:5.   35. M. Miq. 6:2.
36. M. Miq. 6:6.   37. M. Miq. 6:7.

N. he brings a knee-shaped pipe on one side, and a knee-shaped pipe on the other side, and a pipe in the middle —

O. and he touches [the water of the one to that of the other],

P. and descends and immerses.[38]

5:6 A. A wall is between two immersion-pools which was cracked horizontally — it joins together.

B. And [if it was cracked] perpendicularly, it does not join together.

C. R. Yosé b. R. Judah says, "The matters are reversed."

D. [If] they flow together into one another —

E. Rabban Simeon b. Gamaliel says, "A full handbreadth over the [whole] breadth of the split [is required for intermingling of water]."[39]

5:7 A. [If] the corpse is in the bath house, the furnace-room is unclean.

B. [If] the corpse is in the furnace-room, the bath house is unclean,

C. because of the outlet.

D. He who touches the outlet is unclean, but he is clean when he ascends [from the water].

E. R. Simeon says, "He who touches the outlet is clean, for it was only made to serve when affixed to the ground."

5:8 A. The filter which is in the bath —

B. the lower one is full of drawn water —

C. and the upper one is full of fit water —

D. and on condition that it be opposite the hole —

E. and it contributes to the measure of forty se'ahs.[40]

F. Snowballs which are sunk down into an immersion-pool — lo, they raise.

G. And R. Judah says, "They do not raise [it]."

H. And R. Judah agrees that one brings thin mud in a trough and touches [it to the water of the immersion-pool] and goes down and immerses.[41]

5:9 A. Water in which food has been pressed or seethed, and olive-water

B. they immerse in it,

C. and on condition that it does not contain sediment of oil.

D. And the grapeskin wine before it has fermented — they do not immerse in it.[42]

5:10 A. An immersion-pool which does not have forty se'ahs [of fit water],

B. and one puts into it wine, and its color changes —

C. it is not made unfit in the measure of three logs.

D. And not only so, but even if its color returned to what it had been,

E. [the pool] is fit [to be added to].

38. M. Miq. 6:8.   39. M. Miq. 6:9.   40. M. Miq. 6:11.
41. M. Miq. 7:1.   42. ibid.

F. [If] there were in it forty *se'ahs* [of fit water], and wine fell in and its color changed in part,

G. he who immerses, whether in the place of the water or in the place of the wine, is as if he did not immerse.

H. [If] three *logs* of wine fell in, it is as if they did not fall in.

I. [If] it was drawn water and one made it touch —

J. [if] he made it touch at the place of the wine,

K. this and this have not become clean.

L. [If] one touched [them together] at the place where the water is located, it is clean.

M. [If he touched it] at the place [at which] the wine [is located], it is not clean.[43]

5:11   A. A jar which broke in the Great Sea,

B. and the color of that place is like the color of that wine —

C. he who immerses in that place is as if he did not immerse.

D. And not only so, but even if a loaf of heave-offering fell there, it is unclean.

5:12   A. An immersion-pool which contains exactly forty *se'ahs,*

B. and two people went down and immersed one after the other —

C. the first is clean, and the second is unclean.

D. What should one do?

E. While the first still is in the water, one should draw [water in utensils and carry it] on the shoulder and put it into it, and it is clean.

F. R. Judah says, "If the foot of the first is still in the water, the other descends and immerses and is clean."[44]

5:13   A. [If] one immersed in it a large kettle.

B. lo, this is unclean,

C. because the water gushes forth.

D. What should one do?

E. He puts it in with its mouth downward and turns it over,

F. and immerses it, and raises it up by its bottom.[45]

5:14   A. He who jumps into an immersion-pool, lo, such a one is blameworthy.

B. He who immerses twice in an immersion-pool, lo, this one is blameworthy.

C. This one says to his fellow, "Press your hand down on me in the immersion-pool" — lo, this one is blameworthy.

D. R. Judah says, "Press your hand down on him until his soul goes forth."[46]

43. M. Miq. 7:3.   44. M. Miq. 7:6.   45. *ibid.*
46. M. Miq. 7:7.

6:1   A. Samaritan territory [in the Land of Israel] is clean, [and] its immersion-pools and its dwellings and its paths are clean.

B. The land of the gentiles [in the Land of Israel] is unclean, [and] its immersion-pools and its dwellings and its paths are unclean.

C. The immersion-pools of the gentiles which are outside of the Land are fit for those who have suffered a pollution,

D. and unfit for all [other] unclean Israelites.

E. Those in the Land of Israel which are outside the town gate are fit for all unclean people, and it does not need saying, for an Israelite who has had a seminal emission.

F. "And those which are inside the gate are unfit for those who have had a seminal issue, and, it does not require saying, for all unclean people," the words of R. Meir.

G. R. Judah says, "They are fit for those who have had a seminal emission, for one who has had a seminal emission immerses in forty *se'ahs* in any place."

H. And those which are outside the town-gate are fit even for menstruating women.[47]

6:2   A. Rabban Simeon b. Gamaliel says, "I do not have the law [in hand], but a precedent [is in hand], concerning the [immersion-pool] in the garden of a certain extortioner in Damin,

B. "that the priests were climbing over the fence, going down, and immersing in it."

C. Said R. Judah, M'ŚH B: "An immersion-pool [was] between Usha and Shefar'am, and it belonged to Shefar'am.

D. "And R. Dosa would set two disciples of sages to supervise it so that there should be forty *se'ahs* [of fit-water] in it [at all times]."

6:3   A. ŠWB M'ŚH B: [A pool on] the height (RWM) of Bet 'Anat in which more than two thousand *kor* [of water] were gathered, and they came and asked R. Ḥanina b. Teradion, and he declared it unfit, "For I say that gentiles have gone in and emptied it by night, and then have gone and filled it with the water of a swape-well."

B. WM'ŚH B: Rabban Gamaliel and Onqelos the proselyte came to Ashkelon. And Rabban Gamaliel immersed in the bath, and Onqelos the proselyte immersed in the sea.

C. Said R. Joshua b. Qevusai, "I was with them, and Rabban Gamaliel immersed only in the sea."

6:4   A. A bath whose bath-attendants are gentiles,

B. when its filters are open to the private domain, is unclean.

C. [When they are open] to the public domain, it is clean [fit].

D. A bath whose bath-attendants are gentiles, and which an Israelite

47. M. Miq. 8:1.

entered in the morning and touched [the waters of which to a fit immersion-pool] —

E. even though this [gentile] goes in and the other comes out, is clean.

F. [If] it was locked or if it was designated as private property, it is unclean.

6:5 A. He who dreams erotic dreams by night and arose and found his flesh hot is unclean.

B. [If] he dreamt erotic dreams but was not heated, or [if] he was heated but did not dream erotic dreams, he is clean.

C. R. Yosé says, "In the case of one who was ill or an old man, he is unclean.

D. "In the case of a youth or a healthy person he is clean."[48]

6:6 A. "She who discharges semen on the third day is clean," the words of R. Eleazar b. 'Azariah.

B. R. Ishmael says, "Sometimes they are six."

C. R. 'Aqiva says, "They are always five.

D. "And if part of the first season has passed, they reckon that part of the sixth season completes it."[49]

6:7 A. The semen of an Israelite under all circumstances, lo, this is unclean.

B. And that of a gentile, under all circumstances, is clean,

C. except for the urine in which it is located.

D. All those concerning which they have said that they are clean [are clean] for unconsecrated food and unclean for heave-offering,

E. except for the woman who discharges semen, who is unclean for unconsecrated food.[50]

6:8 A. R. Yosé b. R. Judah says, "She who discharges semen is clean for unconsecrated food."[51]

B. And as [to the things about which] they have said, "They interpose," and as [to the things about which] they have said, "They do not interpose"

C. they do not convey uncleanness and do not receive cleanness, except for the membrane on the sore.[52]

D. And the bandage which is on the sore, and the splints which are on the fracture, and the chains, and the ear-rings, and the beads, and the rings,

E. when they are tightly-bound, interpose, and when they are loosely bound, they do not interpose.

F. R. Simeon Shezuri says, "[As to] the privy parts of the woman —

G. "in the case of a married woman, they interpose, and in the case of the unmarried woman, they do not interpose."

6:9 A. A dry poultice which is on the sore,

---

48. M. Miq. 8:3.   49. *ibid.*   50. M. Miq. 8:4.
51. *ibid.*   52. M. Miq. 9:4.

B. and the eyepaint which is in the eye —

C. lo, these do not interpose.

D. The blood, and the ink, and the honey, and the milk, and mulberry-juice, and fig-juice, and sycamore-juice, and carob-juice —

E. when they are dry, interpose,

F. and when they are moist, they do not interpose.

G. And all other juices, whether wet or dry — lo, these interpose,

H. for they are gummy.

I. Stains of fruit-juice,

J. and the eyepaint which is outside the eye —

K. lo, these interpose.[53]

6:10 A. And excrement under the fingernail which is not opposite the flesh, the mud, and the dough under the fingernail even opposite the flesh do [not] interpose.

B. The downy hair of an adult, about which he is not fastidious, and the limb and flesh which are dangling in the case of a man, lo, these do interpose.

C. R. Jonathan b. Joseph says, "A fingernail, most of which has detached — lo, it does not interpose."[54]

6:11 A. Whatever [substances] interpose in utensils, interpose in the case of the menstruating woman and in the case of the convert at the time of immersion.

B. And in connection with [immersion for eating] unconsecrated food, they do not interpose.

6:12 A. A ring which one put into a brick of wet mud, and which one immersed, is clean.

B. If it was miry clay and [mud] like it, it is as if one did not immerse it.

6:13 A. A flagon which is full of unclean water, and moist mud is placed on its mouth —

B. if the water reaches down into the mud, and one dunked it, it is clean.

C. If it was miry clay and its equivalents, it is as if one did not immerse it.

D. R. Yosé declares unclean in the case of potter's clay, because they rub cracks of utensils with it.

6:14 A. And what are the pegs by the road-sides?

B. Those on which people walk in the rainy season,

C. and they are rubbed against [and stick to the garments].[55]

D. As to clothing:

E. [mud] on one side does not interpose.

F. On both sides, it interposes.

G. R. Judah says, in the name of R. Ishmael [says], "Even on one side."

53. *ibid.*   54. M. Miq. 9:2, 4.   55. M. Miq. 9:2.

H. R. Yosé says in the name of R. Ishmael, "[Mud on clothing] of construction workers on one side [interposes].

I. "Even in that of a farmer: in the case of a large one, on one side, and in the case of a small one, on both sides."[56]

6:15   A. Pitch which is on the cup and which is on the flask —

B. [if] it is on its inside, it interposes; and [if] it is on the outside, it does not interpose.

C. Under what circumstances?

D. At the factory.

E. But [if it belongs to] the householder, whether it is inside it or on its outer parts, lo, this interposes.

F. In the case of a tray and dish, whether it is on the inside or whether it is on the outside,

G. whether at the factory or at home,

H. lo, this interposes.[57]

6:16   A. Gum of myrrh and resin, whether in the case of a cup or in the case of a flask, or whether in the case of the tray, or whether in the case of the dish, whether on the inside, or on the outside, whether at the factory or at home — lo, these interpose.

B. [Mud] on the sandal: — [if it is] on its inside and above, it interposes, and [if it is] on the lower part [of the inside], it does not interpose.

C. And [mud] on the bench: [if it is] on top [or] on the sides, it interposes, and if it is below, it does not interpose.

6:17   A. [As to] pieces of excrement which are on the toilet and on the chairs [or: pots] —

B. those which are pressed down —

C. whether on the inside or on the outside,

D. whether below or on the sides,

E. lo, these interpose.

F. Those which are on the bed of the householder —

G. R. 'Aqiva says, "[If it is] on the outer frame, it interposes, and [if it is] on the inner, it does not interpose."

H. [If it is] on the aprons of the tree-trimmers —

I. R. 'Aqiva says, "Even [if it is only] on part of it."

J. R. Simeon says, "Even that which is on those of the olive-workers is like them."

6:18   A. Moist wine lees which are in the cup and the flask,

B. and the fluff on a chain or a bell, and the mud and the dough which are on the handle of the ax and on the handle of a shovel — lo, these do not interpose.

C. [If] they turned solid, lo, they interpose.

---

56. M. Miq. 9:6.   57. M. Miq. 9:5.

6:19   A. All handles of utensils which are affixed in the ordinary way, lo, these do not interpose.

B. [If] one put pitch or wax,

C. whether in the place of the hollow [of the handle] or whether in the place of the spout,

D. lo, these do not interpose.

E. [If] one put them in not in the normal way, lo, these interpose.

F. [If] one put pitch or wax, whether in the place of the hole or in the place of the spout, lo, these interpose.[58]

6:20   A. All handles of utensils which broke,

B. for example, the handle of the sickle,

C. and the handle of the knife,

D. if they serve their original function,

E. interpose,

F. and if not, they do not interpose.

6:21   A. The sickle, the handle of which was broken within that part of the handle which is indispensable in using the tool, does not interpose,

B. because it is equivalent to the private parts.

C. [If it is broken] beyond the indispensable part of the handle, if it serves its original function, it does not interpose; and if not, lo, this interposes.

D. [If] one joined it with reed grass or with rope, lo, this interposes.

E. [If] one affixed it with resin, lo, this does not interpose.

6:22   A. A utensil which is narrow on both ends and broad in the middle,

B. for example a quarter-measure and a half-quarter measure —

C. can never have purification,

D. until one will turn it on its side.

E. A flask, the rim of which is flattened downwards into its midst,

F. and the shoulders of which are high,

G. and so a flagon, the rim of which is flattened downwards into its midst and the shoulders of which are high —

H. can never have purification until one will turn it [on its side].[59]

6:23   A. A flask the lip of which is turned outward —

B. (And) "One immerses it and raises it by its bottom," the words of R. 'Aqiva.

C. R. Yoḥanan b. Nuri says, "One immerses it in the normal manner, and one does not scruple, because it is like the private parts."[60]

6:24   A. A flask, the rim of which is turned down inward —

B. R. Yosé says in the name of R. Yoḥanan b. Nuri, "One immerses it in its normal way and does not scruple, because it is like the private parts."[61]

58. M. Miq. 10:1.   59. *ibid.*   60. *ibid.*
61. *ibid.*

7:1   A. [If] one tied his hands and feet together and sat down in a stream of water —

B. if the water covered his whole [body], he is clean.

C. And if not, he is unclean.

D. [If] his hands and feet were covered with dust, and he went down and immersed in an immersion-pool which contains forty *se'ahs,* he is clean.

E. [If] he rubbed [his hands or feet], or [if] he immersed in hot water, he is unclean.

F. A kettle which is full of soot and which one immersed is unclean.

G. [If] one polished it or immersed it in hot water, it is clean.

7:2   A. Baskets of the wine-press and of the olive-press — [when] they [the holes therein] are tightly packed [by grapes or olives] —

B. one needs [to clean them by] picking.

C. And [when] they are loose, one needs to shake [them loose, so water will permeate the basket].

D. The knots of the money-bag and of the bands, and the knots of the shoe and sandal, and the knots of the hole of a shirt [of a woman] — these interpose.

E. The knots of the fringes of a money-bag, and bands, and the knots of the thongs of the shoe, and the sandal, and the knot of the undergarment which is on the shoulder, and the sheet the fringes of which one tied up, lo, these interpose.

F. [If] they were knotted on their own, lo, these do not interpose.[62]

7:3   A. The knots of the poor person about which he is fastidious and [those] of the householder — lo, these interpose.

B. And the knots of the householder about which he is not fastidious and those of the poor man — lo, these do not interpose.[63]

C. And R. Judah says, "One has to immerse the whole thing on account of [the place where the handle is intended to be] lopped off."

D. And so did R. Judah say in the name of R. Ṭarfon, "One has to immerse the entire ring."[64]

7:4   A. A utensil which is full of wine and which one immersed, if its [the wine's] color is [so diluted as to be] annulled, it is clean, and if not, it is unclean.

B. [If] it was filled with white wine or milk, if it [the water of the immersion-pool that enters the utensil] exceeds it [the wine or milk], it is clean. If not it is unclean.

C. R. Judah says, "They regard it as if it were [red wine] in water. If its color is annulled, it is clean, and if not, it is unclean."

D. [If] it was full of white wine and milk, if it [the water of the immersion-pool that enters the utensil] exceeded it [the wine or milk] —

---

62. M. Miq. 10:3—4.   63. *ibid.*   64. M. Miq. 10:5.

E. Said R. Yosé, "I have heard that even if it is a utensil which holds a *kor* and it contains only a quarter-*log,* it is as if it did not immerse."[65]

7:5 A. All foods join together to render the body invalid in the measure of a half a loaf —

B. in the time that it takes to eat a loaf.

C. [If] one ate and went back and ate again and went back and ate again,

D. if from the beginning of the first act of eating to the end of the last act of eating, [the time has elapsed which is] sufficient for eating a loaf, they join together, and if not, they do not join together.

E. And they do not require him who eats less than the required measure to go down and immerse.

F. But one who eats in accord with the established measure goes down and immerses.

G. [If] one ate less than the established measure and goes down and immerses in the middle, he is unclean.[66]

7:6 A. They permitted a woman who is pregnant to taste a small quantity [of unclean food], because of the danger to life.

B. And how much is a loaf?

C. "Two eggs' bulk, less a bit," the words of R. Judah.

D. R. Yosé says, "Two laughing [large-sized] eggs."

E. And Rabbi [gave the] measure at two eggs and a bit more.[67]

7:7 A. All liquids join together to render the body invalid for eating heave-offering — in [the case of one who] drinks a quarter-*log* in the time it takes to eat a loaf [or: to drink a quarter-*log*].

B. [If] one drank and went and drank again and went and drank again, if [the time elapsed] from the beginning of the first act of drinking to the end of the last act of drinking is sufficient for the drinking of a quarter-*log* [or: to eat a loaf], they join together, and if not, they do not join together.

C. They do not make him liable who drinks less than the established measure to go down and immerse.

D. But he drinks in the established measure and goes down and immerses.

E. [If] one drank less than the established measure and went down and immersed in the middle, he is clean.

F. They permitted a woman who touches something which has touched an object unclean with corpse-uncleanness to suckle her child, and he is clean.[68]

7:8 A. [If] one swallowed an olive's bulk of corpse-matter and entered a house, it is clean, for whatever is swallowed by man or cattle or beast or fowl

65. M. Miq. 10:6. 66. M. Miq. 10:7. 67. *ibid.*
68. *ibid.*

is clean.

B. [If] it decomposed or emerged from below [the rectum], it is clean.

C. [If] one drank unclean water and vomited it up, it is unclean, because it was made unclean when it went out.

D. [If] one immersed, or [if] it decomposed or it came out below, it is clean.

E. [If] one drank other [unclean] liquids even though he immersed and vomited them out, they are unclean, because they are not made clean in the body.

F. [If] they decomposed or went forth, they are clean.[69]

7:9 A. A cow which drank unclean water and vomited it up — it is unclean, because it is not made clean in the body.

B. [If] it decomposed or went out below, it is clean.[70]

C. He into whose knee an arrow penetrated —

D. Rabbi [Judah] says, "It does not interpose."

E. And sages say, "Lo, this interposes."

F. Under what circumstances?

G. In the case of one made of metal.

H. But in the case of one made of wood, lo, this interposes.

I. And if the flesh formed a membrane over it, all agree that it does not interpose,

J. for whatever is swallowed up in man, cattle, beast, and fowl is clean.

K. [If] pieces of gravel or splinters went into the cracks beneath his feet,

L. R. Jacob ['Aqiva] says, "It does not interpose, because it is like the privy parts."[71]

7:10 A. A soothing poultice and a bandage which is on the privy parts —

B. Rabbi says, "It interposes."

C. R. Yosé b. R. Judah says, "It does not interpose."

D. He who mats [hair] on his head —

E. Rabbi says, "It interposes."

F. And R. Yosé b. R. Judah says, "It does not interpose."

G. [If] there was a single hair outside of the sore, and its head cleaves to the sore,

H. or [if] there were on him two hairs, and their tops cleaved to the knots surrounding the anus or excrement,

I. lo, these interpose.

J. [If] there were on him two hairs on his eyelids below, and they pierce a way through to the eyelids above —

K. this was a case, and five sages in Lud took a vote concerning it and declared it unclean.[72]

---

69. M. Miq. 10:8.   70. ibid.   71. ibid.   72. M. Miq. 9:2.

7:11 A. A cow which drank purification-water, and one slaughtered it within twenty-four hours —

B. This was a case, and R. Yosé the Galilean did declare it clean, and R. 'Aqiva did declare it unclean.

C. R. Ṭarfon supported R. Yosé the Galilean. R. Simeon ben Nanos supported R. 'Aqiva.

D. R. Simeon b. Nanos dismissed [the arguments of] R. Ṭarfon. R. Yosé the Galilean dismissed [the arguments of] R. Simeon b. Nanos.

E. R. 'Aqiva dismissed [the arguments of] R. Yosé the Galilean.

F. After a time, he [Yosé] found an answer for him ['Aqiva].

G. He said to him, "Am I able to reverse myself?"

H. He said to him, "Not anyone [may reverse himself], but you [may do so], for you are Yosé the Galilean."

I. [He said to him] "I shall say to you: Lo, Scripture states, 'And they shall be kept for the congregation of the people of Israel for the water for impurity.'

J. "Just so long as they are kept, lo, they are water for impurity, and not when a cow has drunk them."

K. This was a case, and thirty-two elders voted in Lud and declared it clean.

L. At that time R. Ṭarfon recited this verse:

M. "'I saw the ram goring westward and northward and southward, and all the animals were unable to stand against it, and none afforded protection from its power, and it did just as it liked and grew great' [Dan. 8:4] —

N. "[This is] R. 'Aqiva.

O. "'As I was considering, behold, a he-goat came from the west across the face of the whole earth, without touching the ground; and the goat had a conspicuous horn between his eyes.

P. "'He came to the ram with the two horns, which I had seen standing on the bank of the river, and he ran at him in his mighty wrath. I saw him come close to the ram, and he was enraged against him and struck the ram and broke his two horns' — this is R. 'Aqiva and R. Simeon b. Nanos.

Q. "'And the ram had no power to stand before him' — this is 'Aqiva.

R. "'But he cast him down to the ground and trampled upon him' — this is R. Yosé the Galilean.

S. "'And there was no one who could rescue the ram from his power' — these are the thirty-two elders who voted in Lud and declared it clean."[73]

73. M. Par. 9:5.

TOHOROT

1:1 A. Said R. Simeon, "Why did they say, 'Food which is made unclean by a Father of uncleanness and that which is made unclean by an Offspring of uncleanness join together with one another'?

B. "Because it is possible for that which is unclean in the third remove to be made unclean in the second remove. And it is possible for that which is unclean in the second remove to be made unclean in the first remove.

C. "And why did they say, 'The creeping thing and the carrion and the corpse do not join together with one another'? Because it is not possible for a creeping thing to become carrion, and carrion cannot become a corpse."[1]

1:2 A. A piece of dough which was unclean in the third remove, and one stuck others to it —

B. they all are unclean in the third remove so far as Holy Things are concerned.

C. [If] that which is unclean in the third remove separated, all [the others] are clean.

D. And what is the one which sticks?

(And) the one which removes anything at all from it.

E. But if they were mashed together,

F. for example, the ring of pressed figs and the dates and the figs and the raisins —

G. lo, these are not connected.

H. Why did they say concerning olives that it is a matter of connection?

I. For in the first place one placed them only so that they should suck [draw moisture] from one another.[2]

1:3 A. All the same is one who has immersed on the selfsame day on account of a stringent uncleanness and the one who has immersed on the selfsame day on account of a lenient uncleanness,

B. and even one who has immersed on the selfsame day because of the Zab and because of the Zabah and because of the rest of the sources of uncleanness which are mentioned in the Torah —

C. lo, they are like one who has immersed on the selfsame day on account of being made unclean by the dead creeping thing.

D. One who has immersed on the selfsame day and one who is made unclean through a corpse and one who has had intercourse with a menstruant — he works at the olive press,

E. except for one who is made unclean because of the Zab and because of the Zabah — (and even) on his seventh day [after being made unclean], lo, such a one should do nothing,

---

1. M. Toh. 1:5−6.   2. M. Toh. 1:7−8.

263

F. and if he has done it, lo, this is suspended.

G. And all the same is one who is clean, whose hands are unclean and one who has immersed on the selfsame day —

H. he renders unclean liquid of unconsecrated produce and renders unfit heave-offering-foods.

I. And R. Eleazar b. R. Simeon says, "[The rule governing the uncleanness of] hands does not apply to the one who has immersed on the selfsame day."[3]

1:4 A. Abba Saul says, "One who has immersed on the selfsame day is in the first remove so far as Holy Things are concerned."

B. R. Meir says, "One who has immersed on the selfsame day renders Holy Things unclean and spoils heave-offering."

C. And sages say, "Just as he renders unfit liquid of heave-offering and foods of heave-offering, so he spoils liquid of Holy Things and foods of Holy Things."[4]

1:5 A. The creeping thing renders unclean at three removes and unfit at one [further remove] in connection with Holy Things; and renders unclean at two removes and unfit at one [further] remove in connection with heave-offering. It renders unclean at one remove and unfit at one remove in connection with unconsecrated food.

B. Liquid renders unclean at two removes and unfit at one remove in connection with Holy Things.

C. It renders unclean at one remove and unfit at one remove in connection with Heave-offering.

D. And it spoils unconsecrated food.[5]

1:6 A. The hands convey uncleanness at one remove and render unfit at one remove in connection with Holy Things,

and render heave-offering unfit,

and [the rule governing the uncleanness of] hands [has] no [bearing upon] unconsecrated food.

B. R. Simeon ben Eleazar says in the name of R. Meir, "The hands are unclean in the first remove so far as Holy Things are concerned and are unclean in the second remove so far as heave-offering is concerned."

C. In respect to what sort of Holy Things did they speak?

D. Concerning Holy Things of the sanctuary which are sanctified, for example, loaves of thanksgiving and the wafers of the Nazir over which the sacrifice has been slaughtered and meal-offerings which were mixed in a utensil.

E. But loaves of thanksgiving and wafers of a Nazir over which the sacrifice was not slaughtered and meal-offerings which were not mixed in a utensil are like neither Holy Things nor unconsecrated food, but they are

3. M. Toh. 2:1.   4. *ibid.*   5. M. Toh. 2:3—7.

like heave-offering.

F. And the dead creeping thing renders unclean at two removes and spoils at one remove in their case.[6]

1:7 A. The dough-offering and the first fruits and what is brought as restitution for heave-offering and its fifth, lo, they are like heave-offering.

B. The edibles forbidden pending the separation of sacred gifts and the edibles with which heave-offering has been mixed and that which grows from heave-offering and second tithe, lo, they are in the status of unconsecrated food.[7]

C. Loaves of Holy Things —

in their holes [is liquid] —

D. and the [aforementioned] liquid of Holy Things is made unclean in the case of one of them by a dead creeping thing —

E. they all are in the first remove of uncleanness.

F. In the case of heave-offering, it imparts uncleanness at two removes and spoils [heave-offering] at one [further] remove.

G. In the case of unconsecrated food, it imparts uncleanness at one remove and spoils [heave-offering] at one [further] remove.

H. You have no liquid (of Holy Things) which touches something unclean in the third remove [and is] unclean except for Holy Things alone.[8]

I. R. Eleazar b. R. Ṣadoq says, "He who eats food in the second remove of uncleanness should not work in the olive press because he produces uncleanness in the second remove.

"And that which is unclean in the second remove renders liquid unclean so that it conveys uncleanness in the first remove."

J. But food which is unclean in the second remove which touched the liquid of the olive-press — it [the liquid] is unclean.[9]

2:1 A. Said R. Joshua to R. Eliezer, "Where do we find a form of uncleanness in the Torah which produces another uncleanness which is like it [at the same remove, and not at one remove of diminished virulence], that you say, 'It produces [uncleanness in] the first remove'?"

B. He said to him, "Also you say, 'It [that which is unclean in the second remove] produces something unclean in the second remove'!"

C. He said to him, "We find that that which is unclean in the second remove renders liquid unclean to produce uncleanness at the first remove, and the liquid renders food unclean to produce uncleanness at the second remove.

D. "But we do not find something unclean in the first remove which makes something else unclean in the first remove in any instance."[10]

6. *ibid.*   7. *ibid.*   8. M. Toh. 1:9.
9. M. Toh. 2:8.   10. M. Toh. 2:1.

2:2 A. Cress and bean mash, when one stirs them in the pot, receive uncleanness as food.

B. [If] one put them into a dish and liquids exude from them, the liquid which exudes from them receives uncleanness as liquid.[11]

2:3 A. Oil is neither food nor liquid.

B. In what way have they said,

C. "Oil is always in the first remove of uncleanness"?

D. For if it is wiped away and nothing remains of it but as much as a bean, that which exudes from it receives uncleanness as liquid.[12]

2:4 A. It comes out that one rules:

B. There are three traits in respect to liquid.

C. Grease and milk and bean mash, when liquid runs [from them], lo, they are in the first remove of uncleanness.

D. [If] they congeal, they do not require intention [to receive uncleanness] as foods.[13]

2:5 A. Honey which oozes from the hive of bees receives uncleanness as liquid.

B. [If] one gave thought to it as food, it receives uncleanness as food.

C. Oil is neither food nor liquid.

D. [If] one gave thought to it to make use of it as food and not as liquid, his intention is of no effect.

E. Blood which congealed is neither food nor liquid.

F. [If] one gave thought to it to make use of it as food, it receives uncleanness as food.

And [if one gave thought to use it as] liquid, his intention is null.

G. The honey of palms is neither food nor liquid.

H. [If] one gave thought to it to make use of it for food, it receives uncleanness as food.

I. And [if one gave thought to it to use it] for liquid, his intention is null.

J. And as to all other fruit juice, [it is] neither food nor liquid.

K. [If] one gave thought to it, whether for liquid or for food, his intention is null.

L. [Sens:] Snow is neither food nor liquid. If one gave thought to it for food, his intention is null. For liquid — it receives uncleanness as liquid.

M. [If] part of it is made unclean, the liquid is made unclean.

N. [If] part of it is made unclean, the whole of it is not made unclean.

O. [If] part of it is clean, the whole of it is clean.

2:6 A. Purification-water which froze over and does not contain running liquid is clean.

B. [If] it melted, it has returned to its former uncleanness.

C. An immersion pool of drawn water which froze over is clean in

---

11. M. Toh. 3:1.   12. *ibid.*   13. *ibid.*

respect to drawn water.

D. [If] it melted, it is fit to be added to.

2:7 A. He who gives thought to the milk which is in the udder — it is clean.

B. And [he who gives thought to the milk] which is in the maw — it is unclean.

C. The hide and the placenta do not receive uncleanness as food.

D. The hide which one boiled and the placenta to which one gave thought [for use as food] receive uncleanness as food.

3:1 A. Peat and grapeshells which were prepared in a state of cleanness and from which one squeezed liquids are clean.

B. And those which were prepared in a state of uncleanness and from which one squeezed liquids are unclean.

C. And R. Simeon declares clean.

D. Said to them R. Simeon, "What difference does it make to me that they are prepared in a state of uncleanness or that they are prepared when they are in a state of cleanness?"

E. They said to him, "When they are prepared in a state of uncleanness, liquids drip down from under the beam, and when he raises the beam, they go back and are absorbed in the peat."

F. He said to them, "Also when they are prepared in a state of cleanness, the Zab comes and presses on them. The liquids which drip down from under the foot of the Zab when he raises his foot go and are absorbed in the peat."

G. They said to him, "Liquid which exudes at one's intent is not like liquid which exudes not by intent."

H. He said to them, "This and this have never been unclean."

3:2 A. Grapes which are jammed in a wedge by the basket —

B. they fell into the airspace of the clean oven —

C. it is unclean.

D. Olives which are jammed in a wedge by the press —

E. and they fell into the airspace of a clean oven —

F. it is clean.

G. This and this [fell into the airspace of a clean oven], if there is on them running moisture —

H. the oven is unclean.

3:3 A. Unclean pots which fell into the airspace of the oven, whether whole or broken,

even when it is heated up —

it is unclean.

B. When it is not heated up — it is clean.

C. And [if] one made use of them in cleanness, and they are made unclean, and they fell into the airspace of the oven —

D. when it is heated up, it is unclean.

E. When it is not heated up, it is clean.

F. And those which are broken,

G. even when it is heated up — it is clean,

H. for it does not contain liquids by which it will convey uncleanness.

3:4 A. All the unclean things are adjudged as they are at the moment at which they are found, and in accord with every place [in which they are found].

B. [If] one lost a needle which is polished and came and found it full of rust, lo, this remains in its presumption [of being] polished,

C. until one may say, "It is clear to me that it was full of rust."

[Sens, *TR* IV, p. 56, adds:] If it was lost when full of rust and one came and found it polished, lo, it remains in the presumption of being polished until one will say, "It is clear to me that it has put forth rust."

D. And so in the case of a creeping thing.

E. And so in the case of a rag.

F. [If] one left it unclean in this corner and found it in another corner,

G. the first corner is unclean,

H. until one will state, "It is clear to me that it was uprooted from here."

I. The second corner is unclean,

J. until one will state,

K. "It is clear to me that it did not come here."[14]

3:5 A. If an olive's bulk of corpse-matter was lost in the house —

B. they sought and did not find it —

C. the house is clean.

D. When it will be found, the house conveys uncleanness retroactively.

3:6 A. The woman is raking stubble in the courtyard and a creeping thing is found inside the stubble —

B. she is clean.

C. [If it is found] on top of the stubble,

D. she is unclean.

E. [If] she was winnowing wheat in a sieve and a creeping thing is found in the sieve,

F. she is clean.

G. [If it is found] on top of the sieve,

H. she is unclean.

3:7 A. A child who was holding on to his father's hand or was riding on his father's shoulder —

B. a matter of doubt concerning him is unclean,

14. M. Toh. 3:5.

C. because his father may be interrogated about him.

D. A deaf-mute, an imbecile, and a child — a matter of doubt concerning them is clean,

E. because they do not have intelligence to be interrogated.

F. Said R. Simeon, "In this case the rule of justice is smitten!"[15]

3:8 A. Four [stages of] doubts have the sages stated in connection with the minor:

B. [If] his mother left him and came and found him as he was, he is clean.

C. Said R. Judah, "Under what circumstances? When she left him dirty. But [if] she left him clean, he is unclean, because menstruating women hug him."

D. They said to him, "Even if he was dirty, [it] also [should be the rule], because they move him out of the way of the feet of men and the feet of cattle."

3:9 A. [If] he began to go out and come in,

B. his clothing is clean.

C. But they do not prepare clean things depending upon his being clean.

D. And Israelites did not refrain from this point [onward].

E. [If] he has intelligence to be consulted about his condition, a matter of doubt concerning him in private domain is resolved in favor of uncleanness; in the public domain, it is resolved in favor of cleanness.

3:10 A. [If] he knew how to keep his body,

B. food which is on his body is clean.

C. [If he knew how] to keep his hands, food which is on his hands is clean.

D. And how do they examine him?

E. They immerse him and give him unconsecrated food, saying that it is heave-offering.

F. If he knows how to guard his body, food which is on his body is clean.

G. [If he knows how] to guard his hands, food which is on his hands is clean.

3:11 A. A blind man and one who is sleeping and one who walks by night

B. matters of doubt which concern them are resolved in favor of cleanness, because they have intelligence to be consulted.

C. An ass which was standing in a clean place, and it is possible for him to pass over into an unclean place —

D. utensils which are on him are clean.[16]

3:12 A. A child who is found standing at the side of a basket of dough —

B. [or] at the side of a jar of liquids —

15. M. Toh. 3:6.   16. M. Toh. 3:7.

C. R. Meir declares clean.

D. And sages declare unclean,

E. for it is the way of a child to slap [dough].

F. R. Yosé says, "If he can spread forth his hands and touch [or: take] it, it is unclean.

G. "And if not, it is clean."[17]

3:13 A. More than this did R. Yosé say, "If he was found far from the dough, even though there is dough in his hand, it is clean,

B. "for I say, 'Someone else took and gave it to him.'

C. "And if one said, 'It is clear to me that no one came here,' it is unclean."

D. R. Ilai said in the name of R. Eliezer b. Jacob, "With respect to a dog, lo, this is clean,

E. "for he [the dog] would say, 'Any time water is available, but food is not available any time.'"[18]

3:14 A. Whatever is suspended and whatever is dragged — matters of doubt concerning them are resolved in favor of uncleanness,

because they are [regarded] as if they were lying.

B. And whatever is thrown — a matter of doubt concerning it is clean;

C. except for an olive's bulk of corpse-matter,

D. and whatever overshadows —

E. they convey uncleanness from above as from below.

F. But if something clean was thrown over an olive's bulk of corpse-matter — it is clean.[19]

4:1 A. [If a person] was wrapped in his cloak,

B. with unclean things and clean things at his side,

C. and unclean things and clean things above —

D. there is doubt whether he touched or did not touch —

E. his matter of doubt is deemed clean.

F. And if it is not possible for him [not to come] into [contact],

G. his matter of doubt is deemed unclean.

H. R. Dosa says, "They say to him that he should do it again."

I. They said to him, "They do not [attempt a] repetition in matters of cleanness."

4:2 A. Rabban Simeon b. Gamaliel says, "[There are] times that he does repeat."

B. (How so?)

C. [If] there was a creeping thing suspended between the walls, and it is not possible to pass without touching —

D. [if there] is doubt whether one touched or whether one did not touch

17. M. Toh. 3:8.   18. *ibid.*   19. M. Toh. 4:3.

E. his matter of doubt is deemed clean.

F. And if it is not possible [to pass] there [without touching] —

G. his matter of doubt is deemed unclean.

H. R. Dosa says, "[They say] to him that he should repeat."

I. They said to him, "They do not repeat in matter of cleanness."

4:3 A. [If] there was a [live] creeping thing suspended between the walls

B. one rubbed against it, and it fell on his garments or on a loaf of heave-offering —

C. it is clean.

D. And if they found it dead before him, it is unclean.

E. And if they saw it that it was alive between the walls, even though one found it dead before him, it is clean.

F. [If the dead creeping thing] rested on his shoulder, lo, this one is unclean.

4:4 A. A loaf of heave-offering which was placed on top of the board —

B. something unclean with *midras*-uncleanness is set beneath it —

C. and it is not possible for it [the loaf] to fall without touching that which is unclean with *midras*-uncleanness —

D. and one came and found it on top of something else which is unclean with *midras*-uncleanness —

E. it [the loaf] is clean.

F. For I say, "Another person took it and placed it on that place."

G. And if one said, "It is clear to me that no man has come here," it is unclean.

4:5 A. A creeping thing in the mouth of the weasel and it walks on top of loaves of heave-offering —

B. it touches it —

C. there is a doubt whether it is alive or whether it is dead —

D. Rabbi declares unclean,

E. for the presumption concerning creeping things is that they die in the mouth of the weasel.

F. And sages declare clean.

G. Under what circumstances?

H. When it took it and went on its way.

I. But if one found it dead in its mouth —

J. if one saw it alive in its mouth —

K. even though it [then] is found dead in its mouth —

L. it is clean.[20]

4:6 A. R. Simeon b. Leazar says, "A creeping thing in the mouth of the snake —

B. "it is crawling on top of loaves of heave-offering —

20. M. Toh. 4:2.

C. "there is a doubt whether it touched or whether it did not touch —

D. "its matter of doubt is deemed clean.

E. "For thus is the way of the snake, to raise its neck and crawl along."

4:7 A. The creeping thing is in the mouth of the chicken —

B. and a bit of carrion is in the mouth of the dog —

C. they pass through the courtyard —

D. they do not convey uncleanness retroactively.

E. For I say, "From some other place did they bring them."

F. [If] they were pecking at them on the ground,

G. they do convey uncleanness retroactively.[21]

4:8 A. A person went into an alley and made dough, and afterward a creeping thing was found —

B. and the person said, "If it were here, I would have seen it" —

C. Rabban Simeon b. Gamaliel declares clean.

D. And Rabbi declares unclean,

E. until he will state, "It is clear to me that it was not here beforehand."

F. Lo, he who immersed and went up, and afterward there was found on him something which interposes [between his flesh and the water], even though he was occupied with that very sort of thing after he immersed, lo, this one is unclean,

G. until he will state, "It is clear to me that it was not on me before hand."

4:9 A. A grave which is discovered conveys uncleanness retroactively.

B. If a person came and said, "It is clear to me that it was not here twenty [years ago],"

C. it is unclean only from the time that it was discovered and thereafter.

4:10 A. An unclean olive-pit which was found inside a loaf on top of a boiling stew,

B. even though flowing liquid is not on it [the pit], it [the loaf] is unclean.

C. [If] it was discovered on top of a loaf inside of a cold broth,

D. even though there is flowing liquid on it, it is clean.

E. This is the general principle:

F. Whatever is discovered in something which is boiling, even though there is running liquid on it, is unclean.

G. [Sens:] Whatever is found in something which is boiling, even though there is no flowing liquid on it, is unclean. [If] it is found in a loaf in a cold broth, even though there is flowing liquid on it, it is clean.

H. A pit which is in the house — they follow the majority.

4:11 A. Flax which a menstruating woman has spun —

---

21. M. Toh. 4:3.

B. he who moves it is clean.

C. And if it was moist,

D. he who moves it is unclean,

E. because of the liquid which is in his [better: her] mouth.

F. R. Judah says, "Even he who wets it [the flax] is unclean because of the liquid in her mouth."

G. They said to him, "Once they put it into water, it [the water] has formed the greater part, and it is clean."

5:1   A. Unclean blood which was mixed with clean blood —

B. "Blood does not annul blood," the words of R. Judah.

C. And sages say, "They regard it as if it were wine in water. If its color is diluted, it is clean, and if not, it is unclean."

D. Unclean spit which was mixed with clean spit —

E. "Spit is not annulled," the words of R. Judah.

F. And sages say, "They regard it as if it were water. If its color is diluted, it is clean; and if not, it is unclean."

G. [If] it fell into water, [if] it remains cohesive, it is unclean. [If] it dissolved, if its taste and its color are diluted, it is clean, and if not, it is unclean.

5:2   A. Urine which was mixed with wine —

B. they [do not] regard it as if it were water.

C. [If] it was mixed with water, they regard it as if it were wine.

D. If its color is diluted, it is clean, and if not, it is unclean.

E. Urine of a gentile [mixed with other urine] — they follow the status of the majority [of the mixture].

F. R. Judah says, "A quarter-*log* in two *se'ahs* is unclean; more than that is clean."

5:3   A. They purchase and borrow urine from any source, and they do not take account of the possibility that it derives from menstruating women, for the daughters of Israel are not suspected of collecting their urine when they are menstruating.

B. The chamber pot of a Zab and of a Zabah —

C. the [water of] the first and of the second [washings of the pot] convey uncleanness.

D. The [water of the] third [rinsing] is clean.

E. Under what circumstances?

F. When he put water into it.

G. But when he did not put water into it [but washed it with urine] —

H. even up to the tenth [rinsing] —

I. it is unclean.

J. R. Eliezer b. Jacob says, "The third, even though he did not put water into it, is clean."

5:4   A. A Zab who put his mouth on the mouth of the cup and changed his mind and did not drink it —

B. he who moves it is clean.

C. [If] he drank from it any amount at all —

D. whoever moves it is unclean,

E. because of the spit of his mouth.

F. R. Simeon says, "The liquid which is in it forms the greater part over the liquid which is in his mouth [and it is clean]."

G. [If] he bit from the bread or from the onion —

H. he who moves it is clean.

I. [If] he bit off a piece of gourd or cucumber,

J. he who moves it is unclean, because of the spit of his mouth.

K. R. Simeon says, "The liquid which is in it forms the greater part over the liquid which is in his mouth [and it is clean]."

L. And shells of beans and shells of beets which the gentile has shelled

M. he who moves them is unclean.

N. And as to those in the market-places —

O. they follow the status of the majority.

P. R. Judah b. Beterah says, '[If we know that] he has certainly touched. them in private domain, they burn [heave-offering]."

5:5   A. Two drops of spit, one unclean and one clean,

B. and one touched one of them,

C. or carried it on a sherd —

D. R. Judah says, "Since it dripped on him, its status upon him is regarded as if it were on private property."

E. All the same is private and public domain: They suspend.

F. [If] they were dried, or one moved them on a chip,

G. in private property they suspend;

H. and in public property they burn.

I. [Sens, *TR* IV, p. 65:] R. Yosé says, "In private domain they burn."

[If there] is doubt whether he touched or did not touch, whether he moved or did not move, in private property they suspend, and in public property it is clean.

R. Yosé the Galilean says, "In private property, they burn."

J. [If] there was a single drop of spit —

K. there is doubt whether one touched it or whether one did not touch it

L. there is doubt whether one moved it or whether one did not move it

M. in private property they suspend.

N. In public property it is clean.

O. R. Yosé says, "In private property they burn it."[22]

5:6   A. And just as they declared clean a matter of doubt concerning

22. M. Toh. 4:6.

uncleanness floating on the surface of the water,

B. whether it is in utensils or whether it is on the ground,

[Sens supplies: so they have declared clean a matter of doubt concerning cleanness floating on the surface of the water, whether it is in utensils or on the ground] —

C. how so?

D. A trough which is unclean with corpse-uncleanness —

E. a loaf of heave-offering wrapped in bast or wrapped in paper is in it

F. and the rains came and it was filled up, and it [the loaf-wrapper] is unfolded [by the flow's force] —

G. lo, this [loaf] floats on the surface of the water —

H. there is doubt whether it touched the sides of the trough or whether it did not touch —

I. its matter of doubt is deemed clean,

J. because it is a matter of doubt concerning something clean which was floating.

K. R. Simeon says, "In the case of utensils, it is unclean, and in the case of the ground, it is clean —

L. "except for the case of an olive's bulk of corpse and [except for] all things which overshadow, which render unclean above as below."[23]

5:7 A. R. Judah says, "If the doubt concerns his descent, he is unclean, because the water is stirred up,

B. "and it is not possible for him not to touch it;

C. "if the doubt has to do with his ascent, it is clean, because the water pushes it [the uncleanness] to the sides."[24]

5:8 A. And what is the doubt concerning creeping things which the sages declared clean?

B. This is a matter of doubt concerning things which are thrown.[25]

C. R. Dostai b. R. Yannai said in the name of R. Yosé, "[If] one went into an alley and prepared dough, and afterward an insect was found there

D. "this is the doubt concerning creeping things."[26]

E. And he who eats heave-offering which is suspended is clean.

F. And any one whose matter of doubt is deemed clean — a matter of doubt concerning its offspring is clean.

G. Anything the matter of doubt concerning which is unclean, a matter of doubt concerning its offspring likewise is unclean.[27]

5:9 A. And just as he who eats food unclean in the first remove and food unclean in the second remove and drinks unclean liquids,

B. and he whose head and greater part enter into drawn water,

C. and the clean person on whose head and the greater part of whose

___

23. M. Toh. 4:8.   24. *ibid.*   25. *ibid.*
26. M. Toh. 4:12, M. Toh. 3:5.   27. M. Toh. 4:11.

body three *logs* of drawn water are thrown —

D. [as] a matter of doubt concerning his conveying uncleanness to others is deemed clean,

E. so too:

F. liquids which touch him —

G. a matter of doubt concerning their rendering other things unclean is deemed clean.

H. And R. Yosé b. R. Judah says, "Liquids which touch him are as if they touch a creeping thing."[28]

5:10 A. And just as that which is unclean in the first remove produces something unclean in the second remove, and something unclean in the second remove produces something unclean in the third,

B. so a matter of doubt concerning something unclean in the first remove produces a matter of doubt concerning something unclean in the second remove, and a matter of doubt concerning something unclean in the second remove produces a matter of doubt concerning something unclean in the third remove.

C. "A matter of doubt concerning liquids, as to whether they have contracted uncleanness, is unclean, and [a matter of doubt] concerning whether they have been made clean is clean," the words of R. Meir.

D. And so did R. Eleazar rule in accord with his opinion.

E. And R. Judah says, "For all it is unclean."

F. R. Yosé and R. Simeon say, "A matter of doubt concerning liquids:

G. "as to food, it is deemed unclean.

H. "And as to utensils, it is deemed clean."[29]

5:11 A. A staff which is full of unclean liquids and one threw it among clean loaves —

B. it is a matter of doubt whether it touched or whether it did not touch

C. this is not the matter of doubt concerning liquids about which sages have disputed.

D. But what is the matter of doubt concerning liquids about which sages have differed?

E. Two jars —

F. one unclean, and one clean —

H. it is a matter of doubt whether he made the dough from the unclean water or whether he made the dough from the clean water —

I. this is the matter of doubt concerning liquids:

J. [if it concerns] foods, it is unclean.

K. And [if it concerns] utensils, it is clean.[30]

5:12 A. [If] one went into an alley and prepared dough,

28. *ibid.*   29. M. Toh. 4:10.   30. M. Toh. 4:9—10.

B. and afterward a creeping thing was found there —

C. it is a matter of doubt whether he touched or whether he did not touch it —

D. a matter of doubt concerning foods and liquids is deemed unclean;

E. and [a matter of doubt concerning] utensils is deemed clean.

F. And one who had immersed on the selfsame day who put his hand into the airspace of a jar —

G. it is a matter of doubt whether he touched or whether he did not touch —

H. concerning foods and liquids, the doubt is deemed unclean,

I. and concerning utensils, it is deemed clean.

5:13   A. Two jars, one unclean and one clean —

B. and they were broken,

C. and [the liquids therein] came onto clean things —

D. it is a matter of doubt whether it is [liquid of the] unclean [jar] or whether it is [liquid of the] clean —

E. a matter of doubt concerning foods and liquids is deemed unclean;

F. [a matter of doubt concerning] utensils is deemed clean.

G. A jar which is half filled with clean liquids

H. and liquids fell into its airspace —

I. it is a doubt whether they are clean or whether they are unclean —

J. the liquids [in the jar] are clean,

K. for they convey uncleanness only on account of the jar.

L. [If] they fell on liquids [in the jar],

M. the liquids are unclean, but the jars are clean.

5:14   A. [If] one baked a loaf of bread in an oven,

B. and liquids fell into its airspace —

C. it is a matter of doubt whether they were unclean or whether they were clean —

D. the bread is clean,

E. because it is made unclean only on account of the oven.

F. [If] they fell on the loaf of bread,

G. the bread is unclean, and the oven is clean.

5:15   A. He who sprinkles his house with unclean water, and there were clean things there —

B. it is a matter of doubt whether it [the water] splashed or whether it did not splash —

C. its matter of doubt is deemed clean.

D. [If] it is not possible for him to [sprinkle unless the water does touch the clean things],

E. its matter of doubt is deemed unclean.

F. R. Dosa says, "They say to him that he should repeat."

G. They said to him, "They do not repeat in a matter having to do with cleanness."

H. R. Simeon b. Gamaliel says, "There are times that he does repeat."

5:16   A. A person who launders his garment —

B. and washes his hair —

C. and boils his flax —

D. and there were clean things there —

E. it is a matter of doubt whether they splashed or whether they did not splash —

F. their matter of doubt is deemed clean.

G. [If] it is not possible for him [to do so without splashing] —

H. its matter of doubt is deemed unclean.

I. R. Dosa says, "They say to him that he should repeat."

J. They said to him, "They do not repeat in a matter having to do with cleanness."

K. R. Simeon b. Gamaliel says, "There are times that one does repeat."

5:17   A. [If] a person splashed unclean and clean liquids in the house,

B. and afterward liquids were found on a loaf of heave-offering —

C. and [if] one took it [forthwith] to inquire concerning it,

D. lo, this is clean.

E. [If] he waited for it until it dried off, lo, this is unclean.

6:1   A. The bits of carrion and of properly slaughtered animals in a village

B. they follow the status of the majority.

C. Rabban Simeon b. Gamaliel says, "Even [if] a single piece of carrion is sold in a village — all the meat which is found in the village, lo, it is regarded as belonging to carrion,

D. "because bits of carrion [indeed] are located [there]."

E. Unclean and clean drops of blood in the house —

F. they follow the status of the majority.

G. M'ŚH Š: Drops of blood were found on loaves of heave-offering, and the case came before sages, and they declared it clean, for it is only the blood of living creeping things.

6:2   A. Nine creeping things and one frog are in the public domain —

B. and one touched one of them —

C. and it is not known which of them he has touched —

D. his matter of doubt is deemed clean.

E. One of them separated to private domain —

F. its matter of doubt is deemed unclean.

G. [One of them separated] to the public domain —

H. its matter of doubt is deemed clean.

I. And in the case of that which is found: they follow the status of the majority.

J. Nine frogs and one creeping thing in the private domain —

K. and one touched one of them, and it is not known which of them he touched —

L. his matter of doubt is deemed unclean.

M. One of them separated to the private domain —

N. his matter of doubt is deemed unclean.

O. To the public domain —

P. his matter of doubt is deemed clean.

Q. And in the case of that which is found: they follow the status of the majority.[31]

6:3   A. An unclean loaf which was mixed with nine clean loaves —

B. and five people ate the five first ones —

C. and afterward five ate the five latter ones —

D. and one of them was made unclean —

E. and it is not known [which one] —

F. the first ones are unclean,

G. for they have no [mitigating factor] on which to depend,

H. and [the ones who ate] the latter [loaves] are clean.

I. This is the general principle:

J. A man with a man,

K. clean things with clean things,

L. a man with clean things,

M. and clean things with a man —

N. lo, these prove [which must be unclean].

O. [If] the first ones are eaten,

P. [if] they were made unclean, or if they were lost

Q. before the second ones were made,

R. the second are clean.

S. [If this happened] once the second were made —

T. the second are suspended.[32]

6:4   A. Two paths, one unclean and one clean —

B. and one walked in one of them and prepared clean things — [Sens: they are clean.]

C. [One walked] in the second and prepared [clean things] —

D. they are to be burned.

E. In the first [did he walk], but he did not prepare [clean things], [then he walked] in the second, and he prepared [clean things] —

they are to be burned.

F. [He walked] in the first and [then] in the second and [then] prepared clean things —

G. [if] these and these are lying before him,

H. the first are clean, and the second are to be burned.[33]

---

31. M. Toh. 5:1.   32. M. Toh. 5:3—4.   33. ibid.

6:5 A. Two paths, one unclean and one clean —

B. and one walked in one of them and prepared clean things,

C. and his fellow came and walked in the second and prepared —

D. [if] these and these are lying [before them, still available] —

lo, these prove [the condition of one another; the first is clean, the second burned].

E. [If] the first ones were eaten, [or] made unclean, or lost, before the second were prepared —

F. the second are clean.

G. [If this happened] after the second are prepared —

H. the second are suspended.[34]

6:6 A. [If] both of them prepared a single [item in conditions of] cleanness — lo, this is unclean.

B. [If] both of them prepared two clean things —

C. "[If] this one comes and is interrogated by himself —

D. "one says to him, 'It is clean.'

E. "And [if] this one comes and is interrogated by himself,

F. "one says to him, 'It is clean.'

G. "[If] the two of them are interrogated together, one says to them, 'It is unclean'" —

H. the words of R. Judah.

I. R. Yosé says, "If both of them said, 'We were two, and we walked in two separate paths and we prepared two separate clean things,' one says to them, 'It is unclean,'

J. "because even if one unclean thing is mixed together with a hundred clean things, they all are unclean."[35]

6:7 A. Two paths, one unclean and one clean.

B. and one walked in one of them, and entered the sanctuary —

C. he is clear [of punishment].

D. [If he walked] in the second [and then entered the Temple], he is liable.

E. [If he walked] in the first and did not enter [the sanctuary], and [then he walked] in the second and entered [the sanctuary], he is liable.

F. [If he walked] in the first and entered, [then] was sprinkled and the sprinkling was repeated, and he immersed,

G. then he walked in the second and entered the sanctuary —

H. he is liable.

I. R. Simeon declares free in this case.

J. And R. Simeon b. Judah declares free in all cases, in the name of R. Simeon.[36]

K. M'ŚH B: They were bringing a dying man from Genossar to Ḥam-

34. *ibid.*   35. M. Toh. 5:5.   36. *ibid.*

matan,

    L. and the groups of bearers were changed for him,

    M. and at the end he was found dead by them,

    N. and the case came before sages,

    O. and they declared unclean only the last group of pall-bearers alone.[37]

6:8   A. [If] one touched someone at night and did not know whether he was alive or dead,

    B. and at dawn he got up and found him dead —

    C. R. Meir declares him clean,

    D. [for] a matter of doubt involving the public domain is deemed clean.

    E. And sages declare unclean,

    F. for all matters of uncleanness are adjudged in accord with their condition at the time they are found.

    G. Sages agree with R. Meir that if he saw him alive in the preceding evening, even though dawn came and he found him dead, he is clean,

    H. for this is a matter of doubt involving the public domain.[38]

6:9   A. [If] one fell asleep on a rock in public domain —

    B. at dawn (and) he found on it a creeping thing or a drop of spit —

    C. R. Meir declares clean, because a matter of doubt in public domain is deemed clean.

    D. And sages declare unclean, for all matters of uncleanness are adjudged in accord with their condition at the moment that they are found.

    E. And sages agree with R. Meir that if they saw it, that it was clean in the preceding evening, even though he came at dawn and found on it a creeping thing or spit,

    F. that he is clean, for this is a matter of doubt in the public domain.[39]

6:10   A. "[If] there is one [female] idiot in the village, all the drops of spit which are in the village are unclean," the words of R. Meir.

    B. R. Judah says, "If she was accustomed to go into a certain alley, that alley in particular is in the presumption of being unclean, but all [the other] alleyways are in the presumption of being clean."

    C. And R. Simeon says, "All the alleyways are in the presumption of being unclean, except for a courtyard which is guarded."

    D. And R. Eleazar b. R. Simeon [Sens: b. R. Ṣadoq] says, "Even a courtyard which is guarded is in the presumption of being unclean,

    E. "until one will give evidence, stating, 'It is clear to me that I have not come to this place.'"[40]

6:11   A. He who bumps against millstones in which a gentile is located —

    B. [or] in which a menstruating woman is located —

---

37. M. Toh. 5:7.   38. *ibid.*   39. *ibid.*
40. M. Toh. 5:8.

C. his garments are unclean with *midras*-uncleanness.

D. What are millstones?

E. Any which one uproots and moves from its place.

F. [If] one spit and tread,

G. on account of his spit, they burn the heave-offering,

H. and as to his garments, they follow the status of the majority.[41]

6:12　A. He on whose garments a woman has stepped —

B. his garments are unclean with *midras*-uncleanness.

C. R. Dosetai b. R. Judah says, "If she spit and wiped away her spit, when she spit, his clothes are unclean with *midras*-uncleanness,

D. "for thus is the way of the daughters of Israel:

E. "they wipe up their spit when they are menstruating.

F. "[If] she did not wipe up her spit, his clothing is clean."[42]

6:13　A. Two say to him, "You were made unclean," and he says, "I was not made unclean" — he is clean.

B. But they do not say to him, "You prepare clean things." But he should watch out for himself.[43]

6:14　A. A man brings an offering in behalf of his son and his adult daughter and his Hebrew slave and maid servant,

B. and he contradicts them.

C. He is believed concerning himself.

D. How so?

E. They said to him, "You have vowed," and he says, "It was subject to an unstated condition" —

F. they accept his statement.

G. "You have vowed," and he said to them, "I did not vow," and when they came, he said, "It was subject to an unstated condition" —

H. they do not accept his statement.

I. "Your wife has vowed," and he says to them, "She did not vow," and when they came, he said, "I intended to annul her vow for her" —

J. they do not listen to him.

6:15　A. One is believed to say, "This son of mine is nine years and one day old," "This daughter of mine is nine years and one day old,"

B. [if] he is liable to bring an offering for them.

C. But for flagellation, and for punishments,

D. lo, this one is not believed.

6:16　A. [If] his asses and his workers were bearing clean things and passing [some distance] before him, even if they were more than a mile away, lo, these are clean,

B. because it is in the presumption of being guarded.

C. If he said to them, "Go out, and I shall come after you," once they

---

41. *ibid.*　　　　　　42. *ibid.*　　　　　　43. M. Toh. 5:9.

have left his eyesight, lo, these are unclean.

6:17 A. Two say, "He was made unclean," and two say, "He was not made unclean" —

B. [if the matter of doubt concerns] private domain, he is unclean.

C. [If the matter of doubt concerns] public domain, he is clean.

D. They asked Ben Zoma, "Why is [a doubt in] private [domain deemed] unclean?"

E. He said to them, "What is the status of the wayward wife in respect to her husband?

["Has she] certainly [committed adultery] or [has she only] possibly [committed adultery]?"

F. They said to him, "[She has only possibly committed adultery.] It is a matter of doubt."

G. He said to them, "We find that she is prohibited to her husband."

H. On this basis you may reason on a matter involving a creeping thing:

Just as in this case, in the private domain [we deem a matter of doubt to be unclean], so in the other case, in the private domain, we deem a matter of doubt to be unclean.

I. [If you argue;] Just as here, that is the case where there is intelligence for interrogation, so in the other case, where there is intelligence for interrogation —

J. on this basis have they said, "A matter in which there is intelligence for interrogation involving the private domain — a matter of doubt is deemed unclean, and in the public domain a matter of doubt is deemed clean."

K. "And why is a matter of doubt in the public domain deemed clean?" [The students asked].

L. He said to them, "We find that the community prepares the Passover in a state of uncleanness when the larger numbers of them are unclean.

M. "And if a matter of certain uncleanness is permitted for the community, all the more so a matter of doubtful uncleanness."

N. Rabban Simeon b. Gamaliel says, "On what account is a matter of doubt in the private domain deemed unclean, and a matter of doubt in the public domain is deemed clean?

O. "Because it is possible to interrogate an individual, and it is not possible to interrogate a crowd."[44]

7:1 A. The dying man who is placed in a shop and entered the stoa —

B. it is clean.

C. [If] they brought him out of the stoa and brought him back to the shop a second time —

---

44. *ibid.*

D. it is unclean.

E. And R. Simeon declares clean.

F. For R. Simeon says, "The public domain intervenes retroactively,

G. "for one cannot say, 'He was dead in the private domain and then he was [alive] in the public domain.'"[45]

7:2   A. There are things in the public domain which they have treated as private domain.

B. A basket in the public domain which is ten handbreadths high,

C. and the uncleanness is in it —

D. it is a matter of doubt whether he touched or whether he did not touch —

E. his matter of doubt is deemed clean.

F. [If] he put his hand into it —

G. it is a matter of doubt whether he touched or whether he did not touch —

H. his matter of doubt is deemed unclean.[46]

7:3   A. If there was a basket [Sens: on his shoulder], and a loaf of heave-offering was wrapped in bast or in paper and placed in it —

B. it is a matter of doubt whether another [person] touched or did not touch —

C. its doubt is deemed clean.

D. [If] he put his hand into it —

E. it is a matter of doubt whether he touched or whether he did not touch —

F. its matter of doubt is deemed unclean.[47]

7:4   A. An ass in the public domain, ten handbreadths high —
and uncleanness is placed on top of it —

B. it is a matter of doubt whether he touched or whether he did not touch —

C. its matter of doubt is deemed clean.

D. [If] he stretches out his hand on top of it —

E. it is a matter of doubt whether he touched or whether he did not touch —

F. its matter of doubt is deemed unclean.

G. A rock in public domain, ten handbreadths high —
and uncleanness is placed on top of it —

H. it is a matter of doubt whether he touched or whether he did not touch —
his matter of doubt is deemed clean.

I. [If] someone climbed up to its top —

J. it is a matter of doubt whether he touched or whether he did not

---

45. M. Toh. 6:1.   46. M. Toh. 6:3.   47. *ibid.*

touch —

K. his matter of doubt is deemed unclean.[48]

7:5   A. This one was riding on his ass, and the other was riding on his ass

B. one is unclean and one is clean —

C. it is a matter of doubt whether this one touched that one or whether he did not touch him —

D. R. Jacob declares unclean.

E. And R. Yosé declares clean.

F. The son of this one was riding on his shoulder,

G. [and the son] of that one was riding on his shoulder —

H. one is unclean and one is clean —

I. it is a matter of doubt whether they touched one another,

J. or whether they did not touch —

K. R. Jacob declares unclean.

L. And R. Yosé declares clean.

M. There was a bundle on his shoulder —

N. And spit was cleaving ten handbreadths above —

O. it is a matter of doubt whether he moved it or whether he did not move it —

P. R. Jacob declares unclean.

Q. And R. Yosé declares clean.[49]

7:6   A. Utensils are lying on the public domain above ten handbreadths, and the unclean person passes —

B. it is a matter of doubt whether he moved or whether he did not move [them] —

C. R. Jacob declares unclean.

D. And R. Yosé declares clean.

E. For R. Jacob would say, "A basket which is ten handbreadths high in the public domain, lo, it is regarded as the private domain."

F. And R. Yosé says, "Whoever has taken his way through the public domain is clean."[50]

7:7   A. [If] one entered the valley in the rainy season,

B. and uncleanness is [in] a certain field —

C. They said before R. Eliezer, "Lo, it belongs to a private person."

D. R. Merinus explained in his name, "Any field which has a name unto itself."[51]

7:8   A. And what is the dry season?

B. Once the crop is gathered from it.

C. And what is the rainy season?

D. Once the second rain falls.

---

48. *ibid.*   49. *ibid.*   50. *ibid.*
51. M. Toh. 6:5.

E. [If] there were there clear fields —

F. if one could stand on one side and see those that enter and those that leave on the other side —

G. it is private property with respect to the Sabbath and public domain with respect to uncleanness.

H. And if not, it is private property with respect to both.[52]

7:9   A. The paths which lead down to the wells, caves, and cisterns, and winepresses, and threshing floors, are private domain for the Sabbath and public domain for uncleanness.

B. R. Eleazar says, "When they lead down, they are public domain for both;

C. "and they do not lead down, they are private domain for both,

D. "and public domain for uncleanness."[53]

7:10   A. Alleys which go down to the sea or to the river, even though they are fenced off on either side, and the public climb over the fences and walk therein

B. are private domain for the Sabbath and public domain for uncleanness.

7:11   A. The roofs of the village on which a public path passes are private domain for the Sabbath and public domain for uncleanness.

B. A garden, when it is guarded, is private domain.

C. If it is not guarded, it is public domain.

7:12   A. A basilica which they open by day and lock by night — so long as it is open, it is public domain.

B. [When] it is locked, it is private domain.

C. You come out to rule, By day [a doubt concerning] it is clean, and by night [a doubt concerning] it is unclean.

D. A basilica the doors of which are directly opposite one another,

E. and so too a stoa which is fenced on either side and there is a space between the pillars —

F. R. Judah says, "If one stands on one side and sees those that enter and leave by the other side, it is private domain for the Sabbath and public domain for uncleanness.

G. "And if not, it is private domain for both."[54]

7:13   A. A basilica, the two doors of which are directly opposite one another —

B. "The middle area of it is private domain for the Sabbath and public domain for uncleanness,

C. "and the sides are private domain for this and for that,"

D. the words of R. Meir.

E. And sages say, "All the same is the rule applying to the middle and to

---

52. *ibid.*, M. Toh. 6:7.   53. M. Toh. 6:6.   54. M. Toh. 6:8.

the sides:

F. "it is private domain for the Sabbath and public domain for uncleanness."[55]

7:14   A. And R. Meir agrees with sages concerning a basilica, the two doors of which are not directly opposite one another —

B. for example, the courtyard of Bet Gaddi and Ḥammata —

C. that all the same is the rule of the middle and the side:

D. they are private domain for the Sabbath and public domain for uncleanness.

E. And sages agree with R. Meir concerning a courtyard belonging to an individual which is interrupted by the public way —

F. for example, the courtyard of Bet Gaddi —

G. the middle is public domain for uncleanness, and private domain for the Sabbath, and the sides are private domain for this and for that[56]

8:1   A. R. Simeon says, "He who gave a key to an 'am ha'areṣ — the house is unclean."

B. [If] he gave him the [key to the] outer [room] and did not give him [the key to] the inner [room], the outer one is unclean.

C. And as to the inner, unclean is only [the space] up to the place to which he can stretch out his hand and touch.

D. [If] there were there shelves ten handbreadths high and niches ten handbreadths high, unclean is only [the space] up to the place to which he can stretch out his hand and touch.

E. [If] the outer room belongs to one [person] and the inner room to another [person], even though the clean things are placed on the side of the door of the inner [room], lo, they are clean.

F. He who enters without permission, even though he stands at the side of clean things —

they are clean.

G. And so in the case of a gentile: one does not take into consideration [the possibility of his touching things] in connection with wine used for purposes of idolatry.[57]

8:2   A. A ḥaber who was sleeping in the house of an 'am ha'areṣ, with his clothing folded up and lying under his head, and his sandals and his jug before him — lo, these are clean,

B. because they are in the presumption of being guarded.[58]

8:3   A. A ḥaber who said to an 'am ha'areṣ, "Go and sleep in the house"

B. the whole house is in his domain.

C. "Go and sleep on such-and-such a bed" —

55. ibid.   56. ibid.   57. M. Toh. 7:1.
58. M. Toh. 7:2.

D. unclean is only that very bed, and the space up to which he can reach out his hand and touch from the bed.

E. [If] he said to him, "Keep this cow for me, that it not enter the house" —

F. "Keep this heifer for me, that it not break the utensils" —

G. lo, these are clean,

H. for he gave him only the task of guarding the cow alone.

I. But if he said to him, "Guard this house for me that the cow should not enter it" —

J. "Guard these utensils for me that the cow should not break them" —

K. lo, they are unclean.

L. Rabbi says, "Workers whose way is to gather pebbles and sherds in the house — all the house is regarded as in their domain."[59]

8:4 A. The wife of an 'am ha'areṣ grinds [grain] with the wife of a ḥaber when she is unclean, but when she is clean, she should not grind [wheat with her].

B. R. Simeon [b. Eleazar] says, "Even when she is unclean, she should not grind,

C. "for even though she does not eat, she gives to other women, and they will eat."

8:5 A. The tax-collectors who went into the house —

B. if they said, "We entered the house, but we did not touch anything,"

C. lo, these are believed,

D. for the testimony which prohibited is the testimony which permitted.

E. If there were others giving testimony concerning them that they entered the house, and they said, "We did not touch anything," they are not believed.

F. When the pledge is in their hand, even though others do not give testimony about them, they are not believed, because the pledge gives testimony about them.

G. If there was a gentile with them, even though the pledge is in their hand,

H. even though the gentile gives testimony concerning them that they entered,

I. and they said, "We did not touch anything,"

J. lo, these are believed,

K. because the fear of the gentile is upon them.[60]

8:6 A. The thieves who entered the house —

B. "all the house entirely is unclean," the words of R. Meir.

C. And sages say, "Unclean is only [the space] up to the place to which they can stretch out their hands and touch from the place of the robbery."

---

59. M. Toh. 7:3.   60. M. Toh. 7:6.

D. [*TR* IV, p. 84:] Rabban Simeon b. Gamaliel says, "The whole house is unclean because of the theft."

E. Rabbi says, "Unclean is only the place of the robber."

F. R. Meir agrees concerning shelves and niches,

G. that "a place for the feet of the thieves" does not apply to them,

H. that unclean only is the space to which they can reach out their hands and touch.[61]

8:7   A. He who leaves an *'am ha'areṣ* in his house to guard it,

B. and this one is immobile or tied up —

C. when he can see those that enter and those that leave,

D. unclean is only [the space] up to the place which they can make unclean.[62]

E. Said R. Judah, "R. Eleazar b. 'Azariah agrees with the sages concerning the niches of the bath house, which are open from one to another [at the back or sides] —

F. "if the utensils were detached [hanging out] from them,

G. "that they are unclean.

H. "And sages say, 'One way or the other, they are unclean.'"[63]

8:8   A. He who leaves his utensils in the wall niches of a bath house —

B. he locked and sealed —

C. even though he came and found the lock open,

D. and the seal spoiled —

E. it is clean.

F. The seal of which they spoke [suffices] even if [it is] of mud,

G. even if [it is] a spindle.[64]

H. He who stuffs his utensils in the wall niches of a bath house —

I. they are [Sens:] unclean,

J. because the gentile may be interrogated concerning them.

K. R. Yosé b. R. Judah says, "Even if one thread goes forth from them, they are unclean,

L. "for pressure brings uncleanness to itself in any measure whatsoever."

8:9   A. He who purchases utensils from gentile craftsmen, and he who gives over utensils to gentile craftsmen —

B. they are unclean with *midras*-uncleanness [Sens: and clean] of corpse-uncleanness.

C. And he who purchases utensils from craftsmen who are *'ammé ha'areṣ* and he who gives over utensils to craftsmen who are *'ammé ha'areṣ*

D. they are unclean with *midras*-uncleanness and unclean with corpse-uncleanness.

61. *ibid.*   62. M. Toh. 7:5.   63. M. Toh. 7:7.
64. *ibid.*

E. [If] one left his utensils before an 'am ha'areṣ and said to him, "Guard these for me" — they are unclean with midras-uncleanness and unclean with [Maimonides: clean of] corpse-uncleanness.

F. [If] he put them on his shoulder, they are unclean with midras-uncleanness [and unclean with] corpse-uncleanness.

8:10 A. Said R. Dosetai b. R. Yannai, "The House of Shammai [and the House of Hillel] did not disagree concerning one who deposits [utensils] with an individual, that they are unclean;

B. "and concerning one who leaves them before the public, that they are clean.

C. "Concerning what did they differ?

D. "Concerning one who deposits [utensils] in the public domain and concerning one who leaves [utensils] in the domain of the private person, for:

E. "The House of Shammai declare unclean.

F. "And the House of Hillel declare clean."

G. M'ŚH B: Someone forgot utensils in the synagogue, and the case came before sages,

H. and they declared [them] clean.

I. For it is not wholly property of the 'am ha'areṣ.

8:11 A. [If] one left his utensils in the bath and came and found them as they were [originally left] —

B. lo, these are clean.

C. But they instruct him not to do so with clean things.

D. [If] one left his wine-press and his cistern [Sens: house] and entered the town, even though he came and found an 'am ha'areṣ beside them,

E. they are clean.

F. And so in the case of a gentile:

G. One does not take into consideration the matter of wine used for the purposes of idolatry.[65]

8:12 A. An 'am ha'areṣ who came to be sprinkled — they sprinkle on him and on his utensils only after three days.

B. But a ḥaber who came to be sprinkled — they sprinkle on him and on his utensils forthwith.

C. Said R. Judah, "Under what circumstances? When it was in the presumption of being [purification for] heave-offering-foods. But [if] it was in the presumption of being [purification for] unconsecrated food, they sprinkle on him forthwith and on his utensils once he will guard [them]."

8:13 A. [If] one was dressed in a shirt and wrapped in a cloak, and he said, "My concern was for the shirt, and my concern was not for the cloak"

B. the shirt is clean, and the cloak is unclean.

65. ibid.

C. [If] a basket was on his shoulder, and a shovel was in it, [if] he said, "My concern was for the basket, and my concern was not for the shovel,"

D. the basket is clean, and the shovel is unclean.

8:14 A. [If] one was making use of the jar in the assumption that it was of unconsecrated food and afterward it was found to contain heave-offering, lo, this is clean, and it is prohibited to be eaten,

B. because it is a matter of doubt concerning one who has immersed on the selfsame day and awaits sunset for the completion of purification.

C. [If] they said to him concerning that which was clean, "It is suspended" — lo, this is unclean.

D. And if he said, "Lo, I shall leave it until I shall inquire concerning it" — lo, this is clean.

8:15 A. Unclean and clean liquids [are] in the house — they follow [the status of] the larger part.

B. WM'ŚH B: A woman filtered unclean and clean liquids into a jar of heave-offering,

C. and the case came before sages.

D. And they did not declare it unclean,

E. because she did not cease to be concerned for it.

8:16 A. Said R. Eleazar b. Pilah, "On what account does R. 'Aqiva declare unclean? Because women are gluttonous.

B. "A woman opens the pot to know what her girl-friend is cooking."[66]

9:1 A. A *haber* and an *'am ha'areṣ* who were dwelling in a courtyard and who forgot utensils in the courtyard —

B. that which is suitable to become unclean with *midras*-uncleanness is [deemed to have been] made unclean with *midras*-uncleanness,

C. and that which is suitable to become unclean with corpse-uncleanness is [deemed to have been] made unclean with corpse-uncleanness.

D. This one has a *sukkah* before his door, and that one has a *sukkah* before his door —

E. this one has a partition before his door, and that one has a partition before his door —

F. this one leaves his utensils in his *sukkah,* and that one leaves his utensils in his *sukkah;*

G. this one leaves his utensils by his partition, and that one leaves his utensils by his partition —

H. all [the objects] are clean.

I. And R. Simeon says, "Even though there is no *sukkah* and no partition, they are clean,

66. M. Toh. 7:9.

J. "for this one leaves before his door, and that one leaves [objects] before his door."[67]

9:2 A. This one has a *sukkah* or partition before the door of his fellow, and that one has a *sukkah* or partition before the door of his fellow —

B. this one leaves his utensils in his *sukkah* or partition before the door of his fellow, and that one leaves his utensil by the *sukkah* or partition before his fellow's door —

C. lo, these are unclean, .

D. for this one has the right to enter, and that one has the right to enter.[68]

9:3 A. A *haber* who left food and liquid on a well and went down to drink

B. they are clean,

C. for others do not handle them.

D. But a *haber* who was selling food and liquid at the door of his shop and went inside [the shop] —

E. lo, these are unclean,

F. because others do handle them.

9:4 A. An *'am ha'areṣ* is believed concerning the immersion of something unclean with corpse-uncleanness, but he is not believed concerning the immersion of something unclean with *maddaf*-uncleanness.

9:5 A. A *haber* who died and left produce — they follow the status of the greater part of that which is brought in [to storage].

B. If the greater part of that which is brought in [to storage] is unconsecrated food, [the whole is regarded as] unconsecrated food,

C. and if the greater part of that which is brought in [to storage] is heave-offering, [then the whole is deemed] heave-offering.

9:6 A. [If] he [a *haber*] left clean [foods], lo, they are [regarded as] clean [foods].

B. [If] he left utensils, lo, they are regarded as unclean,

C. for I say, "They were sprinkled, but not repeated[ly sprinkled], or repeated, but not immersed,

D. "or possibly he did not sprinkle them at all."

E. A *haber* who died and left produce, even if on that very day he gathered them in, lo, they are in the presumption of having been properly prepared [tithed].

F. An *'am ha'areṣ* who took on himself [the obligations of the *Ḥaber*], and who had clean foods, and who said, "It is perfectly clear to me that they have not been made unclean" —

G. (Delete: but) When others had been engaged therewith, they are prohibited to him and prohibited to everyone else.

H. [If] only he himself [was engaged therewith], they are permitted to

67. M. Toh. 8:1.   68. *ibid.*

him and prohibited to everyone else.

I. (Delete: if they are prohibited to everyone).

J. R. 'Aqiva says, "[If] they are permitted to him, they are permitted to everyone else; [if] prohibited to him, they are prohibited to everyone else."

9:7   A. A gentile who converted and who had wine and who said, "It is perfectly clear to me that it has not been made unclean" —

B. when others were engaged therewith, it is prohibited to him and prohibited to everyone else.

C. [If the man] himself [was engaged therewith], it is permitted to him and prohibited to everyone else.

D. R. 'Aqiva says, "If it is permitted to him, it is permitted to everyone else. If it is prohibited to him, it is prohibited to everyone else."

9:8   A. He who loses [something] and finds [it] —

B. in private property —

C. and a night passed over it —

D. it is unclean with *midras*-uncleanness and unclean with corpse-uncleanness.

E. [If he lost them]

F. in public domain —

G. and a night passed over them —

H. they are unclean with *midras*-uncleanness, and clean in regard to corpse-uncleanness.

I. R. Simeon declares clean.

J. For R. Simeon says, "[If] one lost a needle and found a needle, it is clean,

K. "for I say, 'The needle which is lost is the very needle which is found.'"[69]

9:9   A. And sages agree with R. Simeon in the case of one who leaves or one who forgets in the public domain,

B. that, even though the night passed over them —

C. (that) they are clean.

D. And in the case of one who leaves or forgets them in private domain and a night passed over them —

E. they are unclean with *midras*-uncleanness and clean of corpse-uncleanness.

F. He who loses something and finds it inside the house — lo, this is clean,

G. because they are in the assumption of being guarded,

H. for the entire house is in the status of that which is set apart.[70]

9:10   A. "Utensils laid out to dry in the private domain higher than ten handbreadths are clean," the words of R. Simeon [Sens: Meir].

69. M. Toh. 8:3.   70. *ibid.*

B. R. Judah [Sens: Simeon] says, "Even above a hundred *amot*, they are unclean."[71]

9:11   A. The roof of a *ḥaber* is beside the roof of the *'am ha'areṣ* —

B. the *ḥaber* lays out utensils there and leaves clean things there,

C. and on condition that the *'am ha'areṣ* cannot reach out his hand and touch.

D. The roof of the *ḥaber* is above the roof of the *'am ha'areṣ* —

E. even though the *'am ha'areṣ* can reach out his hand and touch —

F. the *ḥaber* lays out utensils there and leaves clean things there.

[Sens: And so with a gentile: one does not take into consideration the possibility of wine used for idolatrous practice.]

G. R. Simeon b. Gamaliel says, "[If] the roof of the *ḥaber* is higher than the roof of the *'am ha'areṣ*,

H. "the *ḥaber* lays out utensils there and leaves clean things there,

I. "and on condition that the *'am ha'areṣ* cannot reach out his hand and touch."

9:12   A. [If] his dipper fell into the well of an *'am ha'areṣ* — lo, this is unclean.

B. But it is clean when it comes up.[72]

C. R. Eleazar says, "[If] the liquid is putrid, lo, this is clean."

D. They said to him, "[Putrid] liquid does not restrain the cow and also not fowl."[73]

9:13   A. Wheat which comes out with the turds of the oxen and barley which comes out with the turds of the cattle —

B. even though one gave thought to them to make use of them for food,

C. are not susceptible to uncleanness [with the uncleanness affecting] food.

D. [If] one gathered them for food, they are susceptible to uncleanness [with the uncleanness affecting] food.

E. Urine —

even though one gathered it for drink —

his intention is null.[74]

9:14   A. A young pigeon which fell into the pit of the wine-press —

B. "if one gave thought concerning it [to toss it] in the garbage-heap,

C. "it is [in]susceptible to uncleanness.

D. "And [if one gave thought to it to make use of it for food] for a dog, it is insusceptible to uncleanness," the words of R. 'Aqiva.

E. And R. Yoḥanan b. Nuri declares it susceptible to uncleanness.

F. This was an actual case, and five sages took a vote concerning it and declared it susceptible to uncleanness.[75]

71. *ibid.*   72. *ibid.*   73. M. Toh. 8:6.
74. *ibid.*   75. *ibid.*

9:15 A. A kneading-trough which is unclean with corpse-uncleanness —

B. they do not knead in it grain of unconsecrated food,

C. and they do not lay out in it dough of heave-offering.

D. But if one wants, he may bring grain of unconsecrated food and put it in it, and lay on it dough of heave-offering,

E. and on condition that the dough should not touch the trough.

F. R. Simeon b. Eleazar says in the name of R. Meir, "The gutter which was receiving and discharging liquids —

G. "and an unclean person came and broke [it] apart —

H. "the upper ones are unclean,

I. "because they are guided by his hands;

J. "and the lower ones are clean."

K. A staff is wholly covered by unclean dripping liquids —

L. R. Judah says in the name of R. Joshua, "Once one has stuck it into the immersion-pool, it is clean."[76]

10:1 A. Rabban Gamaliel says, "When its preparation will be completed," and the law is in accord with his words.[77]

10:2 A. He who completes [work on] his olives on that very day —

B. we have returned to the opinions of the House of Shammai and of the House of Hillel.[78]

C. R. Jacob says, "Sap is a liquid, and why did they declare clean sap which exudes from the olives before its work is completed?

"Because a person does not want to keep it."

D. And R. Simeon says, "Sap is fruit-juice.[79]

10:3 A. "And why did they say that sap which exudes from the bale [of olives made up] for the olive-press is susceptible to uncleanness?

B. "Because it is not possible for the serial fluid of olives not to contain particles of oil."

C. Sap which exudes from oil is susceptible to uncleanness.

D. That which exudes from the vat is insusceptible.

E. [If] one gathered it and made it into a bale [of olives for the press], it is susceptible to uncleanness.[80]

10:4 A. He who packs his olives in two groups —

B. once one of them is completed, they [the olives in that group] are susceptible to receive uncleanness.

C. He who cuts his olives in the Upper Galilee and is going to bring them down to Lower Galilee —

D. they do not receive uncleanness until he brings them down to Lower Galilee.

---

76. M. Toh. 8:9.   77. M. Toh. 9:1.   78. *ibid.*

79. M. Toh. 9:2.   80. *ibid.*

E. If before he cut them he gave thought to them, they are insusceptible to uncleanness.

F. [If he did so] after he cut them, they have been rendered susceptible to receive uncleanness.

G. [Delete:] 'WRRW.

H. He who completes work on his olives and is going to sell them — they are insusceptible to uncleanness.

I. [He who completes work on his olives and is going] to adorn them with leaves, they are susceptible to receive uncleanness.[81]

10:5 A. He who purchases a vat of olives from the gentile, if he is gathering them on the ground, [or: if there are olives to be gathered, lying on the ground,] let him prepare it in cleanness.

B. [And he who purchases] from an Israelite, [the Israelite] is believed to say, "I did not complete work on it."

C. [If] he had a clump of olives and wants to prepare them in cleanness,

D. even though he is going to add [only] a *qab* or two *qabs* of olives to the clump,

E. lo, these are insusceptible to uncleanness;

F. and on condition that he not practice deception;

G. but if he practiced deception, lo, these are susceptible to uncleanness.

10:6 A. He who stacks his olives in the domain of an *'am ha'areṣ* and locked and placed a seal —

B. he does not scruple lest there is there another key or another seal.

C. And even though he came and found the lock open, or the seal disarranged, it is insusceptible to receive uncleanness.

D. The seal of which they spoke may be even a bit of mud, and even a spindle of wood.

10:7 A. [If] there were there holes and cracks, he does not scruple lest one have thrust in a reed and moved the [olives] about.

B. [If] there were there windows of four handbreadths, they are treated as doors.

10:8 A. He who stacks [his olives] in his house — he prepares a partition for them from the ground to the beams.

B. And on condition that they should [not] be shaken up on account of the partition.

C. R. Simeon b. Gamaliel says, "If it was ten handbreadths high, even if it does not reach to the beams, it is insusceptible to receive uncleanness."

D. He who stacks [his olives] in the press is like him who stacks in his house.

10:9 A. He who completes work on his olives and left one basket —

B. let him give it before the priest,

81. M. Toh. 9:3.

C. and bring him the key —

D. "Forthwith," the words of R. Meir.

E. And R. Judah says, "That whole day."

F. And R. Simeon says, "The whole of a twenty-four-hour period."

G. Even more said R. Simeon, "Even if he completed work on his olives on the eve of the Sabbath at six hours — let him bring him the key forthwith,

H. "(and) at the end of the Sabbath at six hours."[82]

10:10 A. R. Simeon b. Judah says in the name of R. Simeon, "The House of Shammai and the House of Hillel did not differ concerning him who leaves his olives in a basket,

"to let them putrify and salt them —

"that they are not rendered susceptible to uncleanness.

B. "Concerning what did they differ?

C. "Concerning the case of one who left them so that they may be easy to press,

D. "for the House of Shammai say, 'They are not rendered susceptible to uncleanness.'

E. "And the House of Hillel say, 'They are rendered susceptible to uncleanness.'"[83]

10:11 A. The olive which one crushed with unclean hands — it has not been rendered susceptible to uncleanness.

B. [If he did so in order] to dry them with salt — (and) it has (not) been rendered susceptible to uncleanness.

C. [If he did so] in order to know whether there is water in it, it has not been rendered susceptible to uncleanness.

D. R. Judah says, "It has been rendered susceptible to uncleanness."[84]

E. [If] he had a mass of olives and is going to turn it over, once he has driven a stake into it,

F. even if there are many clumps in it,

G. lo, these are not connected to one another.

H. Once he has turned it over, and they have been made a mass —

I. Rabbi says, "It is not connected."

J. And R. Yosé b. R. Judah says, "It is connected."

10:12 A. Shriveled olives which are soaked in water and made into a mass

B. Rabbi says, "It is not connected."

C. R. Yosé b. R. Judah says, "It is connected."

D. If, before the work of preparing them has been completed, he gave thought to them,

E. and he wanted to take from them [enough olives for] one pressing or for two —

---

82. M. Toh. 9:4.   83. M. Toh. 9:5.   84. *ibid.*

F. The House of Shammai say, "Let him set apart in uncleanness and cover in cleanness and bring it to the press."

G. And the House of Hillel say, "Also: he covers in uncleanness."

H. And on condition that he not uproot the whole clump.

I. But in a place in which they are accustomed to leave a sufficient amount for a pressing, one leaves enough for a single pressing.

J. In a place in which they are accustomed to leave a sufficient amount for a small olive press, one leaves sufficient for a small olive press.

K. [If they are accustomed to leave enough for] a small olive press with a cylindrical beam, one leaves enough for a small olive press with a cylindrical beam.

L. And on condition that one not uproot the whole clump.

M. And if one has uprooted the whole clump,

N. lo, these are susceptible to uncleanness.

O. R. Ishmael b. R. Yosé in the name of his father says, "Even though one has uprooted the whole clump, lo, these are insusceptible to receive uncleanness."

P. And on condition that one not practice deception.

Q. And if one has practiced deception, lo, these are susceptible to uncleanness.

R. And he who stacks in the press is like him who stacks in his house.[85]

11:1   A. "[If] one was stowing away [olives] from the vat and bringing [them] up to the roof —

B. "and a dead creeping thing is found on the roof —

C. "the vat is clean.

D. "[If] it is found in the vat, [that which is on] the roof is unclean,"

E. the words of Rabbi.

F. And sages say, "[If] a dead creeping thing is found on the roof, unclean is only the roof. [If it is found] in the vat, unclean is only the vat."

G. [If] it is found in a clump [of olives] and on the roof —

H. [if found in the next] three days, the vat is unclean.

I. [If it is found] after three days, the vat is clean.[86]

11:2   A. "He who cuts pieces from the dough, and a dead creeping thing is found in the piece, the dough is clean. [If it is found] in the dough, this piece which is cut off is unclean," the words of Rabbi.

B. And sages say, "[If] it is found in the dough, unclean is only the dough. [If it is found] in the piece which is cut off, unclean is only the piece."

C. [If] it is found inside the piece which is cut off, the whole is unclean.

11:3   A. "He who empties out from vessel and a dead creeping thing is found in the lower one — the upper one is clean. [If it is found] in the upper

85. M. Toh. 9:7.   86. M. Toh. 9:9.

one, the lower one is clean," the words of Rabbi.

B. And sages say, "[If] a dead creeping thing is found in the upper one, unclean is only the upper one.

"[If] it is found in the lower one, unclean is only the lower one."

C. [If] it is found on clods and touched as much as an egg's bulk [of crumbs], it is unclean.

D. Clods which are on clods —

E. even though it touched as much as an egg's bulk —

F. unclean is only the place which it touched.[87]

G. What does one do?

H. R. Eliezer b. Jacob says in the name of R. Ḥanina b. Kinai, "While the dead creeping thing is still there, he sticks in a twig-basket."

11:4 A. Grapes — until when do they receive uncleanness as food?

B. Until the time that they will trample them, warp and woof.

C. And [if] there remain of them whole dried berries, they receive uncleanness as food.

D. Olives — until when do they receive uncleanness as food?

E. Until one will press them.

F. And R. Simeon says, "Until one will have crushed them."

G. [If] one has crushed them but there remain of them whole dried berries, they receive uncleanness as food.

11:5 A. And what are uncrushed olives and grapes?

B. Those that exude from under the beam or from under the peat and from the grape-skins.

C. [If] one gathered them for food, they receive uncleanness as food.

D. And the grape pits and the skins, even though one has gathered them for food — his intention is null.

11:6 A. He who weighs grapes in the balance, even though wine flows on his hands —

B. and even though he gave thought to it — it is insusceptible.

D. He who presses grapes in a jug, even though [the juice] flows on his hands — it is insusceptible.

E. And so with respect to the gentile:

F. One does scruple on account of wine used for idolatrous purposes.

11:7 A. He who cuts grapes of his vineyard for the market —

B. if he did not find a market for them, he returns them to the vat.

C. [He who cuts] olives for the market —

D. [if] he did not find a market for them,

E. he returns them to the press.

F. Even though he brings them to the market in unclean baskets and in unclean containers, they are clean.

---

87. *ibid.*

G. [When] they have entered the domain of the vat and the domain of the press, they are made susceptible to receive uncleanness.[88]

11:8   A. He who purchases from that which is lying on the ground —

B. [if he purchases] from an Israelite, let him do the work in uncleanness.

C. [If he purchases them] from a gentile, let him do the work in cleanness.

D. [He who purchases] from what is lying on the ground on leaves —

E. whether from an Israelite or from a gentile,

F. let him prepare them in uncleanness.

G. And R. Yosé b. R. Judah says, "[He who purchases them] from what is lying on leaves is like one who purchases them from what is lying on the ground;

H. "[in the case of purchasing them] from an Israelite, let him prepare them in uncleanness.

I. "[In the case of purchasing them] from the gentile, let him prepare them in cleanness."[89]

11:9   A. He who purchases [olives] from what is lying on the ground from an Israelite —

B. [intending] to make them into dried olives —

C. lo, this one prepares his olives in cleanness.

D. He who eats [grapes] from the baskets and from what is lying on the ground —

E. [if] he ate and left over as much as a *se'ah* or two *se'ahs,*

F. even though he spread them out for the vat,

G. and threw them into the vat,

H. [even though he spread them out for the vat] and the wine spurts on the grapes,

I. it is clean.

J. And so in the case of the gentile:

K. one does not scruple on account of wine used for idolatrous purposes.

11:10   A. [If] a single berry fell from it —

B. if it has a seal, it is clean.

C. [If] it does not have a seal, it is unclean.

D. Under what circumstances?

E. When one [who is unclean] has touched the place on which the liquid is located.

F. [If] one did not touch the place on which the liquid is located, it is clean.

11:11   A. R. Yosé says, "Even if four or five eggs fell from it and one

88. M. Toh. 10:5.   89. *ibid.*

trampled them all in a single vat —

B. "liquid which exudes from them is clean.

C. "Since one has trampled on them, they have been annulled.

D. "For the liquids have nothing by which they will be made unclean."[90]

11:12   A.   He who was standing and talking on the edge of the pit and spit drooled from his mouth —

B. it is a matter of doubt whether it reached the pit or whether it did not reach the pit —

C. [if it is a pit] of oil, the matter of doubt is deemed unclean.

D. [If it is] a vat of wine, its matter of doubt is deemed clean,

E. since the air [Sens: rim] of the cistern retains it.[91]

11:13   A.   He who empties the cistern one by one [filling one jar at a time]

B. and the dead creeping thing is found in the first jar —

C. they all are unclean.

D. [If it is found] in the last jar,

E. the last jar is unclean, but the rest of them are clean.

F. [If it is found] in the middle jar, from it and following, the jars are unclean;

G. from it and the foregoing, the jars are clean.

H. Under what circumstances?

I. When one examined but did not cover, or covered but did not examine.

J. [If] he was examining and covering,

K. and a dead creeping thing is found in one of them, it alone is unclean.[92]

11:14   A.   A dead creeping thing which is found floating on the rim of the cistern of a vat for heave-offering —

B. its matter of doubt is deemed unclean.

C. [If it is doubt as to] the workers, the matter of doubt is deemed clean,

D. because it is a matter of doubt concerning that which floats.[93]

11:15   A.   The upper cistern is public domain, and the lower is private domain—under what circumstances?

B. When the public enter through one way and leave through another.

C. [If] there is there only a single door,

D. or only a single breach,

E. this and that are private domain.[94]

11:16   A.   He whose wine-vats and olive-presses were unclean and who wants to clean them:

B. [as to] the boards and the two posts supporting the beams of the press and the troughs —

90. *ibid.*   91. M. Toh. 10:6.   92. M. Toh. 10:7.
93. M. Toh. 4:5.   94. M. Toh. 10:8.

C. he dries them, and they are clean.

D. The cylinders of twigs and of hemp —

E. he has to dry out.

F. The cylinders of bast and of reeds —

G. he has to leave unused.

H. And how long does he leave them unused?

I. Twelve months.

J. Rabban Simeon b. Gamaliel says, "From one wine-vintage to the next, and from one pressing season of olives to the next."

K. R. Yosé says, "If one wants to clean them forthwith, he should pour over them boiling water or scald them with water of olives."

L. Rabban Simeon b. Gamaliel says in the name of R. Yosé, "He places them in a river whose waters flow a whole season or under the spout whose waters flow."

M. And just as he dries for cleanness, so he dries for wine used for idolatrous purposes.[95]

95. *ibid.*

MAKHSHIRIN

1:1 A. He who shakes the tree in order to bring down liquids from it —

B. and they fell on those [pieces of fruit] which were detached, which were on it [the tree] and on those [vegetables] which were attached [to the ground], which were under it [that tree] —

C. The House of Shammai say, "It is under the law, If water be put."

D. And the House of Hillel say, "As to those which were detached, [they are] under the law, If water be put.

E. "And as to those which were attached [to the ground], they are not under the law, If water be put."[1]

1:2 A. Said R. Yosé b. R. Judah, "The House of Shammai and the House of Hillel did not dispute concerning the case of one who shakes the tree in order to bring down from it liquids,

B. "and they fell on the detached [pieces of fruit] which were on it, and on those which were attached to the ground which were beneath it,

C. "that they are [GRA deletes: not] subject to the law, If water be put.

D. "[Nor did they dispute of the case in which] one detached them after they were dried off, that they are not subject to the law, If water be put.

E. "Concerning what did they differ?

F. "Concerning the case of him who shakes the tree to bring down from it pieces of fruit, and they [drops of moisture] fell from one press to another, or from one *sukkah* to another, in that very same tree —

G. "for the House of Shammai say, 'It is subject to the law, If water be put.'

H. "And the House of Hillel say, 'It is not subject to the law, If water be put.'"[2]

1:3 A. Said the House of Hillel to the House of Shammai, "All agree concerning one who brings up a single upright sack, and who placed it on the side of the river,

B. "that, even though the water descends from the upper side to the lower side, (that) it is not subject to the law, If water be put."

C. The House of Shammai said to them, "Do you not agree concerning one who brings up two sacks which are upright and placed them on the bank, one on top of the other, and the water descends from the upper to the lower, (that) the lower is under the law, If water be put?"[3]

1:4 A. R. Yosé says, "All the same is the law covering one sack and two sacks:

B. "The House of Shammai say, 'It is under the law, If water be put.'

C. "And the House of Hillel say, 'It is not under the law, If water be

---

1. M. Mak. 1:1–4.   2. *ibid.*   3. *ibid.*

303

put.'"

D. R. Judah says, "R. Eliezer says, 'This and that are under the law, If water be put.'

E. "R. Joshua says, 'This and that are not under the law, If water be put.'

F. "R. 'Aqiva says, 'The lower one is under the law, If water be put. And the upper one is not under the law, If water be put.'"[4]

1:5   A. He who rubs off [in the wetness] of the press and of the leek,

B. even though the water descends from the upper side to the lower side — it is not under the law, If water be put.

C. [If] they [the drops of moisture] were detached [from the leek or press], lo, this is under the law, If water be put.

D. R. Yosé says, "A Zab and a Zabah who were walking along, and rain fell on his hair and on his garment,

E. "even though the water is detached from the upper side to the lower, lo, they are clean.

F. "For they [drops of water] are taken into account only after they have exuded from all of it.

G. "[Supply: Once they have exuded from all of it], lo, these are susceptible to uncleanness, and they are clean.

H. "For they are taken into account only after they have exuded."[5]

1:6   A. He who sets up jars in a vaulted chamber, even though they absorbed more than a *log* — it does not fall under the law, If water be put.

B. So far as the matter of purification-water is concerned, one does not take account of the possibility that they have absorbed [water].

C. Others said in the name of R. Neḥemiah, "If they were glazed, they do not drink up."[6]

1:7   A. "Fruit juice into which a drop of water of any amount has fallen is deemed susceptible to uncleanness," the words of R. Meir.

B. And sages say, "They follow [the status of] the majority."

C. R. Eliezer b. Jacob says, "Even a pitful of brine into which fell a drop of water of any amount at all is susceptible to uncleanness.

D. "[If] [Sens:wine,] honey, or milk fell into it, they follow the status of the majority [of the mixture]."[7]

1:8   A. He who plasters his roof

B. and he who launders his garment —

C. when does he know whether or not rain-water has formed the greater part?

D. At first it drips in gentle drops.

E. And now it flows drop after drop [in a torrent].

4. *ibid.*   5. M. Mak. 1:5.   6. M. Mak. 2:1.
7. M. Mak. 2:3.

F. [If] he found meat in it, they follow the status of the majority of the butchers.

G. In the case of meat in strings, they follow the status of the majority of those who eat meat.

H. [If] one found in it an abandoned [child] —

I. half and half —

J. they impose upon it the stringencies of both [gentiles and Israelites].

K. R. Judah says, "If there was a single gentile woman or a single maidservant, she is suspected of having abandoned [the baby]."[8]

2:1   A. A jar which is full of pieces of fruit and placed in liquids —

B. Said R. Yosé, "Under what circumstances? In the case of a jar made of earthenware.

C. "But in the case of all other utensils, they do not absorb [liquids].

D. "And stone utensils which are soft — lo, they are deemed equivalent to earthenware utensils."[9]

2:2   A. A sheet which one stretched on top of the pipe of the potter to wet down grains of wheat thereby —

B. if [the wheat is wet down] on account of the water, it is under the law, If water be put on.

C. If [the wheat is wet down] on account of the sheet, it is not under the law, If water be put on.[10]

2:3   A. He who sprinkles his house with [*TR* IV, p. 110; deletes: unclean] water and [afterward] put into it ears of grain and they became damp —

B. if there is on them flowing liquid, lo, this is under the law, If water be put, and if not, it is not under the law, If water be put.

C. R. Simeon says, "Even though there is flowing liquid on it, it is not under the law, If water be put."

D. Sages agree with R. Simeon in the case of one who wets down his threshing floor, that it is [supply: not] under the law, If water be put.

E. And in the case of one who gets up early in the morning to bring refuse —

if [he did so] on account of the drops [of dew] on it, lo, this is under the law, If water be put;

F. and if it is so that he might not be disturbed in his work, it is not under the law, If water be put.[11]

2:4   A. A beast that went down on its own account —

B. water which comes up in its mouth and in its moustache is under the law, If water be put.

C. [Water which comes up] on its foreleg and hindleg is not under the law, If water be put.

D. R. Judah says, "The water which comes up on the feet of man invariably imparts susceptibility to uncleanness."

E. R. Simeon b. Eleazar says, "Water which comes up on the hooves of the unclean beast invariably imparts susceptibility to uncleanness."[12]

2:5 A. He who draws water with a jug —

B. the water which comes up on its outer parts and on its rope wound round its neck and on the rope which is needed lo, it is (not) subject to the law, If water be put.

C. As to purification-water, one does not scruple lest [the water which is drawn in respect to the aforenamed parts of the jug be deemed water] which has [not] been drawn by means of a utensil.[13]

2:6 A. A trough into which water dripping from the roof has fallen —

B. "the drops of water which splash out and those which overflow are subject to the law, If water be put on.

C. "[If] one took it in order to pour it out —

D. "the House of Shammai say, 'It is subject to the law, If water be put.'

E. "And the House of Hillel say, 'It is not subject to the law, 'If water be put.'

F. "Under what circumstances?

G. "In the case of a clean [trough].

H. "But in the case of an unclean [trough],

I. "all agree that it is under the law, If water be put," the words of R. Meir.

J. R. Yosé says, "All the same is the clean and the unclean —

K. "The House of Shammai say, 'Lo, it is under the law, If water be put.'

L. "And the House of Hillel say, 'It is not under the law, If water be put.'"[14]

2:7 A. He who touches a piece of carrion which is in the midst of the immersion-pool is unclean, and he is clean when he ascends [from the water].

B. He who touched a bed or a chair [which is unclean] in the immersion-pool is unclean, and he is clean when he ascends [from the water].

C. A Zab who stepped [exerted pressure] on a bed or a chair in the midst of the immersion-pool — it is unclean, and it is clean when it ascends.

2:8 A. Pieces of fruit which fell into a water-channel,

B. and one whose hands were unclean reached out and took them —

C. his hands are unclean and the pieces of fruit are clean.

D. And if he gave thought that his hands should be rinsed off, his hands are clean, and the pieces of fruit are subject to the law, If water be put.[15]

---

12. M. Mak. 3:8.   13. M. Mak. 4:1.   14. M. Mak. 4:5.   15. M. Mak. 4:7.

2:9   A. He who draws water with a swape-pipe —

B. R. 'Aqiva explained, "If it was dried forthwith, they are clean, and if it was not dried off, even after up to thirty days they are unclean.

C. "Under ordinary circumstances — three days."[16]

2:10 A. Pieces of wood which absorbed [GRA: (on which) fell] unclean liquids,

B. and rains fell on them —

C. and they were more —

D. they are unclean.

E. Abba Yosé b. Dosa'i and R. Yosé b. Hammeshulam say, "[If] they were more, they are clean.

F. "He may kindle them, even with unclean hands.

G. "[If] he took them out so that rains might fall on them, and the clean [liquids] were more, [in any event] he should kindle them only with clean hands."[17]

2:11 A. R. Simeon says, "If they [the pieces of wood] were wet, and one kindled them,

B. "and the liquids which exuded from them were more than [following Sens:] the water which they absorbed, they are clean,

C. "by reason of an argument *a fortiori:*

D. "Now if rain-water, which is destined to receive uncleanness — lo, it imparts cleanness when it forms the greater part,

E. "fruit juice, which is not going to receive uncleanness —

F. "is it not logical that it should preserve cleanness when it forms the greater part?"

G. They said to him, "No. If you have said so in the case of rain-water, which imparts cleanness to unclean things [in an immersion-pool], will you say so in the case of fruit juice, which does not impart cleanness to unclean things?"[18]

2:12 A. He who immerses in the sea or in a river,

B. even though he went out more than a mile,

C. lo, [water which is on him] is under the law, If water be put.

D. [If] he crossed another river —

E. [if] his fellow pushed him

F. or if rain fell on him

G. and they were greater [in volume than the original water] —

H. the second [infusion of water] imparts insusceptibility to the first.[19]

2:13 A. The *tarnegilah* [?] and the pestle which had unclean water in them

B. and one immersed them —

C. the first [drops of water on] are made clean, but [those on] the second

16. M. Mak. 4:9.   17. M. Mak. 4:10.   18. *ibid.*
19. M. Mak. 5:1.

are susceptible to uncleanness.

D. "He who makes a bird in the water —

E. "the drops that splash out and those which remain in it are not subject to the law, If water be put," the words of R. Meir.

F. R. Judah says, "Both this and that are subject to the law, If water be put."

G. R. Yosé says, "The water which splashes out is not subject to the law, If water be put.

H. "And that which is in it, lo, this is under the law, If water be put."

I. He who makes a channel among pieces of fruit — [the liquids which flow down it] are not under the law, If water be put.[20]

2:14 A. He who measures the cistern.

B. "whether [to find out] its depth or [to find out] its breadth —

C. "[water which comes up on the measuring rod], lo, it is under the law, If water be put," the words of R. Tarfon.

D. R. 'Aqiva says, "[If he did so] to measure its depth, [the water which comes up on the rod] is under the law, If water be put. [If he did so to measure] its breadth, [the water which comes up on the measuring rod] is not under the law, If water be put."

E. Said to him R. Tarfon, "What difference does it make to me whether he measured it to find out its depth or whether he measured it to find out its breadth?"

F. He said to him, "When he measured it to find out its depth, he wants the liquid which is on the mark [of the measuring rod].

G. "When he measured it to find out its breadth, he does not want the liquid which is on the mark [of the measuring rod]."

H. He said to him, "If so, let the liquid on the mark [of the measuring rod] be unclean. [Let the liquid on the measuring rod] below the mark be clean."

I. He said to him, "Do you not agree that:

"he who draws water in a jug — the water which goes up [on its outer parts] and on the rope that is bound about its neck and on the rope which is needed for using the bucket —

"that the liquid is subject to the law, If water be put?

J. "For it is not possible for the water to pour into it until it touches its outer parts.

K. "If so, it is not possible for the liquid [to be] on the mark until it will be below the mark [of the measuring rod]."

L. R. Tarfon reverted to teach in accord with the opinion of R. 'Aqiva.[21]

2:15 A. [If] one let down a rope into a cistern to find out whether there is water in it —

20. M. Mak. 5:2.   21. M. Mak. 5:4.

B. [water which comes up on the rope] is under the law, If water be put.

C. [Water which is] on his hands and his feet is not under the law, If water be put.

D. [If] one let down the lifter to bring up with it a bucket or a ladle —

E. [or if he let down a basket] to bring back a chicken on it —

F. [water which comes up] is not under the law, If water be put.

G. And if he shook [it], lo, [water which is detached from the rope] is under the law, If water be put.[22]

2:16 A. [If] one brought a nail out into the rain in order to extinguish it['s heat], [the rain which falls on it] is not under the law, If water be put.

B. If [he did so] in order to temper it, lo, [the rain which falls on it] is under the law, If water be put.

C. He who leaves the burning brand in the rain to extinguish it — [rain which falls on it] is not under the law, If water be put.

D. If [he did so] in order to turn it into charcoal, lo, this is under the law, If water be put.[23]

3:1 A. He who brings up bundles of vegetables to the roof so that they will stay fresh —

[Supply: It is not under the law, If water be put].

B. [If he gave thought to them] to tie them up —

C. lo, this is under the law, If water be put.

D. And R. Judah says, "It is not under the law, If water be put [until he actually does the deed]."

E. He who brings [fruit] up to the roof to have it washed in dew and in rain, lo, this is under the law, If water be put.

F. [If] he brought them up to keep them free of maggots, and rain fell on them —

G. if he was happy, it is under the law, If water be put.

H. R. Judah says, "It is not possible that he should not be happy. [Supply: But (it is not under the law, If water be put) until he turns it over]."

I. While the dew or rain is still on them, if he gave thought to it, lo, it is under the law, If water be put.[24]

3:2 A. An imbecile, a deaf-mute, and a minor who brought up their pieces of fruit to the roof to have them washed in the dew and in the rain — lo, this is under the law, If water be put.

B. [If] they brought them up to keep them free from maggots, and dew or rain fell on them,

C. even though they gave thought to it,

D. it is not under the law, If water be put,

E. for they have the power of deed but not the power of intention.[25]

22. M. Mak. 5:5.   23. M. Mak. 5:7.   24. M. Mak. 6:2.   25. *ibid.*

3:3 A. Ḥilfata b. Qavinah says, "Ba'albeki garlic is subject to the law, If water be put,

B. "because they sprinkle water on it and afterward they twist it [into strings of garlic]."

C. Said sages, "If so, let it be susceptible to uncleanness to Ḥilfata b. Qavinah, but insusceptible to uncleanness to all Israel."

3:4 A. Joshua b. Peraḥiah says, "Wheat which comes from Alexandria is susceptible to uncleanness.

B. "because of their irrigation-wheel."

C. Said sages, "If so, let it be susceptible to uncleanness to Joshua b. Peraḥiah and insusceptible to uncleanness to all Israel."

3:5 A. Said R. Yosé, "At first the bundles of cucumbers and of gourds which were in Sepphoris were deemed susceptible to uncleanness,

B. "because they clean them off with a sponge when they pluck them up from the ground.

C. "The men of Sepphoris undertook not to do so."

3:6 A. "At first a paste of beans and of a kind of pulse of Sepphoris was deemed susceptible to uncleanness,

B. "because they used to soak them in water when they made them into a paste.

[C. Sens: "The men of Sepphoris undertook not to do so."]

3:7 A. The pieces of fruit in every place, lo, they are assumed to be insusceptible to uncleanness.

B. All the same [is the rule which applies to the fruit of the] gentile, the Samaritan, and the Israelite.

C. Even though they said, "A man is not permitted to impart susceptibility to uncleanness to his fruit," they permitted a householder to impart susceptibility to uncleanness to some small thing and to put it into a basket.

3:8 A. All bundles of vegetables deriving from the villages, which come from the marketplaces, are susceptible to uncleanness.

B. "And not concerning the place of the binding alone did they speak, but it is entirely [unclean], because it grows loose, and one goes and ties it up," the words of R. Meir.

C. Rabban Simeon b. Gamaliel says, "If the law is in accord with the opinion of R. Meir, then the sheaves are insusceptible to uncleanness."[26]

3:9 A. Sumac berries in every place, lo, they are in the presumption of being susceptible to uncleanness.

B. Cucumbers and gourds which are suspended by reed-grass on the doors of stores, lo, they are deemed susceptible to uncleanness.[27]

3:10 A. Vegetables which are sold with whatever can be eaten raw in front of a store, lo, they are susceptible to uncleanness,

26. *ibid.*   27. *ibid.*

B. because they water them when they sell them.

C. And the *etrogs* of Caesarea, lo, they are in the assumption of being insusceptible to uncleanness.

D. "The eggs of a storekeeper who sells [them] with them both wet and dry [produce], lo, they are susceptible to uncleanness," the words of R. Meir.

E. And R. Judah declares them insusceptible.[28]

3:11 A. Said R. Simeon b. Eleazar, "It is not that R. Meir declared susceptible in the case of [selling] both wet and dry [produce].

B. "But the child imparts susceptibility to uncleanness to them with the liquid which is in the cup."

C. All eggs are in the assumption of being insusceptible to uncleanness.

D. And the egg paid to the bath-housekeeper is in the assumption of being susceptible to uncleanness.[29]

3:12 A. How do they catch fish in the assumption of insusceptibility to uncleanness?

B. Whether one catches them with a net or whether one catches them with a cage or whether one catches them with a trap,

C. [if] one did not shake off the trap over them, lo, they are in the assumption of being insusceptible to uncleanness.

D. But they are always in the assumption of being susceptible to uncleanness until one will intend to catch them in a state of insusceptibility.

F. And the *'am ha'areṣ* is not believed to testify, "I did not shake the snare over them."[30]

3:13 A. The blood of the boil and the blister and what is squeezed out of the flesh,

B. and fruit juice and salt which melted [Maimonides: do not] receive uncleanness and do not impart susceptibility to uncleanness.

C. The urine of cattle does not impart uncleanness and does not impart susceptibility to uncleanness.

D. R. Yosé b. R. Judah says, "If they collected them in a utensil, lo, they impart susceptibility to uncleanness."[31]

E. Said R. Yosé, "'Onymus, brother of R. Joshua, the grit-dealer said to me,

3:14 A. "'He who slaughters the raven to practice [slaughtering] on it —

B. "'Its blood imparts susceptibility to uncleanness.'"

C. And R. Eleazar [Sens: Eliezer] says, "All blood deriving from slaughter invariably imparts susceptibility to uncleanness."

D. "The blood of a corpse imparts uncleanness in any measure at all," the words of R. Meir.

28. M. Mak. 6:3.   29. *ibid.*   30. *ibid.*
31. M. Mak. 6:7.

E. And R. Yosé says, "In the measure of a quarter-*log*."

F. Said Rabbi, "The opinion of R. Meir appears to me better in the case of a minor uncleanness, to impart uncleanness at one remove and to render unfit at one [further] remove, and the opinion of R. Yosé in the case of a major uncleanness, to impart uncleanness at two removes and to render unfit at one [further] remove."

3:15 A. [All] liquid which exudes from the corpse is clean, except for his blood.

B. And anything with the appearance of blood in connection with the corpse, lo, it is unclean.[32]

C. Said R. Joshua b. Qebusai, "All my days have I read this verse, 'The clean person shall sprinkle on the unclean person' [Num. 19:19], and I only discovered its meaning with regard to the storehouse of Yavneh.

"And from the storehouse of Yavneh I learned that one clean person sprinkles even on a hundred unclean persons."

32. T. Ah. 4:9.

ZABIM

1:1 A. He who sees one appearance of flux —

B. The House of Shammai say, "He is like a woman who awaits day against day."

C. And the House of Hillel say, "He is like one who has had a nocturnal emission."

D. And these and those agree that he immerses and eats his Passover in the evening.

E. The House of Hillel said to the House of Shammai, "Do you not agree that he immerses and eats his Passover in the evening?"

F. The House of Shammai said to them, "Do you not agree that if he sees [flux again] on the next day, that he is unclean? Lo, he is like a woman who awaits day against day, for if she should see [a drop of blood] the next day, she is unclean."[1]

1:2 A. He who moves the appearance [of flux] —

B. The House of Shammai say, "[His status is deemed to be] suspended."

C. And the House of Hillel say, "He is clean."

D. His bed and his chair —

E. The House of Shammai say, "[Its status is deemed to be] suspended."

F. And the House of Hillel say, "It is clean."[2]

1:3 A. [If] one saw two appearances [of flux] —

B. "He who moves both of them is unclean," in accord with the words of the House of Shammai.

C. And the House of Hillel say, "He who moves the first is clean, and [he who moves] the second is unclean."

D. Beds and chairs [on] which [he sat] between the first and the second [appearance of flux] —

E. The House of Shammai declare unclean.

F. And the House of Hillel declare clean.

G. [If] he saw one as profuse as two —

H. "He who moves the entire mass is unclean," the words of the House of Shammai.

I. And the House of Hillel say, "Unclean is only the one who moves the last drop alone."[3]

1:4 A. Said R. 'Aqiva, "The House of Shammai and the House of Hillel did not disagree concerning him who sees two or one as profuse as two, and then on the second day it ceased, and on the third day he saw one, that he is entirely a Zab.

---

1. M. Zab. 1:1.   2. *ibid.*   3. *ibid.*

B. "Concerning what did they disagree?

C. "Concerning him who saw one [flux] on the first day, and on the second it ceased, and on the third he saw two —

D. "The House of Shammai say, 'He is entirely a Zab.'

E. "And the House of Hillel say, 'He imparts uncleanness to bed and chair,

"'and requires entry into running water,

"'but is free of the obligation to bring a sacrifice.'"[4]

1:5 A. When R. 'Aqiva was arranging laws for disciples, he said, "Whoever has heard a reason from his fellow should come and state it."

B. In his presence did R. Simeon state in the name of R. Eleazar b. R. Judah of Bartuta, "The House of Shammai and the House of Hillel did not disagree concerning him who saw one [flux] on the first day, and on the second it ceased, and on the third he saw two, that such a one is not entirely a Zab.

C. "Concerning what did they disagree?

D. "Concerning him who sees two, or one as profuse as two, and on the second day it ceased, and on the third day he saw one."

E. He said to him, "Not just anyone who jumps forward is to be praised, but only one who gives the reason [for his ruling]."[5]

1:6 A. R. Simeon said before him, "Thus did the House of Hillel say to the House of Shammai [by way of a reason]:

B. "'What difference does it make to me that he saw one at first and two at the end or that he saw two at the outset and one at the end?'

C. "[The House of Shammai] said to them, 'When he saw one at the outset and two at the end, the clean day annuls [the effects of] the appearance, and he has in hand two appearances.

D. "'When he saw two at the first [instance] and one at the end, since he is obligated to count seven [clean days], the appearance [of flux] thereby annuls the effects of the clean [day], and he has in hand three appearances [of flux].'"

E. R. 'Aqiva reverted to teach in accord with the words of R. Simeon.[6]

1:7 A. R. Eleazar b. R. Yannai said in the name of R. Eleazar Ḥisma before Rabbi, "The House of Shammai and the House of Hillel did not disagree concerning him who saw one [flux] on the first day and one on the second, and on the third it ceased, and on the fourth he saw one.

B. "Or concerning him who saw one on the first day, and on the second it ceased, and on the third and on the fourth he saw two, that this one is not entirely a Zab.

C. "Concerning what did they disagree?

D. "Concerning him who sees two or one as profuse as two, and on the

4. *ibid.*   5. *ibid.*   6. *ibid.*

second day it ceased, and on the third [GRA deletes: and on the fourth] he saw one."[7]

1:8 A. Said one disciple of the disciples of R. Ishmael before R. 'Aqiva in the name of R. Ishmael, "The House of Shammai and the House of Hillel did not differ concerning him who sees semen on the second day, that he loses the day before it, or concerning him who sees [semen] on the fourth day, that he loses only that day alone.

B. "Concerning what did they disagree?

C. "Concerning him who sees [semen] on the third day."[8]

1:9 A. Any semen which imparts uncleanness in the case of priests causes the loss [of a day] in the case of the Zab.

B. The Zab is permitted to have sexual relations on the day of the completion of his counting, and [if he does so], loses only that day alone.

C. How so?

D. [If] he saw [semen] [even] at the eve of the eighth day, he counts as at the first and brings another sacrifice.

E. [If] he saw on the eighth day, he counts as at the first and brings two offerings.[9]

F. How much is sufficient time for immersion and drying off?

G. Sufficient time for one to descend and to immerse and to ascend and to dry off.[10]

1:10 A. And how much is the measure of a profuse appearance [of flux]?

B. As [much time as it takes to go] from Gad Yon to Shiloaḥ,

C. which is the same [as the amount of time required for] two immersions and two acts of drying off.

D. R. Simeon says, "Sufficient [time for] circumambulating the house on the inside."[11]

1:11 A. [Rabbi says,] "They made a parable. To what is the matter comparable?

B. "[It is comparable] to a rope of a hundred 'ammot in length."

C. [Following Sifra Zabim 1:4, *TR* IV, p. 121, to 1s. 14/15:] "How so?

D. "[If] one saw at the beginning a hundred, and at the end fifty, and at the end a hundred 'ammah, lo, this is entirely a Zab.

E. "[If] one saw at the beginning a hundred, in the middle fifty, and at the end, a hundred,

F. "or at the beginning a hundred and afterward fifty and at the end a hundred, lo, this is not entirely a Zab.

G. [Following Sens:] "[If] it ceased and one saw between one appearance and another sixty 'ammah or seventy 'ammah and afterward he sees [flux], all the more so is it his uncleanness."

7. *ibid.*   8. M. Zab. 1:2.   9. *ibid.*
10. M. Zab. 1:4.   11. *ibid.*

H. This is the principle: So long as it is profuse, all the more so is it his uncleanness.[12]

1:12 A. How so?

B. [If] he saw three appearances [of flux], if there is not sufficient time between the first and the third for immersion and an act of drying off, he has at hand only one [flux].

C. [If] he saw one profuse as two —

D. [if] there is sufficient time from the beginning of its [flow] to its end for immersion and an act of drying off, he has in hand two appearances.

E. If not, he has in hand only one.

F. And R. Yosé says, "He has in hand only one."[13]

1:13 A. And R. Yosé agrees that, if he saw one at twilight, even though its flow is not so long as the time required for an immersion and an act of drying off, there are in it two appearances [of flux] because two distinct days divide it.

B. And so did R. Yosé rule, "[If] he saw one [flux] at twilight, it is a matter of doubt as to uncleanness. He is free of liability to bring a sacrifice.

C. "[If he saw] two at twilight, it is a matter of doubt as to uncleanness and a matter of doubt as to sacrifice.

D. "[If] one [flux] was certain and two were at twilight, or one was at twilight and two were certain,

E. "[then] it is a matter of certainty as to uncleanness and doubt as to sacrifice.

F. "[If] two were certain and one was at twilight,

G. "or two were at twilight and one was certain,

H. "[then] he is certain as to uncleanness and certain as to the obligation to bring a sacrifice."[14]

2:1 A. The gentiles and the convert and the resident alien are not susceptible to uncleanness through flux.

B. But even though they are not susceptible to uncleanness through flux, they [in fact] are unclean like Zabs in every respect.

C. And on their account they burn heave-offering.

D. But they are not liable on their account for contamination of the sanctuary and its holy things.[15]

2:2 A. A ṭumṭom and an androgyne who saw either white or red flow — on their account they do not burn heave-offering.

B. And they are not liable on their account for contamination of the sanctuary and its holy things.

C. [If] they saw white and red flow simultaneously, they do burn heave-

12. *ibid.*   13. M. Zab. 1:5.   14. M. Zab. 1:5—6.
15. M. Zab. 2:1.

offering on their account.

D. But they are not liable on their account for contamination of the sanctuary and its holy things.[16]

2:3 A. He who touches semen and red flow and enters the sanctuary is free [of obligation].

B. He who touched his own white flow and red flow and entered the sanctuary is liable.

C. [If] he was counting [clean days] on account of white flow and saw red flow, [or if he was counting clean days] on account of red flow and saw white flow, lo this one does not lose [the day on which the one or the other appeared].

2:4 A. And what is the difference between flux and semen?

B. Flux comes from a limp penis, and semen from an erection.

C. Flux is like the white of a crushed egg, and semen is congealed like the white of an egg which is not crushed.

D. Red semen is clean, and the woman attributes [red flow] to it.

2:5 A. As to a Zab, they attribute it to food — and to any kind of food.

B. R. Eliezer b. Pinḥas says in the name of R. Judah b. Beterah, "Milk and cheese and fat meat and old wine and bean-mash and eggs and brine lead to the matter of flux."[17]

2:6 A. As to a child, they attribute [his flux] to five things:

B. to food, to drink, to a carrying something, and to jumping during his and his mother's illness.

C. R. Simeon b. Judah says in the name of R. Simeon, "Exactly as they attribute [flux] to semen during the twenty-four hour period, so [they attribute it] to something he has seen or fantasized about during the twenty-four hour period.

D. "But [as to attributing flux to] food and drink and carrying something and jumping, they attribute it to such causes only so long as he is affected [by such things]."[18]

2:7 A. A gentile who saw semen and converted — forthwith is he susceptible to uncleanness by reason of flux.

B. Under what circumstances?

C. When he converted when already circumcised.

D. But if he was circumcised and afterward saw [semen], they attribute it to it so long as he is distressed [recovering from the circumcision],

E. whether he is gentile or Israelite.[19]

2:8 A. He who finds a corpse lying across the breadth of the path —

B. a Nazir and one who is going to eat his Passover is clean.

C. And as to heave-offering, he is unclean.

16. *ibid.*   17. M. Zab. 2:2.   18. *ibid.*

19. M. Zab. 2:3.

D. Under what circumstances?

E. [If] there is no place to pass [except across the corpse itself].

F. But [if] there is a place to pass, even for heave-offering is he clean.

G. Under what circumstances?

H. When he goes by foot.

I. But [if] he carries or rides on a beast, he is unclean.

J. For the one who goes on his own two feet may possibly not touch and not overshadow and not move [the corpse].

K. But it is not possible for him [who carries or rides] not to touch and not to overshadow and not to move [the corpse].

L. [If]it is not possible for him not to touch, overshadow, and move, he is unclean.

M. And in the case of a corpse which is spread about in bits and pieces, he is clean.

N. Under what circumstances?

O. In the case of the uncleanness of the nethermost depths.

P. But if it is a case of certain uncleanness, he is unclean.

2:9   A. What is the uncleanness of the nethermost depths?

B. That [is a case in which] no one else anywhere in the world knew about the presence of the corpse-matter.

C. But [if] anyone else in the world knew about the presence of corpse-matter, this is not deemed uncleanness of the nethermost depth.

D. [If] one found it buried in straw or in dirt or in pebbles, lo, this constitutes uncleanness in the nethermost depths.

E. But a corpse which is buried in water and in darkness and in the crevices of rocks — this is not deemed a grave in the nethermost depths.

F. A grave in the nethermost depths applies only to the corpse alone.

3:1   A. A more strict rule applies to the Zab than to the Zabah, and [a more strict rule applies] to the Zabah than to the Zab.

B. For the Zab must [for purification] enter into running water. But the Zabah need not enter into running water.

C. The Zab is susceptible to uncleanness through flux on the very day that he is born. But the Zabah [is not susceptible until] ten days [after birth].

D. If the Zab saw three occurrences of flux in three days, he is made unclean by them. But the Zabah sometimes sees three appearances on three successive days and is not made unclean by them.

E. As to the Zab, his days do not stand before him, which is not the case for the Zabah.

F. The Zab's sort [of fluid] does not cause him to lose a day, which is not the case for the Zabah.

G. The Zab is made unclean by white [flow], which is not the case with the Zabah.

3:2 A. More strict is the rule applying to the Zabah than to the Zab:

B. For the Zabah imparts uncleanness to bed and chair on account of an appearance of unclean flow of any amount at all.

C. She imparts uncleanness to the one who has intercourse with her.

D. And she imparts uncleanness during the antecedent twenty-four hour period.

E. And she imparts uncleanness internally as externally,

F. And she imparts uncleanness in cases of inadvertence.

G. And she imparts uncleanness through red flow —

none of which is the case for the Zab.

3:3 A. More strict is the rule applying to the Zab than to one unclean by corpse-uncleanness, and [more strict is the rule applying to] the one unclean by corpse-uncleanness than to the Zab:

B. For the Zab makes a bed and chair under him render man unclean and render garments unclean and [imparts] to what is above him *maddaf*-uncleanness and makes food and drink unclean — [forms of uncleanness] which the corpse does not impart.

C. His flux and his spit and his urine impart stringent uncleanness.

D. And he imparts uncleanness by means of contact to a utensil which is subject to purification by rinsing, and by means of shifting to a clay utensil.

E. And he is liable for a sacrifice and is required to enter running water for his purification, which is not the case for the one who is unclean by reason of corpse-uncleanness.

F. More strict is the rule applying to one unclean by corpse-uncleanness:

G. For the one suffering corpse-uncleanness requires sprinkling [with purification-water] on the third and seventh day, which is not the case for the Zab.

3:4 A. More strict is the rule applying to the Zab than that applying to the *meṣora'*, and [more strict is the rule applying] to the *meṣora'* than applies to the Zab:

B. For the Zab requires purification through entry into running water, which is not the case for the *meṣora'*.

C. More strict is the rule applying to the *meṣora'*:

D. For the *meṣora'* imparts uncleanness through entry, which is not the case for the Zab.

3:5 A. More strict is the rule applying to the Zabah than to the *meṣora'at*, and [more strict is the rule applying] to the *meṣora'at* than to the Zabah:

B. For the Zabah imparts uncleanness to one who has intercourse with her, which is not the case for the *meṣora'at*.

C. More strict is the rule applying to the *meṣora'at*:

D. For the *meṣora'at* imparts uncleanness through coming into a house.

E. And she requires sprinkling with running water, which is not the case for the Zabah.

4:1 A. "An unclean person who hits the clean person, and the clean person who hits the unclean — the clothes of the clean person are unclean," the words of R. Meir.

B. And sages say, "[If] a clean person hits the unclean, the clothes of the clean person are clean. [If] an unclean person hits the clean,

C. "since if the clean person draws back, lo, the unclean person falls down,

D. "the clothes of the clean person are unclean."[20]

E. R. Simeon says, "[If] he hits him with knuckles, he is unclean. [If] he hits him with the back of his hand, he is clean."

F. R. Judah says, "A four-sided house, two corners of which touch the ground, and the middle part of which rocks —

G. "[if] the unclean person and the clean person sit in it —

H. "the clothes of the clean person are clean."[21]

I. And sages say, "[There is no transfer of uncleanness] until this one pushes and that one opens."

J. They raise one another from the pit —

K. And R. Simeon declares clean.[22]

4:2 A. R. Simeon agrees in the case of two who were grinding with millstones propelled by an ass or with a handmill.

B. [If] they unload an ass or load it up,

C. when their burden is heavy,

D. the clothes of the clean person are unclean.[23]

4:3 A. [R. Simeon says,] "[If] the hair of the unclean person is on the hair of the clean person, he is clean.

B. "[If] the hair of the clean person is on the unclean person, he is unclean.

C. "[If] the hair of the unclean person is on the hair of the clean person,

D. "if the unclean person arose, he is clean.

E. "And if the clean person arose, he is unclean.

F. "[If] the hair of the clean person is on the hair of the unclean person,

G. "whether the unclean person arose or whether the clean person arose, he is unclean."[24]

4:4 A. Three things did R. Eleazar Ḥisma declare unclean in the name of R. Joshua, and did sages declare clean:

B. (1) A menstruating woman who sat with a clean woman on the bed the cap which is on her head —

C. R. Eleazar Ḥisma declares unclean in the name of R. Joshua.

D. And sages declare clean.

E. (2) [If] she sat down on the boat, utensils which are on the top of the

20. M. Zab. 3:3.   21. M. Zab. 3:1.   22. M. Zab. 3:2.
23. *ibid.*   24. M. Zab. 5:4.

mast of the ship —

F. R. Eleazar Ḥisma declares unclean in the name of R. Joshua.

G. And sages declare clean.

H. (3) A trough which is full of clothing, when its burden is heavy —

I. R. Eleazar Ḥisma declares unclean in the name of R. Joshua.

J. And sages declare clean.[25]

K. A Zab who was lying on six chairs —

L. [if they are set] lengthwise, they are clean, for no one of them bears the greater part of his [weight].

M. R. Simeon says, "If the middle one was higher [than the others], it is unclean, because the greater part of his [weight] is borne on it."

N. R. Simeon agrees that if he sat on the frame of the bed, four cloaks which are under the four legs of the frame are unclean.

O. In the case of a beast, under two forelegs and a hindleg, under two hindlegs and a foreleg.[26]

4:5   A. A Zab who knocked against a tree which is infirm, and against a branch which is infirm —

B. [if] there fell from them unripe figs or branches, and on them is flowing liquid, they are unclean.[27]

4:6   A. [If a Zab] knocked against an oven —

B. [if] from it fell a loaf of heave-offering, it is clean.[28]

C. And if there was sherd cleaving onto it, it is unclean.

D. [If a Zab] knocked against the door-pin, the lock, and the door, they are unclean.

E. [If a Zab knocked against] the chest, box, or cupboard,

F. even though they hold [the requisite] volume — [they are unclean].

G. R. Neḥemiah and R. Simeon declare clean.

H. And if they were shifted, they are unclean.

I. This is the principle: Whatever is through the force of trembling is clean; through the force of shaking is unclean.[29]

4:7   A. [R. Judah says,] "The beam of the olive-press, when it is reenforced, is clean."

B. R. Yosé says, "Also: the beam of the bathhousekeeper, when it is loosened, [is unclean].

C. "If it is not loosened,

D. "it [the loaf] is clean."[30]

4:8   A. [If] the Zab is on one side of the scale and a bed or a chair is opposite him, if the Zab goes down, it imparts uncleanness at one remove and renders [heave-offering] unfit at one.

B. And if it outweighed the Zab, it imparts uncleanness at two removes

25. M. Zab. 4:1.   26. M. Zab. 4:4.   27. M. Zab. 4:3.
28. M. Zab. 4:2.   29. M. Zab. 4:3.   30. M. Zab. 4:2.

and renders [heave-offering] unfit at one remove.

C. In the case of a man, whether he outweighs the Zab or whether the Zab outweighs him, he imparts uncleanness at one remove and renders [heave-offering] unfit at one remove.[31]

4:9 A. [If] a Zab is on one side of the scale and food and drink are on the second side,

B. even if it is only slightly distant from the ground,

C. they impose upon it the stringent rulings applying to that which [who] carries and the stringent rulings applying to that which [who] is carried.[32]

D. [If] he [a Zab] sat on top of a small press with a cylindrical beam, utensils which are in the roller are unclean.

E. [If he sat] on the fuller's press when it is loaded with stones, utensils which are under it are clean.

F. And R. Neḥemiah declares unclean.

G. When it goes back over the utensils [clothes], utensils which are under it become unclean.[33]

5:1 A. The Torah has imposed a more stringent rule upon food and drink and *maddaf* [an object not used for sitting and lying] which are above the Zab,

B. than upon food and drink and *maddaf* which are under the Zab;

C. upon bed and chair which are under the Zab,

D. than upon bed and chair which are above the Zab;

E. and upon *maddaf* [an object not used for lying and sitting] which is above the Zab,

F. than upon bed and chair which are above the Zab;

G. upon man, whether above the Zab or below the Zab,

H. than upon bed and chair which are above the Zab.[34]

I. [If] something connected to the unclean person is on a clean person,

J. on part of him,

K. [if] something connected to a clean person is on the unclean person

L. on part of him —

M. in the case of the Zab, he is unclean,

N. in the case of the bed, he is clean.

O. [If] the greater part of the unclean person is on the clean person,

P. on part of him,

Q. [if] the greater part of a clean person is on the unclean person,

R. on part of him —

S. whether on the Zab or on the bed —

31. M. Zab. 4:5.   32. M. Zab. 4:6.   33. M. Zab. 4:7.
34. M. Zab. 5:2.

T. he is unclean.

U. [If] part of the unclean person is on a clean person, on part of him,

V. [if] part of the clean person is on the unclean, on part of him —

W. in the case of the Zab, it is unclean. In the case of the bed [of the Zab], it is clean.

X. R. Simeon says, "Also: if part of an unclean person is on a clean person, even in the case of the Zab, he is clean."[35]

5:2   A. What are the connectors?

B. They are the teeth, the fingernails, the hair, and the backbone.

C. What are the parts?

D. They are the fingertips of the hands and the toes.[36]

E. His phlegm, and his mucous, and his saliva, and his snot, lo, they are like his spit.

F. His tear and the blood of his wound and the milk of a woman [*TR* IV, p. 136:] and blood which exudes from his mouth and from his penis impart uncleanness as liquid.

G. His flux, his spit, and his urine impart stringent uncleanness.

H. His semen —

I. R. Eliezer says, "It does not impart uncleanness when it is carried."

J. And sages say, "It imparts uncleanness when it is carried,

K. "because it is not possible for semen to be emitted without a trace of urine to be contained therein."[37]

5:3   A. Utensils which touch the Zab and the Zabah and the menstruating woman and the woman after childbirth and the *meṣora'* and the bed and the chair impart uncleanness at two removes and spoil [heave-offering] at one [further remove].

B. [If] they separated, they impart uncleanness at one remove and render unfit at one remove.

C. He who touches, and he who carries, and he who shifts on account of carrying —

none of these applies to them.[38]

5:4   A. He who touches the flux of the Zab and his spit and his semen, his urine and the blood of the menstruating woman imparts uncleanness at two removes and renders unfit at one.

B. [If] he separated, he imparts uncleanness at one remove and renders unfit at one remove.

C. All the same is the one who touches and the one who carries.

D. He who carries and he who shifts — [these] do not apply to them.

E. For you have nothing not animate which imparts uncleanness through shifting.

35. M. Zab. 5:4—5.   36. *ibid.*   37. M. Zab. 5:7.
38. M. Zab. 5:6.

F. And you have nothing which imparts uncleanness through shifting except for something which is animate.[39]

5:5   A. He who touches the fringes of the saddle and the wool of carrion [and] purification-water which contains sufficient volume for sprinkling imparts uncleanness at two removes and renders unfit at one.

B. [If] he separated, he imparts uncleanness at one remove and renders unfit at one.

C. In the case of the horn of carrion and the wood of the saddle and purification-water which lacks sufficient volume for sprinkling, he imparts uncleanness at one remove and renders unfit at one remove.

D. [If] he separated, he imparts uncleanness at one remove and renders unfit at one remove.[40]

F. He who touches one who has had intercourse with a menstruating woman and [who touches] an idol imparts uncleanness at one remove and renders [heave-offering] unfit at one remove,

G. whether man or utensils.

5:6   A. An idol is [unclean] in the status of a dead creeping thing, and its appurtenances likewise are unclean in the status of a dead creeping thing, as it is said, "You shall utterly detest it" [Deut. 7:26].

B. R. 'Aqiva says, "It is of the same order of uncleanness as a menstruating woman, as it is said, 'You shall cast them away as a menstruous thing; you shall say to it, Get thee hence' [Is. 30:22].

C. "Just as the menstruating woman imparts uncleanness when she is carried, so an idol imparts uncleanness when it is carried."

5:7   A. He who pokes his head and the greater part of his body into a temple of idolatry is unclean.

B. Utensils which he stuck into the contained airspace of a temple of idolatry are unclean.

C. The stools and chairs, the greater part of which he put into a temple of idolatry, are unclean.

5:8   A. Wine which one saw a gentile offer up as a libation,

B. if it is of the volume of an olive's bulk,

C. imparts stringent uncleanness.

D. And if not, it imparts only the uncleanness of liquid.

E. And the remainder of the gentile's wine, even though it is prohibited on account of wine used for idolatrous libations, imparts only the uncleanness of unclean liquid alone.

5:9   A. He who eats of the carrion of a clean bird, bones, sinews, the cluster of eggs, blood and flesh —

B. [if] it is alive, he is clean.

C. [If] he eats of the ovaries, crop, intestines,

39. M. Zab. 5:7.   40. M. Zab. 5:8.

D. or [if] he melted the fat and swallowed it,

E. he is unclean.

F. [If] he wrapped it in bast and swallowed it, he is clean.

G. [if] he wrapped it in lettuce and swallowed it, he is unclean.

H. [If] he vomited it up and swallowed it, he imparts uncleanness at two removes and renders unfit at one [further remove].

I. [If] he swallowed it and went and vomited it up and it is located in his gullet, he imparts uncleanness at one remove and renders unfit at one remove.

J. [If] he swallowed it, and it is not of the volume of an olive, he is clean in every respect.

K. [If] he took a claw and ate it, if it is of the volume of an olive, he is unclean, and if not, he is clean.

5:10　A. [If] the carrion of a beast is inside [him] and in his mouth, he is unclean.

B. [If it is] in his gullet, he is clean.

C. [If] the carrion of the fowl is inside [him] and in his mouth, he is clean.

D. [If] it is in his gullet, he is unclean.

E. You come out to say that in a situation in which this imparts uncleanness, the other imparts cleanness, and in a case in which the other imparts cleanness, this imparts uncleanness.[41]

5:11　A. The carrion of clean fowl is in the measure of an olive in respect to the gullet.

B. And this is one of the thirteen things which have been stated in connection with the carrion of the clean fowl.

C. The carrion of the unclean fowl is in the measure of half of a loaf to render the body unfit.

D. "In the measure of an egg it imparts the uncleanness of food," the words of R. Joshua.

E. R. Eliezer says, "This and that are in the measure of an olive."

F. R. Ḥoniah says, "This and that are in the measure of an egg."

5:12　A. He who eats a limb from a living animal,

B. whether from beast or wild animal or clean fowl —

C. in any measure at all, [he is liable].

D. [If] they are unclean, [he is clean] until they are of the volume of an olive.

E. "He who eats of the carrion of the unclean fowl, lo, this one incurs eighty [stripes]," the words of R. Judah and R. Eleazar.

F. And sages say, "He incurs only forty stripes."

41. M. Zab. 5:9.

YADAYIM

1:1 A. "[To render hands clean], a quarter-*log* of water do they pour for one, but not for two.

B. "A half-*log* of water do they pour for three, but not for four.

C. "A *log* of water do they pour for five, but not for ten, and not for one hundred.

D. "They add [the water used] for the first [pouring] but they do not add [to the water used for] the second," the words of R. Yosé.

E. R. Meir says, "A quarter-*log* of water do they pour for hands, even for two, and a half a *log* for three, even for four, a *log* for five and ten and a hundred."[1]

1:2 A. They add to the second but they do not add to the first —

B. How so?

C. [If] one poured the first [water] and rubbed off [his hands] and went and poured the second,

D. and it [the water] is not sufficient to reach the wrist, lo, this one adds to it.

E. All the same is one who washes one of his hands and one who washes two of his hands,

F. [all the same is] the hand of a large person and the hand of a small one —

G. he must pour out a quarter-*log* [of water].

H. Rabban Simeon b. Gamaliel says, "Two hands of two individuals are regarded as if they were of two men."

I. How so?

J. [If] two people washed their two hands with a quarter-*log*, the second one should not go and wash his hands with what is left of the quarter-*log*.[2]

1:3 A. One who pours water on his hands must rub his hands off.

B. [If] he rubbed one hand on the other, it is unclean.

C. [If he rubbed it] on his head or on the wall, it is clean.

D. [If] he went and touched them, it is unclean.

E. "He who pours water on his hands with a single rinsing has to wash with a quarter-*log* [of water]," the words of R. Meir.

F. R. Yosé says, "In the case of both hands, he has to pour a quarter-*log*. In the case of one hand, even if he washed with the remnant of the quarter-*log* of water, it is fit."[3]

1:4 A. Whatever interposes in the case of the body interposes in the case of the hands,

B. with reference to the sanctification of the hands and feet for the Tem-

---

1. M. Yad. 1:1.   2. *ibid.*   3. M. Yad. 2:1.

ple House.[4]

1:5 A. He who washes his hands [for unconsecrated food prepared in accord with cleanness required for] Holy Things must pour out a quarter-*log* of water.

B. And as to the sanctification [washing] of hands and feet, there is no fixed measure.[5]

1:6 A. A stopper which one made for a utensil — they pour out water from it for hands.

B. The waterskin and the tub, even though they are broken down — they pour out from them water for hands.

C. The sack and the basket, even though they hold [liquid] — they do not pour out water from them for the hands.

D. A chest, box, and cupboard, when they hold [requisite measure to be insusceptible to uncleanness], even though they are not deemed as Tents — they do not pour out water from them for hands.[6]

1:7 A. Priests sanctify in the sanctuary only with a utensil.

B. And they force the suspected wife to drink, and they purify *meṣora's* [only with a utensil].

C. The sides of a wooden utensil and a bone utensil and glass utensil — they do not pour out from them water for hands.

D. If one smoothed them, sanded them, and made them into utensils, and they can hold a quarter-*log* of water, they do pour out water from them for hands.

1:8 A. Sherds of earthenware utensils which can hold a quarter-*log* of water —

they pour out from them water for hands.

B. Sherds of metal utensils, even though they can hold a quarter-*log* of water —

they do not pour out from them water for hands.

1:9 A. He who hews out a water-channel and made in it a receptacle, even though the water uprooted it and attached it —

B. they do not draw with it water for the purification-rite,

C. and they do not mix in it,

D. and they do not sprinkle from it [purification-water onto someone made unclean by the corpse],

E. and it does not require a tightly-sealed cover,

F. and they do not pour out water for hands from it.

G. [If] one uprooted it and affixed it and gave thought to it to make use of it as a utensil after its uprooting —

H. they do draw with it,

I. and they do mix in it,

---

4. M. Yad. 2:2.   5. M. Yad. 1:1.   6. M. Yad. 1:2.

J. and they do sprinkle from it,

K. and it does require a tightly sealed cover [in the Tent of the corpse],

L. and they do pour water for hands from it.[7]

1:10   A. Water which has been made unfit for cattle to drink —

B. R. Simeon b. Eleazar says, "[If] it is on the ground, they immerse [in it], but they do not pour from it water for hands."[8]

C. Water which is before the baker, even though its color has not changed —

they do not pour from it water for hands.

D. And when he takes it with his hands and pours it on loaves,

E. if its color changes, it is unfit.

F. And if not, it is fit.[9]

1:11   A. Water which is before the smith,

B. even though its color has not changed —

C. they do not pour from it water for hands,

D. for it is certain that work has been done in it.

E. Water which is before the scribe, if its color has changed, is unfit, and if not, is fit.[10]

1:12   A. All are fit to pour out water for hands, even a person unclean by reason of corpse-contamination, even a man who has had intercourse with a menstruating woman.

B. Whoever does not impart uncleanness to water when he carries it is fit to pour out water for hands.[11]

1:13   A. [If] the one who takes the water intends and the one who pours out the water does not intend [that by his act the water will clean the hands],

B. [if] the one who pours out the water intends, and the one who takes the water does not intend [that the water should clean the hands],

C. his hands are deemed clean.

D. R. Yosé says, "His hands are unclean."[12]

1:14   A. [If] one broke open the caldron and poured out water for hands from a pipe which contains a place capable of containing a quarter-*log* of water —

B. his hands are clean.

C. And R. Yosé says, "His hands are unclean."

D. And R. Yosé agrees that if he left a jar between his knees or in the crook of his arm and poured out water, his hands are clean.[13]

1:15   A. [If] there were before him two glasses [of water] —

B. with one of them work had been done, and with one of them work had not been done —

7. T. Par. 5:8.   8. M. Yad. 1:3.   9. M. Yad. 1:5.
10. *ibid.*   11. *ibid.*   12. *ibid.*
13. *ibid.*

C. [if] he poured [water] from one of them onto both of his hands and prepared foods requiring cleanness —

D. they are held in suspense.

E. [If he poured out water] from the second and prepared [foods requiring cleanness], they are clean.

F. [If he poured out water] from the first and did not prepare foods requiring cleanness,

G. [and if he then poured out water] from the second and prepared [foods requiring cleanness], they are clean.

H. [If he poured out water] from the first and prepared,

I. from the second and prepared,

J. [if] these and those are lying [before him],

K. these and those are clean.[14]

1:16 A. [If] one poured out [water] from one of them on to one of his hands and prepared foods requiring cleanness, they are held in suspense.

B. [If he did so] from the second and prepared [foods requiring cleanness], they are clean.

C. [If he did so] from the first and did not prepare,

D. from the second and did prepare [foods requiring cleanness], they are clean.

E. [If he poured out water] from the first and prepared,

F. from the second and prepared,

G. [if] these and those are lying [before him],

H. these and those are clean.[15]

1:17 A. [If] there were before him two glasses [of water], one unclean and one clean.

B. and he poured out [water] from one of them for one of his hands and prepared foods requiring cleanness,

C. they are held in suspense.

D. [If he did so] from the second and prepared [foods requiring cleanness], they are clean.

E. [If he did so] from the first and did not prepare,

F. from the second and prepared [they are clean. (If he did so) from the first and prepared, from the second and prepared] —

G. [if] these and those are lying before him,

H. lo, they determine [the status of one another].

I. [If] he ate the first [foods which he prepared], or they were made unclean, or they were lost, before the second [foods requiring cleanness] were prepared, they are clean.

J. [If this took place] after the second were prepared, the second are kept in a state of suspense.

14. M. Yad. 2:4.   15. *ibid.*

K. [If] he poured out water from one of them on to one of his hands and prepared things requiring foods requiring cleanness, they are kept in suspense.

L. [If he poured out] the second and prepared [foods requiring cleanness], they are clean.

M. [If he did so] with the first and did not prepare,

N. with the second and did prepare,

O. [if] these and those are lying [before him],

P. [supply: lo, they determine (the status of one another).][16]

1:18 A. [If] one of his hands was unclean, and one of his hands was clean,

B. and before him were two glasses, one unclean and one clean,

C. and he poured out water from one of them on to both his hands and prepared foods requiring cleanness, they are kept in a state of suspense.

D. R. Yosé says, "The unclean one remains in its established status of uncleanness."

E. [If] one of his hands was unclean, and one was clean,

F. and before him were two loaves of bread, one unclean and one clean,

G. and [if] his two hands touched one loaf, whether simultaneously or in succession,

H. or one of his hands touched both of the loaves, in succession,

I. the hands and the loaves are kept in a state of suspense.

J. [If] one of his hands touched the two loaves simultaneously,

K. the hands remain as they were, and the loaves of bread are to be burned.[17]

2:1 A. The priests sanctify in the sanctuary, in regard to the hand, up to the wrist, and in regard to the foot, up to the calf.

B. He who pours out water on his hands should not say, "Since the first [water] is unclean [anyway], lo, I shall pour out unclean [water to begin with]."

C. If he did so, lo, he must dry off his hands.

D. He who pours out water on his hands must dry his hands.

E. But he who immerses his hands does not have to dry off his hands.

2:2 A. He who pours water on his hands must raise his hands so that the water does not flow beyond the wrist and go back and render his hands unclean.

B. But he who immerses his hands does not have to raise his hands.[18]

2:3 A. He who pours out water on his hands, if he had proper intention, his hands are clean, and if not, his hands are unclean.

B. But he who immerses his hands, one way or the other — his hands are clean.[19]

---

16. *ibid.*   17. *ibid.*   18. M. Yad. 2:3.   19. *ibid.*

C. Rabban Simeon b. Gamaliel says, "[If] one poured out the first [water] and on his hand was found a red insect which originates in the water, his hands are clean."[20]

2:4   A. He who pours water on his hands —

B. if the water goes up to the wrist, his hands are clean, and if not, his hands are unclean.

C. [If] he poured out the first water on this [hand] by itself and changed his mind and poured out the second water on both hands simultaneously,

D. they render one another unclean.

E. [If] he poured out the first water on both hands and changed his mind and poured out the second [water], this on this hand by itself and that on that hand by itself,

F. if he had proper intention in the matter, his hands are clean, and if not, his hands are unclean.[21]

2:5   A. [If] one poured out the first water, and one of his hands was made unclean,

B. lo, this one pours out the second water on the second hand and does not scruple in the matter.

C. [If] he poured out the first water, and it flowed beyond the wrist, and then he poured out the second water on it, and a loaf of bread fell from the wrist and inward, it is unclean. [If it fell] from the wrist and outward, it is clean.[22]

2:6   A. [If] he poured out the first water and the second water beyond the wrist, and a loaf of heave-offering bread fell, it is unclean.

B. But logic requires that it be clean:

C. Now if the (first) [rain] water, which does not impart cleanness to water which is on the hand, imparts cleanness to water which is on the ground,

D. the second water, which does impart cleanness to the water which is on the hand, logically should impart cleanness to water which is on the ground.[23]

2:7   A. They pour out water for four or five people, one beside the other,

B. and they do not scruple on account of four things:

C. lest it be made unclean;

D. lest work have been done with it;

H. lest it not be poured from a utensil;

F. and lest a quarter-*log* not be poured out on a hand.

G. But he who takes and he who pours out for his fellow with his cupped hands —

H. his [the fellow's] hands are unclean,

20. M. Yad. 2:2.   21. M. Yad. 2:3.   22. M. Yad. 2:2.
23. *ibid*.

I. for in the first place the water has not been poured from a utensil.[24]

2:8 A. Two who poured out water for two hands, this one from [a measure of] an eighth of a *log,* and this one from an eighth of a *log,*

B. even though it goes and is mixed together in a spout —

C. their hands are unclean.

D. For in the first place [the water] was not poured from a quarter-*log.*[25]

2:9 A. These spoil [heave-offering]:

B. hands, food in the first remove, *maddaf*-objects, and liquids.[26]

C. R. Simeon b. Judah says in the name of R. Simeon, "He who touches the strap is clean, unless he touches the knot."

D. R. Zakkai says in the name of R. Jacob, "He who touches the knot is clean, unless he touches the box."[27]

2:10 A. A scroll which wore out,

B. if one can gather from it eighty-five letters,

C. such as the paragraph, "And it came to pass when the ark set forward" [Num. 10:35f.],

D. imparts uncleanness to hands.

E. A scroll in which are written eighty-five letters,

F. such as the paragraph, "And it came to pass when the ark set forward,"

G. does (not) impart uncleanness to hands.

H. [If] one attached to it other sheets, it imparts uncleanness to hands.

I. But the remainder does not impart uncleanness to hands.[28]

2:11 A. R. Judah says, "The blank space which is at the beginning of the scroll and is of the breadth of the entire [scroll] imparts uncleanness to the hands."

B. He who writes *Hallel* and the *Shema'* for child's practice — even if it is not permitted to do so —

C. it imparts uncleanness to hands.[29]

2:12 A. The thongs and straps which one sewed onto a scroll, even though it is not permitted to keep them, impart uncleanness to hands.

B. The container of a scroll and the box of a scroll and the wrappings of scrolls, when they are clean, impart uncleanness to hands.

C. The [segments used for] blessings, even though they contain letters of the divine name and of many passages which occur in the Torah, do not impart uncleanness to hands.

2:13 A. The Gospels (GYLYWNYN) and books of heretics do not impart uncleanness to hands.

B. And the books of Ben Sira and all books written thenceforward do not impart uncleanness to hands.[30]

24. M. Yad. 2:3.   25. *ibid.*   26. M. Yad. 3:1.   27. M. Yad. 3:3.
28. M. Yad. 3:5.   29. M. Yad. 3:4.   30. M. Yad. 3:5.

2:14 A. R. Simeon b. Menassia' says, "The Song of Songs imparts uncleanness to hands, because it was said by the Holy Spirit.

B. "Qohelet does not impart uncleanness of hands, because it is [merely] the wisdom of Solomon."

C. They said to him, "And did he write only this alone? Lo, it says, 'And Solomon uttered three thousand proverbs and his songs were a thousand and five' [I Kings 5:12].

D. "And it says, 'Do not add to his words lest he rebuke you and you be found a liar' [Prov. 30:6]."[31]

2:15 A. Ammon and Moab give poor-man's tithe in the Sabbatical year.

B. And [in] all other lands and in Babylonia, one tithes [second tithe].

C. [As to] Ammon and Moab and all other lands during the other years of the septennial cycle, [if in the Land they give] poorman's tithe, [they are to give] poor-man's tithe, and [if in the Land they give] second tithe, [they are to give] second tithe.[32]

2:16 A. Said R. Yosé the Damascene, "I was with the former elders [going thereafter] from Yavneh to Lud, and I came and found R. Eliezer.

B. "For he was sitting in the stall of bakers in Lud.

C. "He said to me, 'What new thing was there in the *bet hammidrash?*'

D. "I said to him, 'Rabbi, We are your disciples and drink from your water.'

E. "He said to me, 'Even so — what new thing [did you hear]?'

F. "I reported to him the laws and responsa and the vote.

G. "And when I came to this matter, his eyes filled with tears. He said, "'The secret of the Lord is with those that fear him' [Ps. 125:14]. And it says, 'Surely the Lord God does nothing without revealing his secret to his servants the prophets' [Amos 3:7].

H. "Go and say to them, 'Do not be anxious about your vote. I have a tradition from Rabban Yoḥanan b. Zakkai, which he received from the pairs, and the pairs from the prophets, and the prophets from Moses, a law [revealed] to Moses at Sinai:

"'They tithe the tithe of the poor man in the Sabbatical year.'"[33]

2:17 A. On that day:

B. Judah an Ammonite proselyte stood up before them in the *bet hamidrash.* He said to them, "Am I allowed to enter the congregation?"

Rabban Gamaliel said to him, "You are prohibited."

R. Joshua said to him, "You are permitted."

Rabban Gamaliel said to him, "Lo, it is written, 'An Ammonite or a Moabite shall not enter into the assembly of the Lord [even to the tenth generation]' [Deut. 23:3]."

R. Joshua said to him, "And are Ammon and Moab still standing in

31. *ibid.*   32. M. Yad. 4:3.   33. *ibid.*

their place? Already has Sennacherib, king of Assyria, come up and mixed up all the nations, as it is said, 'And I have removed the bounds of the people and have robbed their treasures and have brought down as a valiant man them that sit on thrones' [Is. 10:13].''

Rabban Gamaliel said to him, "Scripture says, 'But afterward I will bring again the captivity of the children of Ammon' [Jer. 49:6]. And have they not yet returned?"

Said to him R. Joshua, "Scripture says, 'And I will return the captivity of my people Israel and Judah, says the Lord' [Amos 9:14].

"Just as these have not yet returned [to their homeland], so those [Ammonites and Moabites] have not yet returned to their homeland."[34]

2:18 A. Judah the Ammonite proselyte said to them, "What shall I do?"

B. They said to him, "You have already heard the ruling of the elder. Lo, you are permitted to enter into the congregation."

C. Rabban Gamaliel said to them, "Also an Egyptian proselyte is in the same status as this one."

D. They said to him, "In the case of the Egyptians [in any event], it [Scripture] has set a limit to the matter for them, as it says, 'At the end of forty years I shall gather together Egypt' [Ezek. 29:13]."[35]

2:19 A. Said to them Rabban Yoḥanan b. Zakkai, "The preciousness of Holy Scriptures accounts for their uncleanness,

B. "so that a man should not make them into bedding for his cattle."[36]

2:20 A. The Boethusians say, "We complain against you, Pharisees.

B. "Now if the daughter of my son, who inherits on the strength of my son, who inherits on my account, lo, she inherits me — my daughter, who comes on my account [directly], logically should inherit me."

C. Say Pharisees, "No. If you have said so in regard to the daughter of the son, who shares with the brothers, will you say so of the daughter, who does not share with the brothers?"

D. Those who immerse at dawn say, "We complain against you, Pharisees.

E. "For you mention the divine name at dawn without first immersing."

F. Say Pharisees, "We complain against you, those who immerse at dawn.

G. "For you make mention of the divine name in a body which contains uncleanness."

---

34. M. Yad. 4:4.   35. *ibid.*   36. M. Yad. 4:6.

TEBUL YOM

1:1 A. He who puts pieces of dough-offering [into a basket, collecting them from door to door], whether intending to separate them from one another or not intending to separate them from one another —

B. [if] they stuck together,

C. they are made unfit by counting [the sequence of removes of uncleanness].[1]

D. In addition to them: rice, and pounded barley when not husked.

E. Rabban Simeon b. Gamaliel says, "Also beans are like them" —

F. "They are clean [when touched] by a Father of uncleanness, and it is not necessary to say, By a Tebul Yom," the words of R. Meir.

G. And sages say, "They are clean [when touched] by a Tebul Yom,

H. "and it is not necessary to say, [by] all other sources of uncleanness."[2]

1:2 A. In addition to them: rice and pounded vetchlings when husked.

B. Rabban Simeon ben Gamaliel says, "Meir would state, 'Under what circumstances? In the case of loaves produced domestically. But in the case of baker's loaves, unclean are only the black cummin and the garlic and the sison alone.'"[3]

1:3 A. All the same are liquid which is made unclean by a Father of uncleanness and liquid which is made unclean by an Offspring of uncleanness — lo, it is always deemed unclean in the first remove.

B. It imparts uncleanness to its fellow, and its fellow to its fellow, even though they are one hundred [sequences of contact].

C. [This rule applies] except to liquid of the Tebul Yom, which is unfit and does not impart uncleanness.

1:4 A. More strict is the rule which applies to hands than that which applies to the Tebul Yom:

B. For the hands are in the first remove of uncleanness in respect to unconsecrated food;

they impart uncleanness at one remove and impart unfitness at one [further] remove in respect to Holy Things;

and they render heave-offering unfit;

and they impart uncleanness to liquid, putting it in the first remove of uncleanness, as if it was water.

C. And anything which is not deemed connected in the case of the Tebul Yom is (not) deemed connected in the case of hands.

1:5 A. More strict is the rule pertaining to foods than that pertaining to liquids, and more strict is the rule pertaining to liquids than that pertaining

1. M. T.Y. 1:1.   2. M. T.Y. 1:5.   3. *ibid.*

to foods.

B. For foods have handles;

and they do not require intention to be used as foods;

and they impart uncleanness to liquid to put it into the first remove of uncleanness,

C. while liquid imparting uncleanness to foods, puts them into the second remove of uncleanness.

D. And a matter of doubt pertaining to it, in so far as it results in imparting uncleanness to other things, is deemed unclean.

E. They cannot be made clean of uncleanness,

F. which [rule] does not apply to liquid.[4]

1:6   A. More strict is the rule pertaining to liquid:

B. For liquid [which is made unclean] is always deemed to be unclean in the first remove of uncleanness.

C. It imparts uncleanness in any amount at all.

D. And there are some [sorts] of them which are made unclean as a Father of uncleanness so that they impart uncleanness to clothing, impart uncleanness to man, and impart uncleanness to food.

E. It imparts uncleanness to a utensil which is cleaned by rinsing if it touches its outer parts, and to a clay utensil if it comes into its contained airspace,

F. which [rules] do not apply to foods.

1:7   A. More strict is the rule applying to water than applies to [other] liquids and more strict is the rule applying to liquids than applies to water.

B. For water becomes a Father of uncleanness so that it imparts uncleanness to man and imparts uncleanness to clothing;

C. and it renders the immersion-pool unfit in the measure of three *logs,* and liquids in the measure of three *logs;*

D. which is not the case for [other] liquids.

E. And more strict is the rule concerning [other] liquids.

F. For liquids are not made clean in the body,

G. and they cannot be made clean of uncleanness,

H. and they are not made clean along with the body;

I. and they render the immersion-pool unfit if they change its color;

J. which is not the case for water.

1:8   A. The outer parts of utensils which are made unclean by liquids —

B. R. Eliezer says, "They render liquids unclean but do not render food unfit."

C. And the law follows his opinion.

D. R. Joshua says, "They render liquids unclean and they render foods unfit,

E. "by reason of an argument *a fortiori:* Now if a Tebul Yom, who

4. M. T.Y. 2:1.

does not impart uncleanness to liquid which is unconsecrated, does impart unfitness to foods of heave-offering, the outer parts of utensils, which do impart uncleanness to unconsecrated liquid, all the more so should impart unfitness to food of heave-offering."[5]

1:9 A. Shema'iah the brother of 'Azariah says, "Matters are reversed:

B. "Now if the Tebul Yom, who renders unfit foods of heave-offering, does not impart uncleanness to unconsecrated liquid, the outer parts of utensils, which do not impart unfitness to heave-offering food, all the more so should not impart uncleanness to unconsecrated liquid."[6]

1:10 A. Said R. Yosé, "See, in the case of this law, how the early fathers debated the matter and reasoned concerning it, drawing inferences from the teachings of the scribes in connection with the teachings of the Torah, and from the teachings of the Torah in connection with the teachings of the scribes."[7]

2:1 A. A piece of dough, the dough-offering of which one designated at the northern corner,

B. and so too: a cucumber, the heave-offering of which one designated at its southern corner —

C. lo, this is (not) deemed connected [to the remainder of the mass of the food].

D. If one removed its dough-offering from within it and returned it,

E. lo, this is [not] deemed connected.[8]

2:2 A. The porridge [and] the cake of unconsecrated food, and the garlic and the oil of heave-offering float over them, [and] a Tebul Yom touched the oil — he has spoiled only the oil.

B. R. Yoḥanan b. Nuri says, "Both of them are deemed connected to one another."[9]

C. Meat of Holy Things on which a layer of jelly formed,

D. and so too oil which floated on the surface of wine,

E. R. Ishmael the son of R. Yoḥanan b. Beroqah says, "The House of Shammai say, 'It is connected [when touched] by a Tebul Yom,'

F. "And the House of Hillel say, 'It is not connected [when touched] by a Tebul Yom.'"[10]

2:3 A. A Tebul Yom who raised up the heave-offering [wine] out of the cistern,

B. and a jar of heave-offering [wine] fell from him and sunk down into the cistern of wine,

C. [if it lands] from the rim and inward, it is deemed connected.

D. From the rim and outward, it is not deemed connected.

5. M. Toh. 8:7. 6. *ibid.* 7. *ibid.*

8. M. T.Y. 2:4. 9. *ibid.* 10. M. T.Y. 2:5.

E. And if it was a *pithos*-jar, even a jar which contains a hundred *kor*, the entire thing forms a single connector.[11]

2:4   A. A jar which was perforated, whether at its rim or at its bottom or at its side, and which a Tebul Yom touched, is unclean.

B. R. Judah says, "[If he touched it] at its rim or at its bottom, it is unclean —

C. "at its rim, because the liquid is drawn into his hand;

D. "at its bottom because the liquid is led down on to his hand.

E. "But [if it is perforated] at the sides, it is neutralized in a hundred and one parts [of clean wine]."[12]

2:5   A. A bubble which is in a [clay] jar which was perforated

B. directly through from inside to outside —

C. R. Judah says, "In the case of all of them, [if the hole is] at the sides, it is neutralized in a hundred and one."

D. M'ŚH W: There was a bubble of wine in the upper [part], and they came and asked R. Judah (b. Baba), and he said, "It is neutralized in a hundred and one."[13]

2:6   A. Produce which was severed but which was attached in part —

B. if it has a handle, they hold it by the handle.

C. [If it has] a leaf, they hold it by the leaf.

D. [If] it has both this and that, they hold it with both this and that.

E. [If] it has neither this nor that —

F. R. Meir says, "[They hold it] by the larger part [thereof]."

R. Judah says, "By the smaller part."

G. R. Neḥemiah says, "[They take it by the part that is] clean."

H. Sages say, "[They take it by the part that is] unclean."

I. Under what circumstances?

J. In the case of the Tebul Yom.

K. But in the case of all other sources of uncleanness, lo, this is deemed connected.

L. Rabbi says, "All the same is the Tebul Yom and all other sources of uncleanness:

M. "That which is drawn up with it is deemed connected, and that which is not drawn up with it is not deemed connected."[14]

2:7   A. "Dough which was mixed with heave-offering dough or which was leavened with heave-offering yeast

B. "is liable for dough-offering, but is not made unfit by the Tebul Yom," the words of R. Meir and R. Judah.

C. R. Yosé and R. Simeon declare unfit.[15]

2:8   A. Said R. Menaḥem b. R. Yosé, "I stated before father: Do you not

11. M. T.Y. 2:6.   12. M. T.Y. 2:7.   13. M. T.Y. 2:8.
14. M. T.Y. 3:1.   15. M. T.Y. 3:4.

agree in the case of a porridge and cake of unconsecrated food, and garlic and oil of heave-offering are floating on their surface, that if a Tebul Yom touched part of them, he has rendered unfit only the place which he touched?"

B. He said to me, "This is one kind, but that involves two separate kinds."[16]

2:9   A. A vegetable which is of heave-offering, and a beaten egg is placed on top of it —

B. "The entire upper row is deemed connected," the words of R. Yosé and R. Simeon.

C. R. Judah and R. Meir say, "Connected is only the stalk which is over against his hand."

D. Said R. Yosé, "Not concerning this item did he give testimony, but concerning that which was made like a cap, that it is not deemed connected."[17]

2:10   A. The streak of an egg which formed a crust on the side of a pan and which a Tebul Yom touched —

B. [if he touched it] from the lip and outward, it is not connected.

C. R. Yosé says, "Even [if he touched it] from the lip and inward, [only] the streak and whatever is peeled off with it are connected.

D. "[If he touched it] from the rim and outward, the streak and all that is connected with it are not connected."[18]

2:11   A. Eggs which were cracked open into a dish, lo, this [mass] is not deemed connected.

B. [When] one began to beat [them], it [still] is not connected.

C. [If] one beat them with liquids, it is deemed connected.

D. Eggs which one cracked open into the pitcher, lo, they are not connected.

E. [If] one began to beat them, it is not connected.

F. [If] one beat them with liquids, it is connected.

G. [If] one beat them with their own water, they are made susceptible to uncleanness.

H. Lo, they are comparable to the ring of dried figs.

2:12   A. Rings of dried figs, on part of which liquids fell —

B. "Lo, one removes three fingerbreadths' thickness by an entire fig's width," the words of R. Judah.

C. And sages say, "One removes from it only the place on which the liquid fell alone."

D. Said Rabbi, "The opinion of R. Judah seems best in the case of a thick ring of figs which one did (not) pulverize, and the opinion of sages seems best in the case of a thick ring of figs which one pulverized [into

16. *ibid.*   17. M. T.Y. 3:2.   18. M. T.Y. 3:3.

bits]."

2:13   A. The liquid of a Tebul Yom is like that of a clean person.

B. And R. Yosé b. R. Judah says, "[It is] like [that of an] unclean person."[19]

2:14   A. The woman who is a Tebul[at] Yom kneads dough, and cuts off a piece as dough-offering, and sets it aside, and leaves it in a basket or on a board, and brings it near and designates it by name—because it is in the third remove, and that which is in the third remove is clean so far as unconsecrated food is concerned.[20]

B. A kneading trough which is in the status of that which has been immersed on the selfsame day — they knead dough in it, and cut off from it dough-offering, bring it near, and designate it by name, because it is in the third remove, and the third remove is clean so far as unconsecrated food is concerned.[21]

C. Said R. Joshua, "A new thing did the scribes innovate, and I do not have an answer [for their critics]."[22]

2:15   A. He who raises up heave-offering from the cistern and set it in a place from which it would roll down and reach the cistern, and [then] went and put it in a place from which it would not roll down and reach the cistern

B. [if] it spilled, lo, this is deemed [to have been removed from the cistern] in safety.

C. [If] he was raising up heave-offering from the cistern and the jar cracked or poured out, if a sufficient volume of it to be considered heave-offering trickled down from it [back into the pit], lo, this [not] deemed [to have been removed from the cistern] in safety, and if not, this is (not) deemed [to have been removed from the cistern] in safety.[23]

2:16   A. [If] he was raising up as heave-offering four or five jars, even though a sufficient amount of each one of them did not trickle back [into the cistern] to be deemed heave-offering, lo, this is deemed [to have been raised from the cistern] in safety,

B. because it is deemed that he made a condition to govern each one of them.

C. Under what circumstances?

D. In the case of heave-offering of the first [vintage] of wine or oil, for the heave-offering of the first [vintage] is taken only from that which is nearby.

E. But in the case of heave-offering of all other produce, this is not deemed [to have been taken up] in safety.[24]

2:17   A. [If] one separated heave-offering and Heave-offering of tithe simultaneously —

19. M. T.Y. 3:6.   20. M. T.Y. 4:1.   21. M. T.Y. 4:2.
22. M. T.Y. 4:6.   23. M. T.Y. 4:7.   24. *ibid.*

B. in the case of all other produce, lo, this is deemed [to have been raised up] in safety.

C. R. Yosé says, "In the case of all of them, if he was a common person and did not state the condition [referred to herein], [it nonetheless is deemed to prevail as] a condition [of the act of giving heave-offering laid down] by the court [and so applies]."[25]

25. *ibid.*

UQSIN

1:1 A. The prick of the grape imparts uncleanness and is made unclean and joins together.

B. The leaves of garlic [and of] onions and the leeks when wet are made unclean and impart uncleannes and join together.

C. [When they are] dry, they are not made unclean and do not impart uncleanness and do not join together.

D. The roots of the dill do not impart uncleanness and are not made unclean and do not join together.

E. The roots of the lettuce and the parsnip and the long radish and the round radish impart uncleanness and are made unclean and join together.

F. R. Judah says, "He who touches the column is unclean. [He who touches] the fibre-like roots and the hair is clean."[1]

1:2 A. R. Eleazar says, "The growth of grape clusters and of downy growth join together, because it guards the food."

B. The roots of all things which are uprooted are not made unclean and do not impart uncleanness and do not join together.

C. R. Judah says, "The outer husks of corn in any amount whatever, lo, they join together, because they are chewed."

D. [If] one bound a sheaf, whether within the limit or beyond the limit — unclean is only that which is up to the limit alone.[2]

1:3 A. He who plucks ripe ears to bring them into his house — their measure is a handbreadth.

B. The handle of the stem of the brush of the palm-tree on which one left a single date is susceptible to uncleanness.

C. And the entire handle is joined to it.

D. And the fruit-stalks are not connected to one another.[3]

1:4 A. The handle of the broom of a palm-tree which is longer than four handbreadths,

B. and the reed of the sheaf which is longer than three handbreadths,

C. and all other things which are uprooted

D. do (not) impart uncleanness and are (not) made unclean but do not join together.

E. R. Yosé says, "[If] one gathered them to transplant them in his marriage-canopy or at the door of his shop, lo, they join together."

F. And so did R. Yosé say, "The roots of the inferior grapes, the apples, and the *etrogs* which one gathered to transplant in his marriage-canopy or at the door of his shop, lo, they join together."[4]

---

1. M. Uqs. 1:1–4. [M. Toh. 10:5.]   2. *ibid.*   3. *ibid.*   4. *ibid.*

1:5 A. Grain which one threshed in the threshing floor does not impart uncleanness and is not made unclean and does not join together.

B. R. Yosé says, "It joins together, because one turns it over with a pitchfork."[5]

1:6 A. And so did R. Yosé say, "The roots of the young shoots of a beet are susceptible to uncleanness because it is eaten with it."

B. And so did R. Yosé say, "The handle of a pumpkin is susceptible to uncleanness because it is sold with it."

C. R. Simeon says, "The handle of a *marḥapit* [?] is susceptible to uncleanness because it is sold with it."

D. R. Eleazar bar Ṣadoq says, "The handle of the artichoke is three handbreadths."[6]

1:7 A. A stem of [a bunch of] garlic, on one [bulb] of which liquid fell, is susceptible to uncleanness, but the [garlic] joined to it is not susceptible to uncleanness,

B. because connection effected by man is no connection.

C. An *etrog* which burst and which one stuck onto a spindle — this is not deemed connected,

D. because connection effected by man is no connection.[7]

1:8 A. Dough which was kneaded with fruit juice is insusceptible to uncleanness.

B. You have nothing which joins together foods except seven [specified] liquids alone.[8]

C. They said to R. Judah, "It is not a handle nor a protector, and it does not impart uncleanness, and it does not become unclean, and it does not join together."[9]

D. The prick of a pomegranate is susceptible to uncleanness.

E. R. Eleazar says, "That which touches the nipple is susceptible to uncleanness. [That which touches] the hair and the comb is insusceptible to uncleanness."

2:1 A. The soft date, part of which is eaten, and part of which remains —

B. [That part of the pit which is] near the food joins together.

C. [That part which is] not near the food does not join together.

D. "As to a dry one, [that part which is] near the food is susceptible to uncleanness.

E. "[That part which is] not near the food is insusceptible to uncleanness," the words of R. Meir.

F. And sages say, "[As to] a dry one, the whole is insusceptible to uncleanness."[10]

---

5. M. Uqs. 1:5.   6. *ibid.*   7. M. Uqs. 2:5.
8. *ibid.*   9. M. Uqs. 2:1.   10. M. Uqs. 2:1.

2:2 A. The fresh date, part of which turned rotten and part of which remains —

B. [that part of the pit which is] near the food joins together.

C. [That part which is] not near the food does not join together.

D. What is the part which is near the food?

E. Rabbi says, "Up to the empty space."[11]

2:3 A. Bundles of savory and marjoram and thyme —

B. [that part which is] near the food joins together,

C. [and that part which is] not near the food does not join together.

D. What is deemed to be near the food?

E. Rabbi says, "Up to the empty space."[12]

2:4 A. A bone on which is meat,

B. and so [marrow in] the brain which is in the head and which is in the thigh-bone —

C. [that part which is] near the food joins together,

D. [and that part which is] not near the food does not join together.

E. What is the part which is near the food?

F. If there is there empty space, it is up to the empty space.

G. [If there] is not there empty space, unclean is only the uppermost layer of the bone alone.[13]

2:5 A. R. Judah says, "A thigh-bone on which is an olive's bulk of meat leads the whole to [become] susceptible to uncleanness."

B. [*TR* IV, p. 177:] And sages say, "Even though there is on it only so much as a bean, it leads the whole thing to become susceptible to uncleanness."

C. R. Ishmael says, "They regard the meat which is on it, for

D. "if it is stretched out, and there is in it sufficient [flesh] to cover the circumference for as much as the breadth of the thread of a woof, then that which is near it joins together."[14]

2:6 A. The bones and the sinews and the horns and the hooves join together [to form the requisite bulk] to impart the uncleanness of food but not to impart the uncleanness of carrion.

B. But they are made [serve as] handles to impart the uncleanness of carrion.[15]

2:7 A. The soft date which one put on top of pieces of meat to moisten them,

B. and so [too] beans which one put on top of pieces of bread to congeal them —

C. that which touches either the soft date or the pieces of meat, or the [congealed] bread or the beans —

---

11. M. Uqs. 2:2–3. 12. M. Uqs. 2:2. 13. *ibid.*
14. *ibid.* 15. M. Toh. 1:4.

D. the whole is deemed connected.

E. Dates and dried figs which one boiled so that they were turned into a congealed mass —

[the mass] is deemed connected.

F. [Rabbi says, "If one did so] in order to moisten them, it is deemed connected.

G. "[If one did so] in order to extract their juice, [the mass] is not deemed connected."[16]

2:8   A. Dates, nut, almond, and palm which rattle are measured just as they are.

B. He who cuts off [produce] in order to cook it,

C. once he has cut if off — it is not deemed connected.

D. [If he did so] to pickle or seethe it or leave it on the table, it is deemed connected,

E. until it will begin to fall apart.

F. [If] he began to take it apart, this one on which he began is not deemed connected.

G. And the remainder is deemed connected.[17]

2:9   A. The shells of beans and of sesame, if they contain food-matter, receive uncleanness as food.

B. [If] they do not contain food-matter, they do not receive uncleanness as food.[18]

2:10   A. The shells of squash, even though they contain food, do not receive uncleanness as food.

B. The pits of olives and the pits of dates which one boiled do not receive uncleanness as food.

C. [If] one mixed them together with food, they do receive uncleanness as food.

D. Pits of carobs, even though one boiled them, do receive uncleanness as food.

E. Grape-pits and grape-skins, even though one mixed them up with food — his intention is null.[19]

2:11   A. Vegetables which dried up in their roots,

B. for example, carob and gourd which dried up in their roots [while still attached to the ground-root],

C. do not receive uncleanness as food.

D. [If] one gathered them, and they then dried out, they do (not) receive uncleanness as food.[20]

2:12   A. A piece of wood which became soft, half of which is rotten, and half of which remains — lo, this is not connected.

---

16. M. Uqs. 2:5.   17. *ibid.*   18. M. Uqs. 2:4.
19. M. Uqs. 2:4, 3:6.   20. M. Uqs. 3:8.

B. [If] the middle part became soft and the sides remain, the sides are not deemed connected to one another.

C. A pomegranate, part of which turned rotten and part of which remains, lo, this is not connected.

D. [If] the middle turned rotten and the sides remain, the sides are not deemed connected to one another.[21]

E. A tree which was cut down and on which were pieces of fruit — lo, they are as if they were detached.

F. [If] the tree dried up, and pieces of fruit are on it, lo, they are is if they were attached to it.

2:13   A. [If] one began to take nuts and to strip off the onions,

even though there are before him a hundred *kor* —

B. [once] he began with a single one of them, [the whole] is not deemed connected.

C. [If] there were two or three and he began with one of them, this one with which he began is not deemed connected, but the remainder are deemed connected.

D. Ben 'Azzai says, "The three of them have been rendered insusceptible to uncleanness."[22]

2:14   A. A melon which one cut and put on the table is deemed connected until one will begin to take it apart.

B. [Once] one has begun to take it apart,

C. the segment and everything that is pulled up with it are (not) deemed connected, but the remainder is [not] deemed connected.

D. The lower knob is connected with its own, but it is not deemed connected to the segments.

E. [If] there were two or three, and one began with one of them, this one with which he began is not deemed connected, but the remainder is deemed connected.

F. Ben 'Azzai says, "The three of them have been rendered insusceptible to uncleanness."

G. R. Yosé says, "Even [if he said], 'I shall eat half of it at dawn and half of it shall I eat at twilight,' this one with which he began is (not) deemed connected, but the remainder is [not] deemed connected."[23]

2:15   A. Nuts and almonds, even though one has crushed them are deemed connected, until one will begin to separate them.

B. A boiled egg and an egg baked down to the size of a pill are deemed connected until one will begin to scale off the shell.[24]

2:16   A. An egg which was spiced in its shell, lo, this is deemed connected.

B. Wool which is on the head of sheep and on the beard of goats, even

21. M. Uqs. 2:3.   22. M. Uqs. 2:5.   23. *ibid.*
24. *ibid.*

though one scorched it in fire, is deemed connected, until one will begin to pull it up.[25]

C. R. Judah says, "The wings of locusts and the scales of fish, even though one passed a knife across them, are deemed connected until one will begin to remove the scales."

2:17 A. A perforated pot which one set on top of two pegs, even if they are a cubit above the ground, does not render seeds susceptible to uncleanness.

B. Under what circumstances?

C. When [the hole] is below.

D. But if it is at the side [of the pot], it [the pot] does render the seeds susceptible to uncleanness.

E. If there is on the hole [in the pot] any amount of dirt at all, it does not render the seeds susceptible to uncleanness.[26]

2:18 A. A tray on which is a rim and which one tipped on its side does not impart susceptibility to seeds.[27]

B. [If] there was liquid in the pot which is not perforated,

C. [If] liquids fell on top of a cucumber [in the pot] and it was made susceptible to uncleanness,

D. [and if a root then] grew large and went outside the pot,

E. it is insusceptible to uncleanness.[28]

3:1 A. Clean fish and clean locusts in every location,

B. unclean fish and unclean locusts in the villages

C. require preparation but do not require intention.

D. The fat of a dead [beast] in every place requires intention and does not require preparation,

because it is like [or: from] its body.

E. Fat of a slaughtered beast in the villages requires intention and preparation.

F. [B. Hul. 128a supplies: R. Judah said,] "R. 'Aqiva did teach concerning fat of a slaughtered beast in the villages that it requires intention but does not require preparation, because it already has been prepared [for susceptibility] by means of [proper] slaughter."[29]

3:2 A. "I [Judah] said before him, 'Rabbi, you have taught us:

B. "'Endives which one gathered for cattle and to which one afterward gave thought for human consumption do not require preparation.

C. "For I say, 'If there is dripping liquid on them, they [already] have been prepared [to receive uncleanness].'"

D. R. 'Aqiva reverted to teach in accord with the opinion of R. Judah.[30]

---

25. M. Uqs. 2:6.   26. M. Uqs. 2:10.   27. *ibid.*
28. M. Uqs. 2:9.   29. M. Uqs. 3:9.   30. *ibid.*

3:3 A. The fat of an unclean beast is unclean.

B. The fat of a wild animal, whether it is unclean or whether it is clean, lo, it is equivalent to its body.

C. The fat of carrion and the fat of an animal improperly slaughtered is clean, as it is said, "The fat of an animal that dies of itself and the fat of one that is torn by beasts may be put to any other use, but on no account shall you eat it" [Lev. 7:24].[31]

3:4 A. He who tears meat off a limb of a living creature and gave thought to it — it does not require preparation.

B. [If] he gave thought to it and afterward tore it off, it requires preparation.[32]

3:5 A. Said R. Yosé, "On what account did they say, 'The carrion of a clean bird does not require preparation?'

B. "Because it imparts severe uncleanness, and whatever imparts severe uncleanness does not require preparation."[33]

3:6 A. What are olives and grapes which have turned hard?

B. They are those which exude from under the beam and the peat and the grapeskins.

C. [If] one gave thought to them for food, they [nonetheless] do not receive uncleanness as food.

D. [If] one gathered them for food, his intention is null.

E. Grape pits and skins, even though one has gathered them [for food] — his intention is null.[34]

3:7 A. R. Yoḥanan b. Nuri and R. 'Aqiva agree concerning unripe figs and grapes which one pressed before the season of tithes has come that they do not receive uncleanness as food.

B. Hard pears, Crustumenian pears, quinces, crab-apples [follow] their season for tithes and do not receive uncleanness as food earlier than that [time].

D. And [if] one seethed them, they do receive uncleanness as food.[35]

3:8 A. R. Neḥemiah says, "Unripe olives which one pressed before they reached the season of tithes —

B. "liquid which exudes from them is insusceptible to uncleanness,

C. "since it is nothing more than sap."[36]

3:9 A. The sprouts of the service-tree and of carobs, before they have turned sweet, do not receive uncleanness as food.

B. Once they have turned sweet, they do receive uncleanness as food.

B. But arum, mustard, and lupines, and all other things which are pickled, whether or not they have turned sweet, do receive uncleanness as food.[37]

31. *ibid.*   32. M. Uqs. 3:1—3.   33. *ibid.*   34. M. Uqs. 3:6.
35. *ibid.*   36. *ibid.*, M. Toh. 9:3.   37. M. Uqs. 3:4.

3:10   A. Palm-sprout is purchased with money of [second] tithe, but it does not receive uncleanness as food.

B. Unripened dates are not purchased with money of [second] tithe and are free of tithes.[38]

3:11   A. (Delete: Said R. Yoḥanan b. Nuri) In the case of all of them did R. Judah say, "Palm-sprout — lo, it is like wood in every respect, but it is purchased with money of [second] tithe.

B. "Lo, they are like fruit in every respect but they are free of tithes."[39]

3:12   A. Mixed seeds of the vineyard and the ox which is to be stoned to death and the heifer whose neck is to be broken and the bird-offerings of the meṣora' and the hair of the Nazir and the first-born of the ass and meat boiled in milk

B. receive uncleanness as food.

C. R. Simeon says, "All of them do not receive uncleanness as food."

D. And R. Simeon agrees in the case of meat cooked in milk that it receives uncleanness as food.

E. R. Simeon did say, "There is notar [that which is left over of the sacrifice] which receives uncleanness as food, and there is notar which does not receive uncleanness as food.

F. "How so? [If] a night passed before sprinkling the blood, they do not receive uncleanness as food. [If] after sprinkling of blood, they do receive uncleanness as food.

G. "As to piggul [flesh of the sacrifice which the officiating priest has formed the intention of eating at an improper time] of Most Holy or Less Holy things, it does not receive uncleanness as food.

H. "The piggul in the afternoon offering receives uncleanness as food."

3:13   A. "Vetches receive uncleanness as food," the words of R. Judah.

B. And R. Simeon says, "It does not receive uncleanness as food."

C. Said to him R. Judah, "Do you know of something which is liable to tithes and does not receive uncleanness as food?"

D. Said to him R. Simeon, "Do you know of anything which does not receive uncleanness as food and is liable to tithes?"

E. Said to him R. Judah, "Also you have denied the law."[40]

3:14   A. As to fenugreek, all agree that it does not receive uncleanness as food.

B. Vetch does not receive uncleanness as food.

C. Palm-sprout which one seethed or fried does receive uncleanness as food.[41]

D. Dates and dried figs which one put into the pot as spices do receive uncleanness as food until they cease to be edible by man.

---

38. M. Uqs. 3:7.   39. ibid.   40. M. Uqs. 3:5.
41. M. Uqs. 3:7.

E. R. Judah says, "Locusts which one put into the pot and which are spoiled receive uncleanness as food until they are unfit for human consumption."

3:15 A. Said R. Judah, "R. Eliezer and sages did not disagree about honeycombs, that they are not susceptible to uncleanness in their spread out parts.[42]

3:16 A. "In all the days of the priests they did not refrain from examining wine in them in a state of uncleanness and then going and scraping off the honey in a state of cleanness.

B. "Concerning what did they disagree?

C. "Concerning the Sabbath and the seventh year, for:

D. "R. Eliezer says, 'Lo, it is equivalent to immovable property.'

E. "And sages say, 'Lo, it is equivalent to a [movable] utensil.'

F. "[If] it was attached [to the ground] with plaster, all agree that it is equivalent to immovable property in every respect.

G. "[If] it was set on two pegs, all agree that it is equivalent to a [movable] utensil in every respect."[43]

---

42. M. Uqs. 3:10   43. *ibid.*

355

BABYLONIAN TALMUD